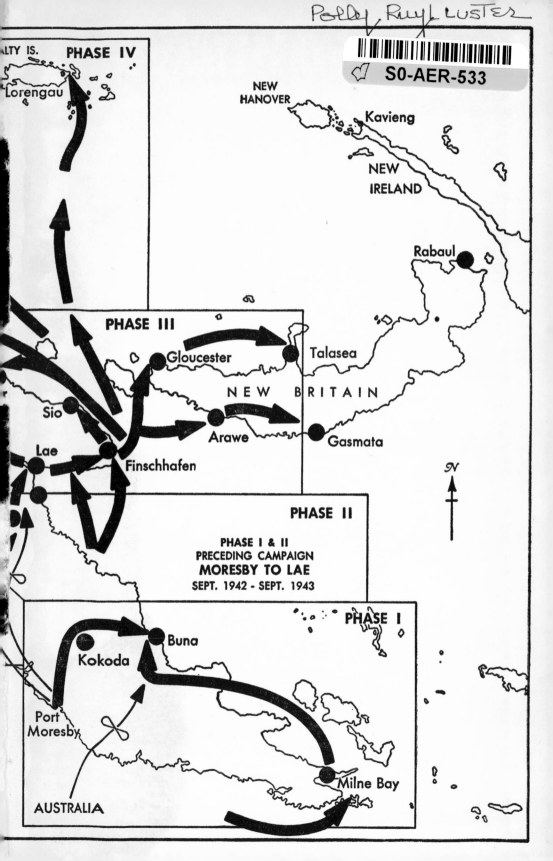

PHASE IV

ALTY IS.

Lorengau

NEW
HANOVER

Kavieng

NEW
IRELAND

Rabaul

PHASE III

Gloucester — Talasea

NEW   BRITAIN

Sio

Lae

Arawe — Gasmata

Finschhafen

N

PHASE II

PHASE I & II
PRECEDING CAMPAIGN
MORESBY TO LAE
SEPT. 1942 - SEPT. 1943

PHASE I

Buna

Kokoda

Port
Moresby

Milne Bay

AUSTRALIA

MacArthur: 1941-1951

General MacArthur with General Willoughby (by *Life* Photographer Carl Mydans
© TIME, Inc.)

MacArthur
1941-1951

MAJOR GENERAL CHARLES A. WILLOUGHBY
and JOHN CHAMBERLAIN

McGraw-Hill Book Company, Inc.

NEW YORK   TORONTO   LONDON

SECOND PRINTING

MacArthur: 1941–1951

Copyright, 1954, by Major General Charles A. Willoughby. All rights in this book
are reserved. It may not be used for dramatic, motion-, or talking-picture purposes, without written authorization from the holder of these rights. Nor may the
book or parts thereof be reproduced in any manner whatsoever without permission in writing, except in the case of brief quotations embodied in critical articles
and reviews. For information, address the McGraw-Hill Book Company, Inc.,
Trade Department, 330 West 42d Street, New York 36, New York.

Library of Congress Catalog Card Number: 54-11277

Published by the McGraw-Hill Book Company, Inc.

Printed in the United States of America

Preface

MODERN military staffs—the tools of generals—consist of four functional sections that reflect the basic elements of war. They are, respectively, Personnel (G-1), Intelligence (G-2), Operations (G-3), and Supply (G-4). These sections are held together by a plenary executive, the Chief of Staff.

Any one of the chiefs of section could write an authentic story of general headquarters. Through an immediacy of association, they are aware in greatest detail of the inner springs in the mechanism of war. As G-2 at MacArthur headquarters for a full decade, I had a close-up opportunity to watch the planning and development of all the MacArthur campaigns, from Bataan to the battle for North Korea. This book reflects the immediacy of the personal experience of that decade. However, the book is more than an eye-and-ear-witness account; it has a broader base than mere personal observation.

All major military headquarters maintain small research groups to prepare histories of the command. In Tokyo the function of creating and maintaining such a group was assigned to G-2 in 1946. At the time of MacArthur's dismissal this group had extensively documented the operational history of MacArthur's campaigns from Bataan to Tokyo; they had prepared administrative histories of general headquarters and of certain phases of the Occupation of Japan; they had thoroughly sifted the official Japanese war records; they had translated the *ex post* revelations of Japanese generals and admirals who were assigned to the project of writing a story of Japanese operations in the Southwest Pacific and elsewhere from their own point of view; and they also prepared a General Intelligence Series running to some 6,000-odd pages for use in the service schools. As editor-in-chief (in addition to my other duties), I directed all of these projects, personally editing the more important works. The enormous range of research, source development, and manuscript of all the Tokyo projects is evident in a stupendous aggregate of about 30,000 pages of text, nearly nine million words.

The so-called "MacArthur Histories," which were developed to the galley stage, subject to MacArthur's final edit, and which were interrupted by the Korean War, represent about 5 per cent of the grand statistical aggregate. These include two volumes covering the campaigns in the Pacific from Bataan to Tokyo, a volume on the military occupation of Japan, and a volume separately devoted to a Japanese history of the war condensed from Japanese war records and voluminous depositions made by Japanese officers after the war. The authors of this book have used the "MacArthur Histories" as a general guide and for pertinent quotation in the portions of the narrative that deal with operational Army history up to 1946. In general, the movements of armies, corps, and divisions have been merely touched upon; they are already covered in Dr. Louis Morton's scholarly Pacific War Series, in General Krueger's *From Down Under to Nippon*, and in General Eichelberger's *Our Jungle Road to Tokyo*. We have dealt in this book with a lesser-known field: the considerations of "high command," the analysis of the political, strategic, and economic factors that influenced General Mac-Arthur's major decisions in the Pacific, in Japan, and in Korea during the period 1941 to 1951. This is a "headquarters story."

As such it has been supplemented by recourse to leading figures in the drama, many of whom have supplied written documentation to clear up disputed points. Besides the numerous contributions of military and civil staff officers, there are extracts from many unpublished wartime manuscripts ranging from captured Japanese diaries to depositions made by intrepid officers who were charged with penetrations into the heart of enemy-held territory.

The study was initially undertaken with the encouragement of General MacArthur; it is expanded from an original group of ten chapters which were read and annotated by him. The material, however, is not to be regarded as in the nature of the General's memoirs. In correspondence with the publishers, General MacArthur remarked: "Willoughby was the intelligence officer on my staff for ten years and as such was in a position to acquire a wealth of information of broad general and historical interest and to establish him as an authority whose narration of events within the sphere of his responsibility is entitled to full public acceptance. In addition, in their own rights, he and Mr. Chamberlain are authors of note."

The MacArthur histories were turned over to the Department of the Army. On the quality of this collection, the Army historians commented as follows: ". . . All of the material . . . constitutes a unique and extremely valuable body of records which derives its value as much from the organization and assembly as from its contents. Tremendous effort was expended in the creation of this collection, in order to facilitate research and reference into the history of the war in the Pacific. . . ."

As regards the General Intelligence Series, the Washington G-2 had this to say: ". . . MacArthur's area produced a number of intelligence agencies and techniques which could have served as models for other areas of operations. . . . Scarcity of intelligence source material at the Service Schools was one of the greatest hindrances to proper training in the period between world wars. The Intelligence Series not only furnished background information on operations but also point up to the students the valuable lessons learned in the Far East which can be adapted with some modifications elsewhere. . . ."

I take this occasion to acknowledge the contribution of a succession of able assistant editors in the period 1946 to 1951: Cols. W. F. Niederpruem, Donald F. Ring, F. H. Wilson, and F. H. Svensson, USA; Dr. G. W. Prange, University of Maryland; Dr. Mitsutaro Araki, University of Tokyo; and Lt. Gen. T. Kawabe, Vice Chief of Staff, Imperial Japanese Army.

CHARLES A. WILLOUGHBY
Major General U.S. Retd

Contents

Illustrations

xi

Frontispiece: General MacArthur with General Willoughby

Photographs: (FOLLOWING PAGE 162)

American troops landing on New Guinea

The conference in Hawaii: President Roosevelt, General MacArthur, and Admirals Leahy and Nimitz

En route to Leyte: Generals Kenney and Sutherland, President Osmena, General MacArthur, and Colonel Romulo

Wading ashore at Leyte

General MacArthur with General Krueger

Awaiting the Surrender aboard the USS *Missouri:* Generals Derevyanko (USSR), Krueger (USA), Blamey (RAA), Sutherland (USA), Percival (UK), Wainwright (USA), and MacArthur

Japanese troops, repatriated from the South Seas area, carrying the ashes of dead comrades

Flotsam of war: displaced Japanese civilians

At Inchon: General MacArthur with Marine troops

Restoring the capital of Korea to Syngman Rhee: Generals Hickey, MacArthur, Almond, Walker, and Barr with President Rhee and Ambassador Muccio

Press conference in Korea: Generals MacArthur, Whitney, and Ridgway

Flying over the Yalu: Generals MacArthur, Wright, and Stratemeyer

On Formosa: Generals Willoughby, Almond, Stratemeyer, and MacArthur with Generalissimo and Madame Chiang Kai-shek

Japanese civilians bidding good-by to MacArthur

MacArthur leaves Japan

1 The War of Distances

LONG before it was ever fought, the Pacific war excited the minds of men. It fascinated Franklin D. Roosevelt, who once turned to the map and said to Gen. Hugh Johnson: "Look, Hugh, this is the place where we can beat the Japs!" It fascinated British naval writers, one of whom wrote a book called *The Great Pacific War*. And it drove Homer Lea, the strange little American hunchback who had taken service in the Chinese armies fighting the fierce old Dowager Empress, to his amazing 1909 work of prophecy, *The Valor of Ignorance*, which accurately forecast the lines of attack the Japanese would follow in the Philippines some thirty years later in 1941.

Clairvoyant to the point of specifying the precise bays and beaches the Japanese would use to debark their troops, Lea's dour manifesto was destined to become one of those works of art to which life goes for imitation.

As the conquest of Cuba [so Lea wrote in his best vein of magisterial gloom] was accomplished by landing forces distant from any fortified port, so will the Philippines fall. Lingayen Gulf on the north coast of Luzon, or Polillo Bight on the east coast, will form the Guantanamo Bays of the Japanese. . . . Japan, by landing simultaneously one column at Polillo Bight and another column at Dagupan, would, strategically, render the American position untenable. These two columns converge on Manila at right angles. . . . If the American forces should remain behind their lines at Manila, they would, in two weeks after the declaration of war, be surrounded by overwhelming numbers.

Although the Lea forecast was forgotten for an entire generation by the American public, it formed the basis of plan and counter-plan in military and naval circles. The American General Staff came

I

up with a defense concept called the "Orange Plan," which had the United States fleet encounter the Japanese Navy in Far Eastern waters in a single sea battle to settle everything. It was assumed that American and Filipino forces in the Philippines would resist the Japanese invasion, and it was taken as a certainty that the United States would have a large Pacific Fleet intact. There were no doubts whatever that the whole U.S. Fleet (not merely units that could be spared from Atlantic warfare) would be free to carry the fight westward across the Pacific into Japanese waters. The siege of the Philippines would thus naturally be raised, and all the Philippine garrison had to do was to dig in until the Navy had carried through their rescue work.

The Orange Plan was rendered almost totally academic on December 7, 1941, when the Japanese shattered the Sunday morning calm at Pearl Harbor by their sneak attack on Admiral Kimmel's Pacific Fleet. Caught short by events (he was only in the sixth year of carrying out his ten-year plan of preparation for the defense of the Philippines), General MacArthur was forced to improvise. He could, indeed, look forward to fighting a delaying action in the Philippines—the persistent defense of the Bataan Peninsula and the island of Corregidor at the entrance to Manila Bay exceeded any of Washington's most optimistic expectations—but beyond that everything was shrouded in murk.

This epic operation in Bataan and Corregidor became a decisive factor in the ultimate winning of the war. First and foremost, it gave the United States a needed image of courage. Hong Kong fell in two weeks, Singapore (to the vocal consternation of Winston Churchill) in two months—and in a single day the British lost the backbone of their Far Eastern naval strength when Japanese planes sank the battleship *Prince of Wales* and the battle cruiser *Repulse* off the east coast of Malaya. Yet Bataan held on. The Japanese timetable, which called for quick conquests throughout a great fanshaped territory reaching from the Indian Ocean past the long 3,000-mile stretch of the Malay Barrier deep into the Pacific, was disrupted in a way that was to prove crucial. Because of Bataan the Japanese never managed to detach enough men, planes, ships, and matériel to nail down Guadalcanal at the eastern tip of the Solomons. Nor did they ever succeed in mopping up New Guinea or seizing a foothold in Australia.

The new American posture of defense involved a quick recasting of the whole theory of Pacific war. Despite MacArthur's insistence that he stay with his troops, a Presidential order lifted the General from Corregidor and sent him to Australia, where he was placed in command of all the Allied forces in the Southwest Pacific. There, looking upward, so to speak, from a distant "down under" part of the world that could not be reached from America save by ships that had to skirt thousands of miles of menacing Japanese flank, Douglas MacArthur had an opportunity to look at the coming Pacific war in its entirety. What he saw was a staggering problem. And it was the more staggering in that he proposed to win the war by returning to the Philippines and moving on to Japan, not by resting on the defensive in Australia and hoping that the Japanese would somehow spend themselves by going out into the "blue" in the Australian desert in the manner of the Germans reaching for Stalingrad in 1943.

First of all, MacArthur was confronted by the terrifying facts of geography. The magnitude of the Southwest Pacific Theater can best be appreciated against a background of comparative geographical distances. To grasp the immense distances and the ticklish, often baffling, logistical problems involved in getting men across mountain ranges, jungles, and typhoon-menaced seas, MacArthur's staff in Brisbane frequently superimposed a map of the United States on one of the Southwest Pacific. Against this comparative geographical background, the logistical difficulties of the Southwest Pacific Theater in the conduct of the war loomed as something tremendous. To quote from the records: "Not only was the line of communications from the United States to the scene of operations one of the longest the world has ever seen, but the entire route was by water at a time when the Japanese Navy was undefeated and roaming the Pacific almost at will."

The shortage of water transportation was probably the most difficult problem of all. There was not enough shipping to mount operations rapidly or to support the troops in dispersed places. Tremendous logistic risks were taken in making decisions for plan-

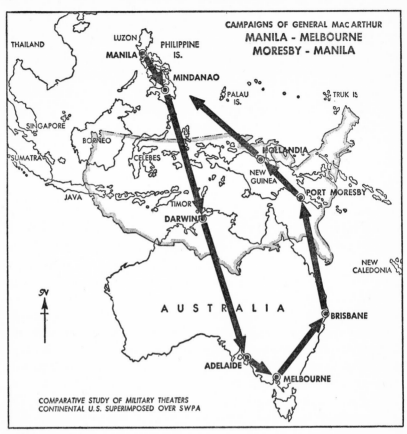

COMPARATIVE STUDY OF MILITARY THEATERS
CONTINENTAL U.S. SUPERIMPOSED OVER SWPA

ning and launching operations. These were "forced risks" which had to be taken if the war was to be pursued aggressively and if the Allies were to seize the initiative and hold it. There were shortages of combat equipment and of service troops; ports, bases, and airfields had often to be hacked out of the jungle.

The distances involved were terrible enough to contemplate in sheer mileage quantity, but they were even more staggering when surveyed from the standpoint of quality. To begin with, they were largely unmapped. On the scale of Europe, MacArthur's war took him roughly from the English Channel to the Persian Gulf—a distance at least twice that encompassed by Napoleon, Julius Caesar, or Alexander the Great in their most extended campaigns. When Gen. J. J. Twitty of the Hawaiian Intelligence Center remarked on the ease with which information could be obtained on the Normandy beaches or Anzio as compared with collecting terrain data on Tarawa, he voiced a complaint that was relevant all over the Pacific. To solve the problem of the nonexistent terrain studies, the necessary Baedekers of war, MacArthur's G-2 had to start absolutely from scratch. Before the war was over in August 1945, G-2's Allied Geographical Section, one of the great unappreciated workhorses of the war, had turned out a grand aggregate of 193,555 terrain studies, terrain handbooks, and special reports, most of which had to be done on forced printing deadlines and hurried to troops and staffs on fixed dates, agreed upon for irrevocable operations. Throughout most of the war the documents were flown from Australia hundreds and even thousands of miles to the front, on split-second schedules.

The unmapped terrain of New Guinea and the other islands was more often than not just about as tough and tenacious as the Japanese themselves. To quote from a draft prepared in Tokyo for the MacArthur historical records:

In New Guinea the great mountain ranges with their high peaks and deep gorges, the dense jungles which cover almost all of the huge island, the reeking nipa and mangrove swamps—"a stinking jumble of twisted, slime-covered roots and muddy 'soup' "—the hazardous jungle trails, the vast patches of kunai grass, with its sharp-edged blades growing to a height of six or seven feet, the swollen streams, the ever-present mud, the dangerous off-shore reefs, most of them uncharted, the poor harbors —these terrain characteristics exerted a constant and adverse influence on troops and military tactics.

The problems of climate and health were no less severe. The penetrating, energy-sapping heat was accompanied by intense humidity and frequent torrential rains that defy description. Health conditions were among the worst in the world. The incidence of malaria could only be reduced by the most rigid and irksome discipline and even then the dreaded disease took a heavy toll. Dengue fever was common while the deadly blackwater fever, though not so prevalent, was no less an adversary. Bacillary and amoebic dysentery were both forbidding possibilities, and tropical ulcers, easily formed from the slightest scratch, were difficult to cure. Scrub typhus, ringworm, hookworm and yaws all awaited the careless soldier. Millions of insects abounded everywhere. Clouds of mosquitoes, flies, leeches, chiggers, ants, fleas and other parasites pestered man night and day. Disease was an unrelenting foe.

Merely to combat the anopheles mosquito, the carrier of malaria, was enough to tax any man's genius. It was a sanitary battle involving science and discipline, waged by the troops, both officers and men, under an indomitable leader. During the first stages of the New Guinea campaign, malaria had been as bitter and deadly a foe as the enemy. On the Papuan front, it was responsible for more noneffectives than any other factor. By the time General Mac-Arthur was ready to go into the Philippines, however, it was conquered.

This remarkable achievement, comparable with Goethals' and Gorgas's triumph over yellow fever, was accomplished by the co-operation of everyone who served in New Guinea. The Medical Department surveyed, researched, lectured, demonstrated, and recommended, and general headquarters issued the necessary directives to ensure the success of the struggle. General MacArthur appointed a special committee of representatives from both the Australian and the American medical services, to formulate the general principles under which the campaign would be carried out. Medical officers, malaria control units, and malariologists provided expert advice to unit commanders. Troops were educated with posters and pamphlets and every man was urged to wage his own personal war against the mosquitoes. The result was an astounding success.

Japanese efforts along these same lines were ineffective. Their malaria casualties assumed enormous proportions, despite the fact that they had captured huge quantities of quinine in the Netherlands East Indies. As General MacArthur stated: "Nature is neutral in war but, if you beat it and the enemy does not, it becomes a powerful ally."

When MacArthur was ordered by President Roosevelt from the Philippines to Australia, he made a simple statement: "I came through and I shall return." Below the surface of the statement there was, as the events described in this book were to prove, a simple yet profound strategical concept—that of an arrow-straight axis of advance from Australia to the Philippines that would result in severing the

Japanese supply lines from the oil, rubber, tin, and rice of the Indies, Indo-China, and Malaya. MacArthur held to this economical view of strategy despite Navy importunings that he strike westward through the Netherlands Indies toward Singapore, while the fleet moved directly through the Central Pacific. The Navy wished to subordinate everything to the requirements of the Central Pacific. The Marianas, Formosa, and the Chinese mainland were the Navy goals. This view of strategy would have bypassed the Philippines. In the end MacArthur and the Navy compromised by pushing their separate strategies as mutually supporting operations, the Navy moving through the Central Pacific to the Marianas and Okinawa, while MacArthur converged on Luzon. In addition to the economy and the quick action which MacArthur's strategy guaranteed at a time when men and means were short and America was desperately hungry for victories, there were moral and psychological factors involved that were transcendently important.

After his first battles with the Japanese in New Guinea, MacArthur took a long look at the scene in the light of his straitened supply of troops and planes. The Papuan campaign had exhausted many of his men and much equipment. Replacements trickled in slowly, providing only the minimum essentials with which to conduct immediate operations. To push back the Japanese perimeter of conquest by direct pressure against the mass of the enemy-occupied islands would be a long and costly effort. MacArthur envisioned an entirely different strategy:

My strategic conception for the Pacific Theater contemplates massive strokes against only main objectives, utilizing surprise and air-ground striking power supported and assisted by the fleet. This is the very opposite of what is termed "island hopping," which is the gradual pushing back of the enemy by direct frontal pressure with the consequent heavy casualties which will certainly be involved. Key points must of course be taken, but a wise choice of such will obviate the need for storming the mass of islands now in enemy possession. "Island hopping" with extravagant losses and slow progress is not my idea of how to end the war as soon and as cheaply as possible. New conditions require for solution, and new weapons require for maximum application, new and imaginative methods. Wars are never won in the past.

The appeal of the MacArthur strategy was that it combined flexibility and economy at a time when these had to be substituted for strength. While its central feature was its military directness—"the principle of the objective," in bleak staff-school language—it allowed for all sorts of strategical and tactical deception in furthering the objective. What MacArthur proposed to do was to jump around strong points along the central axis of advance without throwing his forces out beyond his own air umbrella. Broadly speaking, he sought to split the Greater East Asia–South Sea Empire of the Japanese by penetration along interior lines. But, lacking the facilities to fight the Japanese head-on, he proposed no frontal strokes at Japanese strong points. What he sought for each individual battle was an opportunity to get around and behind the enemy, striking him obliquely on the flank and grappling for his supply lines. The whole MacArthur theory of maneuver was a hark-back past the man-devouring frontal assaults of World War I to the fluidity of Napoleonic times.

Napoleon's campaigns are filled with maneuvers against flank and rear. The strategic and tactical results were generally absolutely crushing or decisive, such as Bassano, Arcole, Marengo, Ulm, Austerlitz, Jena, Friedland, Landshut, and Montmirail. All succeeded in driving the enemy far to the rear and gaining large amounts of territory.

Similarly, the New Guinea campaign from Lae via Finschafen, Saidor, and Aitape to Hollandia contains brilliant examples of the Napoleonic maneuver against the flank and rear of the enemy. The double envelopment of Lae—by parachutists at Nadzab and a beach landing at Hopoi—was designed to cut the enemy's escape routes to the east and west. The landings at Saidor, Arawe, and Talasea were in the rear of the enemy and sharply astride his lines of communication and retreat.

The big jump at Hollandia and Aitape was encompassed by placing a force deeply in flank and rear of the Japanese Eighteenth Army. The Japanese communication by land, sea, and air was completely cut and his forces humiliatingly defeated and subjected to complete disintegration.

Throughout these actions ran the central theme of the whole master plan, a relentless advance that began at Finschafen and paused, for the moment, at Morotai, after an advance of 1,100 miles, before moving on to Leyte and Manila.

A staff paper, prepared in 1944 before the landings in Leyte, sums up the phases of the MacArthur operations and gives a contemporary view of the nature of the Commander in Chief's strategy:

Major elements frustrated, their defensive dispositions outmaneuvered . . . [the Japanese] have exhausted themselves in trekking tardy reinforcements to futile frontal attacks on organized beachheads, a historical predicament that has always invited heavy losses. Continuous combined air-sea attrition of coastwise barge traffic has exacted further casualties, and has driven demoralized enemy remnants into the jungle, over native trails, tortuous, disease-ridden, devoid of population or food, leading only to utter extinction. MacArthur has made use of unique geographic time and space factors, indigenous to this theater; he converted a hostile climate and terrain into dynamic offensive weapons by maneuver which lured a numerically superior enemy into ultimate self-destruction with negligible losses to allied troops; there is no greater test of skilled command than the survival of one's own soldiers at the expense of the enemy. The record speaks for itself.

These vast operations were firmly held together by a central theme, a parent idea, a strategical "leitmotif" that permeated the entire composition—the recapture of the Philippines and the restoration of prestige that was shattered at Singapore and Pearl Harbor. The iron continuity in the master plan is evident in a steady progression of Phases.

I PHASE   MORESBY TO BUNA
            26 Aug 42: Milne Bay
            2 Nov 42: Kokoda recaptured
            9 Dec 42: Allies capture Gona
            14 Dec 42: Buna Village seized by Allies

II PHASE   SALAMAUA AND LAE
            11 Sep 43: Salamaua captured by Allies
            16 Sep 43: Lae falls to Allies

III PHASE   FINSCHAFEN TO SAIDOR
            2 Oct 43: Allies capture Finschafen

15 Dec 43: Allied forces seize Arawe
26 Dec 43: Allies land at Cape Gloucester
2 Jan 44: Allies land at Saidor

IV PHASE ADMIRALTIES AND ST. MATTHIAS ISLANDS

29 Feb 44: Allied forces land on Admiralties
21 Mar 44: Allies land at Emirau

V PHASE MADANG TO HOLLANDIA——AITAPE

22 Apr 44: Humboldt Bay, Tanahmerah landings
25 Apr 44: Aitape Village taken

VI PHASE SARMI——WAKDE——BIAK

17 May 44: U.S. Forces land at Maffin Bay
18 May 44: U.S. Forces land at Wakde
27 May 44: Allies land on Biak Island

VII PHASE NOEMFOOR——SANSAPOR

2 Jul 44: Noemfoor Island landing
31 Jul 44: Sansapor landing

VIII PHASE MOROTAI

15 Sep 44: Morotai landing

IX PHASE PHILIPPINES

The incomparable virtue of the MacArthur strategy is that it resulted in large territorial conquests and the systematic wastage of whole Japanese armies (they died on the vine all over the South Seas when their communications disappeared) without involving any butchery of American troops. MacArthur simply could not afford to be a butcher. War is a terrible bookkeeping process. The debit is in lives lost, perhaps squandered. The most brutally outspoken discussion of the gruesome balance sheet of war is to be found in Henry "Rake-hell" Wilson's 1914 to 1918 *Memoirs*. Wilson was Chief of Staff of the British Imperial Forces, a cool professional who occupied highest positions. This cynical bookkeeper of the dead and dying spoke casually of "intake" (*i.e.*, recruits) and "outgo" (the killed and wounded). He recognized scientifically that the abattoir of Flanders was a deadly drain on British manpower, and he became interested in the only remaining reserve—the Americans. MacArthur knew all about Wilson's "intake-outgo" terminology—and was resolved to keep the "outgo" a minimum. In a comparison of total troops, planes, and guns in the shoestring campaigns of MacArthur's "Cinderella" theater, there is irrefutable evidence of the most careful husbanding of means, of a painfully meticulous attention to the saving of lives, which spelled immeasurable comfort to the mothers of Topeka and Albuquerque and Bridgeport whose sons had a unique wartime chance to return home in one piece.

The safety and well-being of his soldiers was all-important to MacArthur. This master craftsman, like Robert E. Lee, was constantly compelled to a sleight-of-hand adjustment of his means to the task. With B-17s taken away (they apparently needed them more in Europe) and P-38s (needed there too), he was left with only limited-range aircraft; consequently he frequently had to fight the Japanese to get additional airdromes close enough to make full use of short-range fighter equipment. The MacArthur strategy and tactics were constantly governed by short flight ranges. If he had had P-38s to accompany bombers to the Japanese strong point of Rabaul, he might not have been forced to take Cape Gloucester or seize Hollandia. But he needed these as rungs in a ladder that needed close rungs.

Given the need for Gloucester and Hollandia, MacArthur landed his men where the Japanese could not fire on them. At Finschafen, in a split-second move, he stepped in before a Japanese reinforced division had a chance to block the landing. At Lae he dropped a parachute regiment behind the Japanese while an Australian division landed unopposed elsewhere. That sort of thing is not chance; it is an exhibition of great tactical skill. It involves deliberation and knowledge. It is generalship. MacArthur did not want losses as a humanitarian. He could not afford them as a commander. He protected his men to the utmost within the scope of human ingenuity. The General who brilliantly led first a brigade and then a division in 1918 in close-in fighting knew the nature of war and appreciated the value of human lives. One cannot improvise experience. MacArthur had respect for death—and his superb technical skill enabled

IMPERIAL RESCRIPT

We, by grace of heaven, Emperor of Japan, seated on the Throne of a line unbroken for ages eternal, enjoin upon ye, Our loyal and brave subjects:

We hereby declare war on the United States of America and the British Empire. The men and officers of Our army and navy shall do their utmost in prosecuting the war, Our public servants of various departments shall perform faithfully and diligently their appointed tasks, and all other subjects of Ours shall pursue their respective duties; the entire nation with a united will shall mobilize their total strength so that nothing will miscarry in the attainment of our war aims.

To insure the stability of East Asia and to contribute to world peace is the far-sighted policy which was formulated by Our Great Illustrious Imperial Grandsire and our Great Imperial Sire succeeding Him, and which We lay constantly to heart. To cultivate friendship among nation and to enjoy prosperity in common with all nations has always been the guiding principle of Our Empire's foreign policy. It has been truly unavoidable and far from Our wishes that Our Empire has now been brought to cross swords with America and Britain. More than four years have passed since China, failing to comprehend the true intentions of Our Empire, and recklessly courting trouble, disturbed the peace of East Asia and compelled Our Empire to take up arms. Although there has been re-established the National Government of China, with which Japan has effected neighbourly intercourse and co-operation, the regime which has survived at Chungking, relying upon American and British protection, still continues its fratricidal opposition. Eager for the realization of their inordinate ambition to dominate the Orient, both America and Britain, giving support to the Chungking regime in the name of peace, have aggravated the disturbances in East Asia. Moreover, these two Powers, inducing other countries to follow suit, increased military preparations on all sides of Our Empire to challenge us. They have obstructed by every means our peaceful commerce, and finally resorted to a direct severance of economic relations, menacing gravely the existence of Our Empire. Patiently have We waited and long have We endured, in the hope that Our Government might retrieve the situation in peace. But our adversaries, showing not the least spirit of conciliation, have unduly delayed a settlement; and in the meantime, they have intensified economic and military pressure to compel thereby Our Empire to submission. This trend of affairs would, if left unchecked, not only nullify Our Empire's efforts of many years for the sake of the stabilization of East Asia, but also endanger the very existence of Our nation. The situation being such as it is, Our Empire for its existence and self-defense has no other recourse but to appeal to arms and to crush every obstacle in its path.

The hallowed spirits of Our Imperial Ancestors guarding Us from above, We rely upon the loyalty and courage of Our subjects in Our confident expectation that the task bequeathed by Our Forefathers will be carried forward, and that the sources of evil will be speedily eradicated and an enduring peace immutably established in East Asia, preserving thereby the glory of Our Empire.

The 8th day of the 12th month of the 16th year of Showa

Signature	Title
TOJO, Hideki	Prime Minister, Minister of War
HASHIDA, Kunihiko	Minister of Education
SUZUKI, Teiichi	Minister of State
INO, Sekiya	Minister of Agriculture and Forestry
KOIZUMI, Chikahiko	Minister of Health and Social Affairs
IWAMURA, Michiyo	Minister of Justice
SHIMADA, Shigetaro	Minister of Navy
TOGO, Shigenori	Minister of Foreign Affairs
TERASHIMA, Takeshi	Minister of Communications
KAYA, Okinobu	Minister of Finance
KISHI, Nobusuke	Minister of Commerce and Industry
HATTA, Yoshiaki	Minister of Railway

Japan declares war

him to dodge its worst ravages. His balance sheet was that of a great economist; he gained the objective at a low cost in lives, in men, in equipment, in aircraft—all of which could also be expressed in terms of money and taxation, of easing the burden of the national debt for those who come after us. The statistics of comparative Japanese and American casualties show an almost incredible ratio in killed and wounded in favor of the American soldier. It is interesting, too, that MacArthur had only 12 per cent of the troops abroad and he received less than 9 per cent of the supplies sent overseas from America. In three months North Africa received more than the SWPA in an entire year. MacArthur received five tons per man; Africa fifteen tons per man.

The central theme of "too little—too late" is sharply audible in the abortive defense of the Philippines, though the psychological impact on the Filipinos—indeed on all of Asia—was incontestable. There is no better appraisal of the action in the Philippines, as a summation statement, than the following, and no critic is better qualified than Carlos Romulo, resident Commissioner of the Philippines in Washington and later the presiding officer of the United Nations. On the occasion of the reconquest of the Philippines, he said:

Manila is only a long-range gunshot away. From Manila and back to Manila again—that was his pledge of faith made to eighteen million Filipinos, and he has kept that rendezvous.

Whatever the rest of the world may have thought when Douglas MacArthur made the promise, "I will return," in Filipino minds there was no misunderstanding. They knew he would be back.

To them, in the Far East, he was the living symbol of the integrity of America. He had won their confidence and their trust through his faith in the Filipinos' ability to take their place among the free nations of the world. . . .

In 1935 he came to Manila and surrounding him then like a halo were the glories of five campaigns in World War I, the Rainbow Division triumphs in France, his career as Superintendent at West Point and as Chief of Staff of the United States. He began the work of forming half a million men into an army that could, if need came, be the vanguard of American freedom in the Far East.

He remained in the Philippines to see the job of defense through. What held him there? His knowledge of the true character of Japan. He knew that the day would come when his America would need a loyal Philippines that had been trained to fight America's way. He was convinced that the Philippines could be defended.

Douglas MacArthur knew the Filipinos. He was their friend; they were his. He answered his critics, "You are talking nonsense. The Filipinos will use their guns, yes, for America, if ever the time shall come."

Thank God, when the time came, enough were trained and armed to help him hold until the last words came from Corregidor: "Men fighting under the banner of an unshakable faith are made of something more than flesh, but they are not made of impervious steel . . . the flesh must yield. . . ."

All he believed in has been vindicated by time. All he has done has been justified. . . .

The strategy he followed is history. It is almost personal history, for much of it was done without defenses and with empty hands. The enemy had a hundred bombers to one of ours, and a thousand fighters to our one. They had equipment and all the panoply of war. The Japanese had everything they needed to drive democracy out of the Far East.

We who saw him on Corregidor with that worn, embroidered, much-maligned cap pushed back, no protection under that lethal sky, counting the Japanese planes dropping their bombs over our ravaged Rock—there on that nub of stone in Manila Bay stood America, endangered, entrapped, but indomitable.

We knew, in the Philippines, how at first he could not bring himself to leave Corregidor even under orders. We heard of that strange imperiled journey by PT boat and by plane to Australia, and how, landing there, he sent back his pledge: "I will return."

The promise of a man separated from them by two thousand miles of sea held them together, and the assurance given them by the President of the United States regarding their freedom led them on, while everywhere else, in the Far East, natives turned against the white man who had lost face and power. . . .

While they kept the faith with him, what was he doing in Australia?

He had been sent to Australia with orders to hold that endangered continent. Without MacArthur, Australia might have become a second Bataan. The Australians knew that. They hailed him as a savior. Australian soldiers were fighting elsewhere; while they were fighting in Europe, the continent Down Under was practically undefended.

All this time Japan was growing richer and huger and more terrible.

General MacArthur prepared to hold Australia, while Corregidor collapsed, and in Melbourne, we saw one another's tears. Again, he was building bricks without straw.

Men, equipment, guns, planes—all these were lacking. The vast distances out there were his enemies. How could his frail defenses span and hold.

Again, he not only held, he attacked. At first the faint pattern of his offensive may have been imperceptible from America, but the Southwest Pacific area felt the shape of it as mighty pincer arms, built out of practically nothing in the beginning, began stretching out over hundreds of miles.

He had to make every man and every mile count. Not a man died without need. Fighting an entrenched and powerful enemy, MacArthur's lines cleared the air, sea, and jungle ahead mile by mile, cut supply lines, sucked in the invading forces, felt their way through starvation, blockade and superior forces past the Japanese objectives. Gona, Buna, Lae, Salamaua, Finschafen, New Guinea, Kolombangara, Rabaul, Hollandia, Biak, and then Leyte, Mindoro, Marinduque and Luzon—where in history has one man done so much with so little?

When on Christmas he sent his message to his men, he revealed a source of his power. "On this Christmas Day, the anniversary of the birth of our Lord, Jesus Christ, I pray that a merciful God may preserve and bless each one of you."

That came from a deeply religious man who regarded the protection of every man set under him as a holy responsibility. . . .

Words spoken for Filipinos echoing a promise. "I have returned." In Tagalog: *"Eumalik ako."* Words that reached into the barrios and jungle hiding places all over the Philippines.

He said, on Leyte, when matters progressed with apparent slowness: "I could take Leyte in two weeks. But I will not take by sacrifice what I can win by strategy. I owe too much to the mothers and wives in America to risk needlessly the lives of their men. . . ."

And he pointed out a Filipino guerrilla and an American soldier walking arm in arm, and said: "See, in Washington, the Filipino patriots fought for equality. You won social equality on Bataan."

2 Sideslip to Bataan

WHEN the Japanese attacked the Philippines on December 8, 1941, Gen. Douglas MacArthur, who had been named Commander of the United States Armed Forces in the Far East on July 27, was still in the midst of a zealous eleventh-hour struggle to build up enough "muscle" to repel the enemy. He had spent six years in the islands as military adviser to Manuel Quezon—which was four years short of the time he deemed necessary to build the Filipino Army into a fighting force competent to throw the troops of a major invading power into the sea. Starved for funds that were anywhere near commensurate with preparations for modern warfare, MacArthur lacked the guns, planes, and PT boats that might have made the inland waters of the 1,400 islands impregnable and the outer beaches a terrible hazard to the presumptive invader. Nor had the United States sent him much after making him chief of USAFFE in July. A few P-40s and Flying Fortresses, a small fleet of PTs, a few trained officers, two transport loads of troop reinforcements—and that was about all.

Nevertheless, the combined Filipino and American forces held out in Bataan and Corregidor for virtually six months, denying Manila Bay to an enemy that was frantic to use the local docks as staging intermediaries in its thrusts to the South Seas. That six-month period of successful delaying action was precisely the task set for the Filipino-American forces in the Orange Plan for the defense of the Philippines. In the Orange Plan, the Navy was counted on to lift the siege of the islands within half a year.

Looking back on the long Bataan days, MacArthur had many eloquent things to say about the heroism of his commanders and his gaunt men, but nothing is perhaps more eloquent than the following General Staff evaluation of the defense of the Philippines:

Sideslip to Bataan

In complete justice to the gallant men on Bataan and other outposts, a flat comparison will have to be made between the op forces, their combat experience, quality and equipment. The Japanese forces were fought to a standstill by February and sp reinforcements had to be rushed in from other fronts, disrupting Tokyo's strategic time tables severely. Comparison by divisions are not truly descriptive. The Filipino divisions were not thoroughly integrated, trained, equipped or armed; the indefinable moral and technical qualities that make an officer corps cannot be improvised in a few months. Comparisons by total are more indicative. Fil-Americans: 50/60,000. Japanese: 191,939. A ratio of roughly four to one . . . , a discrepancy that Americans in the Orient would take on as almost routine for the next ten years.

In the latter days of the Pacific war, the Americans held a technological advantage over the Japanese that did much to offset the discrepancy in sheer manpower. But in the Philippines from December 1941 to April 1942 MacArthur was forced back on the intangibles of will, heart, and intellect. Besides the fighting stamina of his men, the General had two things on his side that were worth many divisions. The first was his knowledge of the Japanese mind—a knowledge that dated back to the days of the Russo-Japanese War when he was an observer in Manchuria with his father, Gen. Arthur MacArthur. The second was an encyclopedic knowledge of previous campaigns in the Philippines, with particular reference to what Homer Lea had written about them. Knowledge of the first helped MacArthur to parlay the second into the long six-month struggle to hold Bataan and Corregidor, which saved the day until Allied defenses could be reorganized in Australia.

A sharp clue to the early Manila staff reading of the Japanese mind is contained in a translation of the Japanese war song, "Umi Yukaba," which someone in the Far Eastern Theater thought worth filing away for future reference after it had been picked up by radio listeners in 1941. All of Japan went to war singing this song. Roughly translated, "Umi Yukaba" goes:

> Across the sea,
> Corpses in the water;

Across the mountain,
Corpses heaped upon the field;
I shall die only for the Emperor,
I shall never look back.

The song aroused the attention of MacArthur's staff because it
seemed an accurate revelation in capsule of the whole Japanese
warrior character. The Commander in Chief knew all about the
hold of the Emperor on Japanese soldiers; he had seen mutinous
troops come to heel in the days of the Russo-Japanese War at the
mere whisper of the Emperor's wish. (It was the memory of his
experiences in Manchuria in 1904 that prompted MacArthur to
land unarmed at Atsugi Field, near Tokyo, on August 30, 1945,
after the Emperor had proclaimed the surrender.) But there was
more than Emperor-worship implied in "Umi Yukaba"; there was
also the implication that Japanese tenacity had another face, in a
rigidity that could be exploited by the Americans to their infinite
advantage. "Umi Yukaba," in short, was a prophecy, quite literal
in its truth, of the war to come. The Japanese *would* heap their
corpses across the sea; they *would* never look back, even when the
Americans had run around and beyond them. The whole inelastic
overextension of the Japanese campaigns was there in "Umi Yukaba," which is one reason why it was preserved in the MacArthur
historical staff compilations.

The Japanese, of course, were quite oblivious to the prophetic
aspects of "Umi Yukaba" as they sent their veteran divisions of the
China War southward in long lines of convoys to smash the tottering colonial outposts at Singapore, Surabaya, Hong Kong, and
Manila. Working on the assurance that Hitler was about to take
Moscow and knock the Russians out of the war, the Japanese commanders thought they had all the time in the world to consolidate
an empire that was to reach from Burma in the west to the Bismarck
Archipelago and the Gilbert Islands in the South Pacific. They remembered the words of their elder statesman who had prophesied
that great advantages would come to the Japanese Empire from the
"confusion of Europe." They could not foresee the smashing of
their aircraft carriers at Midway, the fierce ebb and flow of the
fighting on Guadalcanal, the loss of whole divisions of troops in

New Guinea from malaria and starvation as their communications dwindled under growing American control of sea and air.

They could not count, in advance, the bodies that were to be burned by flame throwers in the caves of Tinian and Iwo Jima; nor could they guess that their monster 72,000-ton battleships, the *Musashi* and the *Yamato*, would go to watery graves without ever having an opportunity to close with the smaller battleships of the American fleet. They had no notion that the as yet uninvented napalm, or jellied gasoline, would consume many a Japanese encampment all over the South Seas, or that fire bombs would lay waste whole cities on Honshu, or that the unimaginable splitting of the atom would, in due course, doom the middle-sized towns of Hiroshima and Nagasaki. But MacArthur knew that the Japanese hand, once its fingers had closed into a fist, would never relax its grasp upon an object. This tenacity dictated a stand-and-die Japanese strategy that, however formidable it might be, could be turned to the American advantage by a commander who was light on his feet and nimble in his head. A hand that closes never to open again is useless when the fighting turns to catch-as-catch-can wrestling.

If MacArthur knew what the Japanese would do in general, he also had a fairly clear notion of what they would do in the Philippines in particular. He knew how the Americans had taken Manila in 1898. He knew what Homer Lea had written in *The Valor of Ignorance* as long ago as 1909. He knew that general staffs everywhere, including the Japanese, had read Lea's extraordinary forecast.

In many a pre-Pearl Harbor staff conversation at the General's Manila military headquarters in gloomy old Fort Santiago, Lea's "invasion map" of the Philippines—a pincer movement on Manila beginning with landings to the north at Lingayen Gulf and to the southeast at Polillo Bight—was discussed. The name of Homer Lea popped up most prominently when the whole of Manila society was buzzing about a Japanese espionage case and an alleged betrayal that involved a Filipino officer, a graduate of West Point.

In pleading for lenience toward the Filipino West Point graduate on the ground that his "secrets" were public knowledge that "could be had in a bookstore," MacArthur's staff had reference to the particular passage in Homer Lea that has been quoted in Chapter 1.

Knowing the rigidity of the Japanese mind, MacArthur counted on the enemy to follow Homer Lea to the end. As for himself, he would follow another course, based on a quite different historical reference. When Douglas MacArthur was a cadet at West Point, he had thrilled to the story of his father's exploits as the first military governor of the Philippines. It was Gen. Arthur MacArthur who had been handed the task of pacifying the islands after the Spaniards had lost Manila to the United States in 1898. Presiding in Manila, Gen. Arthur MacArthur knew that he couldn't presume to govern Luzon as a whole until he had tracked down Aguinaldo, the Filipino insurgent patriot.

This wily precursor of the Filipino independence movement had holed up in the rocky jungle fastnesses to the north of the Bataan Peninsula. It took a deal of plotting and maneuvering on Arthur MacArthur's part to enable General Funston to dig Aguinaldo out of the jungle.

Forty years after the capture of Aguinaldo, Gen. Douglas MacArthur held the name of Bataan as a shining beacon star in his mind. The U.S. plan was to let the Japanese repeat the strategy which had been used in 1898 to beat the Spaniards; as for the Americans and the Filipinos, they would follow the far more intelligent course of the insurgent Aguinaldo. To put it briefly, MacArthur's forces wouldn't bother to defend the indefensible city of Manila at all; they would "sideslip" into Bataan when the time came and hold out from there.

MacArthur said of the initial stages of the campaign:

My concept for the initial defense of the Philippine Islands was to defeat the enemy on the beaches where he would be at his weakest in any attempted amphibious landings. There were three possible areas in Luzon for such landings—north, south and, of much lesser potentiality, southeast. My forces were meager. I deployed the partly equipped and only partially trained I Corps in the north under General Wainwright, the II Corps to the south under General Jones, and local Philippine forces to the southeast.

The Ist Corps was unable to prevent the enemy from securing beachheads in the north and was being gradually forced back toward Bataan from one defensive line to another. No major attack had developed on the south line but reports reached me about midnight that a landing had been made in the southeast and our forces there were unable to hold the enemy driving rapidly west toward Manila. This would have split the II Corps from the I, divided my forces and subjected them to destruction in detail. I immediately ordered Jones to withdraw by forced marches from the south to Bataan through Manila and Wainwright to temporarily stand in the north at all cost to hold clear the roadnets leading to Bataan until the II Corps could take position there and our base of supplies be moved from Manila to Mariveles and Corregidor. When these moves had been successfully accomplished, I evacuated Manila and declared it an open city to save it from destruction. This decision and its brilliant implementation by the field commanders involved made possible the months of delay to the Japanese advance caused by the sieges of Bataan and Corregidor. I have always regarded it as the not only most vital decision of the Philippine campaign but in its corollary consequences one of the most decisive of the war.

With Homer Lea at their elbows, the Japanese came on in all confidence after December 8, rigidly following a plan laid down in its essentials in the days of Teddy Roosevelt. When they struck, MacArthur had barely reached the halfway mark in his ten-year plan for the defense of the Philippines. MacArthur's hurried efforts to whip his rice farmers into shape sometimes caused more apprehension than reassurance, for it was obvious that the Filipino recruits were mere amateurs when stacked up against the Japanese veterans of the China War.

There were open scoffers in the islands who spoke of the rice farmers as "MacArthur's Boy Scouts." The "Boy Scouts" turned out to be individually brave beyond all reckoning, but in the nature of things they could never be welded into a really formidable force. Of the 110,000 native Filipino soldiers, organized into ten divisions, of variable quality, only 50,000 were on the island of Luzon—the rest were scattered around on the numerous islands of the Visayas and on Mindanao. Dialect differences made command of these troops an extremely difficult matter: at the very minimum there were twenty-seven dialects spoken by MacArthur's Filipino troops. Even on Luzon the dialect differences were many: an Ilocano soldier could not necessarily understand a command given in Tagalog. The 6,000 American regulars in the islands—not enough to amount to a division—were, with very rare exceptions, completely unconversant with the Tagalog of the Manila area. The Philippine Scout division, composed of long-term professional Filipino soldiers, was a brilliant exception and played a conspicuous role on Bataan until decimated by battle losses.

Following upon General MacArthur's recall to active duty as a U.S. Army officer in July, Japanese intelligence noticed a marked acceleration in the organization and training of Philippine Army units. The Japanese espionage organization of that time was almost openly arrogant in its surveillance of the American war preparations. To quote from a staff report of the period:

The Philippines were overrun with potential Japanese spies . . . businessmen, sidewalk photographers and bicycle salesmen; in small towns and hamlets throughout the Islands, one was sure to see some stocky, slightly bowlegged figures usually in dark alpaca suits and crumpled hats, wearing tinted glasses presumably to protect them from the harsh tropical glare but also very convenient for having a good look around. We had spotted the clearing houses, the rendezvous and principal operators in Manila, but there was nothing of an immediate or tactical nature. However, the interest of their observers in certain coastal areas, in the Ilocos and in the Bicols, was significant: they seemed to be following Homer Lea's plan.

As Pearl Harbor approached, we got many of the intercepts of that period; there was a considerable time lag, since they all came via Washington; we set up our own plant during the war and eventually cut the decoding time on all local items. We were fortunate in having a real expert in our midst, the chief signal officer, General Spencer Akin, long associated with this very sensitive type of work. Spencer looked like a younger edition of Lincoln and had much of that great man's dry grassroots humor. . . . We saw some of the intercepts in Manila, on a relay through special channels. . . . It was known that the Japanese Consul in Honolulu cabled Tokyo reports on general ship movements. In October his instructions were "sharpened." Tokyo called for specific instead of general reports. In November, the daily reports were on a grid-system of the inner harbor with co-ordinate locations of American men of war; this was no longer a case of diplomatic curiosity; co-ordinate grid is the classical method for pin-point target designation; our battleships had suddenly become "targets."

Spencer Akin was uneasy from the start. We drew our own conclusions and the Filipino-American troops took up beach positions long before the Japanese landings.

As the G-2 files show, American pursuit interceptor planes began night patrols on December 4. To quote from the official records:

Each night [the interceptor planes] located Japanese bombers from twenty to fifty miles out at sea, but the enemy planes turned back before actual contact was made. The last of these night flights was intercepted and turned back at the exact time of the attack on Pearl Harbor. When war broke on December 8 . . . enemy bombers were guided in by sympathizers or espionage agents located near military objectives. Complete reports on American air fields and troop dispositions, procured by an extensive espionage net just prior to hostilities, enabled the Japanese to concentrate their attacks accurately on the most important objectives.

One of these objectives was Clark Field, Luzon headquarters of the American Far Eastern Air Forces. The American air fleet, which consisted of fewer than 150 planes of varied combat quality, was never a ponderable element in plans for the defense of the Philippines; even so, the husbanding of the thirty-five bombers and seventy-two fighters was an important consideration. The bombers were ordered to Mindanao at the very outbreak of hostilities to dispersed landing fields then available. The obviously exposed Luzon fields were expected to be used in hit-and-run tactics only, *i.e.*, as "forward staging areas."

MacArthur's orders, however, were not carried out. And the loss of seventeen bombers on the ground at Clark Field even before hostilities were well begun was a tragedy whose repercussions are still debated by veterans of the Philippine campaign. The official records shed some light on the controversy, but the crisscross of claims still goes on, as it probably will forever.

When Lt. Gen. Lewis H. Brereton, the American air commander, was awakened sometime after two in the morning on December 8 by a telephone call from Gen. Richard K. Sutherland, MacArthur's coolheaded Chief of Staff, and informed that Pearl Harbor had been attacked, he dressed hastily and reported to MacArthur's head-quarters. It was Brereton's later recollection that he asked Suther-land to obtain MacArthur's permission to bomb Formosa with the B-17s.

While waiting for word from Sutherland, Brereton sent some of his planes on scouting missions. Recalled for loading with bombs and for reservicing, the planes were on the ground when the enemy attack came in at Clark Field around noon. As a MacArthur intel-ligence report says:

The bombers were on the ground around the luncheon hour . . . they failed to have fighter cover over the field while the bombers were being serviced. As to the Japanese approach, the air-warning system reported their flight almost continuously, without interruption.

Col. "Pappy" Gunn, a veteran of more than two hundred trips in and out of Clark Field in the first weeks of the war, left a curious deposition bearing on the bomber losses in the MacArthur files. In 1944, when MacArthur was being boomed against his will for president, the story was repeated that the General had issued orders for the planes to remain on the ground. Personnel at Clark Field reported that they had heard this said by air officers. In "Pappy" Gunn's long, somewhat scrambled statement of his wartime experi-ences, there is a cryptic bit:

One thing that really sits hard with me: General Brereton—he was a good man—he did not say this, but any man who has put himself up as a Southwest Pacific combat man and is organizing a group to combat General MacArthur in the next election and calling on veterans to help him and saying anything about orders issued to B-17s on Clark Field— I know no such orders were issued because part of the group were at Del Monte, so there could have been no orders issued not to take off Clark Field. I was at Del Monte and saw them there. I was not in the Army at the declaration of war, but I know what I actually saw the next morning after the attack. I was in Del Monte and saw them on the ground. We had about 16 or 17 at Del Monte and 16 or 17 at Clark Field. There were six on the field when I got there. Sixteen planes were knocked out completely at Clark Field.

Despite the fact that the Clark Field planes were caught in the face of previous orders from MacArthur to fly them south to Del Monte field on Mindanao, MacArthur has always defended Brereton, who, as the air commander, was of course entirely and solely responsible for the security of his planes. In 1943, when criticisms of this officer were called to his attention in Australia, he said:

General Brereton had in the Philippines only a token force which, excluding trainers and hopelessly obsolete planes, comprised but 35 bombers and 72 fighters. He was further greatly handicapped by the lack of airdromes, there being only one on Luzon, Clark Field, that was usable by heavy bombers, and only five usable by fighters. Many airdromes were under construction in the Philippines, but they were not completed and available by December 7. . . . At this time, and during succeeding days, a number of our airplanes were destroyed on the ground while landing for gas, or while down for essential maintenance . . . but never as a result of negligence.

But if MacArthur always insisted on defending Brereton against those who claimed he was guilty of carelessness, he could not, in the nature of things, have granted permission to bomb Formosa. When asked "to clear up the mystery of the order Brereton wanted but never got," he wrote:

My orders were explicit not to initiate hostilities against the Japanese. The Philippines, while a possession of the U.S., had, so far as war was concerned, a somewhat indeterminate international position in many minds, especially the Filipinos and their government. While I personally had not the slightest doubt we would be attacked, great local hope existed that this would not be the case. Instructions from Washington were very definite to wait until the Japanese made the first "overt" move. Even without such a directive, practical limitations made it unfeasible to take the offensive.

The only possibility lay in striking from the air. The relative weakness of our air situations precluded any chance of success for such an operation. Our only aggressive potential consisted of about 36 B-17s. Their only possible target was the enemy's fields on Formosa. Our advance fields in Luzon were still incomplete and our fighters from our other fields in Luzon were too far away from Formosa to protect our bombers in a Formosa attack. They did not have the necessary radius of action. The enemy's air force based on excellent fields outnumbered ours many times. In addition, he had a mobile force on carriers which we entirely lacked.

Our basic mission directive had confined our operations to our own national waters so no outside reconnaissance had been possible. The exact location of enemy targets was therefore not known. Our air force was in process of integration, radar defenses not yet operative, and personnel raw and inexperienced. An attack under such conditions would have been doomed to total failure. *As a matter of fact, I had for safety reasons ordered the bombers to withdraw from Luzon to Mindanao to be out of the enemy range.* This was in process of accomplishment when the enemy's air attacked. I did not know it at the time, but later understood that General Brereton had suggested to the Chief of Staff, General Sutherland, that we should initiate operations by an attempted "strike" at Formosa. Had such a suggestion been made to me, I would have unequivocally disapproved. In my opinion it would have been suicidal as well as in direct defiance of my basic directive.

The attempt has been made to equate the loss of seventeen bombers at Clark Field with the loss of the battleships at Pearl Harbor. But there is really no comparison; Brereton's pitiful number of planes was never enough to affect the issue in the Philippines, and they would soon have disappeared through attrition even with the most careful husbanding. As an intelligence report has said about the proposed Formosa raid:

Even if the B-17s had taken off, nothing decisive could have been expected. Takao [on Formosa] had a complex of air fields and could not possibly have been knocked out in a single raid and our planes would have run into hundreds of Japanese fighters of the calibre that hit Pearl Harbor.

The American air strength in the Philippines had been closely watched by the Japanese and was a factor in their prewar calculations. Rear Admiral Tomioka stated: "If MacArthur had an air force of 500 planes or more, we would not have ventured to strike the Philippines. Long experience had taught us that a 3 to 1 ratio was necessary to attain air supremacy." The Japanese provided for this figure; in the course of operations they employed 307 first-line army planes and 444 navy planes—a total of 751 first-class aircraft, of the same quality that hit Pearl Harbor.

As early as the spring of 1941, secret British-American diplomatic understandings had relegated the Philippines to a secondary theater —and potential doom in the event of war with Japan. This was not known by MacArthur. He never could understand the defeatist Far Eastern military strategy pursued in those early days of 1942 by the high command, both military and diplomatic, in Washington. Lacking knowledge of the motivations of Washington, MacArthur simply carried on as he had always done. With his appointment in July to command the American forces on the islands as well as the Filipino contingents, defense plans were accelerated and improved. MacArthur's local variant of the Orange Plan necessarily became part of the larger U.S. Pacific defense strategy—which was to fight in Philippine outposts until the Navy could engage and defeat the main Japanese battle fleet. Estimating that the Japanese would land in force both in the Lingayen Gulf area of northwest Luzon and to the south and east of Manila, the Orange Plan visualized delaying actions by Filipino-American forces at the beachheads. MacArthur knew he didn't have the power to throw the Japanese back into the sea anywhere, but he could fight long enough to cover the retreat into Bataan Peninsula.

When the time came for the "sideslipping" movements into Bataan, MacArthur made skilled use of the only small-tank group which he had at his disposal. Virtually useless in jungle or rice-paddy country, the tanks could be utilized just to the north of Manila to cover the bottleneck of the Calumpit Bridge. At Calumpit the roads from Manila and from northern Luzon converged to lead into Bataan; the bridge had to be kept open to the very last if the troops south of Manila were to join their comrades of the north in the prepared positions of the Bataan mountains.

The brief and violent tank action at Calumpit was decisive: the Japanese were stalled until the trucks and taxicabs of Manila had

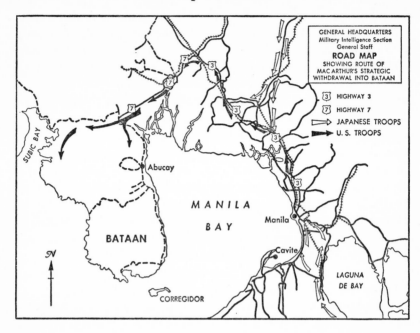

GENERAL HEADQUARTERS
Military Intelligence Section
General Staff
ROAD MAP
SHOWING ROUTE OF
MAC ARTHUR'S STRATEGIC
WITHDRAWAL INTO BATAAN

[3] HIGHWAY 3
[7] HIGHWAY 7
⟹ JAPANESE TROOPS
➤ U. S. TROOPS

completed their ferrying mission. Trucks roared across the bridge
for the better part of three days; then, on New Year's morning of
1942, Gen. Hugh ("Pat") Casey's dynamiters blew up the bridge
as the Japanese were marching out upon it.

In one of the reports of the period, weary and embittered men
remarked on empty trucks rolling into Bataan. The withdrawal of
some of Wainwright's divisions was so precipitate that there was
no time to salvage or collect supplies. Brig. Gen. C. C. Drake, the
chief supply officer who was captured by the Japanese, has testified
to the reason for the deficiency of supplies on Bataan and the empty
trucks:

Although the U.S. Army took the field well equipped in comparison
with the Philippine Army, it had very little of the War Reserve to call
upon when it fell back into Bataan. It just disappeared like the snows
of Winter on a balmy day in Spring. A good bit of it went to equip the
Philippine Army. More of it went down with the SS *Corregidor* when
it sunk after striking a mine off Corregidor bound for Cebu with supplies and equipment for the troops in the Southern Islands. Still more was
lost when we destroyed our advance depots at Tarlac, Los Banos and

Guagua as the troops retired for lack of motor transport and rail under our control . . . More of it destined for the troops in the field went to Corregidor instead of Bataan. It happened this way: On December 23rd, Dick Marshall called me into his office and informed me that General MacArthur had decided to withdraw the troops into Bataan and for me to begin stocking Bataan with all the supplies I could get my hands on. However, and he emphasized this: "No supplies would be shipped to Bataan until after all supplies were shipped to Corregidor to complete a six months' supply for a garrison of 10,000 men." That was 3,000 more than we had planned for and of course reduced by that much those destined for Bataan. We (Ward and McConnell QMC) got the supplies over there in 24 hours and then we started with what we had left and what we could beg, borrow and steal to ship to Bataan. Most of the supplies went by barge across Manila Bay, a tedious and slow job even at its best. Crews deserted their tugs and stevedores the waterfront in the Manila Port Terminal Area. Ward and McConnell did the work with volunteers they got by radio broadcast appeals. . . .

When we needed a motor transport pool to evacuate the supplies over the highways we found the pool empty. There were just 26 motor vehicles left of the 1,000 which the MTO had assembled at the beginning of the war. They had all been hi-jacked by the troops as motor convoys endeavored to move our supplies from Manila Base Depots to the Motor Heads in the division areas and the Advance Depots at Tarlac, Guagua and Los Baños. Dick Marshall called me up and said: "Charlie, you have no motor transport left. What are you going to do about it?" I replied that I was very well aware of that fact. There were no more vehicles in the Manila area and we had no facilities or personnel to go out into the "bosque" and "buscar" them. My recommendation to him was to get the division commanders to round them up in their areas, and return us our trucks and busses. I assumed he did nothing about it, except to send out orders that troops would stop hi-jacking motor vehicles, because none came back to the Manila Pool. When the MTO moved to Bataan he had just 20 trucks left to make the move. On the 2nd round trip to Bataan the vehicles had to be abandoned at San Fernando because the Engineers had blown up the bridges and they couldn't get through. However, Brezina, the Department QM, Chuck Lawrence, commanding our Advance QM Depot at Tarlac and the QM's at Stotsenberg and McKinley did get their hands on a few trucks and did heroic work moving supplies from these points to Bataan.

Now as to why "trucks arrived on Bataan empty." . . . Upon learning of the truck situation from the MTO through Kalakuka who was acting as "trouble shooter" for me in Manila, and realizing what a blow that would be to our transportation needs, I prepared a radio [message] for General MacArthur's signature directing Force Commanders to notify their division commanders to use their Field Trains (mostly our hi-jacked trucks and busses) and all other vehicles they could gather together—they had been previously authorized by USAFFE to requisition in the field such vehicles as they needed to augment their trains and to stop seizing our motor vehicles—to forage extensively for food supplies, especially rice and sugar, and to stop on their way to Bataan and pick up the supplies at QM installations as they passed by. On reaching Bataan they were to deliver these supplies to the QM Dump at Limay. Needless to say, not an ounce of food or other supplies was turned in by the division trains. . . . But the Divisions did bring in all the motor vehicles they could get their hands on, many of them empty. Later on a spot-check was made by the MT people on Bataan and they turned up well over 1,000 motor vehicles brought in by these divisions and concealed in their division areas. Now [it can be seen] why that "tank major" reported seeing empty trucks moving into Bataan.

There was an even more important collateral reason why Bataan's supplies were short: the entire preparation for defense, allocation of means, equipment, and supplies, was limited to the war-plan concept to defend for a maximum period of six months only, to hold the entrance to Manila Bay for the rescue Navy that never came.

In MacArthur's opinion, the Navy could—and should—have come. Despite the power of the Japanese in the Western Pacific, the situation in late 1941 and early 1942 seemed fluid to MacArthur; there were several things that could have been done to check the Japanese and to prepare for the relief of the Philippines.

First of all, there was the possibility of bringing diplomatic pressure to bear on the Russians. As early as December 13 MacArthur wired Secretary of War Henry Stimson to force the Soviet hand. As MacArthur puts it:

. . . the Russians had turned back the Germans before Moscow. Stalin had his great victories, the Germans had been rolled back

200 to 600 miles. That was the time for the Russians to put pressure on the North and so save the Pacific. But Churchill and the American government were against it. I was as insistent on the Russians' entrance into the war at that time as I was against it later when we had the victory in our grasp.

Even discounting the possibility of forcing the Russians to play a part in the Pacific war in early 1942, MacArthur still insists that the United States could have cut through to relieve beleaguered Bataan. The Japanese blockade of the Philippines, he says, was

. . . a paper blockade. Mindanao was still accessible if Washington had made a real effort at relief and reinforcement. The bulk of the Japanese Navy, operating on tight schedules, was headed south for the seizure of Borneo, Malaya and Indonesia. American carriers could have approached the Philippines and unloaded some planes on fields still in our possession in Mindanao. The Navy claims that they had no ships in that period. But the only thing of importance that was lost at Pearl Harbor was the battleship fleet. Actually, the Navy fought the next two years without any new ships. A serious naval effort might have saved the islands. The destroyers were at sea, keeping Japanese submarines under control. But the big ships were kept in harbor, behind nets.

As a matter of record, MacArthur's forces did everything that was provided for in the Orange Plan concept. But, as a staff report put it, they had to do it on short rations because of an unforeseen factor:

Purchase and stockage of food and ammunition would depend on peacetime appropriations against which to buy locally or import from the States but restricted to values of six months' consumption. . . . We had ammunition to the end on Bataan, but food was another story. We had about 150 days' "stocks" on hand or scraped together from Manila commercial warehouses, for about 50 or 60 thousand men. . . . Eventually, the Japanese drove the panicky civilian population of Zambales and Bataan into the Peninsula, knowing full well that we would feed them—a humanitarian measure which cut deeply into our food stocks.

The totalitarian Jap was in some ways like the totalitarian German or Russian; impervious to ordinary standards of compassion, he played it the hard way deliberately, counting on the "soft" moral standards of the West; this put our troops on half rations from the beginning.

If MacArthur did not anticipate that he would have to feed a mass of civilians on Bataan as well as his army, he did accurately make provision for the military defense of the peninsula. Early in 1941 two officers were told to investigate in complete secrecy the possibilities of Bataan as a last-ditch defense area. The officers were Hugh ("Pat") Casey, the chief engineer who later served with MacArthur all the way to Tokyo, and Charles Willoughby, Gruenert's supply officer (G-4) who later became MacArthur's chief of intelligence (G-2). As a result of the engineer and supply surveys, the Bataan road net was

. . . improved and the vulnerable Mariveles Point, a marshy area of canals and bridges, was by-passed with a new interior road cut through the adjacent hills. The China coast was provided with a country road as far as Bagac; it turned out to be extremely valuable to "Skinny" Wainwright later on. Along the inshore road skirting Manila Bay we put up provisional docks at Limay and Cabcaben. Storage warehouses, for ordnance and supplies, were discreetly built. . . . Willoughby would not allow a single tree to be cut in the dense forest area of Km 129 and small ordnance warehouses sprang up in a crazy-quilt of winding roads, quite invisible, concealed under primeval foliage; these warehouses were never hit by enemy aerial bombardment. . . .

In the summer of 1941 mobile transportation was provided by converting the commercial bus and truck companies, then operating on Luzon, into provisional motor transport units, in which every civilian driver and the administrative staff from the chairman of the board to the bookkeeper became "soldiers" overnight. We were thus able to test our ability to shuttle troops from one sector to another in a hurry. The evacuation of the South Luzon force from Batangas–Tayabas Bay area via Manila and the Calumpit Bridge en route to Bataan was handled by these militarized bus lines.

In this connection, an item is noteworthy; in addition to the warehouse and transportation preparations, MacArthur provided specifically for the care of sick and wounded, whether civil or military.

It was on December 27 that MacArthur declared Manila an open city, a declaration which the Japanese never saw fit to honor. His proclamation went:

In order to spare the metropolitan area from possible ravages of attack either by air or ground, Manila is hereby declared an open city without the characteristics of a military objective. In order that no excuse may be given for a possible mistake, the American High Commissioner, the Commonwealth government, and all combatant military installations will be withdrawn from its environs as rapidly as possible.

The Municipal government will continue to function with its police force, reinforced by constabulary troops, so that the normal protection of life and property may be preserved. Citizens are requested to maintain obedience to constituted authorities and continue the normal processes of business.

The declaration was the first inkling the Japanese had that MacArthur did not himself intend to follow Homer Lea and make a fight for the Philippine capital. Caught short by this unforeseen turn in the American strategy, the Japanese drove furiously southward against General Wainwright's north Luzon troops in an attempt to cut off the Calumpit Bridge defile. But they were just too late. To quote from the official records:

The hazardous timing of [the Calumpit] . . . movement was its most notable feature; one slip in the co-ordinated maneuver and the motor columns from southern Luzon would have been cut off and cornered in Manila. The success of this split-second operation enabled the assembly and reorganization on Bataan of the bulk of General MacArthur's forces and contributed to the subsequent brilliant defense of the peninsula. No trained veteran divisions could have executed the withdrawal movement more admirably than did the heterogeneous force of Filipinos and Americans. On January 1 General MacArthur announced the successful completion of the historic withdrawal. . . . "This movement [he said in a press release] will uncover the free city of Manila, which, because of complete evacuation by our forces previously, has no practical military value. The entrance to Manila Bay is completely covered by our forces and its use thereby denied the enemy."

MacArthur and his staff had already left Manila when Operation "Sideslip" into Bataan was set in motion. The headquarters of the Filipino Army on the Calle Victoria, where MacArthur had one of his offices, was actually a part of the old city ramparts; hence they were extremely vulnerable to bombers interested in the pattern of the ancient fortifications within a stone's throw of the harbor area. When the first bombing of the navy yard at Cavite started, the staff was ordered below into air-raid shelters while MacArthur himself walked out on the ramparts with a pair of field glasses to observe the precision of the Japanese flight formations. But this sort of calculated indifference, deliberately designed to buck up troop morale, was tempting fate. And it was also tempting fate for MacArthur to continue living in his suite at the top of the Manila Hotel. So, at midnight on December 22, the General embarked with his staff on a ferryboat for Corregidor, the historic "rock" off the southernmost tip of Bataan at the entrance to Manila Bay.

He left behind in his suite many souvenirs of his own career and that of his father. The latter had been presented with rare vases and lacquer work, gifts of the Japanese Emperor that were easily recognizable by the sixteen-petal gold chrysanthemum that is the Imperial crest. During the occupation no looting hand dared touch the suite containing the Emperor's gifts. They were destroyed when the hotel came under heavy fire in 1945, but their protective magic lasted long enough to enable MacArthur to recover a chest of table silver that might otherwise have been stolen.

As the ferry moved out of Manila Harbor carrying the MacArthur staff to its refuge on the "rock," Pat Casey's engineers started blowing up Manila's warehouses and storage tanks. Behind the group on the ferry, to quote a staff officer's memoirs:

. . . the lights of the Army and Navy Club and the Manila Hotel blinked forlornly against the backdrop of huge smoke columns limned in red, billowing to heights of hundreds of feet, with yellow and green flames stabbing intermittently through the sultry night, while the earth shook with the dull roar of incessant explosions.

There were several officers on the ferry who were destined to serve with MacArthur all through the war. His Corregidor staff included names that were to become famous in Australia, in New Guinea, and in Japan. Sutherland, Marshall, Casey, and Marquat had all been on his staff when he was military adviser to Quezon. Eisenhower had been on this staff and by the flip of a coin might have remained in the Orient. To the original group MacArthur added specialists like Akin, a signal technician. From Gruenert's staff he took over Stivers (G-1) and Willoughby; the latter had first come to MacArthur's attention in the 1930s as a lecturer in military history at the General Staff school at Ft. Leavenworth. As Chief of Staff of the Army, MacArthur had emphasized the value of historical analysis in his annual reports; he liked the use which Willoughby had made of these reports for lecture purposes.

By virtue of his position as Chief of Staff, the figure of Sutherland, the son of a Supreme Court justice, emerged early in the game. Brittle in personality, aloof, a "hard" man, Sutherland could not count on affection but found associates who were willing to work with him on the basis of devotion to the "old man." Sutherland had a difficult temper but kept it under admirable control. He inspired respect from the staff because he was an indefatigable worker, on a sixteen-hours-a-day basis, who demanded nothing from anyone that he was not perfectly willing to do himself. A handsome man with a Roman profile, he would sometimes break the mask of hardness with a sardonic smile and curious flashes of humor. He had played near-professional golf in the better days in the Philippines and kept himself in perfect physical shape. He would listen to MacArthur carefully, ascertain every nuance of his views, and then present them to the other "hard" men on the staff with impeccable *sang-froid*. Like all chiefs of staff, he was sometimes known as the "hatchet man." But in the end he ruffled no personal feelings, for his innate honesty and complete probity were soon recognized by his associates.

Richard Marshall was the next in the hierarchy of the staff. He handled supplies, procurement, and storage, a logical assignment since he belonged to the Quartermaster Corps. On Bataan he took over the forward echelon of the staff, while the rear echelon remained on Corregidor. In Australia he rose to high position, in command of the communication zone and service elements in contradistinction to the forward combat echelon, a comparatively small combined General Staff comprising Army, Navy, and Air head-quarters. As a personality, Marshall was less aggressive, less dominant than Sutherland; it was perhaps in the nature of his work that persuasion, conference methods, and compromise were more essential than the brusque decisions of execution.

Pat Casey, the engineer, handled constantly increasing responsibilities. Every category of engineer construction came under his purview, from temporary camps in Australia to airfield construction in the *kunai* grasslands of New Guinea. A great improvisor, accustomed to operate on a shoestring, his peculiar talent came into full play on Bataan. A man of charming manners and bonhomie, who worked hard and played hard, he enjoyed great popularity.

Marquat was also one of the old Adviser group; his specialty was coast- and anti-aircraft artillery. From Australia onward, he developed the complicated anti-aircraft artillery contingents on an increasing scale. An irrepressible extrovert, with a flair for puns, his sense of humor was welcome in dark hours; one of his friends called him "an oasis of wit in a wilderness of stuffed shirts"—without identifying the shirts.

The warp and woof of MacArthur's headquarters staff, a group that soon developed a recognizable pattern of efficiency, was spun in the elegant atmosphere of prewar Manila. It was put to its first shattering test in the penury and privations of Bataan.

The "rock" at Corregidor, while safer than the Hotel Manila, still left a great deal to be desired as headquarters for the long, desperate stand at Bataan. A first-class coastal installation in 1918, it had had very little added to it since that time:

. . . there was absolutely no comparison with the modern equipment of Singapore or Hong Kong. The water tower was built in pre-aerial days and stood out starkly against the skyline—a perfect target for a Japanese bombing run. The only concession to defense was a coat of camouflage paint which merely gave it a slightly rakish look. The vital cold storage plant which contained practically all our meat supply was equally exposed. We threw up a makeshift earth embankment to give it some protection.

Not only was Corregidor vulnerable to air assault, but MacArthur seemed bent on tempting the gods by placing his small group of senior staff officers in the exposed eyrie known as "Topside." This was the strangest headquarters in the world, on the very top of the Corregidor hills, in the Coast Artillery barracks, a three-story building, rather narrow, about 40 feet across and immensely long. From the air at 20,000 feet it looked like a white chalk line—an excellent aiming point for enemy bombardiers.

Notes taken by a staff officer at the time provide a picture of MacArthur's calculated indifference to the Japanese threat:

His quixotic defiance of the enemy was not an exhibition of Renaissance Italian bravado, but the subtle application of psychology. It was intended as a deliberate act of leadership. At the time when MacArthur moved his senior officers to Topside, the battered Filipino divisions had barely dug in on Bataan. A sense of frustration had already set in, with eyes anxiously directed toward Hawaii. The full extent of the disaster at Pearl Harbor was not known except for a few disquieting rumors, but the radio perorations of Colonel Frank Knox had begun to irritate raw nerves. Filipino citizen-soldiers were completely indifferent to "Hitler first" for the simple reason that the smoke pillars of their burning villages reminded them of the "Philippines now." Night after night fatuous voices crashed into the bruised consciousness of the Filipino soldiers in the Bataan trenches to remind them that they must wait and wait and die, and all because they had kept faith with America, while the substance of America was being channeled into other and distant regions. The MacArthur staff will remember forever the stony, contemptuous silence of the Filipino leader Roxas when the unctuous radio voice of Colonel Knox boasted of the rising airplane production of the United States. And they will never forget the baffled fury of President Quezon when he heard of the enormous tonnage that had begun to move across the Atlantic.

In this atmosphere of emotion, of flickering distrust and bewilderment, the brazen confidence of MacArthur became a symbol of assurance. The contemptuous occupation of the highest point of the island of Corregidor stood out boldly as a calculated affront to the arrogant conqueror.

The challenge was quickly accepted. The American flag fluttering on "Topside" while the embers of Cavite were still smoking must be lowered! With a savage onslaught on December 29 the Japanese started the steady air bombardment of Corregidor.

The previous occupants had prudently abandoned this most conspicuous landmark and had dug in around their batteries. One or two defiant mess-sergeants kept their kitchens going, at night, for a hot meal at least once a day. That, however, didn't last long. Soldiers have a fine nose for coming danger: they had pulled out before the General moved in. Now they gave the place an even wider berth.

The General hoisted his flag defiantly. His senior staff officers occupied the southern corner, first floor, with a few bunks on the second story. The silent emptiness of the immense pile gave it the air of a bedraggled monastery. As in all tropical buildings, there were colonnaded porches; the Americans filled in the arches with a row of sandbags which caved in from time to time for no reason at all but stood up beautifully when the bombardment test came.

The floor plan, at this end of the building, contained two rooms, one occupied by the General and the Chief of Staff, the other by the senior staff heads, G-1, G-2, G-3, and G-4, with a few soldier-clerks. The usual staff headquarters milieu: small folding tables, a desk or two, the spider-web of signal telephone wire hastily strung up for intercommunications. There was a troop lavatory adjacent and, through a hallway, an abandoned troop kitchen.

In the empty dormitory, upstairs, the Americans put up folding cots and hung up their "musette" bags. A few Filipino orderlies completed the menage. The rest of the immense building was abandoned. The general locality of "Topside" is a flat-top hill, with artificial fills for lawns and the parade ground. From the barracks, the usual winding sidewalk led to senior officers' quarters, built in comfortable tropical bungalow style. Most of the men were at their posts in the battery positions; the wives had long been transferred to the States. There was the indefinable air of a bachelor menage about all of them—a little lonely, a little raffish.

The MacArthurs occupied the Commander's villa, in a beautiful location with a view of enchantment over the China Sea. The color values were those of the Cote d'Azur or Miami Beach. Gaily colored tropical birds chirped in the azalea bushes. Brittle palms rustled overhead.

Suddenly at 9:00 A.M. the banshee wail of the air alarm! Of course, the MacArthur staff had been bombed before. While the American headquarters were still in Manila, the Japanese would come over, in perfect geometrical formations, showing off, in insolent exhibition, carefully selecting their targets, the dock area, the river wharves, Cavite, shipping. The white mothlike planes would creep leisurely across the blue sky. Then the tearing boom of the explosions in rapid sequence, brownish geysers or swift rising plumes. The men at Headquarters were sent down to an air-raid shelter deep in the bowels of the old Spanish fortifications, but the General would remain in his office, or take a leisurely walk out on the terrace of the old wall to chat with the anti-aircraft gunners and observe the enemy. However, the savage onslaught on "Topside" at Corregidor on December 29 was something else again. Corregidor is a small island. This was the beginning of as bad a continuous pounding as any suffered by Malta or Coventry.

It was the overture to a demoniac symphony—an oriental opus, libretto by Krupp, lyrics by Pratt & Whitney. Indeed, every feature of the hellish planes that swooped down on Corregidor came originally from the drafting boards or assembly lines of the West. Down they came, the evil birds of death, weaving boldly through the anti-aircraft fire: the pattern of their passes looked like gigantic pretzels. The first bombs crashed into the Corregidor moving picture theater. Soon the MacArthur senior staff heard the crackling of flames. The center of the Barracks was hit. The first floor contained a Post Exchange salesroom, the typical country store, with display counters, glass cases, shelves. Curious caprice of nitrocellulose: the glass cases were left intact, but standing on the rim of a gaping crater!

In a lull the beleaguered staff peeped out through a yellowish haze of pulverized earth that settled slowly. There was absolutely no doubt that the Jap was gunning for the General's barracks. The thin rectangle was a bombardier's dream to line up in a bombsight. The first hits resulted in a shell-pitted lawn; the smoking wreck of a car; strips of corrugated tin roofing scattered around crazily, like bits of waste paper.

Inside, the dust had settled on the tables. The telephone lines were cut. There was nothing to do but wait. The men sat on the floor or threw themselves prone during the worst moments. The officers, all veterans of 1917–18, maintained a fictitious professional nonchalance. Sutherland, the Chief of Staff, a cool hand, came around to chat occasionally. Now and then a specially terrific blast that made the walls tremble and sent horizontal jets of dust blasting through the crevices of the sandbag revetment. Then, curiously exaggerated lulls of silence, as if the earth were breathing. The officers looked out. The streetcar line wound around this end of the building. A 500 or 1,000 pounder had dug a crater across the road, the steel rail and ties were torn upward and twisted like a hairpin. From the General's porch the officers could look into a greenish, smoldering pit. On the opposite corner, there was another crater, even deeper and wider; the blast struck along the wall and literally curled the overhanging roof into rolls, like the curvature of a Chinese pagoda.

One of the boys remarked reflectively: ". . . if that bastard had moved his line of collimation by one horsehair, he would have dropped this thing right into MacArthur's lap. . . ." It was a most reasonable observation!

That made everybody think of the others in the officers' quarters. Of the General. Of his wife and little son. Of still others who were caught in the open or in the battery positions. The ambulances on the road. The nurses in the hospital.

The General was out in the open. He was accompanied by his Filipino orderly. Near his house, the first blast forced him to the ground, in the shallow concrete gutter. The General always disdained to wear a steel helmet. The faithful Filipino put an arm around him protectively; at this moment, his outspread hand was nicked by a steel fragment. The next blast went through the roof of his house. Fortunately, Mrs. Mac-Arthur had been taken to a nearby shelter by Colonel Huff, an aide-de-camp.

Intermittent bombing and strafing: The hailstone rattle of machine-gun bullets overhead. The sharp crack of anti-aircraft guns. The throbbing and screaming of dive bombers. The artificial gloom created by pulverized dust that rose from the tortured earth like a fog. The sun, hung against this yellow curtain like a distorted Chinese lantern. The hours seemed endless. In a lull, the General sent Sutherland to round up the men and find refuge in an adjacent concrete telephone exchange that had a top cover of about fifteen feet of earth, steel doors and a frontal row of sandbags. It wasn't foolproof by engineering standards, but it was better than the barracks.

There the officers passed the rest of the day. The last sortie was made by the enemy toward 4 o'clock. The "forward echelon" of Headquarters then decided to join the "rear echelon" in the tunnel.

An eyewitness story of what this hellish bombardment looked like from the "outside" was reported by Colonel Allison Ind, Air Corps.

On this same Monday, December 29, he was over on Bataan, on the southern slope of Mariveles, in a perfect ringside seat to observe the aerial attack on Corregidor: ". . . It was nearing mid-day when the first wave of the familiar twin-engined bombers came over . . . this must be the bomb release—yes, there they were: those tiny, black dots hurtling downward in a long, forward-sweeping arc . . . a ripping flicker halfway up the dark flank of the island; the earth seemed to swell in a black-brown bubble . . . the ground beneath us quivered to the immensity of the explosion on distant Corregidor across two miles of water.

"This was no nuisance raid. This was the 'real thing,' deadly and enormously destructive . . . high up on 'Topside' the long, white scar that was the concrete structure of the main barracks spat swift jets of dirty, gray smoke from a thousand sudden fractures. . . . Another attack. This time the sky was no longer blue but a mottled gray . . . a gigantic funeral pyre for more than a score of gun crews buried under tons of debris in an improvised bomb shelter . . . for three crazy hours, the man-made storm of lightning and thunder raged over the now almost obscured island. . . ."

On Tuesday, December 30, Ind had this to say: " 'We've re-established communication with the Rock, sir,' announced the Sergeant on duty. His face looked grim in the shaded light of the receiving panel. 'They really plastered the boys over there yesterday,' he continued in a low voice. . . . They blew out most of 'Topside' and for a while there was a rumor that they had General MacArthur and General Sutherland and most everybody else, including Mrs. MacArthur and the boy."

This is how it looked to an "outsider"—miles across the channel. It was a close call; there were other situations quite as deadly, though none quite so spectacular. After the hellish demolition, the General began a curious meandering housemoving. Corregidor is built in terraces; "Topside" was the choicest peacetime locality.

The General left his now wrecked bungalow there to start a definitely downward career, from one terrace to the next, literally shot out from one house to another. It was pure coincidence, of course, but the Jap fire followed consistently. He had a breathing spell for quite a few weeks until the Jap began firing with 155's from the south shore of Bataan. Toward the end, no space on the island was really safe. When the planes had finished, long-range batteries began harassing fire, and lobbed shells in a crazy incalculable pattern day and night. The robots of London must have been just about as erratic.

The tunnel was mainly a 24-hour office; to the end, the officers slept in folding cots outside the entrance or on the winding adjacent trails —until an exploding shell scattered rocks over everybody as a delicate reminder to move on.

MacArthur's senior staff had established a tent space, on the outside, as an al fresco dining room for the rice and carabao stew that became a standard menu twice a day. The General always had at least one meal with the staff and brought Mrs. MacArthur along. The attractive lady made it a point to introduce a note of normal living into the tense atmosphere of danger by always looking well groomed and charming and acting as if this were a peacetime garrison. The staff wondered how she managed to look continually *soignée* in the dusty squalor of the Corregidor catacombs.

The so-called tunnel was, in fact, a wide driveway, with streetcar tracks, cut at an incline through the rocks; lateral shafts radiated from this central artery, some used as hospital wards, others as storerooms and ammunition magazines. One of the laterals was used as the Headquarters, with a row of desks, glaring drop lights and the usual orderly litter of an administrative establishment. Outside, the whir of cars or ambulances or the subdued murmur of men, coming or going; there was always some repair work required and gangs of laborers employed thereon.

When an air alarm sounded, the General usually rose and tagged someone of the staff to accompany him. He then would casually wind his way through the now silent mob, sitting on their haunches in that age-old oriental posture of patience and stolid resignation, step through the sandbag revetment at the entrance, past the sentries and on out along the highway, to watch the firing or shelling or the weaving pattern of the enemy's air formations. There was always a slightly morbid curiosity involved in following the glistening silver moths far up in the sky. The bomb-bays would open, the strings of bombs would cascade downward like obscene streams of monstrous fish eggs.

There is a scientific basis for calculation, the exact point of impact; one quickly learned to judge it, but the tell-tale whistling scream was a better guide; when it reached the crescendo of venom, one had a second or two to jump into a ditch or drop prone to the ground.

To dare the bombs in a sally to the open is a commander's bitter privilege. Noblesse oblige! The men liked it. The subtle corrosion of panic or fatigue, or the feeling of just being fed-up, can only be arrested by the intervention of a true commander. Leadership is often crystallized in an open sacrifice, making a public gesture; like breaking bread as a symbol of hospitality; finally, there is the fraternity of danger, the common denominator of sudden death.

The milieu may change—the obligation of the commander is constant. MacArthur understood and practised a commander's grim prerogative in the France of 1917. In the shadow of defeat, in the Philippines, he resumed his precarious privilege.

Meanwhile, as MacArthur was dodging bombs on Corregidor, the troops fought the long delaying action on Bataan to the north, using the interdiction fire of cleverly placed artillery to brilliant advantage. The story of that protracted, bitter fight, carried on during the latter stages by half-starved men, has been eloquently detailed in books by General Wainwright and others. As the official records sum it up:

The resistance afforded by the American and Filipino forces against successive concentrations of superior strength in all components and branches had developed into an epic of courage and tenacity. . . . For many . . . weeks the line from Bagac to Orion had held steady. The enemy had begun to avoid bloody frontal assaults and to resort to landings on the west coast behind the American-Filipino lines, or to attempted penetration raids, to stab deep into the battle line, only to be sealed off and liquidated. If only help could have reached the Philippines, even in small force, if only limited reinforcement could have been supplied, the end could not have failed to be victory.

To the men in the mud and downpour of the Bataan jungles, the struggle, even if epic to the outside world, often seemed forlorn and hopeless. It seemed even more useless in retrospect to many of the men who lived through the famous "death march" and the voyage by "hell ship" to captivity in Japanese or Manchurian prison camps.

But to the Japanese General Homma, Bataan was not a victory but a defeat. Heavy-set and dominating, bull-like in his reactions, Homma insisted that Bataan must be taken, not merely contained. As Bataan wore on, Homma made wistful remarks on the swiftness of the Japanese victory at Port Arthur in 1904! When Hong Kong fell in two weeks and Singapore in two months, it was a terrible goad to Homma. He pressed and tore at the hasty field fortifications of Bataan. The Japanese acknowledged the important effect of the protracted resistance in the Philippines. Staff officers of the Japanese Fourteenth Army expressed themselves as follows:

Politically it stood as a symbol to the Filipinos and encouraged them to continue their resistance. There was a spiritual influence exerted by the Americans on Bataan. The Japanese at home worried about the length of this resistance.

For this loss of face Homma apparently never forgave Wainwright; it was Homma who became the villain of the infamous "death march" of the captured veterans of Bataan.

By the end of January Homma had to cease operations and call for substantial reinforcements:

General Homma studied documents captured in Manila and realized that Bataan was very strongly defended. General Sugyama, the chief of staff, Imperial Headquarters, personally flew to the Philippines to investigate. It was realized that Bataan could not be taken with available troops. Imperial Headquarters ordered the transfer of the 4th Division and a mixed Brigade, from China, the Kitajima heavy artillery group from Hong Kong, and several aerial bombardment groups from Burma and Malaya.

The impact of the defense of the Philippines began to make itself felt, from Hong Kong to Singapore. Tokyo began to worry.

The extent to which Bataan threw the Japanese off stride became fully apparent in interrogations and the postwar testimony of the Japanese generals, which appear in translation in the MacArthur records:

. . . it was anticipated that General MacArthur would deploy his troops in key positions around Manila and endeavor to hold the capital as long as possible. The Intelligence Section of the Army General Staff also foresaw the possibility of an enemy withdrawal to Bataan Peninsula, but since knowledge was lacking regarding the existence of any prepared defense positions in that area, such a contingency was not regarded seriously. It was estimated that, if such a withdrawal took place, the enemy forces could easily be bottled up and destroyed. . . . General Staff planners took the practical view that [Manila's] capture would largely achieve the main strategic purpose of the Philippine invasion: the quick elimination of American bases. It was also expected that the fall of Manila would exert a strong psychological effect toward demoralizing Filipino resistance, and thereby facilitate the pacification of the Philippines.

What would MacArthur have done if he had been Homma? In the light of the MacArthur leapfrog "hit 'em where they ain't" strategy, as it developed later in the war, he would almost certainly have sealed off Bataan with a holding force and gone on to the south. The Japanese tied up valuable men, material, and ships for six months in the Philippines that might have been used to seize the south coast of New Guinea or the crucial island of Guadalcanal. Australia would thus have been virtually isolated from America. But Homma was not MacArthur—or maybe it was Count Terauchi, Homma's suave, elegant, and aristocratic superior as Japan's Southern Commander, who was not MacArthur. Because the Japanese did not think like MacArthur, the Americans were able to use the protracted delay at Bataan to cover MacArthur's escape by PT boat and plane to Australia, where the "return" to the Philippines was already being planned before the last shell had burst over Bataan or the flag had been struck at Corregidor.

3 The Brisbane Line Is
Not Enough

ON February 22, 1942, President Roosevelt ordered MacArthur out
of the Philippines and told him to proceed to Australia. Two weeks
later MacArthur was still on Corregidor. He didn't want to leave.

Various passages from the MacArthur records describe the General's feelings about quitting the Philippines. He was loath

. . . to leave because he knew that the Japanese had lost heavily on
Bataan and he had planned to organize an early counter-attack against
them. . . . He sensed the slowdown in Japanese resistance and planned
a breakthrough to continue a guerrilla type of warfare in Northern
Luzon.

With his long and intimate acquaintance with the Philippines,
MacArthur knew the meaning of the white, uncharted areas still
on the maps—blank spots where no white man had ever set foot
from the time of the Spanish conquest to the time of the American
occupation. He wanted to put guerrillas in some of these areas.
With such plans stabbing at his mind, he had ignored an earlier
"suggestion" from Roosevelt that he leave Corregidor. The notion
of a breakthrough in Luzon haunted him for a long time; in a message sent to Gen. George C. Marshall from Australia in early April,
MacArthur said:

I am utterly opposed under any circumstances or conditions to the
ultimate capitulation of this [the Bataan] command. If it is to be destroyed, it should be on the field of battle in order to exact full toll
from the enemy. To this end I had long ago prepared a comprehensive
plan for cutting a way out if food or ammunition failed. This plan
contemplated an ostentatious artillery preparation on the left by the
I Corps as a feint and a sudden surprise attack on the right by the II
Corps . . . taking the enemy's Subic Bay positions in reverse simul-

taneously with a frontal attack by the I Corps. If successful, the supplies seized at this base might well rectify the situation. . . . If the movement is not successful and our forces defeated, many increments thereof, after inflicting important losses upon the enemy, could escape through the Zambales Mountains and continue guerrilla warfare in conjunction with forces now operating in the north. . . . I would be very glad if you believe it advisable for me to attempt to rejoin this command temporarily and take charge of this movement.

The guerrilla breakthrough idea was never carried out because both Roosevelt and the Australians were peremptory about the need for an over-all command for the whole Southwest Pacific Area. Grudgingly, the General gave way. By March 11 he had selected those who were to go with him—besides his immediate family there were eighteen servicemen, including his aide, Col. Sid Huff. For the record, this wartime group comprised the following officers: Lieut. Gen. Richard K. Sutherland, C of S; Maj. Gens. Richard J. Marshall, Deputy C of S, Charles P. Stivers, G-1, and Charles A. Willoughby, G-2. Others joined in Australia to complete the General Staff: Lieut. Gen. Stephen J. Chamberlin, G-3; Maj. Gens. Lester D. Whitlock, G-4, and Harold E. Eastwood, G-4; Brig. Gens. Burdett M. Fitch, AG, and Bonner B. Fellers, G-5; and Col. Laurence E. Bunker, ADC.

Two general factors governed the selection of those who were to go out. The first factor was possible contribution to the eventual liberation of the Philippines: such men as Sutherland, Marshall, Casey, Akin, Marquat, and Willoughby were chosen to form the nucleus of a staff capable of planning the return to the islands. The second factor was general usefulness to the United States: Admiral Rockwell and Captain Ray were taken because the Navy wanted them for reassignment. In the case of Colonel Sherr, humanitarian considerations prevailed; Sherr had been a cryptographer to General Akin, and if the Japanese ever got hold of him they would certainly put him to gruesome tortures in order to extract code keys.

In the eyes of the remaining "smoke-begrimed men covered with the murk of battle . . . the grim, gaunt, ghastly men" of Bataan (the words are MacArthur's), it was a matter of grave doubt that the little escape party would succeed in breaking through to Mindanao, whence they could be flown to Australia. The odds were all against them. It was one of the most hazardous chances of history.

On March 10 MacArthur called in his daredevil naval commander, Lt. John Bulkely, to check on the condition of the four remaining PT boats of Squadron Three. The PTs, each of them 70 feet of light plywood from stem to stern, were powered by costly Packard motors, which after long and arduous service were hardly in the best of shape. Clogged with carbon and rust, and no longer able to match the speed of a Japanese destroyer, the PTs represented a real risk in the eyes of most of MacArthur's party. But MacArthur was confident. He had sent President Quezon and Francis Sayre successfully to Australia in submarines, but he chose for himself the more open way. It was a daring choice but understandable to fighting men.

The escape party assembled at the Corregidor dock in the dark of the moon on March 11. Because of bombings the dock had long since been abandoned; it was guarded by a lone sentry in a concrete shelter. That night, however, there were people waiting in the shadows to see MacArthur off. Among those who had been told of the departure at the last minute was Jonathan Wainwright, who was left with the hopeful order to "hold out until I come for you." With tears in his eyes Wainwright accepted the command. MacArthur shook hands with "Skinny" Wainwright and, for the first time, used the words: "I shall return." The scene at the dock was etched unforgettably for those who were there. An eyewitness account tells it as follows:

Corregidor rises abruptly from the water's edge where Bulkely's PT stood by. All boarded promptly except the General, who stopped and turned slowly to look back. What a transformation had taken place in that normally beautiful spot. Its vivid green foliage was gone with its trees, its shrubs, its flowers, all bruised and torn by the hail of relentless and devastating bombardment. That warped and twisted face of scorched rock seemed to reflect the writhings of a tortured body. It had become a black mass of destruction. Up on Topside the heavy guns still rent the air with their red blasts and deep roars. They were commanded by Paul Bunker, MacArthur's classmate at West Point, a famous all-American back on the team MacArthur had managed. He and many others of those thousands were old, old friends, bound by ties of deepest comradeship. What thoughts must have crowded his mind as he looked his farewell. And then I saw him slowly raise his cap in salute, there in the twilight, as he glanced up through the smoky haze with its smell of death and stench of destruction thick in the night air. And it seemed to me that I could see a sudden convulsive twitch in the muscles of his jaw, a sudden whitening in the bronze of his face. I said to the man next to me: "What's his chance of getting through?" "About one in five," was the reply. And then the General's quiet voice as he stepped aboard the boat: "You may cast off, Buck, when you are ready." And then they moved off into the night.

MacArthur's confidence in the PT boats had a very solid background. Since he had been personally responsible for developing the type for a Philippine government that could hardly afford more expensive naval craft, he had a thorough technical appreciation of the PT's power and capacity. A reminiscence of his staff on that particular point:

To some extent he was the father of the PT boat in the Far East. He had worked out the plan of operations with Bulkely. If discovered, there was no intention of running but to attack. The PT carries torpedoes fore and aft—the four of them had sixteen. And there is nothing that a cruiser is more afraid of than a torpedo. Bulkely had planned the formation of the four boats, a lozenge formation predicated on their fire power. If a Japanese cruiser was encountered, the plan was to launch an immediate attack, spreading a torpedo pattern in simultaneous salvos. Then to scatter and run for it.

This was no small scale movement. The General was no youngster chosen to ride from the stockade through the Indian lines. This was the attempt of a Commander-in-Chief and his party to move to another theater of war for other operations. The Japanese themselves had emphasized the significance of such a movement. We had been listening to the broadcasts of "Tokyo Rose." She had been threatening that MacArthur, in case of capture, would be hung in public in the Imperial Plaza in Tokyo, where the Imperial towers overlook the traditional parade ground of the Emperor's Guard Divisions. It was to be five years later at the first parade review of Occupation troops in Japan that General MacArthur as Supreme Commander for the Allied Powers took the salute at the Imperial Plaza on the exact spot where Tokyo

Rose had so dramatically predicted his coming execution in the dark days of 1942.

It is possible that the Japanese had some inkling of the movements on the night of March 11, for as the PT's moved southward toward Mindoro, huge bonfires began to light up along the shores in a chain of improvised signals. The sea was getting rough and visibility was going down as the hours wore on. We knew we must be closing on the Japanese blockading fleet and the growing suspense grew tense. Suddenly there they were, the silhouettes of cruisers against the flickering patches of drifting clouds. Black, sinister blotches of slowly moving monsters bent upon destruction. We held our breath waiting for that first crashing gun to challenge our identity. Ten seconds. Twenty. Sixty. They had not spotted us, we lay so low in the tossing seas. "Put her hard on starboard," came the sharp order, and we slid by in the blackness of the night. But the heavy weather in the open sea with doused navigation lights was becoming too much for our worn-out boats and gradually we became scattered. The contingency had been foreseen and a rendezvous selected.

It was now each boat for itself to reach the appointed spot at the uninhabited Cuyo Islands.

The No. 2 boat was first in. Suddenly through the morning mist zooming in at thirty miles an hour came what appeared to be a Japanese destroyer. Instantly the extra drums containing 500 gallons of gasoline were jettisoned to make a run for it and the torpedo tubes cleared for action. Just as the signal to fire was to be given, the figure of MacArthur was recognized standing in the bow of the onrushing vessel. It was close —a real "squeaker." No. 3 came in later. No. 2, having lost its fuel, was unable to go on and its personnel was crammed aboard the other two before the trip to Mindanao could be resumed. A submarine had been directed to meet the PT flotilla at the Cuyo Islands but failed to make the rendezvous. For hours during the hot day the boats waited, still spots on the water, camouflaged as best could be from the searching eyes of enemy planes.

Despairing of his No. 4 boat, MacArthur finally gave the order to push on south across the Mindanao Sea in an endeavor to reach Cagayan on the North Coast of the great island of Mindanao. The sea was high, the night clear, the going rough indeed. The General said later he felt "as though he were in a cocktail mixer." Suddenly square athwart the way loomed an enemy warship black and menacing. It was too late to dodge, too close to run. The only hope was to cut the engines, lie still, and make the sign of the cross. The seconds ticked slowly, ran into minutes—but no sign from the battleship. We had undoubtedly been taken for one of the native fishing fleet which was putting out its nets. She steamed slowly past, making her leisurely way to the west and opening up the road to safety.

As for the fourth PT, it never did make contact with the main party. Without an experienced navigator, it somehow found its way alone to Cagayan, on the north coast of Mindanao. Willoughby's report on the vagaries of this PT on which he was a passenger reads:

We were behind schedule and reached the north coast of Mindanao in broad daylight. It was a clear, dazzling day. Fortunately no Japanese planes cut across the blue sky, though the enemy was known to make regular mail flights from Mindanao to Luzon. We felt pretty conspicuous as the hours dragged on. Each promontory with a fringe of palms looked like the next one. Based on azimuth bearings in a navigational guide book, I took a few sighting shots with a ruler, only to admit failure. Casting professional naval pride aside, we turned toward the shore. There was a small village. The fish traps cut geometrical patterns in the glittering water. A schoolhouse and a cluster of excited children around the schoolteacher. I gambled on the impact of American teaching and had a sailor flag a signal. Sure enough, a little boy scout popped up and began to wig-wag, slowly but accurately. That's how we got the name of the village and our map location. We were actually close to our destination, Cagayan. One more palm fringe and we could have picked it up ourselves—not to mention the Del Monte cannery at Bugo, with gaping holes in the warehouses. We found out later that a Jap destroyer had shelled the place the day before.

At Del Monte, a makeshift airfield that was camouflaged by day by spotting movable trees about its terrain, the MacArthur party was startled by two developments. Planes from Australia had been directed to be there, but there were no planes. MacArthur's own report of this is deadpan:

Upon arrival at Mindanao we learned that of four planes dispatched, only one had arrived and that without brakes or superchargers, and being unfit for its mission it had already departed. Brett [Commander of Allied Air in Australia] selected three more planes for the trip, of which one developed mechanical trouble and two arrived safely, taking the entire party out. Safe arrival and departure forced us to pass the latitude of Ambon at dawn, but our course was set somewhat to the eastward, enabling the party to escape interception. We landed at Batchellor Field while Darwin was under air raid.

Behind the difficulties of providing planes there is a story of red tape that mystified and angered many on MacArthur's staff. Gen. George H. Brett, air commander in Australia, has left a record of the troubles:

I received a radiogram from General Marshall informing me that General MacArthur would call on me to send a flight of long-range bombers to Mindanao before March 15. . . . From the wreckage of Java I had brought a dozen B-17s of the 19th Group. They were in pretty bad shape. In a fully equipped air force they all would have been scrapped. . . . But they were all we had, and we had to keep them flying, if we tied them together with chewing gum and baling wire. . . . I looked over my B-17s. . . . There wasn't a bomber in the lot fit for the Philippine trip. . . . There was only one way out. Twelve new Flying Fortresses had just arrived in Australia, but they were assigned to the Navy. . . . I went to Admiral Herbert Fairfax Leary and told him I had to get MacArthur out of the Philippines. . . . Could I borrow three of his planes to bring him to Australia. Leary had the reputation of saying no to all requests, unless he could see that the Navy would benefit by his acquiescence. "I'd like to help you, Brett," he said, "but it is quite impossible. We need those planes here and can't spare them for a ferry job, no matter how important it is."

Since Brett had no authority over the Navy, he was compelled to send the best of his old B-17s. One fell into the sea and two turned back because of engine trouble. So Brett went back to Admiral Leary. This time he got the Navy planes; as he says, "Perhaps Leary had heard from Washington . . . the Admiral loaned me four beautiful new bombers. . . ."

The three-day delay at Del Monte might have proved disastrous for the MacArthur party, for it soon became apparent that their

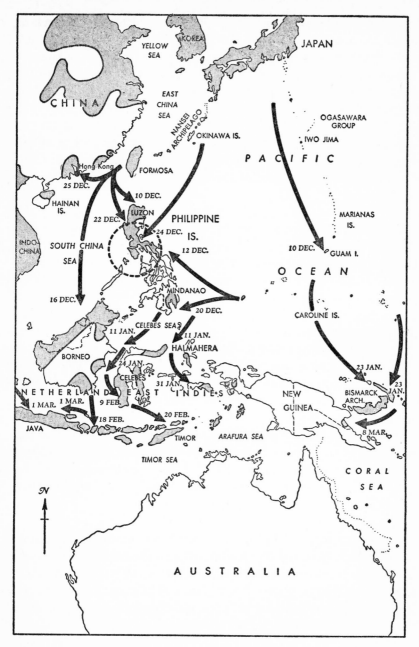

Isolation of MacArthur's forces in the Philippines, and the Japanese
thrust toward the Malay Barrier

arrival on Mindanao was known far beyond the confines of the pineapple plantation where the airfield lies. The Japanese had long been in control of Davao, at the other end of the island, and their patrols had been seen on more than one central Mindanao road. Almost immediately after the MacArthur arrival at Del Monte an old "sunshiner," an American veteran of the War of 1898, came into the post from 25 miles away, with his youngish Moro wife. The Moro lady announced that she had girls in school in Manila, and insisted on talking with Mrs. MacArthur. General Sutherland, fearing treachery, promptly put the Moro woman and her husband under surveillance, which made them extremely angry. They never saw the MacArthurs and were kept under guard until the planes had taken off for Australia. Nothing came of the incident, but the staff has always wondered how MacArthur's arrival at Del Monte could have been known in advance in the interior of Mindanao.

On March 16 two of the Flying Fortresses that had been cadged by Brett from the Navy finally arrived, landing by flare in the darkness. Although the failure of a third plane through engine trouble obviously spelled some more overloading, MacArthur decided to chance it. The last leg of the escape journey began with the General and his party throwing away practically all of their luggage and with the No. 1 plane going down the runway with one engine sputtering and missing before it finally took hold.

As the two Fortresses soared southward in the dark, over Mindanao and out across the Celebes Sea, enemy fighters from Timor rose to get them but failed to close in the darkness. The MacArthur party cast many a backward glance into the night. So much had been done to keep the Filipinos steamed up for continued resistance to the Japanese, yet one could never know. Bataan had been primed to fight to the end, but that was only the forlornest of hopes. The party could only trust that enough had been done on balance to keep the Filipinos inwardly rebellious and disposed to widespread guerrilla activity, even though the Japanese were to overrun all of the islands.

There had been the delicate problem of convincing the Filipino President, Manuel Quezon. On February 28, speaking from Corregidor, Quezon had addressed a message to his people. As it rests in the MacArthur files, the message still has a noble ring:

I urge every Filipino to be of good cheer, to have faith in the patriotism of valor of our soldiers in the field, but above all, to trust America. . . . The United Nations will win this war. America is too great and too powerful to be vanquished in this conflict. I know she will not fail us.

Bringing Quezon to this pitch of confidence in the purposes of the United States, however, had taken quite a bit of doing. For Quezon had been listening to the radio speeches of Franklin Roosevelt and his cabinet. It was the Atlantic war, not the Japanese, that was bothering Washington in those days, and Quezon felt the Philippines were being given the brush-off. Sitting in his wheelchair and racked by tuberculosis, Quezon felt caged and frustrated whenever he heard the suave fireside voice telling Americans about the thousands of aircraft that would shortly be coming from the assembly lines and on their way—to Europe!

One day, when the radio was blaring, MacArthur quietly motioned to Willoughby (who spoke Spanish, Quezon's favorite idiom) to go down and handle the situation. Quezon was livid with rage; Dr. Trepp, his Swiss physician, and Dona Aurora, his devoted wife, were trying to calm him down, but meeting with no success whatever.

"*Ole, llegastes al mejor momento*," shouted Quezon as Willoughby entered the tent. . . . "*Escuchastelo que dicen los sinverguenzas de Washington.* Listen to what the 'shameless' ones are saying in Washington."

A torrent of bitter denunciation poured from his lips. From time to time he pointed to Manila, toward Cavite and the south. It was a typical glittering day. The sea was a brilliant blue as on some Riviera. It was hot and still in the ravine. The birds had long since vanished, driven away by the daily bombing of the Japanese. Far to the south, probably in Ternate, black columns of smoke rose high in the skies above a burning hamlet, where the Japanese had been. He pointed to that ominous plumage and said:

"For thirty years I have worked and hoped for my people. Now they burn and die for a flag that could not protect them. *Por Dios y todos los Santos.* I cannot stand this constant reference to England, to Europe.

. . . I am here and my people are here under the heels of a conqueror. Where are the planes that this *sinverguenza* is boasting of? *Que demonio* —how typically American to writhe in anguish at the fate of a distant cousin while a daughter is being raped in the back room. . . ."

To counter the depressing effect of the Washington broadcasts, MacArthur set up a radio transmitter on Corregidor to proclaim the "Voice of Freedom," Filipino style. Carlos Romulo handled some of the script. To help shore up Filipino morale, on March 3, 1942, a script was aimed at demolishing the legend of the Japanese superman:

. . . when the Japanese hordes swept down . . . the legend was built around the emotional fanaticism of the Samurai which was believed to inspire the soldiers to accomplish the impossible. . . . The legend is now shattered. . . . Physical clashes of the front-line fighters tell the story; Filipinos and Americans, shoulder to shoulder and greatly outnumbered, have stopped and thrown back the Japanese infantry. The Japanese soldier emerges from the shattered legend as a man with feet of clay. We have some revealing statistics on prisoners of war: average weight 125.8 pounds; average height five-foot-three. . . . In the range of occupations: farmers 30 per cent, clerks 20 per cent, mechanics and trades 25 per cent. There are ribbon clerks, cooks and such; there is even a waterfront fish-ball vendor from Osaka who knows and likes American tourists—and they liked his fish-balls, so he boasts. Of such is the stuff which the so-called Japanese superman is made.

With such material, the Voice of Freedom on Corregidor tried to erase the unfortunate effect of the Europe-oriented voices that came drifting through the air from America. Quezon was never satisfied, but eventually he went on to Washington to become his country's representative on the Pacific Council. Consumed by tuberculosis, he died before he could see his native land again. His wife, Dona Aurora, did live to see the liberation and the peace, but only to be murdered by the Hukbalahaps after the war was over.

MacArthur knew, as his planes skirted Ambon and passed over the Malay "Barrier" to sight the Australian continent at dawn, that the original Filipino guerrilla network would tend to disintegrate with the collapse of Bataan. But he knew also that Quezon's final broadcast to the Filipino people would have its effect, provided Japanese cruelties continued unabated. He knew that many Filipino and even islander American agents would manage to survive and form nuclei of resistance and a skeleton for the underground.

There was Joe Stevenot, for example. Stevenot, who happened to be the American manager of the Philippine Long Distance Telephone Company, had joined MacArthur's headquarters on Corregidor as a reserve colonel. To quote from the intelligence files, he had

. . . maintained a telephone line into the main Manila switchboard via the Yacht Club cable terminal and received reports on the Japanese in the city from his intrepid chief operator until the middle of February, when it was felt that it was too risky to expose this faithful woman to an obvious death penalty were she discovered. On the other hand, considering that the main switchboard had thousands of terminals, the tracing of calls would be time consuming, if it were really undertaken; in a foreign language it was probably impossible. However, in such a tense situation, of course, there is always the danger of betrayal; there were many Filipino traitors and informants, drawn from the criminal classes.

Stevenot, who was a noted bon vivant, had smuggled a few bottles of Jerez and Oporto to Corregidor; they were marked "Fragile: Signal Tubes" and were cached under his cot in the tunnel area. When things got too tough, we would have a sip carefully rationed out in paper cups. This slightly convivial gathering usually covered the time when we plugged into the Manila exchange.

Stevenot's voice was of course known to all the operators of the main exchange. The conversation was usually in Spanish:

". . . We are interested in selling some crushed stone if the price is right."

"The manager is not here at the moment" (if the Jap inspector was absent), or: "The manager is here and I will connect you" (if a Jap snooper was in the offing).

"Can you arrange a delivery to the Golf Club?" (This indicated that the Jap was using the place for some barracks or depot and he was likely to be bombed by us as long as our planes lasted, which was not very long.)

Stevenot turned over his wire and repair stocks, machinery and technical paraphernalia of every category running into millions on a pencil receipt by our Signal Officer. This generous and fearless man finally made good his escape from the Philippines, only to die in an airplane crash on Noumea.

Then there was Col. Andres Soriano, who belonged in the same category as Stevenot. A millionaire business executive in civil life, he left immensely valuable properties in Manila to join a Filipino division on Bataan; later on he set up the fiscal and administrative machinery in the Visayas and Mindanao to offset the Japanese occupation. And there was Juan Elizalde, president of the most important Spanish firm in the islands, who headed an information group in Manila; he was eventually betrayed and executed in Fort Santiago with other members of his net.

Before the outbreak of the war, many American businessmen, miners and plantation owners had been enrolled secretly in an intelligence underground with a view to forming a nucleus of information in case the Japanese were successful in overrunning the Islands. Col. Joseph K. Evans, an able intelligence operator on the staff of G-2 (Philippine Department), was very active in the prewar development of this clandestine service. In December 1942, Evans, then in Washington, was one of the first to establish radio contact with the guerrillas in the Philippines—Station WYY: Major Praeger, in northern Luzon.

Several FBI-trained operatives of Japanese ancestry, "Nisei," had been imported from Hawaii in the prewar months to keep the Japanese population in the Philippines under discreet surveillance. Those men later rendered most important services on Bataan in the interrogation of prisoners of war, in the translation of captured documents, and as counterintelligence agents. Their use called attention to the linguistic potentialities of the American Nisei; this was the modest beginning of a later famous institution: the Allied Translator and Interpreter Service.

Close liaison was always maintained with the prewar Philippine

Constabulary; many of its best operatives were later to appear again in the counterespionage and in the guerrilla movement. The Philippine Department employed many special intelligence agents, including a narcotic expert of the U.S. Treasury Department. This man was given an undercover identity, as a soldier, and was later imprisoned, first in Cabanatuan and then in Bilibid. He must have been very lucky indeed; by the sheerest chance he was never recognized, although the Japanese imported many shady characters from Shanghai, where this man had worked for many years; by that token he was able to spot them too.

Under the impact of the Japanese occupation, the initial American network disintegrated; the men were either killed or interned. Many Filipino agents, however, managed to live. A typical prewar agent, Miss Yay Panlillio, an able journalist, survived the Jap occupation, and eventually became the mainspring of the guerrilla group.

The story of Yay, as it exists in the intelligence files, shows why MacArthur's faith in Filipino resistance and resurgence was justified:

Yay worked for us before the war. She had instructions to stay on and make any convenient deal with the Japanese propaganda units. She was pretty well known to the Japanese journalists and businessmen who had drifted in and out of Manila, during the prewar period. It was expected that they would woo her to work on some broadcast program, to offset our "Voice of Freedom."

She went on the air, much to the fury and consternation of the Corregidor people, who did not know the real story . . . and accused her of turning traitor.

The Japanese in those days put great emphasis on "austere living" as opposed to the enervating luxury of American ways. Yay would rattle obediently along those lines and just to make everybody homesick put on a good old syncopated American record. She became more and more reckless, making cracks about the occupation. She was bound to run into trouble; sooner or later some local informer would denounce her.

Suddenly, she went off the air, and we were certain that disaster had overtaken her. However, many months later we picked up her trail again, when her name appeared in other intelligence channels, associated with the guerrilla chief Marking, whom she subsequently married, in her stormy fashion.

Besides a scattering of potential guerrilla agents, MacArthur had left behind him the well-defined group of Brig. Gen. Simeon de Jesus. This had been set up in January 1942, as a nucleus of clandestine activities. The mission of de Jesus's outfit, according to the intelligence files, was

. . . to collect, evaluate and disseminate military information obtained in Bataan, Zambales, Pampangas and other occupied areas, through a chain of agents operating behind the enemy lines. Based on Bataan, de Jesus had under his direct charge about sixty agents, most of whom were former Constabulary officers and enlisted men. These experienced and intrepid men crossed the Japanese lines either on foot or by cutting across the northwestern corner of Manila Bay in "bancas," and proceeded on their itineraries; the system was crude, the main difficulty being communications; it took the agents sometimes a whole week to come back. . . . To expedite communications, de Jesus's men established a radio station in Manila, located in the projection room of a movie theater; the noise in the projection room effectively masked the sounds of the transmitter and the crowds in the theater made possible the movements to this focal point, without attracting attention. This radio station was in operation about six weeks prior to General MacArthur's departure and continued undetected until some time after the fall of Bataan.

The de Jesus group did not cease functioning after the surrender. Although scattered, its members went underground and slowly rebuilt their disrupted organization; even in remnant status, this group set the general pattern which was followed in subsequent intelligence penetration. Many of these brave men died ultimately at the hands of the enemy, the Japanese military police, the dreaded Kempei-tai. . . . Quite early in the war, prominent residents of Manila entered the grim game that only too often ended in the torture chamber of old Fort Santiago. General de Jesus died that way. . . .

Under de Jesus agent after agent slipped across Manila Bay, to mingle with the fishermen of Hagonoy and then trickle back into Manila. They were not always successful. Sometimes, a seemingly empty boat floated ashore below the American lines on Bataan, but sprawled grotesquely in the bottom were the mutilated bodies of our men—a grim reminder that the Japanese Kempei-tai, the gendarmerie, were on the job.

In a typical exploit, Captain Rueda and Major Razon went south to Calatagan, on the mainland, to the Roxas hacienda to pick up the rice harvest only a few hours ahead of the Japanese collectors; using one of the few remaining Q.M. motor launches, they even managed to pick up a few heads of beef on the hoof. The Jap coastal patrols must have been mystified to hear the lowing of distressed cattle through the off-shore mists.

Sergeant Villanueva and Lieutenant Custodio repeatedly crossed Manila Bay via Ternate to fill the prescriptions of Dr. Trepp, President Quezon's personal physician. Trepp was caught in the open, in one of the Jap's frequent bombings of Corregidor; in diving for a culvert, he lost his bag containing special medicines for the treatment of the President, which he always carried with him. These prescriptions were ultimately filled in Manila's "Botica Boe," a well-known drugstore, under the very noses of Japanese officers; it was as simple as that and as hazardous. The metropolitan newspapers were also picked up with some regularity, our agents coming in via Ft. Brooks. Needless to say, we were not looking for social items; the Japanese, of course, controlled the Manila press and it was important for us to know what they were dishing out to the Filipinos.

Resistance movements, however, can only thrive on hope, and what promise of hope for the Philippines would MacArthur find in Australia? The question was already agitating the General when his pilot got word that Darwin was being bombed and that his plane would have to land at an emergency strip, Batchellor Field, some fifty miles away.

The landing at Batchellor Field was for a moment only, for the Japanese, after hitting Darwin, promptly headed that way. Getting off the ground in a hurry, the MacArthur party moved on to Alice Springs, in the hot, sandy interior of the Australian bush. There MacArthur and his family and his immediate entourage transferred to a train for Adelaide and Melbourne; the rest of the party went on by air.

For three days while crossing the Australian continent from north to south, MacArthur ruminated on the possibilities of leading a quick rescue force back to the Philippines. But when Gen. Richard Marshall, his deputy chief of staff who had gone on ahead of him, finally boarded the train at Adelaide, the bad news was broken to MacArthur that Australia had practically nothing with which to fight even a defensive war.

General Brett has left a picture of the substance of Dick Marshall's bad news:

We had flown what was left of our planes out of Java, just as Brereton had flown his out of the Philippines. I took over as commander of the American forces. The situation was, to put it mildly, muddled and unhappy. Australia's defenses were weak, and Australia expected an invasion. There are no better fighting men in the world than the hardbitten soldiers of the island continent, but there were too few of them. The Royal Australian air force was equipped with almost obsolete planes and was lacking in engines and spare parts, as well as personnel. We had only one American infantry division, and that was incompletely trained. When MacArthur arrived he was extremely disappointed in what he found. He had not wanted to leave the Philippines. . . . However, his better judgment prevailed, influenced, possibly, by reports that a great American army was being gathered in Australia for him to lead. It did not take long for him to find out how erroneous these reports had been. There was no great army. . . .

The airmen found it difficult to understand why their country, the greatest industrial nation on earth, could not give them the tools with which to fight . . . nothing much came through in those dreary months. . . . On my way back Stateside, everywhere I went I saw bombers and fighters stacked up waiting to move to Australia. Many had been waiting for a long time.

The planes out of Java to which Brett referred were the B-17 junk piles that were unable to bring MacArthur out from Mindanao. As for the Australian planes, they were extremely primitive: the Australian Gypsy Moth had fabric-covered wings and had to be started by spinning the propeller by hand; the Wirraway, although bigger and stronger, was not much more formidable. The Australian

Army was still in North Africa and the Near East, although frantic signals had gone out to bring it home. To defend their home continent, the Australians had, at the time of MacArthur's arrival, only one ready combat division.

So MacArthur's plans for a quick rescue of Bataan came tumbling down almost before they had been formulated. To give any support to Bataan and Corregidor at all, MacArthur had to rely on adventures like Col. "Pappy" Gunn. Said Pappy in an interview that is in the Tokyo files:

My idea was, we had 18,000 soldiers on Bataan and plenty of beef on Mindanao and I was going to parboil the beef and salt it and fly it in to Bataan at night. I could make two trips a night, but I got shot down and did not get to do much of it. I was shot down at Malakalay and had to walk back. Then they sent me out to get another plane to do the job, but I did not get all the way back. I got as far as Darwin . . . I began, together with Captain Muller, to shuttle back and forth evacuating personnel at night from Del Monte with two aircraft, holding 35 to 45 people, each night. These were two LB-30s.

"Pappy" Gunn was valiant, but he hardly constituted an army. So Bataan and Corregidor were forced to capitulate almost before MacArthur and his staff had settled down to survey the scene from their new headquarters at Melbourne.

Of the surrender on Bataan in April MacArthur said:

The Bataan force went out as it would have wished, fighting to the end its flickering forlorn hope. No army has ever done so much with so little and nothing became it more than its last hour of trial and agony. To the weeping mothers of its dead, I can only say that the sacrifice and halo of Jesus of Nazareth has descended upon their sons, and that God will take them unto Himself.

Almost a month later, on May 6, came the announcement of Corregidor's fall. Said MacArthur:

Corregidor needs no comment from me. It has sounded its own story at the mouth of its guns. It has scrolled its own epitaph on enemy tablets.

But through the bloody haze of its last reverberating shot, I shall always seem to see a vision of grim, gaunt, ghastly men, still unafraid.

A year later, on April 9, 1943, MacArthur was still brooding on Bataan:

. . . the light failed. Bataan starved into collapse. Our flag lies crumpled, its proud pinions spat upon in the gutter; the wrecks of what were once our men and women groan and sweat in prison toil; our faithful Filipino wards, 16,000,000 souls, gasp in the slavery of a conquering soldiery devoid of those ideals of chivalry which have dignified many armies. I was the leader of that Lost Cause and from the bottom of a seared and stricken heart, I pray that a merciful God may not delay too long their redemption, that the day of salvation be not so far removed that they perish, that it be not again too late.

And of Corregidor he said, on May 6, 1943:

Corregidor surrendered a full year ago today. Intrinsically it is but a barren, war-worn rock, hallowed, as so many other places, by death and disaster. Yet it symbolizes within itself that priceless, deathless thing, the honor of a nation. Until we lift our flag from its dust, we stand unredeemed before mankind. Until we claim again the ghastly remnants of its last gaunt garrison, we can but stand humble supplicants before Almighty God. There lies our Holy Grail.

The bad news from the Philippines, although not unexpected, greatly distressed General MacArthur. On landing in Australia he had said:

The President of the United States ordered me to break through the Japanese lines and proceed from Corregidor to Australia for the purpose, as I understand it, of organizing the American offensive against Japan, a primary object of which is the relief of the Philippines. I came through and I shall return.

And it was those magic words spoken so casually at Batchellor Field—"I shall return"—which lit the flame throughout the Philippines. They were on every man's lips, they were painted on the walls, scrolled on the beaches, whispered in children's prayers. They became the symbol around which a nation gathered in indomitable will and at whose altar it finally achieved victory and freedom.

On his arrival in Melbourne General MacArthur was received royally. His popularity with the people was almost unbelievable and it never deserted him. Before the Australian Parliament in brilliant array, the American Ambassador on behalf of the United States Congress and in the name of the President conferred on him our Medal of Honor, highest decoration of the nation.

For conspicuous leadership in preparing the Philippine Islands to resist conquest, for gallantry and intrepidity above and beyond the call of duty in action against invading Japanese forces, and for the heroic conduct of defensive and offensive operations on the Bataan Peninsula. He mobilized, trained and led an army which has received world acclaim for its gallant defense against a tremendous superiority of enemy forces in men and arms. His utter disregard of personal danger and under heavy fire and aerial bombardment, his calm judgment in each crisis, inspired his troops, galvanized the spirit of resistance of the Filipino people and confirmed the faith of the American people in their armed forces.

And in his acknowledgment MacArthur eloquently forged an international link of comradeship which remains one of the main props of a free world in the Far East:

I am deeply moved by the warmth of the greeting extended to me by all of Australia . . . there is a link that binds our countries together which does not depend on written protocol. . . . It is that indescribable consanguinity of race which causes us to have the same aspirations, the same hopes and desires, the same ideals and the same dreams of future destiny. My presence here is tangible evidence of our unity. . . . We shall win or we shall die.

Up to this time the plan of the Australian Chiefs of Staff had been purely defensive. The situation summary they made to General MacArthur reads, in part, as follows:

The bulk of . . . forces . . . [were disposed] in the general region around Brisbane and Melbourne where most of the industries, the principal food producing centers, and the best ports were located. . . . Small forces were stationed in Tasmania and Western Australia and at Darwin, Port Moresby, Thursday Island and Townsville. Because of their relative isolation, the retention of these points on the outer perimeter depended largely upon their garrisons, none of which was strong enough to oppose a major assault successfully. Reinforcing them was impossible, as additional troops could be drawn only from the vital southeastern region which, in the opinion of . . . [the Australian Chiefs of Staff] was inadequately held. . . . The return of the 6th and 7th Divisions from Egypt and the arrival of a division from the United States would allow the strengthening of the forces at Darwin, Western Australia and Tasmania. . . . [The Australians], however, planned to retain two of these units to increase the reserve in Brisbane and Melbourne zone.

This meant that it was planned to sacrifice the great western and northern regions of the Australian continent if necessary. The Australian chiefs had drawn a line in front of Brisbane, halfway up the eastern coast, and they planned to defend that line to the death.

But the Brisbane Line concept was solely one of passive defense which could result in all probability only in defeat and disaster. The Australians had seen Hong Kong fall around Christmas; they had shivered while Thailand and Malaya were occupied, and they had felt the noose pulling tighter when the Japanese moved on to Rabaul in New Britain and into the northern Solomons. The Japanese plans seemed ominously clear; there would be further thrusts to seize eastern New Guinea and New Caledonia. And with New Caledonia in enemy hands, the lifeline to America would be practically severed.

In this atmosphere of terrible apprehension, plans were completed to abandon New Guinea and to scorch the earth above the Brisbane Line. Power-generating facilities in northern Australia were to be blown up, military installations destroyed, docks and harbors incapacitated.

MacArthur was in complete disagreement. He felt that:

Such a concept was fatal to every possibility of ever assuming the offensive and even if tactically successful will bottle us up on the Australian continent, probably permanently. I am determined completely to abandon the plan.

It was one of his greatest decisions; in ultimate effect one of the greatest in world strategy. What he proposed to do was to move forward more than a thousand miles into eastern Papua, on New Guinea, and as he said "beat the Japanese to the punch." Specifically, he planned to stop the Japanese on the rough mountain trails of the Owen Stanley Range of New Guinea and thereafter to attack, move forward, and take the offensive. As he said later: "It was one of the most difficult decisions of the war. Its success came through the Buna–Gona–Milne Bay–Coral Sea battles. From this point on I never doubted our full victory."

MacArthur sent his outline of the situation on to President Roosevelt on May 8:

The fall of Corregidor and the collapse of resistance in the Philippines, with the defeat of Burma, brings about a new situation. . . . At least two enemy divisions and all the air force in the Philippines will be released for other missions. Japanese troops in Malaya and the Netherlands East Indies are susceptible of being regrouped for an offensive effort elsewhere since large garrisons will not be required because of the complacency of the native population. The Japanese Navy is as yet unchallenged and is disposed for further offensive effort. A preliminary move is now under way probably initially against New Guinea and the line of communications between the United States and Australia. The series of events releases an enormously dangerous enemy potential in the Western Pacific. That the situation will remain static is most improbable. I am of the opinion that the Japanese will not undertake large operations against India at this time. That area is undoubtedly within the scope of their military ambitions, but it would be strategically advisable for them to defer it until a later date. On the other hand, the enemy advance toward the south has been supported by the establishment of a series of bases while his left is covered from the Mandated Islands. He is thus prepared to continue in that direction. Moreover, operations in these waters will permit the regrouping of his naval and air forces from the East. Such is not the case in a movement towards India. He must thrust into the Indian Ocean without adequate supporting bases, relinquishing the possibilities of concentrating his naval strength in either ocean.

The military requirements for a decisive Indian campaign are so heavy that it cannot be undertaken under those conditions.

On the other hand, a continuation of his southern movement at this time will give added safety for his eventual move to the West. . . . In view of this situation I deem it of the utmost importance to provide adequate security for Australia and the Pacific area, thus maintaining a constant frontal defense and a flank threat against further movement to the southward. This should be followed at the earliest possible moment by offensive action. . . . The first step in the execution of this conception is the strengthening of the position in this area. . . . If serious enemy pressure were applied against Australia . . . the situation would be extremely precarious. The extent of territory to be defended is so vast and the communication facilities are so poor that the enemy, moving freely by water, has a preponderant advantage. . . . I consider it essential for the security of this country that it be reinforced as follows . . . two aircraft carriers . . . an increase from 500 to 1,000 front line planes in U.S. Air Forces . . . one U.S. Army Corps of three first-class divisions capable of executing a tactical offensive movement. . . . We must anticipate the future or we will find ourselves once more completely outnumbered.

Just how well MacArthur had "anticipated the future" can be seen if his demands are checked against what was actually received in the Southwest Pacific Area during the next few months. Although he never managed to get the "two aircraft carriers" he had asked for his own command, the realism of his request was proved by the Battle of the Coral Sea, where the carriers *Lexington* and *Yorktown* under Navy orders were sufficient to win a tactical and strategic victory during the very week he was sending his outline to Roosevelt.

The increase in the Air Force, signaled by the arrival of Maj. Gen. George C. Kenney on July 28, enabled MacArthur to stage the first big bomber attack on the Japanese base at Rabaul in early August. And with two American divisions and one Australian division, which had arrived home from Egypt, MacArthur felt strong enough to carry the fight to the enemy, in New Guinea. Therefore he moved his headquarters from Melbourne to Brisbane in July and set up forward headquarters at Port Moresby, on the southern side of Papua. His staff at this point had been augmented by the addition of Gen. Stephen J. Chamberlin as chief of operations. Chamberlin was sound, unassuming, a careful detail man—the typical West Point professional.

The Australians received a tremendous lift from the decisions and actions of MacArthur. He was well known to them from World War I when Secretary of War Newton D. Baker called him "the finest front line American General of the War." They had admired his work at West Point both as a cadet and as superintendent, and were entirely in accord with his modernization of the Army during his tour of duty as Chief of Staff. His defense of the Philippines they regarded as an epic, and they were prepared to support his efforts with almost fanatical zeal.

This involved the heaviest sort of draft on the meager Australian

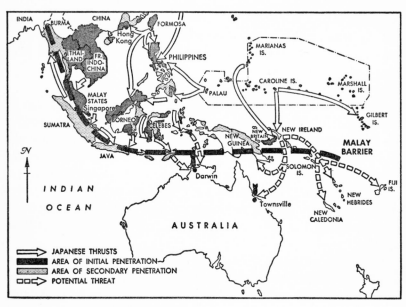

Disintegration of the Malay Barrier and the threat to Australia

population of 7,000,000. After the requirements of the armed forces had been met, the Australians had a working force of only 2,300,000 men. But from this small working force, ably directed by the labor government of Prime Minister Curtin, the man whom MacArthur called "the heart and soul of Australia," great things were to come.

Throughout the whole war Australia gave more to the United States in "reverse" lend-lease than she ever received. In the crucial last three months of 1942, less than 100,000 tons arrived. The supplies to the New Guinea front were assured only because of the extraordinary job done in literally complying with the War Department directive that "local resources will be exploited to the utmost." No American force in any other theater was remotely so self-sufficient or so successful in the assignment of local exploitation as was our Army and Air Force in the Southwest Pacific Area.

In the last six months of 1942, probably 65 to 70 per cent of *all* supplies consumed by United States forces came from local production and resources. In addition, *MacArthur gave to the neighboring Southern Pacific Theater during that critical period a larger tonnage of supplies than the United States shipped to his own area.* In effect, therefore—as far as a drain on the United States is concerned—the Southwest Pacific was 100 per cent self-sufficient.

The supplies secured locally were not simply waiting in warehouses for MacArthur to pick up. The very inadequate supply position of the Australian Army in that year is testimony to that.

By the finest coordination of lend-lease activities, by the superb handling of delicate governmental relations by the Commander in Chief, and by intelligent use of American experts, production essential to the New Guinea battles was created and expanded.

Australia canned some 6,000 tons of meat in 1939; it canned 120,-000 tons in 1944. The canned vegetable production was limited to a very few specialties in 1939; in 1943–1944 the SWPA forces were self-sufficient in vegetables. In 1944 MacArthur used 225,000 board feet of timber drawn from Australian sources, or enough to equal forty Liberty ships. He got some 18,000 vehicles locally. When he could get few service troops, he hired more than 20,000 Australian civilians.

At a time when America was straining to supply Europe, MacArthur got one million pairs of shoes, hundreds of thousands of pairs of blankets, and three hundred thousand automobile tires from Australia. Six out of every ten tons of corrugated iron were locally produced, half the supply of nails, all the cement, all the woolen clothing, fifty or more ocean-going ships, and hundreds of small craft. When the United States would not adjust manufacturing of certain equipment to supply local technical needs, MacArthur did it locally. The fuel tanks that made the victory of Wewak possible had to come from Australia, and U.S. Army technicians brought them into being.

All through these achievements ran the thread of Army technical help, and Army direction of imports of technical equipment to aid in production. Eventually things reached a point where some 15 per cent of the national income of Australia, and consequently 15 per cent of its productive resources, were going to meet United States needs. This was in addition to supplies for the Australian forces and raw material sent to the United States.

The Australian productive record was a great tribute to the Australian Supply Council, to Curtin, to the American Lend-Lease Administration, and to MacArthur himself, whose skillful diplomacy solved many wrangles between various Ministries. Since he had authority over cargo priorities, he was in a good position to make his suggestions effective.

A commentary by William Stix Wasserman, who had charge of early American lend-lease activities in Australia, gives a vivid picture of the Australian supply struggle:

On the first night of my arrival in Australia, I was taken to a hotel in Sydney where a suite had been prepared for me. Almost immediately upon my arrival there, one of the ministers came to see me. . . . He locked the door and in an awed whisper said to me, "Mr. Wasserman, Australia is completely defenseless. In my opinion, we have three more weeks of liberty, after which time the Japanese invasion will commence." The whole country was in a panic and that panic was not stopped until General Douglas MacArthur's dramatic appearance which almost overnight changed the atmosphere of the whole country from one of fear to one of hope and action.

There is another episode which I would like to repeat here. Shortly after my arrival in Australia, the Government formed a Supply Council, the main duties of which were concerned with maintaining an adequate flow of supplies both for the military and civilian population. I was chosen by the Australian Government to represent the United States on the Council, and I sat through a number of meetings which were taken up primarily with the discussion of which Ministry was going to be given the chairmanship of the Council. The meetings usually ended up in a wrangle between the representatives of the various Ministries. One afternoon to the surprise of all of us, General MacArthur himself arrived at our meeting. He patiently sat through the first hour of argument without saying a word, at the end of which time he rose and within five minutes the various questions of procedure and authority were promptly settled. I have never seen a man grasp a problem more quickly or settle it more justly and decisively. The General turned out to be not only a good listener, but a person who could weigh the evidence and reach an accord that was satisfactory to all.

One of the more amusing aspects of my mission occurred shortly after my arrival in Melbourne. I was asked by the Australian Joint Chiefs of Staff to visit them at the Victoria Barracks where they had their headquarters. As I was ushered into the room, I was introduced to a group of men with the most outstanding military names I had ever heard. There was General Steele, General Cannon, General Sturdee, and I have a faint memory of a British Air Marshal's name, but I remember very distinctly he was quite antagonistic to some of the remarks I made, primarily I suspect because he was an Englishman. The first question he asked was what the aims of my mission consisted of. I replied, as far as the military aspect of my mission was concerned, it dealt primarily with seeing to it that the Australians received as far as possible the military supplies they needed in order to carry out their part of the war, subject of course to the over-all requirements of ourselves and our other allies. I was then told that the Australian Army had always obtained its needs from the United Kingdom and that its weapons required British type ammunition. My reply was that England was in no position to supply Australia with any additional arms or equipment. In fact, I remember saying, "the amount of ammunition you will get from the British over the next year you can put in the corner of your eye and it won't make you blink, because every gun and every shell that the British manufacture in England is going to be needed for the defense of the Middle Eastern Forces and Great Britain itself"—and that "the sooner the Australians realize that the United States was their only source of outside supply, the quicker we could get on with our job." I am afraid this answer was none too diplomatic because that night a long cable went out to the Foreign Office in England, sent I believe by the British Air Marshal, to the effect that the United States was attempting to lure the Australians away from the British Empire and bring them completely into the orbit of American influence. The following day I received a communication from the State Department which viewed my activities with alarm, in spite of the fact that such recommendations as I had made were purely for the purpose of military expediency and had no relation to political problems whatsoever.

Later on when I attempted to simplify the review of Australian military requisitions so that they would not have to pass through the channels of Washington first and later those of London, I was once again accused of trying to disrupt the British Empire. You may remember that at the outset of our participation in the war, all military requisitions were first sent to Washington where they were reviewed and then sent to London for a second review. By the time they had gotten through the London review, the British had taken out of the requisitions whatever they felt they could use and what was left was spared to Australia. Eventually this was stopped.

I am proud of the fact that Australia was the one country that actually returned to us more in Lend Lease goods than we gave them. The creation of reverse Lend Lease was my first assignment and I remember quite well sitting up late in the night trying to figure out what things we could get Australia to give to us. I do not think I left very much out, although my inclusion of lodgings for both our officers and men led to a rather amusing episode. . . . Mr. Chifley [who was then occupying the position corresponding to that of our Secretary of the Treasury] came to see me the following day. "Mr. Wasserman," he said, "we are very much disturbed by that section of the Lend Lease agreement whereby we are paying for officers' billets. The American officers have taken over a certain hotel in Melbourne which has approximately 300 rooms and they are paying £1/10 shillings a day. The maximum allowed an Australian officer is £1/– a day." I quickly made a calculation and discovered that Mr. Chifley was complaining about a sum equal to about $300 a day or approximately over $100,000 a year. This item of $100,000 was holding up the Reverse Lend Lease agreement

that would run into countless millions of dollars before it expired. So
I said to Mr. Chifley, "Mr. Chifley, if the American Army assumed
those extra ten shillings, is there anything else standing in the way of
our Reverse Lend Lease agreement?" He said, "No." The matter was
settled. But this little episode throws a light on some of the minutiae
that can hold up a major agreement between powers.

By far the most important of the achievements of the Lend Lease
Mission was the signing by General MacArthur, Prime Minister Curtin,
as well as myself of what later became known as the MacArthur-Curtin-
Wasserman agreement, under which shipping priorities on all materials
destined to Australia from the United States came under the sole jurisdiction of General MacArthur and his staff. This enabled the Lend Lease
Mission to exercise control over Australian imports that was absolutely
essential in view of the demands then being made upon us, since Lend
Lease was besieged with requests for many types of materials that
either were not essential to the war effort or were being used merely
to build up greater stock piles than our mission deemed essential. There
was also a tendency on the part of certain Australian officials to try
to get plant equipment whose primary use would be for the postwar
development of Australia rather than the immediate needs of the services. Each time the Lend Lease Mission protested against this type of
import request, pressure was brought to bear directly in Washington.
The State Department seemed to be far more interested in appeasing
certain foreign government officials than in maintaining the rigid economy that was necessary if the actual needs of the war were to be given
their proper priority. What was true of the State Department, unfortunately, was quite often reflected in the attitude of some of the officials
who were running Lend Lease matters in Washington. In fact, at times
I sometimes wondered whether some of the members of the State Department as well as a few of the officials of the Lend Lease Administration were not more interested in maintaining pleasant social relations
with the officials of foreign governments than in protecting the interests of their own country. However, once control had been transferred
to General MacArthur, whose authority was backed not only with
his great prestige but with the actual facts that his staff was able to gather,
there was a considerable stoppage of unnecessary demands. It is interesting to note that this procedure of giving the General in the field

COMPARATIVE RATIO OF SHIPMENTS
FROM U.S. PORTS TO OVERSEAS THEATERS
1941 TO 1944
PERSONNEL

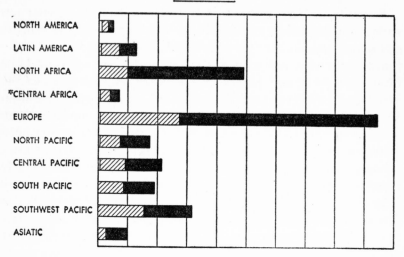

COMPARATIVE RATIO OF CARGO SHIPPED
FROM U.S. PORTS TO OVERSEAS THEATERS
1941 TO 1943
MATERIEL

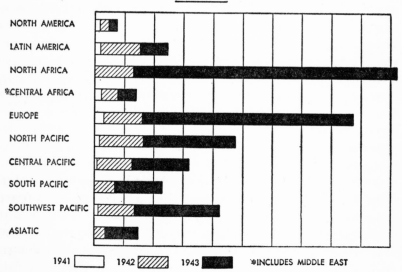

1941 ☐   1942 ▨   1943 ▰   *INCLUDES MIDDLE EAST

75

authority over cargo priorities was later on extended to cover other areas under which Lend Lease was supplied.

The story of this unique achievement in inter-Allied cooperation in the economic field is incomplete without emphasis on the support given by Prime Minister John Curtin of Australia in backing General MacArthur when required. The General often described the Prime Minister, whom he liked and admired tremendously, as "the inner spring of the Australian war effort." Mr. Curtin's personal representative at Headquarters, in Melbourne as well as in Brisbane, handled his difficult position with superb tact and understanding; this was the Hon. Percy Spender, who is now Australian Ambassador in Washington; finally, the lend-lease mechanism was expanded and refined, after Wasserman left, by the Hon. Walter S. Robertson, a Richmond, Virginia, banker, who is now the Assistant Secretary of State for Far Eastern Affairs.

The move to Brisbane and the "north" was successful despite the almost frontier conditions of that part of Australia. Because the railroad gauges ranged from 2 feet 6 inches to 5 feet 3 inches, through shipments were impossible. There was a paucity of sidings, car yards, workshops. Motor roads in the north were principally of the two-lane dirt type. None of them could stand up under military loadings and traffic densities. To the north of Brisbane, the harbors were generally too shallow to accommodate 10,000-ton Liberty ships. And of 47 listed airfields, only six were suitable for combat purposes of any type.

In spite of everything, MacArthur's Chief Engineer Hugh ("Pat") Casey enlarged the airfields, deepened the harbors, and paved the roads in time to support the forces in New Guinea. Air Force repair shops were lifted bodily from the south and moved far beyond Brisbane, to Townsville and Rockhampton—and eventually into Port Moresby on New Guinea. By thrusting his repair depots forward, General Kenney managed to double and then treble the number of sorties his planes could fly to make strategic strikes and to give tactical support to the troops. This, in effect, more than doubled MacArthur's air power without the addition of a single plane from the United States.

The whole effort took the Japanese by surprise. *They* had expected to beat MacArthur to the punch. In the spring of 1942, so said Japanese Captain Ohmae, senior naval staff officer at Rabaul:

. . . the Japanese did not think that General MacArthur would establish himself in New Guinea and defend Australia from that position. They also did not believe that he would be able to use New Guinea as a base for offensive operations against them. The Japanese felt that General MacArthur could not establish himself in Port Moresby because he did not have sufficient forces to maintain himself there and because the Japanese Navy was confident that it could control the Coral Sea and keep him out of New Guinea.

MacArthur had fooled the Japanese once by his "sideslipping" retreat into Bataan, where the Philippine struggle was unexpectedly prolonged for five months. He was to fool them again by taking the offensive in New Guinea at a time when, by all standard tokens, he had hardly enough strength to remain on the defensive in Australia. His spirit at the time, a sort of gay grimness, is best illustrated by his interchange of letters with a boy named Dan Gifford of 1124 Hilton Avenue, Utica, New York:

Dear General:
  I have read all about you and think you are very brave. Jack Fahy, a boy my age, 10, thinks the Japs got Pearl Harbor, so will you please write to me telling that the Japs have not got Pearl Harbor and I will show it to him. . . .

Yrs. truly,
Dan Gifford

To which the General replied:

Dear Dan:
  The Japs "have not got" Pearl Harbor and are not going to get it.

Yours,
Douglas MacArthur

4 MacArthur's Early Decisions

MacARTHUR has never seen fit to grade the big Pacific war decisions in the order of their importance. But, quite aside from Roosevelt's decision to move him from Corregidor to Australia, there are three moves made by the General, in spite of opposition, in the early days of the war that were basic, momentous, and ultimately decisive. The first, as we have seen, was the sideslip from Manila into Bataan, which delayed the Japanese southward thrusts by as much as six months. The second big decision, made at a time when practically every able-bodied Australian thought only to die with his boots on at the Brisbane Line, was, according to MacArthur, to "stop the enemy advances along the Owen Stanley Ridge in New Guinea." This saved Australia from invasion, changed the whole attitude from one of defense to offense, and changed the national morale from despair and defeatism to confidence and victory. And the third crucial decision was to push an "arrow-straight" advance from New Guinea to the Philippines, thus accomplishing a practical unity of our divided command in the Pacific, preventing a dispersion of our forces and objectives, which might well have led to disasters through attacks by a concentrated enemy on our scattered and far-flung units, and greatly reducing our losses by avoiding unnecessary and corollary battles.

Since the second and third big decisions were really phases of a single grand strategy, which he had in his mind as early as March 1942, MacArthur usually brackets them when talking about the Pacific war. The curious thing about it is that the Navy high command in Washington never recognized the relationship between the decision to hold the Owen Stanley Line and the decision to retake the Philippines. The Navy Department saw the Pacific as its own peculiar war: the old Orange Plan had envisaged a westward passage of ships and a great naval victory, to be followed by a rescue or a bypassing of the Philippines and an eventual investment of Japan; and even after the eruption of the Japanese into the Solomon Islands the Navy Department held stubbornly to an Orange Plan revival. Stung by Pearl Harbor, the Navy wanted the lion's share of the fight. In their view, MacArthur's job was to hold in New Guinea, to help out in the Solomons, and then to press westward along the Malay Barrier toward the Indies and Singapore. A side expedition to Mindanao might have been permitted as an offshoot of such a movement, but certainly nothing more.

MacArthur was adamant against this sort of thinking from the very beginning, and fortunately his views prevailed. When the question was put to him point blank, why his forces were not utilized along the south and west coast of New Guinea and in the Netherlands Indies, he answered:

. . . such an axis of advance would have split my command from that of Admiral Nimitz of the Central Pacific and tended to slant away rather than toward the final objective—Japan. Without mutual support between us we did not have sufficient strength. Had I had sufficient forces, it would have been advantageous to have broadened my avenue of advance along both ways, but with the meager command I had this would have been impossible. I therefore chose the one which would permit inter-cooperation with the Central Pacific.

Actually MacArthur thought the entire Pacific Theater should be unified under a single command. He argued for such unification, but without success. He was entirely willing to relinquish his own seniority of command and serve in a subordinate position if it would accomplish the desired result.

His later comments on the amazingly faulty setup were as follows:

Of all the faulty decisions of the war perhaps the most inexplicable one was the failure to unify the command in the Pacific. The principle involved is perhaps the most fundamental one in the doctrine and tradition of command. In this instance, it did not involve an international problem. It was accepted and entirely successful in the other great theaters.

The failure to do so in the Pacific cannot be defended in logic, in theory or even in common sense. Other motives must be ascribed.

It resulted in divided effort, the waste of diffusion and duplication of force, undue extension of the war with added casualties and cost.

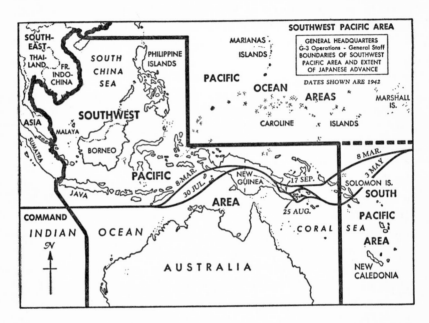

The generally excellent cooperation between the two commands in the Pacific, supported by the good will, good nature and high professional qualifications of the numerous personnel involved was no substitute for the essential unity of direction of centralized authority.

The hardships and hazards increasingly resulting were unnecessary indeed.

As early as June 1942, before the issue had been joined with the Japanese in New Guinea, the long-trend temper of his thinking was obvious:

. . . my plan contemplates a progressive movement, involving primary action against the Solomons and the north coast of New Guinea, in order to protect the naval surface forces and to secure air fields from which essential support can be given to the forces participating in the final phase of the operation; necessary that all ground operations in this area be under my direction; to bring in land forces from other areas with a view to their operation under naval direction exercised from distant points can result in nothing but complete confusion . . . the action projected northwest of Australia [attack on Timor] even if successful, cannot be supported as in the case in the New Britain area [to the north of New Guinea]; doubtful whether Timor could be held under present circumstances in view of nearby Japanese bases and their control of the sea . . . no effort from the northwest coast of Australia should be made until naval and air forces are built up which will insure retention of objectives.

To drive home his fundamental concepts—the importance of eastern New Guinea and the Owen Stanley Ridge, the need for a direct thrust to Manila without diversions toward Timor or Java or Singapore, the desirability of letting his right flank and the Navy's left flank support each other—MacArthur insisted on a good map room. And, since the business of a high command is with strategic decisions more than with tactical decisions, he insisted on grand maps as well as local maps. With his famous cap tilted at its usual rakish angle, whether in the office at Brisbane or in a plywood hut or tent in New Guinea, he would let his own Napoleonic *coup d'oeil* sweep from the bloody circles around the immediate tactical deadlocks in the New Guinea of 1942 and go roving to the far northwest, where Manila lay beckoning over leagues of water. When still thousands of miles from his goal, MacArthur listed Luzon as a "combat zone." Occasionally he would direct his G-2 to arrange with Col. "Pick" Diller, the press-relations officer, to bring the correspondents in for a briefing on phases of the "arrow-straight" advance. But more often he would seek to impress his own staff with the Paul Bunyan, the seven-league-boots, aspects of the Pacific-theater distances.

From Australia on he encouraged the habit of superimposing to scale a map of the United States—or of Europe—over the Southwest Pacific Area. This comparison became standard for tactical or strategic discussion. To quote from a summary in the MacArthur records:

. . . the continental area of the United States will fit roughly between Australia and the Philippines. The distance from New York to San Francisco is approximately the same as from Rabaul to Java. With Miami located at the coastal city of Townsville in Australia, Hollandia will fall on Milwaukee. Biak [where the Japs had ultimately to be routed out of caves] will be south of Minneapolis, and Morotai will

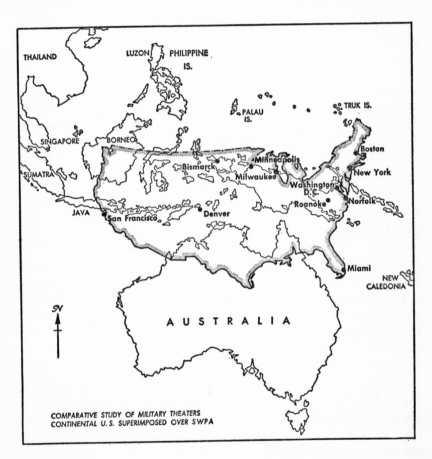

COMPARATIVE STUDY OF MILITARY THEATERS
CONTINENTAL U. S. SUPERIMPOSED OVER SWPA

be near Bismarck, North Dakota. Leyte will be across the Canadian border approximately 300 miles northwest of Regina and Manila will fall some 700 miles north of the United States–Canadian border in Alberta Province.

The inherent tactical and strategical problems of a land and sea advance from Australia and Papua, directed from headquarters at Port Moresby and Brisbane, through New Guinea and the Moluccas to Manila, are comparable to those of a hypothetical American headquarters stationed in the Caribbean Sea 750 miles southeast of Miami, with its advance echelon in the vicinity of Roanoke, Virginia, charged with air strikes on Boston, New York and Washington to points west of Denver, and an advance by land and sea from Norfolk (Milne Bay) via Milwaukee (Hollandia), Minneapolis (Biak), Bismarck (Morotai), and northwest across the middle of Saskatchewan, Canada (Leyte) . . . to northern Alberta (Manila).

What MacArthur forgot to add was a further superimposed comparison: the hypothetical headquarters stationed in "the Caribbean" drew its supplies to bomb Boston and Denver from Venezuela (southern Australia) and from northern Norway (California).

The MacArthur records are eloquent with the difficulties of maneuvering from Miami to Lake Athabaska, or (on the European scale) from Trebizond on the Black Sea coast to Iceland, which is a distance at least twice that covered by Napoleon, Julius Caesar, or Alexander the Great on their longest marches.

. . . the line of communications from the United States to the scene of operations [was] one of the longest the world has ever seen. . . . The time factor alone demanded more than usual foresight in logistical planning and required the application of methods not taught in any of the American service schools . . . there was not sufficient shipping . . . to mount operations adequately and then to support the troops in widely dispersed locations. Allowances of supplies and equipment accompanying troops into battle and also the amounts to be sent later for their maintenance had to be curtailed—at times to the danger point. Factors used for the computation of these requirements in the Southwest Pacific were less than those used in any other theater or area in the world; at times they were less than half the usual figure.

Sometimes MacArthur had moments of near-despair: "Must I always lead a forlorn hope?" he asked bitterly on one occasion in 1942. Washington seemed to have deserted him as coldly and completely as London seemed to have deserted Australia's Prime Minister Curtin. (The two leaders often conferred to plan their respective, though coordinated, pleas to Roosevelt and Churchill for carriers, planes, and landing craft.) But more often than not, the precarious predicament of the Southwest Pacific acted as a stimulant. The MacArthur forces even exulted in their "forced risks" in pushing the "poor man's war," the Operation "Shoestring," the "Cinderella war" (the phrases are those of the staff), in the effort to seize the initiative and hold it:

Shortages of every description necessitated "crisis management" to meet the needs of each individual operation. Other important logistic features which adversely affected the campaigns and operations in the Southwest Pacific Area included shortages of combat equipment and insufficient service troops. There was also a scarcity of equipment and troops for construction of ports, bases and air facilities which often had to be created out of virgin jungle before successive operations could be launched. In certain decisive operations [shades of Korea] there was even a lack of critical calibers of ammunition.

The "crisis management" was to continue far into 1944, long after MacArthur had his advance to the Philippines well under way. But in the spring of 1942 the crisis often teetered toward disaster. In his projected race for the Owen Stanley passes in New Guinea, MacArthur had his eyes on Port Moresby on the southern side of the eastward-thrusting Papuan peninsula. He also wanted Milne Bay, at the very eastern tip of Papua. Accordingly, he sent the inimitable Pat Casey on a personal survey flight to Moresby and Papua as early as March 1942. Casey returned with a report that stressed at least twenty deficiencies for every opportunity. Since anti-aircraft and fighter planes were being hoarded for Europe, Port Moresby could hardly be protected against Japanese bombing. If MacArthur wished to use Moresby as a forward air base, American planes would have to be prepared to get in and get out again between Japanese bombings. This meant that supporting air bases must be built all over the Cape York Peninsula in Australia.

To get the service troops to build airfields, Pat Casey had to enlist civilian Australians. Under American direction these Australians performed prodigies in the summer of 1942; by August 19:

. . . four air fields had been completed at Port Moresby, one for heavy bombers, one for medium bombers, and two for fighters. . . . On Cape York Peninsula two fields for heavy bombers and one for fighters were completed . . . additional service facilities had been completed in the Townsville-Cloncurry area.

MacArthur was thus enabled to bring his characteristic three-dimensional strategy to bear on the Japanese in New Guinea. His complete air-mindedness was

. . . demonstrated by the principle of moving his bomber line forward: (1) advancing in successive bounds, (2) establishing forward air fields, and (3) making the next move under cover of his own air umbrella.

The principle of never moving beyond his own air cover was followed religiously during the advance toward the Philippines until the time came for the Leyte operation, when MacArthur trusted to the Navy and narrowly averted disaster. MacArthur's own meticulousness about air cover made Navy fears that he would dangerously expose the aircraft carriers look just a trifle silly, to say the least.

To move northward in New Guinea, and to take the offensive with the elimination or neutralization of the big Japanese South Sea naval, air, and supply base at Rabaul on the island of New Britain (just north of Papua and to the west of the Solomons), MacArthur's staff developed a series of plans known as "Tulsa B" and "Tulsa Two B." Tulsa Two B envisioned two drives, one along the northern coast of New Guinea, the other following the line of the Solomons to New Ireland, to the north of New Britain and Rabaul. The Navy was to cooperate with the latter by seizing and holding Guadalcanal in the eastern Solomons. But before the more grandiose aspects of Tulsa Two B could be carried out, there was bloody work to be done: Moresby itself had to be nailed down; Buna, across the Owen Stanley Ridge from Moresby, had to be seized; Milne Bay, at the end of Papua, had to be made safe.

The first peril to MacArthur's plans had come in early May of 1942, when the Japanese dispatched a transport and carrier expedition from Rabaul to round the eastern tip of Papua in order to seize

Moresby from the sea. Right here the first big break in the Pacific war occurred. This was the Battle of the Coral Sea—a standoff in ship losses (the Americans traded the aircraft carrier *Lexington* for the Japanese carrier *Shoho*), but a strategic victory for the Americans nonetheless. With the loss of the *Shoho*, the Japanese lost their nerve and sent their troopships back to Rabaul. Later on in the year they attempted to take Milne Bay from the sea, but this water-borne invasion likewise came to grief. The Battle of Midway (June 1942), in which the Japanese lost four large carriers, inhibited their naval action henceforward.

There remained the overland threat to Moresby: intelligence reports soon made it plain to MacArthur that the Japanese planned to cross the 14,000-foot Owen Stanleys along the Kokoda Trail. Thus "the Papuan peninsula would be stitched into the Japanese pattern of quick conquest." MacArthur determined to prevent this at all costs. He moved into Port Moresby personally, along with his staff, to join a handful of Australians and local Europeans who had come to New Guinea to prospect for gold and who remained to fight.

The development of Moresby as a major forward base (it was used as a headquarters until 1944, when the jump to Hollandia in western New Guinea put it too far to the rear) went hand in hand with the establishment of rear-area headquarters in Brisbane. If Brisbane itself could be called an austere establishment compared with the opulent elegance of Melbourne, then Brisbane was in turn a sinecure of lush living as compared with shabby little Moresby. There was a raffish, Conradesque quality to this tropical "port of missing men"; it had scenic beauty, but little else. What the staff first reported to MacArthur was

. . . a native village, huts on "stilts" in the shallow coastal waters; a few warehouses and go-downs; tropical cottages with wide verandas and corrugated iron roofs; a few administration buildings and police barracks . . . hard-eyed native constabulary, strong men in military blouses terminating incongruously in a red blanket-like sarong.

For his own headquarters, MacArthur took over a bungalow of the Colonial government, a building of hardwood floors and wide verandas with bougainvillia creeping along the eaves. The inevitable malice of rumor soon had it that MacArthur was living in luxury, but in actuality the bungalow was, by American standards, no more than a summer cottage. There were no Georgian mansions or French châteaux for military headquarters in the Pacific. The bungalow did, however, have a remarkable library—an index of the culture of its former occupant. Although MacArthur had little time to spare, he could be seen from time to time riffling the pages of expensively bound books in a half-dozen languages, from Zola to Dostoevski, and from Ibsen to Shaw. He also dipped on occasion into a special section dealing with anthropology and native lore and scientific reports on the Papuan aborigines.

The ensuing Papuan campaign, which MacArthur directed partly from Port Moresby and partly from Brisbane, was a mere fragment in the general mosaic of the road to Manila. It was won not by any particular application of strategic genius (this was to come later in the war, when the Americans had more power to achieve local surprise by sea and air), but by hard tactical slogging in the rain and the mud. In anticipation of trouble, the American 32d and 41st Divisions were moved to Brisbane and Rockhampton to train for offensive operations under Lt. Gen. Robert L. Eichelberger, then en route from the States. To forestall the Japanese in Milne Bay, MacArthur secretly dispatched the 18th and the 7th Australian Brigades (Operation "Fall River") under Maj. Gen. Cyril A. Clowes. When the Japanese came on from the sea, landing light tanks, they were surprised by "Fall River." However, before they were finally vanquished, they gave the Australians a taste of the desperate quality of their resistance to come: practically all Japanese were killed and only three were taken prisoner. Wounded Japanese who could not be evacuated were shot by their own men. MacArthur reported on this action:

This operation represents another phase in the pattern of the enemy's plan to capture Port Moresby. This citadel is guarded by the natural defense line of the Owen Stanley Range. The first effort was to turn its left flank from Lae and Salamaua which proved impracticable. He tried to pierce the center in a weak attempt by way of Buna-Gona-Kokoda, subjecting himself to extraordinary air losses. His latest effort was to turn the right flank by a surprise attack at Milne Bay. The move was anticipated. With complete secrecy, the position was occupied by our forces and converted into a strong point. The enemy fell into the trap with disastrous results to himself.

The main Japanese attempt on Moresby over the Owen Stanleys reached Imita Ridge, within twenty miles of the south Papua coast. Looking over the crest of the ridge, the Japanese could see the sea. But behind them their supply lines had stretched taut and snapped; and the Australians were falling back on a reinforced base. The Japanese General Horii, who ran a close second to the Japanese commander in Timor for achieving "furthest south" by land in the war, issued a proclamation that mingled false prophecies of victory with a baffled scream of pain:

Today we firmly hold the heights . . . for more than three weeks . . . every unit forced its way through deep forests and ravines, and climbed scores of peaks in pursuit of the enemy. Traversing knee deep mud, clambering up steep precipices, bearing uncomplainingly the heavy weight of artillery ammunition, our men overcame the shortage of supplies, and we succeeded in surmounting the Stanley Range. No pen or word can depict adequately the magnitude of the hardships suffered. . . . We will strike a hammer blow at the stronghold of Moresby. However, ahead of us the enemy still crawls about. It is difficult to judge the direction of his movement, and many of you have not yet fully recovered your strength.

The "hammer blow" was never struck; the Japanese never did recover their strength. They faded back across the mountains toward Buna.

To seize the initiative after General Horii's futile thrust, Mac-Arthur began an air transfer of troops from Australia to New Guinea in September—"the first large-scale airborne troop movement by the United States forces in a theater of operations." It had to be done that way, for neither the ships nor the docking facilities existed in Moresby to bring men quickly by water. General Blamey, the Australian Commander in Chief, moved his own Allied Land Forces Headquarters to Moresby. By the end of October MacArthur had a total of ten brigades in Papua; he was ready for the big test, the battle to clear the Japanese out of the Buna-Gona-Sanananda area on the north coast of Papua. This also entailed a "battle of the supply depots," a fierce struggle between Japanese-held Rabaul, which was well across the Bismarck Sea to the north of Buna, and Port Moresby on the south side of the Owen Stanleys.

In spite of the lack of service troops, shipping, and virtually everything else, MacArthur won the battle of supply. His air commanders,

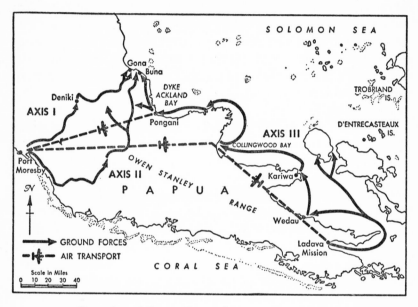

Campaign of Papua: September 1942–January 1943

George Kenney and Ennis Whitehead, worked their few planes around the clock, clearing them safely out of Moresby to bomb the shipping at Rabaul by getting accurate intelligence reports from secretly hidden "coast watchers" on the whereabouts of Japanese planes. When the Japanese tried to take Wau, center of Bulolo gold fields at the western end of the Owen Stanleys, "Whitey" Whitehead's transport planes made fifty-seven landings at the Wau airport under concentrated fire from the Japanese 400 yards away. The entire 17th Australian Brigade was flown in—and the reinforcements drove the Japanese back in disorder.

To win Buna, MacArthur proposed throwing two columns across the Owen Stanleys, one by way of the Kokoda Trail, which General Horii had been unable to conquer, the other by way of the Kapa Kapa Trail to the southeast. A coastal creeping expedition from Milne Bay by way of small Goodenough Island was also part of the plan. A fourth phase, the use of the airlift to land troops at Wanigela south of Cape Nelson on the north coast below Buna, was also utilized.

The struggle to win Buna and clear Papua went hand in hand with the battle of the Marines for Guadalcanal in the Solomons— indeed, one of the reasons for pushing the Buna campaign with the meager forces at hand was to relieve the pressure on Guadalcanal. The strategy served to split the Japanese effort. As the MacArthur records put it:

The Japanese, confused in their estimate of the relative importance of the two theaters of operations and considering each a separate problem, frittered away their strength in uncoordinated and spasmodic reinforcement efforts. General MacArthur, on the other hand, realized that these operations were interdependent and that the utmost cooperation was necessary to insure their success.

In a radio message to the War Department, dated October 17, 1942, MacArthur said:

From its inception I have been acutely aware of the critical situation in the Solomons and in fact anticipated it and reported it with Ghormley in July and in August. . . . I invited attention to the acute danger developing and begged review of the question by the President and the Chiefs of Staff lest it become too late.

Action in [South Pacific] has been supported to maximum capacity of my Air Force, using all planes that can reach targets; Ghormley three times has radioed his appreciation; Turner has also communicated to that effect; while it is impossible to assess all damage it is believed that our bombardment missions have had a vital effect upon the success of operations to date by pounding hostile air and supply installations; the major effort has been expended in Rabaul area, because it can be reached with full bomb loads, while planes going to Solomons area must carry bomb bay tanks, reducing bomb load by 50%; am in constant communication with Ghormley coordinating my reconnaissance with his and have given immediate priority to his requests for reconnaissance and attack; planes capable of affecting his situation have been used exclusively to that end; three times within the last week I have ordered missions on Ghormley's request, using every bomber available during the period; my own operations in New Guinea have been supported only by short-range aircraft. . . .

My operation to capture the north coast of New Guinea in full swing; am greatly hampered by the total lack of light shipping, landing boats, and barges, which I have previously requested; in their absence am moving overland and by air; supply is the controlling factor and must be accomplished by native carrier and by air; improvised landing fields have been and are being prepared . . . supply difficulties incredible and limit speed of movement and size of forces and are of course multiplied by lack of shipping and shortage of transport planes; the possibility of success of the movement and the time factor are still unpredictable; under severe pressure from this Headquarters, much progress has been made beginning with the development of Port Moresby, which had initially a garrison of a regiment of militia, one landing strip without even parking space for planes, and a port capacity of only 500 tons a day. . . .

If we are defeated in the Solomons, as we must be unless the Navy accepts successfully the challenge of the enemy surface fleet, the entire Southwest Pacific Area will be in the gravest danger; information derived from enemy sources indicates that an attack on Milne Bay and possibly elsewhere in New Guinea is contemplated for mid-November; urge that the entire resources of the United States be used temporarily to meet the critical situation; that shipping be made available from any source, that one corps be dispatched immediately; that all available heavy bombers be ferried here at once and that urgent action be taken to increase the air strength at least to the full complement allotted for this area; that immediate action be taken to prepare bases for naval operations on the east coast of Australia; that the British Eastern Fleet be moved to the west coast of Australia.

The story of the capture of Buna at the very end of 1942 has been told in great detail in Gen. Robert Eichelberger's book, *Our*

Jungle Road to Tokyo. But that is the tactician's story, not the strategist's. The job of MacArthur and his staff was to shape up the plan as a whole, then pick good men to carry it out. MacArthur picked Eichelberger after other officers had failed to make the necessary progress at Buna, saying, in effect, that Eichelberger must "take Buna or die."

Buna was a head-on collision of the bloody, grinding type that MacArthur was henceforward to avoid, but it was necessary. The Allied world was starved for victory at the end of 1942, its morale was at its lowest ebb. The Chinese were reported negotiating with the Japanese; the Germans were pushing toward the Volga in southeastern Russia. One more failure and the Chinese would probably sign on the dotted line—and others would follow suit. The world needed a symbol of victory. In World War I, Verdun was such a symbol: it could have been lost without much effect on French organization and supply, but it became a "test," and it took a half million men to pay for it. Buna didn't take as many men, but it was a similar test. And down the line of the Solomons, to the east of Buna, the U.S. Navy and Marines were locked with the Japanese in a battle that had similar symbolic overtones. It became a race between Eichelberger and the Marines under Admiral Ghormley's command to see who would turn in the first important "land" victory of the Pacific war.

The preliminaries to Buna went off more or less on schedule. To quote from the MacArthur records:

At Wanigela, south of Cape Nelson, an airstrip was located which proved to be in sufficiently good order for the landing of transport aircraft . . . landings were successfully carried out on 5 October without the enemy's knowledge or opposition. During the middle of October, plans to move the remainder of the Australian 18th Brigade to Wanigela were changed to speed the operation; instead, Regimental Headquarters and two battalions of the United States 128th Infantry, the Australian 26th Independent Company, and miscellaneous artillery units were substituted and flown from Port Moresby. . . . The remainder of . . . two United States regiments was concentrated north of the Owen Stanleys ready to attack the Japanese in conjunction with the Australian 7th Division.

Concurrently with the advance from Wanigela, a reconnaissance in force was made on Goodenough Island. This force was to locate suitable approaches for supply purposes, to examine the terrain for possible air field sites, and to occupy the island thus denying it to the enemy. . . . Although enemy reaction to the operations along the north Papuan coast was limited to minor resistance at Goodenough Island . . . the Japanese Navy, controlling the sea north of New Guinea, could cut the Allied line of communications almost at will. . . . The advance had to proceed with caution, since withdrawal would be necessary should the supply lines fail. Airstrips were cleared inland at Sapia and Kinjaki primarily for this purpose and supply dumps were established to permit the retirement overland of troops from the coast should the enemy attack in force.

Meanwhile the Allied northward advance over the Owen Stanleys by way of the Kokoda Trail was having greater success than the Japanese southward push over the same terrifying mountain profile had had during previous months. Early in November the Australian 7th Division captured an airfield at Kokoda. The Japanese made a stand on high ground, but by November 10 they were in full retreat. MacArthur described the envelopment of the Japanese forces thus:

The enemy was forced from his main positions near Oivi with heavy loss. His retreat has been blocked by our enveloping troops astride the main track and he is endeavoring to cut his way through the rear. Simultaneously our forces enveloped and destroyed enemy forces trapped south of Gorari.

Our ground troops have reached the vicinity of Ilimor. Here the enemy defending force has been surrounded. Of the enemy detachment which was encircled and destroyed at Gorari, bodies of five officers and more than five hundred men have already been counted in the jungle. In the Oivi pocket several hundred additional dead have been found. Allied fighters cooperating with ground units strafed and silenced enemy positions in the rear areas.

The terrain in which the final battle for Buna and neighboring Sanananda took place is, to quote from the official records,

. . . a low, flat coastal plain stretching inland from Gona and Buna to the foothills of the Owen Stanley Range. It is covered with dense jungle, strips of forest, and large kunai grass patches with extensive sage and mangrove swamps bordering the coast. . . . Movement was generally limited to the few native tracks which, although following the higher ground, were muddy at all times and hopelessly boggy in wet weather.

Throughout November the Allied offensive could not budge the Japanese from the Buna coastal area. In order to break the deadlock, MacArthur put Eichelberger in charge of the attack on December 1. As told in the official records, Eichelberger found that the units of the 32d Division had become badly disorganized during the previous fighting. He proceeded immediately to regroup the scattered units and at the same time reorganize the supply system which had become disrupted and unreliable.

On 5 December General Eichelberger's reorganized forces made a coordinated attack on both fronts in another effort to dislodge the Japanese. They resisted stubbornly, however, determined not to yield a foot of ground. Warren Force made repeated assaults, only to be thrown back exhausted and disheartened. The efforts of Urbana Force proved more successful. By resourceful leadership and daring exploits, a platoon of the 126th Infantry managed to pierce the enemy network of interlacing bunkers and break through to the sea. The enemy counterattacked immediately but the units on the Urbana front held doggedly to their corridor which wedged into the enemy defenses, isolating Buna Village from Buna Mission. For the first time since the beginning of the campaign against Buna, the Japanese line had been breached.

General MacArthur insisted that immediate advantage should be taken of the gains on the Buna front and directed that maximum strength be concentrated in that sector. . . .

The presence of fresh troops in the Buna area made itself felt immediately. On 14 December, Urbana Force launched a heavy attack against Buna Village. Despite fierce resistance and repeated attempts by the enemy to bring in water-borne reinforcements, the village was at last wrested from the Japanese. General MacArthur, describing the first major victory in his coastal offensive, reported as follows:

"Buna Village has been taken. It was occupied by our troops at ten o'clock this morning, December 14. . . . In another attempt by the enemy's naval forces to reinforce their ground troops in the Buna area, the enemy launched a convoy of two cruisers and three destroyers for a landing at the Mambare and Kumusi estuaries. Our air force intercepted this convoy. In heavy bombing and strafing attacks the enemy's landing barges were sunk or disabled. Survivors attempted to reach land by swimming, suffering heavy casualties. Supplies were set afire. Several hits and many near misses were made on the war vessels. The enemy's air force intervened unsuccessfully. . . . It is believed that a major enemy effort was largely parried."

After three more bloody weeks of struggle in the mud and rain, the enemy force in the Buna area finally yielded its positions. On January 2 Buna Mission capitulated. General Eichelberger wrote:

At 4:30 P.M., I crossed the bridge (from The Island) after "C" Company had passed and I saw American troops with their bellies out of the mud and their eyes in the sun circling unafraid around the bunkers. It was one of the grandest sights I have ever seen . . . the 127th Infantry found its soul.

As the MacArthur records say:

It was a fitting culmination to a year of hardship and a propitious beginning for a New Year of hope. The Buna victory was a heartening tonic to the Allies. . . . Secretary of War Stimson sent General MacArthur a warm letter of congratulations:

"The coming of the New Year, coinciding as it does with your success at Buna, impels me again to send you my warmest congratulations and good wishes. Have followed your masterly campaign with close interest and much gratification . . . it is a tremendous satisfaction to feel that American fortunes in SWPA are in such skillful hands; am in constant touch with President Quezon here and we are both beginning to think with encouragement of the time, which now really seems approaching, when we shall redeem our promise to the Filipinos. . . ."

The Buna victory did not end the struggle for the Papua coast; that had to wait upon three more weeks of bitter battle for Sanananda. With Eichelberger taking over command of all the Allied troops north of the Owen Stanleys on January 13, the fight was pushed to the utmost. In the face of three converging Allied columns, the enemy defenses finally began to crumble. MacArthur reported:

The Papuan campaign is in its final closing phase. The Sanananda position has now been completely enveloped. A remnant of the enemy's forces is entrenched there and faces certain destruction. With its elimination, Papua will be entirely cleared of the enemy. One of the primary objects of the campaign was the annihilation of the Japanese Papuan army under Lieutenant General Horii. This can now be regarded as accomplished. This army was approximately 15,000 strong.

And later, with the last Japanese in Papua fleeing and even swimming up the coast toward distant Salamaua, MacArthur said:

The destruction of the remnants of the enemy forces in the Sanananda area concludes the Papuan Campaign. The Horii Army has been annihilated. The outstanding military lesson of this campaign was the continuous calculated application of air power, inherent in the potentialities of every component of the Air Forces, employed in the most intimate tactical and logistical union with ground troops. The effect of this modern instrumentality was sharply accentuated by the geographical limitations of this theater. For months on end, air transport with constant fighter coverage moved complete infantry regiments and artillery battalions across the almost impenetrable mountains and jungles of Papua, and the reaches of the sea; transported field hospitals and the other base installations to the front; supplied the troops and evacuated casualties. For hundreds of miles bombers provided all-around reconnaissance, protected the coast from hostile naval intervention, and blasted the way for the infantry as it drove forward. A new form of campaign was tested which points the way to the ultimate defeat of the enemy in the Pacific. The offensive and defensive power of the air and the adaptability, range and capacity of its transport in an effective combination with ground forces, represent tactical and strategical elements of a broadened conception of warfare that will permit the application of offensive power in swift, massive strokes, rather than the dilatory and costly island-to-island advance that some have assumed to be necessary in a theater where the enemy's far-flung strongholds are dispersed throughout a vast expanse of archipelagos. Air forces and ground forces were welded together in Papua and when in sufficient strength with proper naval support, their indissoluble union points the way to victory through new and broadened strategic and tactical conceptions.

The fight for Buna and Sanananda brought MacArthur smack up against the big problem of New Guinea as a whole. This problem involved not merely the Japanese and their big support base at Rabaul; it was also a question of climate, topography—and the tropics in general. Pat Casey's engineer reports are eloquent of these obstacles:

. . . if the High Command had been conducting war games and had searched for the ultimate nightmare country, Papua must have been the inevitable selection. There was something cynically malignant about the weather and the geography. . . . Through the deep ravines and gorges of these mountains innumerable rivers rush down to muddy coastal plains, smothered in dense tropical forests. This was the country where the Engineers were to build and repair air strips, harbors, bridges, roads and trails.

To help best the anopheles mosquito, MacArthur brought in "Doc" Smith, who had been the health officer of the port of Manila. But the victory over the mosquito was a collective, not an individual, job. The medical services took the mosquito in stride. On the early Papuan front the mosquito was responsible for more "noneffectives" than any other single factor. But by the time MacArthur was ready to invade Leyte, it was reduced to secondary importance as a cause of disablement.

The most immediate difficulty with staff-planning to overcome the enormous distances and the problems of climate and health and the disposition of enemy troops between Australia and the Philippines was sheer lack of information. When the landing was made in Normandy, there were plenty of maps available. But there were few, if any, maps of New Guinea, not even the rudimentary type of Michelin road maps that abound in France. To solve this problem, MacArthur had no time to apply to Washington, to any Coordinator

of Information or Office of Strategic Services, for aid; he realized
that Washington was wrapped up in obtaining data bearing on
North Africa, the Mediterranean, and the Russo-German front.
Since knowledge of the Pacific was in the Pacific, not in libraries
or morgues in the United States, MacArthur wanted his help on the
spot. His G-2 section was handed the job of organizing an Allied
Translator and Interpreter Section (ATIS) to interrogate prisoners
of war and to translate captured documents; an Allied Intelligence
Bureau (AIB) to conduct clandestine operations, sabotage, and
espionage behind enemy lines (a counterpart of OSS); an Allied
Geographical Section (AGS) to gather and publish geographical
information; and a Central Bureau (CB) to provide cryptanalytical
services.

To help get accurate information about what the Japanese were
up to, the Allied Intelligence Bureau took over the Royal Australian
Navy's system of "coast watchers." These men, planted or left
behind enemy lines and armed with radio transmitters, sent in a
constant trickle of messages from places as far apart as Bougainville
and Borneo, or Papua and Palawan. The coast watchers enabled the
thin force of Allied planes to be ready and in the air for Japanese
attacks; they forwarded news of Japanese ship movements in the
area from Rabaul to the Solomons and so helped the Navy and the
Air Force set up their targets at sea.

Fundamental to intelligence, however, was the enormously difficult problem of dealing with the complicated Japanese language.
Few Americans could speak it, much less read its forbidding alphabet
and script. Early in the war, according to the MacArthur records:

. . . the Japanese had found . . . they could label their mine fields,
carry personal diaries, use their spoken language freely, and even handle
military documents with little regard for security.

But MacArthur, unlike the panicky Californian authorities who
insisted on herding second-generation Japanese-Americans (the
Nisei) into concentration camps, had

. . . complete confidence in the Nisei. His G-2 employed hundreds of
second-generation Japanese from Hawaii and California in linguist de-

tachments, to be sent into the field with the combat forces. ATIS intelligence teams accompanied the troops in all initial landing operations. Captured maps and orders processed by ATIS revealed enemy strength and dispositions and plans of attack. Diaries contained excellent clues to the psychology and the state of morale of the Japanese troops. Other documents indicated the enemy's problems of food and supply, his order of battle, the effect of our air attacks, his relations with the natives, the relative effectiveness of Allied and Japanese weapons. . . . Spot interrogations of prisoners taken in battle were at times of such importance that they caused a shift in Allied plans of attack.

Col. Sid Mashbir, a former language student in Tokyo, must be credited with developing ATIS to a high degree of efficiency. The Japanese were not able to match MacArthur's translating services.

To keep his own fingers on the pulse of intelligence, MacArthur made it a habit of going himself or sending his staff officers to the front from time to time. A G-2 report recalls a trip made by Chief Engineer Pat Casey, Signal Officer Spencer Akin, and Willoughby to the Buna front. It is of interest because it shows how MacArthur insisted on keeping his "office" in touch with the realities of war:

Pat Casey . . . and Spencer Akin . . . were on one of these staff jaunts. Pat had climbed up a rope ladder to an Australian artillery observation post, a crude platform lashed to a tree with a few branches to camouflage the observer. Pat probably stayed up there for half an hour, getting a direct view of the innocent-looking, expertly camouflaged low mounds that looked like ancient graves or ant-hills but contained Japanese machine guns. The Australian was directing high-angle fire on them, by telephone. Pat cannot explain why he should have elected to leave, at a precise minute or second; he had no metaphysical warning; he just decided to move on, left his platform and began to climb slowly down; he had not gone half the distance when the Australian officer crashed through the branches to hit the ground with a dull thud, shot and killed by a sniper or some stalking patrol sent for the express purpose of getting rid of the troublesome observer.

During the whole campaign for Buna, MacArthur had the infantryman very much on his mind. On October 19, 1942, he sent a message to I. J. Fox, of the Doughboy Committee in New York, commending the man in the New Guinea mud. It read:

He plods and groans, sweats and toils, he growls and curses, and at the end he dies, unknown, uncomplaining, with faith in his heart, and on his lips a prayer for victory.

But it was Kenney's air force, which had systematically cut down Japanese reinforcements and supplies from Rabaul to Buna, that had finally enabled Eichelberger to crash through on the ground. Observing what Kenney and "Whitey" Whitehead could do to isolate the Japanese and starve them on the battlefield, MacArthur came up after the Buna victory with the decision that he need fight no more Bunas. There would be other tough engagements with the Japanese, but from 1943 on MacArthur elaborated the system of bypassing the Japanese strong points and neutralizing them by pounding them from the air after their communications with Japan had been slowed or cut.

This system of bypassing, which was adumbrated in MacArthur's final statement on Buna, was one of MacArthur's greatest decisions and did much to implement the concept of the "arrow-straight" advance from Papua to Manila. The correspondents who followed him from Australia to the Philippines were quick to call it "leap-frogging." But MacArthur always denied that it was something new in warfare. He said:

The system is as old as war itself. It is merely a new name dictated by new conditions given to the ancient principle of envelopment. It was the first time that the area of combat embraced land and water in such relative proportions. Heretofore, either the one or the other was predominant in the campaign. But in this area the presence of transportation of ground troops by ships as well as land transport seemed to conceal the fact that the system was merely that of envelopment applied to a new type of battle area. It has always proved the ideal method for success by inferior in number but faster moving forces. Immediately upon my arrival in Australia and learning the resources at my command, I determined that such a plan of action was the sole chance of fulfilling

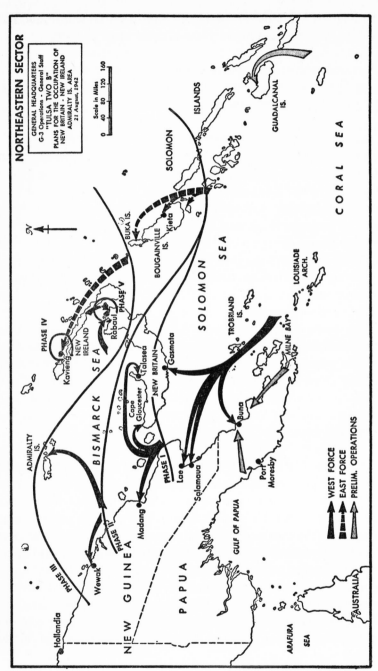

NORTHEASTERN SECTOR

GENERAL HEADQUARTERS
G-3 Operations - General Staff
"TULSA TWO B"
PLANS FOR THE OCCUPATION OF
NEW BRITAIN - NEW IRELAND
ADMIRALTY IS. AREA
21 August, 1942

Scale in Miles
0   40   80   120   160

WEST FORCE
EAST FORCE
PRELIM. OPERATIONS

my mission. For its application it demanded a secure base from which to anchor all operations. Australia was plainly the only possible base. . . . The first actual physical bypass was probably when I had Halsey's forces, which had been placed under my operational control, by-pass the lines of Guadalcanal along the west coast of Bougainville. Probably the first time it attracted general public attention was the Admiralty landings.

The Admiralty landings were bound up with MacArthur's decision to isolate no less a place than Rabaul itself. Steve Chamberlin's (G-3: Plans and Operations) account of the Rabaul bypass decision is rather circumstantial, but the bones of the strategic approach show through the careful G-3 detail:

In compliance with MacArthur's strategic concept and approved by him the details of the plan to isolate Rabaul were developed by General Chamberlin and his chief planners, Captain Ray on the Navy side, and Captain Larr, for the ground force aspects. . . . It was taken to Washington in March 1943, and it was there approved. This plan envisioned a two-prong attack, one along the New Guinea Axis to Hansa Bay, and one along the Solomon Island Axis to North New Ireland. With these two points in our possession, a combined attack was then to be made by the forces of both Axes on the Admiralty Islands. This was to complete the isolation of Rabaul. By the last of December 1943, this joint maneuver was completed to the line Bougainville–Cape Gloucester.

Early in 1944 the plan for the capture of the Admiralty Islands had been partially completed and contemplated the utilization of a lot of amphibious equipment plus battleship and carrier support to be supplied by Admiral Halsey. The overseas operation, of course, was to be accomplished by the Southwest Pacific and the Air Forces of both Axes operating from Hansa Bay, and New Ireland was to cover the attack. Shortly after the first of the year 1944, the Japanese drew back their air from Rabaul to Truk. This permitted Admiral Halsey free action of his fleet around New Ireland and in the straits between New Ireland and New Britain. This free action of Naval forces then gave us the idea of a reconnaissance in force into the Admiralties with the result that after this maneuver we maintained our position in the Ad-

miralties and conquered the islands without the assistance of resources
that had been tentatively set up for later. The South Pacific force then
continued its action into one of the islands to the Northeast of North
New Ireland. . . . Our entrance into the Admiralties and the continuation of the action of the South Pacific completed the isolation of
Rabaul.

MacArthur himself thought the isolation of Rabaul could have
been carried on at a faster pace if he had had some aircraft carriers
under his control. The lack of carriers, he said, affected the SWPA
operations "most seriously":

. . . the very essence of our so-called "island-hopping" method of
advance depended upon securing air control over the area covered in
each forward step. In the present state of development of the art of
war, no movement can safely be made of forces on sea or land without
adequate air protection. The limit of such protection in our case was
the possible radius of operation of our fighter planes. This radius had
to be measured from the actual location of our ground air bases. This
required the seizing or construction of such new bases at each forward
movement. The presence of carriers with their inherent movability
would have immeasurably increased the scope and speed of our operations. I know of no other area and no other theater where they could
have been used to such advantage. The enemy's diversion of his air
forces on many different islands and fields was peculiarly adapted to his
piecemeal destruction which would have been drastically assisted if we
could have utilized the mobility of carriers in surprise concentrations.
For instance, with our over-all inferior air strength, in order to neutralize the enemy's superior combined air strength being linked to
ground air potentiality at Rabaul and Aitape, I had to locate a temporary air base in New Guinea between these two enemy air garrisons
to operate by surprise with my entire force concentrated first on the
one and then on the other. Their combined force could have beaten
me but I destroyed them individually. The presence of carriers would
have entirely altered our potential. Prime Minister Curtin did his best to
persuade Prime Minister Churchill to let us have some carriers, and I
did the same with Washington, but without success. To this day I cannot imagine why the decision was in the negative.

The withdrawal of the Japanese Air Force from Rabaul to Truk gave MacArthur some of the free play he would have had earlier if he had had his own carriers. Steve Chamberlin's account shows how the shrinkage of Japanese air gave MacArthur his first seven-league boots and led to the first big jump of the war, from the Admiralties to Hollandia, bypassing Hansa Bay and Wewak:

. . . our plan for the isolation of Rabaul contemplated the western hinge to be at Hansa Bay . . . after the Admiralties were taken, it became evident to me that we could then with the resources that had been promised for the larger Admiralty invasion go into the attack on Hollandia without any intervening attack. Actually, this was proposed to General MacArthur by me at a conference that he was holding with General Kenney and Dick Marshall [the chief of supply]. The general disposition of the Admiralties with regard to the provision of a Naval base was under discussion and Admiral Halsey was to come the following day to discuss with General MacArthur the subject of a provision of a Naval base at the Admiralties and the further course of tactical and strategic action. . . . General MacArthur in making his decision that day told me to go back to my office and draw up the plan of the attack on Hollandia so that it could be presented the following day to Admiral Halsey. This was done. . . . The next day Admiral Halsey readily agreed to supply the resources that had been intended for the Admiralties to the attack on Hollandia, and they were considerable. . . . We had the carrier force of the entire Pacific fleet in that action, as well as many baby carriers and great assistance in amphibious craft.

Thus the Hollandia campaign was touched off, and thus Mac-Arthur was on his way winging in his first great leap along New Guinea on the road to the Philippines. It had taken a year of desperate slogging and defensive waiting, then a year of "leapfrogging" that grew progressively bolder. Now he was ready for some real leapfrogging. The three basic decisions—the delaying action at Bataan, the defense of the Owen Stanley Ridge, the decision to run the arrow straight from Papua to the Philippines—were paying off. But it was the new water-land-air use of the old tactic of envelopment, the go-around-them-and-get-astraddle-on-their-supply-lines-and-flank that was the wherewithal of the pay-off.

The Japanese saw it more simply. According to Col. Matsuichi Ino of the Japanese Eighth Army staff:

. . . this was the type of strategy we hated most. The Americans attacked and seized, with minimum losses, a relatively weak area, constructed air fields and then proceeded to cut the supply lines to our troops in that area. Our strong points were gradually starved out. The Japanese Army preferred direct assault after the German fashion, but the Americans flowed into our weaker points and submerged us, just as water seeks the weakest entry to sink a ship.

5 The Isolation of Rabaul

AFTER the capture of Buna and Sanananda in January of 1943, MacArthur surveyed the scene and cast up his balance of military profit-and-loss. The loss consisted of a casualty list that was high in its percentage of fever and disease cases. But the gains were solid. American boys from favored temperate climes along the north 42d parallel had learned something about fighting under jungle conditions in tropical downpours. Never again would they gibber in fear at jungle noises, or stand in awe at supposed Japanese "supermen." The victory at Buna and Sanananda, which was gained by the bold use of "shoestring" equipment, meant the end of Japanese power in Papua. With new base and airfield sites on the north coast of New Guinea, the Allies could turn to a different sort of warfare, one that would give scope to what one of his staff officers has termed "MacArthur's peculiar genius for slaughtering large masses of the enemy at little cost in the lives of his own men."

The victory in Papua, however, did not mean that MacArthur could immediately push his master plan of moving along the northwest axis toward the Philippines. There was still a job to do directly to the north, for the Japanese held two sides of the narrow body of water known as Vitiaz Strait, through which convoys from Australia to western New Guinea would have to pass before any Philippines campaign could be contemplated. The western, or New Guinea, side of Vitiaz was controlled by the Huon Peninsula; to the east, the Japanese were anchored in the Cape Gloucester–Arawe region of New Britain, the long island whose trading center and metropolis (at the far eastern end) was Rabaul.

The grand objective of the Allied Forces of the Southwest Pacific in 1943 was to isolate the great Japanese fleet anchorage and supply base at Rabaul. This would not only relieve the pressure on New

Guinea; it would also end the Japanese threat to the Solomons and forever lift the fears of Australians that they might be cut off from America. Members of MacArthur's staff had spent an incredible amount of nervous energy throughout 1942 worrying about Rabaul; they couldn't see how it was to be taken without a vastly augmented army and air force, and they looked forward to casualties even heavier than those involved in the taking of Buna or the defense of Guadalcanal.

When staff members presented their glum forecasts to MacArthur at a famous meeting which included Admiral Halsey, the newly arrived General Krueger, and Australia's Gen. Thomas Blamey, MacArthur puffed at his cigarette. Finally, when one of the conferees said, "I don't see how we can take these strong points with our limited forces," MacArthur leaned forward.

"Well," he said, "let's just say that we won't take them. In fact, gentlemen, I don't want them."

Then, turning to General Kenney, he said, "*You* incapacitate them."

Once the "let-'em-die-on-the-vine" philosophy had been accepted by the staff, the planners fell to their work with a new vigor. The task of reducing Rabaul to impotence was necessarily a dual one, involving close cooperation on the so-called "Elkton Plan" with Admiral Halsey's fleet. After the victory of the Marines at Guadalcanal, which anchored the Americans in the southern Solomons, Halsey was ready to punish the Japanese on New Ireland, to the north and east of Rabaul. MacArthur's own plan was to thrust northward until he could achieve control of the Bismarck Sea. Then he and Halsey would be ready to clamp their proposed bear hug on Rabaul. With the Huon Peninsula in his possession, with the Cape Gloucester–Arawe end of New Britain cleared of Japanese striking power, MacArthur could thereafter address himself to the task of seizing the Admiralty Islands. Then, and only then, would he feel free to turn westward along New Guinea, safe in the knowledge that he could not be rolled up from the rear.

Sensing MacArthur's plan, the Japanese moved heaven and earth to concentrate troops and to build new air strips in the Huon Peninsula and on New Britain. They also poured men into the Solomons to the northwest of Guadalcanal, strengthening Buka and Buin on

Bougainville Island, and Munda on New Georgia, as counters to the U.S. Marines and to Halsey's free-roving fleet.

Now was the time when MacArthur, who still lacked the port facilities, the landing craft, and the men to carry out ambitious sea-land operations, turned to George Kenney's air force. The air would have to carry the offensive brunt during the period of build-up throughout early 1943; after that, MacArthur could return to his more characteristic theory of war, which was to make coordinated use of all three arms of the service to isolate and destroy the enemy on a battlefield of his own choosing.

It was Kenney's immediate job to pound Rabaul. Kenney was the man to do it. Scornful of red tape, an airman of the insouciant "Billy" Mitchell tradition, Kenney had won MacArthur's confidence by his work in putting fifteen B-17s over Rabaul as early as August of 1942, in time to destroy seventy-five planes on the ground at the very moment the Marines were landing in Guadalcanal. This exploit was carried out just eleven days after Kenney's arrival in Australia—and it marked the first time that anything approaching a mass raid had been staged by American bombers. Kenney had done this at a time when most of his sixty-odd B-17s were being overhauled at Mel-

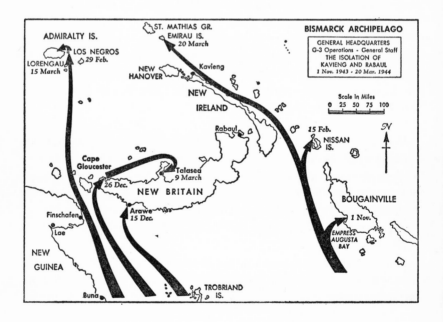

bourne and Brisbane depots, or waiting for new engines and propellers. The air strike at Rabaul had enabled the Marines under Admiral Ghormley's command to get ashore at Guadalcanal with no Japanese air interference. As Kenney put it, the success of the operation made MacArthur "look five years younger than when I had reported to him ten days before."

MacArthur's nickname for Kenney was "the buccaneer," and he sometimes said that "George was born three hundred years too late. He's just a natural-born pirate."

In the early raids on Rabaul the "pirate" had been forced to send his bombers, many of them of "cannibalized" construction, without fighter protection. By the spring of 1943 Kenney had sufficient fighters to give his bombers a protective screen. But the Air Force still needed bases in Kiriwina and Woodlark Islands off the coast of Papua if bombers were to approach Rabaul with adequate fighter convoy. This meant an amphibious operation—the first to be staged under the command of Gen. Walter Krueger, who was subsequently to take the Sixth Army—or the so-called "Alamo Force" elements drawn from the Sixth Army—all the way along New Guinea and into the Philippines. Kenney also needed air strips on Huon itself in order to hit Rabaul with a crisscross of bombing raids from both south and west.

In the fight to clear Huon, MacArthur already had one foot in the door. Ever since March of 1942 a small body of Australians had held the mountain town of Wau in the Bulolo Valley to the southwest of the Japanese coastal stronghold at Lae and Salamaua on Huon Gulf. To quote from the MacArthur records:

Wau . . . had a small air field already constructed and sites suitable for new strips. In Allied hands, it was a valuable outpost for the defense of Port Moresby, and a constant threat to the security of the Japanese positions at Lae and Salamaua. Conversely, if it were controlled by the Japanese, it would provide additional protection for their New Guinea positions and at the same time serve as a strategic intermediate base for a new drive to the south. . . .

Once the Japanese decided to take Wau they moved swiftly . . . the situation was serious . . . the Australian defenders, numerically inferior . . . were forced back toward the airstrip. The Japanese pushed forward until they were within 400 yards of the strip itself and had virtually surrounded the beleaguered Australian garrison.

For days while the Australian "diggers" of the Kanga Force were fighting in the *kunai* grass to hold Wau, a spell of bad weather kept Kenney's planes grounded at Port Moresby. Then came a break. On January 24, 1943, plane after plane took off from Moresby carrying contingents of the Australian 17th Brigade. These reinforcements were

. . . landed in rapid succession on the small air field [at Wau] while the fighting was still in progress. During the first day of airborne reinforcement, fifty-seven landings were made on the Wau airstrip and for several days thereafter Allied air transports shuttled between Port Moresby and Wau carrying additional personnel and material to the sorely pressed garrison. Thus strengthened, the Australians soon shattered the enemy attack and moved forward. By 4 February the Japanese were in full retreat. Beaten and disorganized, they fled in disorder along the jungle trails . . . one-fourth of the original enemy force which had set out to capture Wau was lost . . . the Wau operation had . . . clearly demonstrated the adaptability of air transport not only for conveying needed supplies and ammunition but also for the rapid landing of fully equipped troops under enemy fire. It again proved that air transport had become a strong and trusty weapon of the armed forces. The battle also marked the last attempt by the Japanese to seek new territory in New Guinea. From then on, in anticipation of a major Allied advance, their entire efforts were concentrated on strengthening the positions which they already occupied.

At this point MacArthur told Kenney to watch for the next "front" of heavy weather, when the Japanese could be expected to send a big convoy steaming from Rabaul across the Bismarck Sea to the relief and reinforcement of Lae and Salamaua. Kenney was on his toes immediately. To make ready a proper meeting for the convoy, Kenney's deputy, "Whitey" Whitehead, prepared a special squadron of B-25s by equipping each of them with eight .50-caliber machine guns, the newest thing for air. Other measures were also taken. To quote from the MacArthur records:

Kenney's air forces carried out actual practice maneuvers under conditions similar to those expected, reconnoitering the most advantageous routes of attack so that superiority could be attained at the point of combat. In addition, special preparations were made to carry out a new technique of skip bombing in the event of unfavorable weather and low cloud formations. Extensive rehearsals were carried out in February 1943 until the new method was perfected for the anticipated task.

Meanwhile, Kenney kept his eye on the weather reports. A long-range forecast predicted heavy weather over the northern coast of New Britain toward the end of February. True to MacArthur's prophecy, reconnaissance planes sighted a Japanese convoy about to sail from Rabaul on February 27. The convoy moved south across the Bismarck Sea, protected by tropical rain clouds against the onslaught of high-level bombers. On March 1 the convoy, consisting of eight transports and eight destroyers, was spotted off Cape Gloucester. The next day, according to the MacArthur records:

. . . in spite of haze, rain and thick clouds, the attack was launched according to rehearsed plans. Skip bombing practice had not been wasted. Driving in at low altitudes through heavy flak, General Kenney's planes skimmed over the water to drop their bombs as close to the target as possible.

The Battle of the Bismarck Sea lasted for three days, with Kenney's bombers moving in upon the convoy whenever there was even a momentary break in the clouds. The excited early estimates had it that Kenney's surprise coup accounted for 22 Japanese transports and destroyers, 150 planes, and 15,000 men. But this included duplication of eyewitness accounts that was inevitable in haze and rain. There is a strong possibility that sixteen ships were involved and that an additional group of six vessels were sighted but turned back at Rabaul. When the Japanese records were consulted after the war, it was definitely established that Kenney's raids got a minimum of eight transports and four of the eight destroyers that had left Rabaul. Captured documents disclosed that more than half of the 7,000 to 13,000 troops loaded on the convoy were lost. Only 800 survivors managed to reach Lae. The entire convoy load of aviation

fuel, war materiel, and a four-month supply of food for 20,000 men
went to the bottom of the sea. As the MacArthur records attest:

It was a unique sea battle; not a single Allied vessel was involved . . .
after this disaster, all attempts at running large transports into Lae were
abandoned and the hungry garrisons in eastern New Guinea had to
be satisfied with the thin trickle of supplies and replacements carried
in by destroyers, barges or submarines.

Summing up the Battle of the Bismarck Sea, MacArthur said:

We have achieved a victory of such completeness as to assume the
proportions of a major disaster to the enemy. Our decisive success cannot fail to have most important results on the enemy's strategic and
tactical plans. His campaign, for the time being at least, is completely
dislocated.

Kenney put it in his own characteristic way when he read Mac-
Arthur's summary. "They didn't even leave six for pallbearers," he
said.

Kenney himself has always insisted that at least twenty Japanese
ships were sunk in the Battle of the Bismarck Sea. "Most of the Jap
records," he says, "were destroyed before we got into Japan and
the Japanese who were interviewed on the subject have mentioned
figures all the way from twelve to thirty or forty. . . . But the
actual number is unimportant and the whole controversy is ridicu-
lous. The important fact remains that the Jap attempt to reinforce
. . . their key position at Lae resulted in complete failure. . . . No
quarrelsome statements can alter the fact that the Battle of the
Bismarck Sea was a great victory. . . ."

The Japanese defeats at Wau and in the Bismarck Sea left Lae
and Salamaua vulnerable. But again, before MacArthur could move
on the ground and by sea, there was preliminary work to be done by
the engineers and by air. MacArthur had in mind a combined assault
on Lae by an airborne force operating through the Markham River
Valley and an amphibious force moving up the coast from Buna.
But existing air bases at Port Moresby and Buna were not capable
of furnishing fighter protection for an airborne assault on Lae. To

create the staging fields necessary for the consummation of his plans, MacArthur ordered more air strips to the north and west of Wau. Working secretly throughout the spring of 1943, the engineers planted a fighter strip at Tsili-Tsili—an airdrome which the Japanese never did discover until late in the summer. Other strips were developed at Bena Bena and in the Bulolo Valley. The plans were being set in motion for an airborne landing at Nadzab, in the rear of Lae. Then would come the final amphibious investment of Lae, Salamaua, and the whole Huon Peninsula to the north.

In reviewing the air war in retrospect, General Kenney left a memorandum that still vibrates with the immediacy of cat-ate-canary satisfaction:

At the time of my arrival in July 1942, we felt we would be lucky if we didn't have to fight the Nip in Australia. When I went up to Port Moresby for the first time, the plane stopped rolling just long enough for me to get out. It took off before the enemy could catch it on the ground. Shortly after that the Nip came over and strafed the air field. I may have had a lot of plans and ideas but this attack crystallized one of them—the determination to clear the enemy off our lawn so that we could go across the street and play in his yard.

We did not have the strength to do it then. We were like a smaller and lighter man in the ring with a bigger, heavier opponent. There is only one thing you can do in a situation like that. You box. We boxed with energy. We had to duck the haymakers the Nip was throwing at us and at the same time keep jabbing, looking for openings. It was difficult and heartbreaking work.

From the mainland of Australia, we conducted raids on Lae and Salamaua, using the air fields on the small part of New Guinea which was still ours as hopping-off places. We had to be careful and cautious when we staged our planes, however, else the Nips would catch us on the ground and destroy our aircraft. With all our strength, we set about neutralizing Jap strongholds one at a time.

The first place to be taken out was Buna. During August 1942 the Nip had fixed up a field there and it was a real thorn in our sides. Only 100 air miles from Port Moresby, his planes would come over the 13,000 foot Owen Stanley range and nose over on top of us before our inadequate warning system could give us a chance to get our fighters up. At this time the Japs were within thirty miles of Moresby itself.

The 5th Air Force went to work. Our fighters began to patrol over Buna. If the Nip came up we shot him down. If he did not come up, we strafed him on the ground. In between times, heavies, mediums and light bombers dug holes in his runways, battered down his revetments, burned up his stores and strafed his personnel. The Jap kept filling up the bombcraters and we kept making new ones. He replaced his airplanes and we promptly shot them out of the air or burned them on the ground. Before long, he tired of the game and didn't bother to fill in the holes on the runway. It had cost him around 75 planes and he decided that it was too expensive.

Employing the same procedure, we then started working on his fields at Salamaua and Lae and by November the Nip was out of our front yard. We could now cross the street and play in his. Meanwhile, the Australians had pushed his ground forces back across the mountains and with complete air control we ferried a division of Americans across the mountains and for the next two months, until Papua was regained, supplied them and the Australians by air. Troops, food, ammunition, artillery, jeeps—in fact, everything that would go into the door of a C-47—went over the "hump" and the sick and wounded came back.

In the meantime, Rabaul beckoned. Here was the big supply base for all Jap forces in the Bismarcks, the Solomons and New Guinea itself. With 150,000 tons of shipping constantly in the harbor and a couple of hundred planes on the main airdromes just outside of town, we had plenty of work on our hands. From Rabaul, too, came the convoys; eight in all, that tried to relieve the Nip forces in the Buna area. From August 1, 1942, until Buna fell, we had not only defeated every attempt to bring convoys from Rabaul to that area but had probably sunk or damaged a total of 300,000 tons of shipping trying to run our air blockade or in Rabaul Harbor itself. During the same period we had destroyed 1,888 Jap aircraft. Meanwhile, we had to conserve every bit of striking force we could muster.

Production at home had not yet reached the point where aircraft could be spared for this theater. We rebuilt airplanes so badly shot up they would ordinarily be considered only fit for salvage. We cannibalized the ones we couldn't rebuild and used the pieces to make one or two airplanes that could be made to fly. And we protected those we had in every way we knew how. We built a great air fortress in Port

Moresby, where every airplane was closely protected by earthen revetments, wide-spaced dispersal areas and plenty of anti-aircraft guns and searchlights. We installed warning services, established observation posts up in the hills and maintained our fighters constantly on alert. As soon as we owned the ground on the north coast of Papua, we worked like beavers to build the same kind of fortress in the Buna area—a fortress designed to give us more elbow room and to take a heavy toll of enemy visitors who tried to destroy our planes.

The battle of the Bismarck Sea was not something that just happened. We didn't just see the convoy coming and go out and hit it. It was planned and rehearsed. We prepared. We even picked the spot for the engagement, a location where all of our units could engage the Nips with the maximum efficiency.

Three days before the battle, we rehearsed at full scale. We selected a half-submerged wreck that was exactly the same distance, although in another direction from our bases than the forthcoming engagement would be. Our units took off from their various fields at the same time they would take off three days later. We rendezvoused over the exact spot and, flying with the identical gas and bomb load, we duplicated our flying problem in every possible manner even to the formation and compass headings into the attack.

The Lae operation of September 5, 1943, in which we dropped 1,700 men in one minute and ten seconds thirty miles west of Lae at Nadzab, forced the Nip to give up a base which he had been building for over seventeen months. It meant the abandonment of his major plan to control New Guinea. And it demonstrated that intensive preparation in every phase—bombing, strafing, combined operations, dispersed landings, infiltration and paratroops—pays big dividends.

This operation, too, was rehearsed in full scale.

Whereas the Darwin sector was quiet in comparison to New Guinea, it was of great importance. The reconnaissance work was done not only for the defense of Australia but also for the future operations against the rich islands lying in that direction. This was witnessed by the bombing missions—probably the longest in the world—which our heavies were conducting against the Netherlands East Indies.

Up to April 1943, we were operating on a fairly thin shoestring. About that time, however, production at home got going fast enough to give us some real help. It came just in time. Around the arc from

Soerabaja, Java, to Rabaul the Nip had three times as many airplanes as we had. Why he didn't take us out I don't know. I remember telling General MacArthur that if the Jap didn't ruin me by that August, I would have enough strength to take air control away from him for keeps. But that if we weren't smart enough he would certainly keep us busy trying to survive.

During April 1943 the Nip put on three raids at 75 to 100 planes each in four days. But he put them over three widely separated targets and didn't press them home. We lost half a dozen planes and a couple of boats. It cost the Jap over 100 fighters and bombers. He never appeared again over Moresby in the daytime.

The Nip is not eating so well these days along the north coast of New Guinea. We've got him down. We shall keep him down. Every time he lifts his head we will knock it down again. This is our air wherever we fly. And we are going to keep it that way.

MacArthur's G-2 kept its own records of the air war, complete to periodic reviews of successive phases. Its own papers bearing on the isolation of Rabaul stress the interrelations between air and the other services. The G-2 papers are invaluable for the light they shed on MacArthur's thinking on the subject of the role of air power in what Winston Churchill has called "triphibious" war:

Viewed in perspective, the air war in the Pacific has been marked by contrast and complexity. It has been a battle for inches, as in supporting the initial desperate offensive-defensive in 1942/43, and a battle of bold and extensive vertical envelopment to seize or encircle the enemy's principal air centers in 1943. . . . It has been an air war of improvisation with insufficient aircraft, initially, and later of a calculated use of increasing air strength. Even the climate ran the gamut of extremes, ranging from ever-present equatorial heat, at ground level, to icing conditions at altitude.

Anchored on the important Japanese air bases of Wewak and Rabaul, with intervening, supporting fields—Lae, Gloucester and Admiralties—a Japanese shuttle service by air was possible in any tactical situation. Through Kenney's constant attacks on Wewak and Rabaul, through air blockade and air destruction on the ground and in the air, the Japanese lost approximately 4,000 planes and over a million tons of shipping,

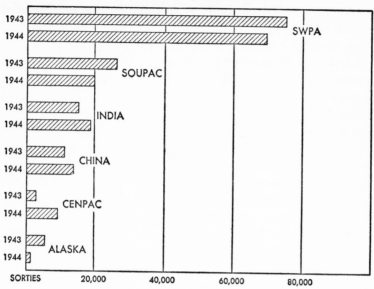

SORTIES FLOWN BY U.S. AIRCRAFT IN PACIFIC THEATERS
FULL YEAR 1943, HALF YEAR 1944

1943
1944 SWPA

1943 SOUPAC
1944

1943 INDIA
1944

1943 CHINA
1944

1943 CENPAC
1944

1943 ALASKA
1944

SORTIES   20,000   40,000   60,000   80,000

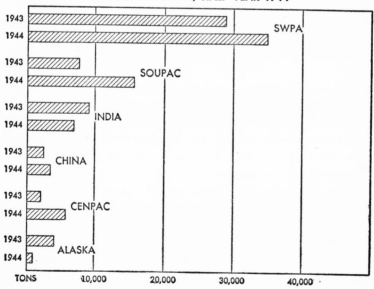

BOMBS DROPPED BY U.S. AIRCRAFT IN PACIFIC THEATERS
FULL YEAR 1943, HALF YEAR 1944

1943
1944 SWPA

1943 SOUPAC
1944

1943 INDIA
1944

1943 CHINA
1944

1943 CENPAC
1944

1943 ALASKA
1944

TONS   10,000   20,000   30,000   40,000

of various classes, fed into this witches' cauldron, to be consumed in fragments, until the staggering total sapped the enemy's vitals. These totals must be viewed in comparison with the historical canard of the "air disaster" at Clark Field in December 1941.

It was realized, from the start and while the Jap was still on the offensive, that shipping was the most lucrative target. It was then the best substitute for hitting the factories and shipyards of Japan. The destruction of the Japanese convoy in the Bismarck Sea Battle, March 2– 4, 1943, will remain the model of execution.

Nevertheless, when necessary, the full weight of our air strength has been diverted to operate as an essential part of our task forces, providing overwhelming air support. The General's use of airborne troops at Nadzab and Noemfoor, and of large-scale air transport for reinforcement and supply, as in the Buna campaign, was originally without precedent in any other theater, but has since been employed as a major feature elsewhere [in the African-European theater]. . . .

The inherent flexibility of air power has been used continuously to throw its full weight in rotation against selected targets, from Java to Truk. Every air operation has been calculated carefully. The result has been the steady advance of the bomber line directly toward the Philippines, each progressive advance determining the scope and distance of the next broad stroke. . . .

Against this background, the successive seizure of Lae, Finschhafen, Gloucester, and a drive through the center of the Japanese line to take the Admiralties represents a tactical and strategical penetration that isolated both Wewak and Rabaul air centers, and knocked out the Japanese Air Force in a first round from which it has never recovered. The enemy made an abortive attempt to rally between Wewak and the Vogelkop, which resulted in an unparalleled destruction of aircraft on the ground at Hollandia, where 475 wrecks were later definitely identified—a total which renders our highly dramatized aircraft losses at Pearl Harbor "chicken-feed" figures.

As the bomber lines moved forward, naval forces mastered the sea lanes and severed the enemy's arteries of reinforcement and supply. Our ground forces then completed the isolation of the enemy's by-passed, blockaded and trapped forces.

This masterly coordination of air, ground and sea forces, despite the difficult space and geographic characteristics of the Pacific Theater, has no parallel elsewhere. . . .

Until the Finschhafen landing, enemy fighter strength in both New Guinea and the Bismarcks-Solomons area averaged 274 per day, maintained rather consistently. With this strength a total of 220 escort sorties were sent out and 287 intercept sorties. This means less than two combat missions per fighter, during the period. Bomber strength, which started low at 260, was strongly reinforced during the operations and was maintained at a daily average of 325. Slightly less than one offensive sortie was made per bomber in the eighteen days of resisting an Allied landing. It should be remembered that these figures are over-all averages. As such, they flatter the Japanese Army Air Service and do injustice to the Naval Air Service. . . .

Our Lae landing, although it was in supposed Japanese Army Air Service territory, drew a sharp reaction from the Japanese Naval Air Service. The initial, and critical, debarkation on the beachhead was unimpeded by air attack; but within a few hours two forces of bombers, both relatively small, were attacking landing craft off shore. In the early afternoon a larger formation of 30 bombers and 40 fighters struck at still more tempting shipping targets at Morobe. . . .

Meanwhile the more ambitious raids came from Rabaul. The Japanese Naval Air Service soon lost interest, however, discouraged by a notable failure on 7 September when Allied interception caused 27 medium bombers, escorted by 30 fighters, to jettison their bombs in sight of, but short of, Allied shipping at Morobe. South Pacific raids of increasing size over Bougainville also accounted for the diversion of the Naval Air Service, which was then throwing fighters up in large numbers to protect its Solomons airdromes. . . .

The air war, as far as the enemy was concerned, appeared to have settled down into an uncomfortable routine. Enemy strength was being maintained fairly evenly. Even with the Wewak losses, daily enemy fighter strength averaged 225; bomber, 306. Fighter sorties were slightly down from those in the Lae period, but bombers held to their mediocre effort of nearly one sortie each in twenty days.

The daylight attack of 12 October on Rabaul, SWPA's biggest strike up to the time, caught airplanes and shipping. This raid, consisting of over 200 bombers and 125 fighters, was the first of a series whose

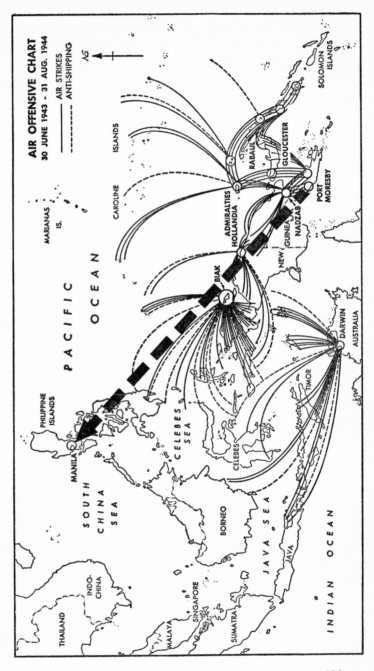

AIR OFFENSIVE CHART
30 JUNE 1943 - 31 AUG. 1944

AIR STRIKES
ANTI-SHIPPING

objective was Rabaul and the Japanese Naval Air Service itself. The enemy failed to understand that air power could have such ambition; he thought the attack was a preparation for an imminent landing. Within three days, therefore, the Naval Air Service put together a considerable striking force of dive-bombers escorted by about 45 fighters, and dispatched them on the 15th to the New Guinea coast, whence it expected the invasion force to sail. Shipping was as usual the target. Sixty of our fighters intercepted and picked off 26 dive-bombers. On the 17th another force of heavily-escorted dive-bombers returned. This time our interception caused all bombs to be jettisoned before the target was reached. . . .

In the latter part of October, enemy bomber strength stood at about 200 on hand, a sharp decrease from previous par, but he was not able to exceed this figure substantially until toward the close of January 1944. Fighter strength was also well down, to 267, on 26 October, but it made a quick recovery within two weeks, indicating the priority and the frame of mind of the Air Services. . . .

By the time Central Pacific forces landed on the Gilberts on 21 November, bomber strength of both the Naval Air Service and Army Air Service combined was down to 169. Fighter strength, however, had declined only slightly, with 215 at the end of the period and an average of 209. The statistical scale of effort remained approximately unchanged from the time of the Lae landing, except for an increase in the number of fighter intercept sorties.

The opening of the Central Pacific theater on a sizeable scale presented a new problem for the Japanese Naval Air Service in the South Pacific. No longer could it expect unqualified first call on reinforcements and replacements. There was a new claimant. . . . [According to a G-2 summary for December 20:]

"Our seizure of Arawe 15 December resulted in a demonstration by the enemy of his conserved air strength in the N.E. Sector. A maximum of 100-odd planes, including possibly 40 dive-bombers, appeared over Arawe within three hours of the landing, and from the 15th through the 17th, around 350 sorties were attempted. Based on the estimate of nearly 500 combat planes within range and available for attack in this sector, these operations represented 70% of the enemy's strength. Only one small Allied vessel was sunk. Fearing more attacks on Rabaul, he would naturally reserve his fighters for defense of this key base on his southern perimeter. Intensive Jap reconnaissance to the south of Long Island and through the Vitiaz Straits indicates some apprehension, also concerning other potential allied moves. . . .

"Evidence of the beginning of a strategic air withdrawal following consistent air defeat, was beginning to develop: Calculated enemy air strength in the South and Southwest Pacific theaters is relatively static at 800–900 airplanes of all types. The greatest strength estimate was 1,071 aircraft 13 September 1943. The significance of these figures is important in that at present the enemy faces serious offensive threats from several quarters while only latent threats were evidenced at the time of his largest concentration. . . .

"The enemy's basic air organization has not expanded materially. His capacity for aircraft production is apparently largely absorbed by the maintenance of air strength in the expensive Southwest Pacific. Until the Gilberts operations, this was his only major air front. Bare maintenance of this air strength, in the face of a fairly constant loss ratio, manifests inability materially to increase this strength under the conditions then existing. The enemy's airplane types have proven qualitatively inferior. The quality of his air crews, while mixed, remains good. Air crews do not appear to be one of his major limitations.

"The pattern of airdrome development and construction for the first two years was one of equal attention to both rear bases and those representing his immediate tactical requirements. Rear bases have been expanded far in excess of his current need. This airdrome plan is an important part of the mounting evidence pointing toward an adopted policy in the air, at least—of a strategic withdrawal. It also gives an indication of the route for this withdrawal, through the Philippines. This has been further emphasized by the readiness of the enemy to abandon air support of ground troops in the face of Allied Air attack. . . ."

6 The Shoulders of a Penetration

THE 1943 offensive, which was designed to drive a great wedge between the Japanese forces at Rabaul on the east and in northern New Guinea on the west, brought Gen. Walter Krueger, new commander of the Sixth Army, into the Pacific picture. Krueger took charge of the Sixth Army on February 16, 1943, establishing his rear-area headquarters in a number of shacks at Camp Columbia, 10 miles to the west of Brisbane. His army units were scattered "from hell to breakfast," as one of MacArthur's staff has described the situation; one division was at Brisbane, another in New Guinea, and there were special units in Melbourne, in northern Queensland, and all over the place in Papua. To negotiate the reaches of his sprawling command necessitated travel over a 2,000 air-mile span, which Krueger covered in a "much-battered, old Netherlands passenger plane," a C-40. It was a long time before the supply situation was such that MacArthur could obtain an armed and protected Flying Fortress for General Krueger.

The new commander of the Sixth Army was MacArthur's own choice. MacArthur had specifically asked for Krueger "because of my long and intimate association with him." Krueger was an immigrant from Germany, self-made and self-educated; the competitive struggle for success, beginning on the plains of Nebraska, had engendered a certain hardness in him that MacArthur liked. A superb military tactician, Krueger insisted on the best performance because he himself could furnish it at any time. Erudite, he had an imposing record as an instructor in the Service schools, for which he had made translations of the best military literature, notably Balck's encyclopedic *Tactics*. But in addition to being a scholar he

123

was a soldier's soldier. He had gone from buck private to three-star general under his own steam. It was Krueger whom MacArthur was ultimately to pick for the job of invading Japan itself—this, after Krueger had turned in a notable series of performances in New Guinea, at Leyte, at Lingayen Gulf, and on Luzon in general. After the war MacArthur said of Krueger:

> I don't think that history has given him due credit for his greatness. I do not believe that the annals of America have shown his superiority as an Army commander. Swift and sure in attack; tenacious and determined in defense; modest and restrained in victory—I don't know what he would have been in defeat because he was never defeated. . . . The great mantle of Stonewall Jackson would certainly fit his ample frame.

From May 1943 to September 1944 Krueger worked in a strange and somewhat confusing dual capacity as head of the Sixth Army and boss of the so-called "Alamo Force," which was composed primarily of Sixth Army troops. The reasons for letting the Sixth Army operate in the field as the Alamo Force were never communicated to Krueger, but they were obviously bound up with international protocol: special task forces could undertake specific missions without complex inter-Allied command adjustments.

The first job of the Alamo Force was the occupation of Woodlark and Kiriwina Islands—small dots of land needed for the development of forward air bases to assist in the reduction of Rabaul. To quote from the MacArthur records:

> It was the first amphibious landing movement assigned to the Southwest Pacific Area and, although neither of the islands was held by the enemy, much advance preparation was necessary. The garrison and construction troops for Woodlark were furnished by the South Pacific Command and arrived at Townsville in northeastern Australia between 21 May and 4 June. The units for Kiriwina were scattered along the Australian mainland and at Port Moresby. Both forces were transported to Milne Bay for staging purposes and movements were carefully coordinated to avoid interference with essential supply activities. The difficulties presented by a poor road net and the inadequate loading fa-

cilities at Milne Bay further complicated the problem. The concentration of troops for the amphibious operation was accomplished in good time, however, and the target date for the main landing was set for 30 June.

Operations were carried out as scheduled. On 23 June, advance engineer and survey construction parties were landed on both islands to prepare for the arrival of the main force. On 30 June, while New Guinea Force was holding the enemy's attention by landings along the New Guinea coast near Nassau Bay and Admiral Halsey's forces were moving toward Rendova Island on New Georgia, Alamo Force carried out the complete occupation of Woodlark and Kiriwina Islands.

Enemy reaction was limited to aerial reconnaissance and one or two feeble bombing raids. Intense attacks by the Allied Air Force on hostile bases during previous months had weakened the enemy's power to organize effectual opposition to the troops of Alamo Force. Besides, the Japanese could not divert their attention from areas of the concurrent Allied operations in New Guinea and New Georgia.

Ground and anti-aircraft defenses on Woodlark and Kiriwina were quickly installed. Work on the airstrips proceeded rapidly, and by 24 July the 67th Fighter Squadron of the South Pacific Command was ready for missions based at Woodlark. On 18 August, the 79th Australian Fighter Squadron was ready for action at Kiriwina.

The seizure of Woodlark and Kiriwina was the prelude to the main task of Elkton III, the master plan for the capture of the Huon Peninsula and western New Britain in MacArthur's territory and New Georgia and Bougainville in the Solomons. To get Elkton III under way involved cooperation between Admiral Halsey and MacArthur, two deeply individualistic men who were to have their differences later over the conduct of operations at Leyte. In spite of their temperamental differences, however, the breezy Halsey and the austere MacArthur got along well for the most part—and they were absolutely at one in their desire to pound the Japanese with everything available. After a personal conference in Brisbane on Elkton, the first meeting between the General and the Admiral, Halsey paid tribute to MacArthur as a man who made quick, strong and favorable impression. To quote from *Admiral Halsey's Story:*

My mental picture poses him against the background of . . . discussions; he is pacing his office, almost wearing a groove between his large, bare desk and the portrait of George Washington that faced it; his corncob pipe in his hand (I rarely saw him smoke it); and he is making his points in a diction I have never heard surpassed.

The plan agreed upon between Halsey and MacArthur was to stage the Kiriwina-Woodlark occupation to coincide with heavy bombing of Bougainville and Buka and with a movement by the Marines to seize a foothold in New Georgia. Meanwhile, as the plan was shaping up, Kenney's air force carried out diversionary raids on Ambon, Timor, and other places in the Dutch East Indies to deceive the Japanese as to the direction of the offensive. A dummy traffic in code signals through radio stations at Darwin and Perth was designed to cause the Japanese to think that some action was being planned from northwestern Australia.

The plan to seize the Huon Peninsula involved some extremely complex hydrographic factors. To quote from the MacArthur records:

Large ship-to-shore movements in the seas adjacent to New Guinea were impractical because of shallow, restricted waters and the danger of major losses from enemy air attack. Shore-to-shore advances were limited by the shortage of small landing craft and overland operations through the mountains were hampered by the impossibility of maintaining a strong supply line. To surmount these problems, it was planned to conduct a combined amphibious, airborne, and overland drive from the east and west, utilizing each type of maneuver where most practical and coordinating the over-all operation to obtain maximum striking power. Again the keynote of General MacArthur's policy was the use of his land, naval and air forces as a composite team.

Early in May [MacArthur] issued Warning Instructions No. 2 which directed the Australians to seize and occupy the area containing Salamaua, Lae, Finschhafen, and Madang. Under the warning order, the Australians were given the code name "Phosphorous" and put under the command of General Blamey with General Herring named as his deputy.

Lae, the gateway to the Huon Peninsula, was the first main objective

for this new advance in New Guinea. This enemy stronghold was protected not only by well-prepared defenses of its own but also by a
cordon of fortified positions at Mubo, Bobdubi, Komiatum, and Salamaua which stood guard over its approaches. It was decided that a
United States amphibious force would be sent along the eastern coast
of New Guinea to effect a landing which would permit a junction with
the Australians already operating along the outskirts of Mubo. . . .

The Japanese tried vainly to prevent the steady closing of the Allied
trap by desperate counterattacks from Mt. Tambu and Roosevelt Ridge.
They knew that if any of their outer defenses were pierced the Allies
would command dominating positions from which to bombard Salamaua itself with direct fire. The Allied forces continued to close in,
nevertheless, and on 19 August the Japanese abandoned Mt. Tambu
and Komiatum Ridge and retreated to a line along the Francisco River.
Salamaua now lay open to assault.

General MacArthur, however, had not planned to take Salamaua
immediately. Its airfield had been rendered useless and the village
proper was of little importance to operations. The main purpose of the
Allied attack on this small isthmus on the east coast of New Guinea was
to siphon off enemy strength from his Lae defenses and lure his troops

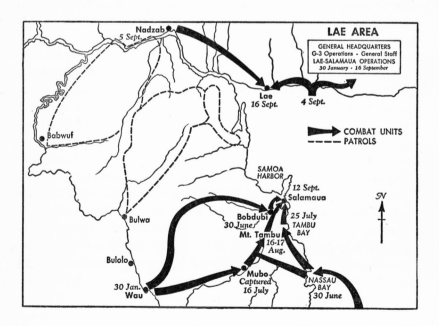

and supplies southward to be cut to pieces on the Salamaua front. It was intended to deceive the Japanese into believing that Salamaua was the prime objective of the Allied advance and this strategy was later to prove most successful. Meanwhile, under cover of the Salamaua operations, the Allies were preparing for the principal drive to capture the strategically important town of Lae. Accordingly, Salamaua was not to be taken until the assault on Lae was actually under way.

When the spotlight of the Pacific Theater focused on operations in the New Guinea area, Japanese Imperial General Headquarters felt that air power in that region had to be considerably strengthened. Consequently, on 28 July, orders were issued for the formation of the Japanese 4th Air Force.

The Allied 5th Air Force, however, suspecting some such move by the enemy, intensified its assaults on key Japanese air bases. On 17 and 18 August, while the Japanese were consolidating their forces on the northeast New Guinea coast to carry out their assigned mission, a strong formation of Allied planes struck suddenly at Wewak. Heavy attacks on its major airdromes destroyed large numbers of planes caught on the ground.

As a result of this successful surprise attack, the sailing of a powerful enemy convoy intended to reinforce the Lae-Salamaua garrison, was delayed and arrived too late to be of any assistance. In commenting on the Wewak raid, General MacArthur said:

"It was a crippling blow at an opportune moment. Numerically the opposing forces were about equal in strength, but one was in the air and the other was not. Nothing is so helpless as an airplane on the ground. In war, surprise is decisive."

Preparations for the Lae operation were intensified during this period. On 20 August General Blamey arrived from Australia to take personal command of New Guinea Force. The amphibious and airborne training of the troops was completed, full-dress rehearsals were held, and the necessary equipment brought forward for loading. A strong United States carrier task force in the South Pacific sortied from Espiritu Santo and Efate in the New Hebrides and began round-the-clock raids on southern Bougainville to divert enemy attention to possible Allied assaults in that area. At the same time, PT boats and submarines struck at enemy barges along the coast and protected Allied waterborne movements against surface and subsurface attack.

The development of the hard-won Allied port at Buna had proceeded rapidly. It was to be the base of operations for the Australian 9th Division in its attack on the enemy's left flank. Actually, the timing of the Lae operation depended to a great extent upon the speed with which Buna could be built up as an intermediate supply base and staging area on the road from Milne Bay to the Lae beaches.

On 1 September, the Australian 9th Division embarked in the transports and assault craft of the 7th Amphibious Force at Milne Bay. After a stop at Buna for reinforcements, fueling, and a final check, the landing force moved forward. On 4 September, under cover of continuous Allied air strikes at Wewak, Hansa Bay, Alexishafen, Madang, and New Britain, the main attack on Lae was launched. The assault troops hit the beaches at Bulu Plantation and at the mouth of the Busu River, less than twenty miles from Lae. Minor opposition from enemy snipers was quickly eliminated and the troops drove on up the coast toward Lae itself.

At the same time that the Allied amphibious assault was being carried out east of Lae, a bold scheme was in progress to strike the enemy simultaneously on his right flank. It was planned to fly the Australian 7th Division directly from Port Moresby and land it in the Markham Valley to attack Lae from the west. The success of this maneuver depended upon the seizure of a prewar emergency landing field located at Nadzab across the Markham River. The previously developed airstrips at Tsili Tsili and Wau were to provide the necessary fighter cover for such an airborne maneuver.

On 5 September, the United States 503rd Parachute Regiment, accompanied by General MacArthur himself, took off from Port Moresby on the first major jump of United States paratroopers in the Pacific War.

Eyewitness accounts of this airborne landing operation stress its spectacular elements. Some 300 planes, taking off from nine different fields, converged seriatim on the picturesque Markham Valley. First came the B-25s, ready to spit deadly fire from their .50-caliber machine guns. Next came the A-20s, prepared to lay down a protective smoke screen as the men sailed to earth. Then came a Flying Fortress, with MacArthur himself inside, his gold-embroidered cap at its usual rakish angle. Kenney followed in another Fortress. Finally came the 100-odd transport planes with the paratroopers and a full battery of artillery. The 4-inch guns of this battery dropped gently to earth, each under its own parachute. MacArthur had insisted on accompanying the great air-drop of men and supplies because, as he said:

I did not want our paratroops to enter their first combat fraught with such hazard without such comfort as my presence might bring to them.

After the drop had been completed, MacArthur radioed his wife at Lennon's Hotel in Brisbane: "It was a honey." The whole show had been unmolested, for a bad fog kept the Japanese planes earthbound at Rabaul.

The MacArthur records complete the tale:

Transport after transport poured out its cargo of fully equipped paratroopers upon the vital airstrip. Watching the multi-colored parachutes spread themselves over the valley, General MacArthur felt the satisfaction of seeing this daring operation carried out with smooth precision. Even before he left the scene, the ground was being prepared for the big transports as flame throwers began to eat away the large patches of tall kunai grass. On the next day, the first of the planes bearing elements of the 7th Division landed on the runway to discharge its precious load of troops and equipment.

The Japanese were surrounded except for one narrow route of escape northward through the dense jungles and almost impassable mountain trails of the Huon Peninsula. As the Allied noose gradually choked them off from all hope of aid, the Japanese yielded their positions and, discarding almost all equipment, began a precipitous flight through jungle and mountains towards Kiari in a desperate effort to escape complete annihilation. On 16 September, Lae was occupied by the Allies. Another valuable link was forged in the chain of air bases that would eventually encircle and render helpless the powerful Japanese war machine.

While the airstrip at Lae was being developed as a new forward base for Allied transport planes, New Guinea Force [Australian] moved onward. Its next objective was Finschhafen—a busy enemy port on the tip of the Huon Peninsula. A keystone in the arch of the Japanese defenses, guarding the western side of the strategic Vitiaz Straits, it was a valuable prize to be plucked from enemy hands.

Plans for the assault of Finschhafen had been mapped well in advance. Immediately after the fall of Lae, the 20th Brigade of the Australian 9th Division which had made the initial Lae landing, started on its next mission. On 22 September it rounded the jutting Huon Peninsula and landed just north of Finschhafen. The beachhead was secured against stiff opposition and the Allied troops, reinforced by another battalion, advanced toward their objective. Moving steadily on against stubborn but hastily prepared enemy counterattacks, Allied forces occupied Finschhafen on 2 October. . . .

The capture of Finschhafen and the subsequent drive up the New Guinea coast together with the simultaneous air-ground movement of 200 miles up the Markham Valley through the center of New Guinea gave the Allies control of the entire Huon Peninsula. The Allied maneuver outflanked and contained all important enemy centers on the Peninsula and rendered impotent his numerous positions and installations along the northeast coast of New Guinea. The speed of this double envelopment apparently caught the enemy unprepared and resulted not only in the serious dislocation of his grip on New Guinea but caused him enormous losses of men and material which he found impossible to replace. . . .

With the ousting of the Japanese from the Huon Peninsula, General MacArthur had secured domination over the western approaches to the Vitiaz Straits. . . .

In preparing for the New Britain landings, the heavy concentration of enemy air strength on the Rabaul air fields constituted a serious menace to Allied operations. In spite of repeated raids on their airdromes, the Japanese continued to send planes aloft in considerable numbers. During the month of November, particularly, their efforts in the air reached a new peak of activity, indicating that plane reinforcements in substantial strength were arriving at Rabaul, Kavieng, Wewak, Hollandia, and Madang.

This resurgence of enemy air power presented an added problem in the guarantee of adequate air coverage for the New Britain operation. There was no illusion that the naval convoy would escape heavy Japanese bombing attacks. To enable the fighter planes of the Allied Air Force, which were based on widely scattered fields, to rendezvous over Vitiaz Straits and maintain a continuous air umbrella over the convoy, General Kenney needed advance reports of Japanese air sorties against Allied landing forces at Arawe and Gloucester. General MacArthur's

G-2 had anticipated this need and had taken steps to develop a comprehensive radio warning net of intelligence agents behind the Japanese lines. Three months prior to the Allied invasion of New Britain the U.S. Submarine *Grouper* had landed 16 Allied Intelligence Bureau operatives and 27 specially trained natives on the island. These operatives had slowly infiltrated inland, and on the day of the Allied landings they were in strategic positions to report on enemy activity and to give ample notice of oncoming enemy air formations.

The requisite troops and amphibious craft of Alamo Force were concentrated at Milne Bay, Buna, and Goodenough Island, while Allied planes began preparatory bombardment. Over 1,500 sorties were flown against Cape Gloucester alone during December and 3,700 tons of bombs were dropped. Gasmata and other positions on the south coast of New Britain were raided frequently, but to avoid alerting the enemy Arawe was not attacked until the day preceding the landing.

On 15 December, the U.S. 112th Cavalry Regiment, with strong air

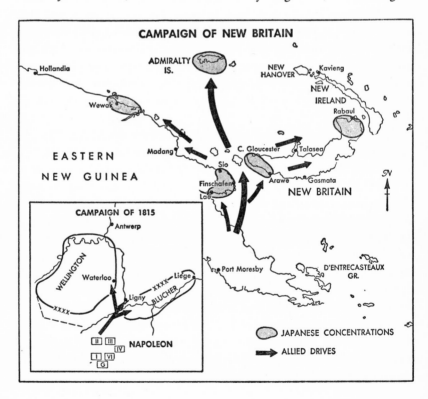

CAMPAIGN OF NEW BRITAIN

and naval support, went ashore at Arawe. Ground resistance was ineffectual and beachhead positions were rapidly consolidated. As predicted by initial intelligence forecasts, however, the Japanese attempted to strike back swiftly and forcibly in the air. An estimated 100 planes appeared over Arawe within three hours after the landing and from the 15th through the 17th approximately 350 enemy sorties were made in one of the largest defensive air operations which the Japanese had thus far engaged upon in the Southwest Pacific. Allied fighters, however, forewarned of the impending strikes, scored heavily against each raid. The Japanese nevertheless continued to expend their plane strength against Arawe until it became apparent that the prime interest of the Allies lay elsewhere.

Persistent Allied raids upon Cape Gloucester marked it clearly as General MacArthur's next objective. Even after the Japanese became aware of the Allies' true intention, they could do little to protect this vital position which guarded the Vitiaz Strait and the lines of communication between Rabaul and New Guinea. The Allied aerial and submarine blockade restricted troop movements to small craft operating under cover of darkness and prevented the concentration of air and naval forces in sufficient strength to resist an attack. The Japanese attempted to reinforce their garrison from the ground troops at Rabaul, but this reinforcement was inadequate to counter the force pitted against it.

The mounting evidence of enemy weakness caused Alamo Force to cancel the airborne phase of the Gloucester operation and to rely entirely upon amphibious assault. On 26 December, two combat teams of the U.S. 1st Marine Division, commanded by Maj. Gen. William H. Rupertus, covered and supported by a heavy naval and air bombardment, landed on the beaches southeast and southwest of Cape Gloucester. The bombardment had proved very effective and the beachheads were secured against minor initial opposition. The main difficulties were presented by the narrow beach, which heavy rains had converted into a sea of mud, and the thick swamp and jungle beyond. At the end of the first day the Marines had established a perimeter approximately 900 yards in from the shore against stiffening resistance. As at Arawe, air reaction was initially strong and determined but after continued successful interception by Allied fighters enemy air activity virtually ceased by the end of December. Both flanks of the vital Vitiaz Straits had been secured, opening the waters of this strategic highway between the Solomon and Bismarck Seas for unrestricted use in the furtherance of Allied plans.

After the recapture of Satelberg and Wareo, New Guinea Force continued to advance along the Huon Peninsula against a steadily retreating enemy. The Japanese, with their supply lines rapidly disintegrating under sweeping Allied assaults, picked their way westward toward Sio and Madang. They were given no opportunity for respite or consolidation; their weary troops were compelled to resume their retreat once more as the Australians moved into Sio on 14 January 1944.

General MacArthur intended that this withdrawal should cost the enemy as high a price as possible. To cut off the main route of retreat and at the same time speed the Allied advance, he directed Alamo Force to make an amphibious landing at Saidor, midway between Sio and Madang.

The landing was made on 2 January and the United States troops turned eastward to meet the fleeing enemy. General MacArthur described the predicament of the Japanese when he reported:

"We have seized Saidor on the north coast of New Guinea. In a combined operation of ground, sea and air forces, elements of the Sixth Army landed at three beaches under cover of heavy air and naval bombardment. The enemy was surprised both strategically and tactically and the landings were accomplished without loss. The harbor and air fields are in our firm grasp. Enemy forces on the north coast between the Sixth Army and the advancing Australians are trapped with no source of supply and face disintegration and destruction."

The Japanese, caught between the closing pincers of the two advancing forces, abandoned the main route of retreat and, trying desperately to reach Madang, scattered in chaotic flight into the jungle. The hundreds of exhausted and starved bodies of Japanese discovered later along the ridges and mountain trails attested to the fact that the jungle had done its part in completing the work of the Allies. The last enemy soldier was squeezed off the Sio-Saidor road when elements of the Alamo and New Guinea forces made contact on 10 February.

Saidor was developed as an advance air and naval base to assist in the further conquest of New Guinea and for penetration into the Bismarck Sea, soon to be the next zone of Allied operations.

The Lae and Salamaua, the Saidor and the Cape Gloucester–Arawe battles yielded a curious loot in the form of numerous captured Japanese war diaries. Translated by ATIS soon after they had fallen into the hands of MacArthur's G-2 officers, they shed a white beam of light on Japanese troop psychology as the battle for the Admiralties and the campaign for the western end of New Guinea were shaping up. They also told MacArthur volumes about the worsening Japanese supply situation, thus enabling him to undertake bolder and bolder strokes with the assurance that the enemy could not adequately feed his men. As taken from the intelligence files, some of the diary entries read:

SALAMAUA

21 May 43: "Friday—clear. Arrived Salamaua. Built temporary shelter in the jungle at the foot of mountain."

30 Jun 43: "Thursday—rain. At 7:30 o'clock, even though it is raining, there are enemy airplanes reported. Recently our friendly airplanes have not come at all. . . ."

10 Jul 43: "Sunday—clear. The aggravating enemy airplanes strafe the Salamaua area as usual. We cannot stand seeing them nonchalantly flying low over the desperately active AA position[s]. Alas for friendly aircraft!"

ARAWE

21 Oct 43: "We are suffering from beri-beri and sudden undernourishment. I have a bowel movement only once in 5 days."

14 Dec 43: "During the morning and continuing for six hours, over 100 airplanes raided us heavily. Among several hundred bombs dropped, a few fell five to six m. from me. Only a few m. away the Coral reef was torn up by the strafing. I was shaken from head to foot by the bomb blast and was buried in sand. I was resolved to die. Because of fatigue and fear, after the bombing, I was spiritually and physically exhausted and felt like a piece of cotton. I felt like a fool. This was my first experience of the horrors of war in a half-year of overseas service."

5 Feb 44: "Situation report: The Det is out of supplies. From beginning of the battle, we have striven to live off the land and to cut down the rations to 200 g a day per person. . . . Many soldiers are getting fever due to the continuous rain and lack of food. Deterioration of arms and uniforms is astonishing. Many are without shoes."

CAPE GLOUCESTER

8 Jan 44: "At last our condiments have been used up. As usual there is continuous withdrawal of the wounded to the rear. The number of men killed in action is large."

17 Jan 44: "The sound of enemy arty and tanks was heard continuously. What will be our destiny tomorrow? Our situation is critical, and the only thing left for us is to fight to the bitter end. If I am worthy to die for my country. I have no regret at dying honorably on this lonely island of the South Seas."

22 Jan 44: "We had no ration today. Many have fallen on the road, weak with hunger and dying. It is a pitiful sight."

20 Mar 44: ". . . The condition is such that even our present position is not known. We have frequently lived on rations mistakenly dropped by the enemy, but there are no more. The Det is living on tree leaves and berries. It is apparent that the enemy is likely to appear. We have to cross a river before we reach Kou. It is doubtful that we can get rations even if we get there. Our future looks very grim. One of the decisive battles will be fought here."

SATELBERG

13 Oct 43: "How many days has it been since leaving Damaine that we have been sleeping on the mountains and living in the field? At our advanced position we find only shells, bombs and machine gun bullets from American planes. Our only pleasure is the food we get when the American forces surrender to us. Seeing the men die one by one by enemy bullets, why is it that I am still alive? Struggling to survive every second is useless in this situation. This terrible malaria—many men falling by the side of the road. The army advancing by automobiles and bicycles, as we saw it in the news in Korea, is a dream. Muddy roads, steep mountain trails—where could there be such hardship outside of war? We cannot even build fires to keep ourselves warm when drenched in the rain and shivering. We are constantly being attacked by malaria mosquitoes and suffering from poisonous insects. The trench, which is the safest place, is filled with rain water. Oh! I am ——. Those detestable American forces! I will not settle it just by killing them alone.

If I should be so unfortunate as to die from an enemy bullet, my soul will positively chew to death the American forces. Until the American forces surrender, I will not be able to go to Yasukuni Shrine feeling at ease."

22 Oct 43: "I eat potatoes and live in a hole and cannot speak in a loud voice. I live the life of a mud rat or some similar creature."

26 Oct 43: "Since leaving Ro High Ground, for one month I have experienced deep suffering undreamed of at the China front. The 'reality,' both spiritual and physical of the present will remain with me throughout my life. The best we can do for food is potatoes planted by the natives. Despite the valiant fighting of the Japanese Army, the situation is beyond imagination. Such must have been the anxiety of Christ in the garden of Gethsemane. The true Japanese as a wise man must take pride in that the more he suffers under such a 'reality,' the more placid he becomes."

27 Oct 43: "I heard that 1 Battalion of the 78 Regiment was annihilated in the Ramu River Sector. Our 80th Regt is down to one-third of its strength. Various units have lost their staffs. The 70th Regiment launched a fierce attack beginning on the 15th and although they did achieve some results, the sacrifice of lives was not slight. I heard that various artillery forces have run out of ammunition. With no reinforcement arriving, our forces, with whatever number of men and amount of ammunition we have left, are determined to achieve certain victory. I understand that the leaders have agreed upon another general attack next month. I am determined to fight and die as long as my body is able to hold out."

31 Oct 43: "Went to the Co. HQ last evening and heard a lecture by the Co. comdr. Heard that the enemy to the northwest is the Australian Force that fought against the Germans and the Italians. The enemy landed in this region totals about 30,000 men. As opposed to this, our force numbers only 10% of this number. Our objective is to capture the Kareki positions, but what happens after we capture it is problematical. The day of the general attack may be postponed, but it is the Co.'s day of extinction. For us it spells death. I entered the army in 1936, and I have had hardships piled one upon another until now, 1943. The operation since landing at Hansa has been a series of hardships consisting of road building and marches. I hope that some day I might be able to laugh and talk about the present fighting, but my

fate has been sealed by this war. I should like to return and flower as
the cherry blossom of Yasukuni Shrine. In spite of the fact that I no
longer value my life, I cannot forget my desire to live. Unreliable reports from the Navy Department: The fate of the Jinno Unit— The
honorable defeat on far off Attu Island and now our fate. There will
be some sacrifices as the result of the great victory for the empire, but
if the safety of the 100 million countrymen is assured, and if the empire
continues to prosper increasingly, then these sacrifices must be considered a glorious deed."

MADANG

10 Apr: "After breakfast we were sitting, watching the waves breaking in the ocean, when suddenly our ears traced a droning engine sound
and we saw airplanes coming directly toward us at about 100 meters
altitude. We didn't think they were enemy airplanes. When the two
airplanes were directly above us we realized for the first time that they
were not painted with our sun flag symbol. At this instant several bombs
exploded all around us. One man died and three were wounded. That
night we slept 2,000 meters inside the jungle away from our billeting
area."

12 Apr: "Arrived Madang."

13 Apr: "Since the attack of the other day, we are only having two
meals a day. . . ."

24 Apr: "Number of men dropping behind and suffering from illness
was numerous. The officers were not aware of the suffering among
men. ORs were the only ones serving the country."

12 May: "I was hungry, but still working. Rations were only one-
third of the usual amount. Potatoes were used as a substitute."

7 Oct: "Both officers and men were in low spirits. Each one in his
own foxhole was passing time dolefully. Is this a battle for Greater
East Asia? What will be the reaction in Japan when they learn of our
defeat?"

24 Oct: "Eating roots and bark of trees. L Bn retreated to Madang.
Not one friendly airplane was protecting us. I regretted deeply the
superiority of enemy dual purpose guns and other weapons. A poor
country is helpless. Enemy reconnaissance is pressing closely on our
position."

5 Nov: "Officers were issued with salt while men received not even potatoes. It seems foolish to work seriously."

Summing up the strategic results of the Huon-Gloucester campaign, MacArthur's G-2 Section once more sought a parallel in Napoleonic strategy (see map, page 132):

Although the General's current consolidation of the Huon Gulf Army was momentarily exposed to air attack on both flanks, from Wewak and Rabaul, the subtle advantage of this position lay in its poised offer of opportunity for a classic operation on interior lines, laying open the strategically important Admiralties as the ultimate breakthrough objective. He drove between the two immediately opposing enemy masses at Finschhafen and on New Britain, which were geographically prevented from significantly reinforcing each other. Turning first to his left flank, he took Finschhafen by direct frontal amphibious assault and set jungle-wise Australian troops to rolling up the battered Jap XVIII Army elements along the coast northwest toward Saidor. That flank secured, the General immediately wheeled to the opposite shore of vital Vitiaz Strait and established beachheads at Arawe and Cape Gloucester on New Britain. After further swift widening of the breach by amphibious envelopment of Talasea and Gasmata the approach to the Admiralties lay miraculously open, with a Japanese Army on each flank rendered powerless to hinder the projected breakthrough.

In this context, "miraculous" is a superficial word. To immobilize with a relatively small force the Japanese Eighth Army on the Rabaul flank represents a professional utilization not only of astute staff intelligence but of time and space factors cannily converted into tactical advantage. It was correctly anticipated that not only would the projected Arawe landing immobilize enemy New Britain reserves in fear of further coastal assaults threatening Rabaul, but that the bulk of enemy opposition to be met at Arawe would be reinforcements caught belatedly en route to Lae. The only other significant portion of the Arawe garrison was known to be elements of the Jap 115th Regiment, 51st Division, which had been dogged with misfortune throughout the Bismarck Sea disaster and the fall of Lae. Further, past experience has shown the enemy's reaction to Allied offensive on New Guinea and Bougainville as an over-all policy of delaying action with reserves committed in piecemeal fashion, and an inability to support with associated arms massed counterattacks. . . .

At the time of our Arawe-Gloucester landings the enemy had a strong cordon about western New Britain coastal arc. Air and naval bombardment smashed it at the selected beaches sufficiently to permit their quick seizure by our Marines. Partially recovering from the stunning Gloucester blow, the enemy within 24 hours counterattacked with but one battalion. Subsequent rapid envelopment of Talasea and Gasmata cut the vital coastal track in four places, isolating all enemy garrisons below Rabaul. With any plan of coordinated military effort disrupted, and contact with the south and east available only by circuitous inland routes, Eighth Army remnants gradually withdrew to Rabaul and eventual starvation. . . .

Finschhafen and Gloucester were preliminaries, the shoulders of a penetration; the dash on the Admiralties was the objective breakthrough that enabled the Allies to roll up both the New Guinea and New Britain flanks; these operations were fought on the ground, though the means were delivered by sea.

The technical pattern, however, remained identical also for the Air Arm. It was equally essential for our Air to split the Japanese aerial front, to interrupt the shuttle service between the great air bastions of Wewak and Rabaul, isolate them and destroy them, in detail.

And through these seemingly scattered actions, there runs a red thread of design, the operative "leitmotif," the flexible, inexorable advance on the Philippines—somewhere—somehow—some time!

The year 1943 had not advanced MacArthur toward the Philippines very far in terms of actual mileage. But it had been a year of vast achievement, nonetheless. The vital breakthrough to the north had been virtually achieved, and the Japanese stood on the defensive everywhere, confused between the attacks of MacArthur on one flank and pressure from Nimitz's navy and marines and Halsey's carriers on the other. As the MacArthur records say:

The year 1943 had fulfilled its early promise. The propitious victory at Buna had presaged the Allied conquests to come. In marked contrast to the slow, uphill struggle of the preceding year, 1943 witnessed long strides by the Allies deep into enemy territory. The goals set at the beginning of the year had been successfully achieved. On his left flank, General MacArthur had moved on from Buna according to plan, seizing in succession Salamaua, Lae, Finschhafen, and the entire Huon Peninsula. His forces were rolling back General Adachi's Eighteenth Army at an accelerating pace all along the coast of New Guinea. On his right flank, the capture of Arawe and Gloucester Bay had placed the southern end of New Britain in his hands. Farther to the east, the Allies controlled the entire stretch of the Solomon Islands and the waters of the Solomon Sea.

Rabaul was being steadily emasculated by a growing Allied air arm which slashed constantly at its vital air fields and harbor installations. Enemy thrusts from that once powerful stronghold were becoming weak and ineffectual and by the end of February 1944, Rabaul had "no air support whatsoever." In spite of replacements and reinforcements the once-powerful "Japanese air force in this area had been driven to the point of extinction." The gradual decimation of the enemy's land-based air power by the Fifth and Thirteenth Air Forces sharply decreased his ability to defend his vital sea lanes and opened the way for Allied naval craft to advance in increasing strength. It was these unrelenting and punishing attacks against major Japanese air fields and ground installations that won the battle in the skies and gradually destroyed the enemy air force in the New Guinea–Solomons area.

The Japanese at the opening of the year had held an advanced line running from Salamaua and Lae across southern New Britain and the Solomon Sea to New Georgia. Now their ground forces were pushed back to Madang, Rabaul, and Kavieng. In the air, the power of the Allied Air Force was increasing rapidly and could drive the enemy from the sky at almost any chosen point. On the sea, Allied Naval units had demonstrated that they could cope with any threat to amphibious operations and defeat the enemy wherever he chose to give battle.

The Japanese had suffered heavily in men and materiel. Huge amounts of discarded and abandoned supplies, guns, and ammunition marked the veering paths of their confused retreat as they were forced from one position after another. Thousands of their dead, killed in battle or stricken by starvation and disease, were left strewn on the battlefields and along the jungle trails. Additional thousands of troops were pocketed on Bougainville, Buka, Choiseul, and the Shortlands, their sting removed by isolation and their whole attention occupied with maintaining their own sustenance. Their transport and supply ships were sunk in increasing numbers as Allied planes and submarines exacted an ever-rising toll for their passage. Clearly, the Japanese had lost the power to conduct any further large-scale offensives in New Guinea.

As supplies kept coming into the Southwest Pacific Area and the shortages which shackled his every plan were gradually being removed, General MacArthur prepared to launch heavier blows against the Japanese.

The story of what MacArthur did in combat with limited resources is matched by the story of how his forces managed to use the Australian economy to support their war. Complete understanding between the General and the Australian government was an essential ingredient in this achievement. As the Australian Prime Minister, Mr. Curtin, said near the end of the campaign:

. . . the position of General MacArthur in Australia is unique. He is a Commander of a foreign though friendly power with his Headquarters located in the country of another Government which has continued to exercise all its sovereign powers, but assigned to him its combat forces which for long constituted the great bulk of his command.

General MacArthur has also looked to the Australian Government for many of his supplies and services and the provision of his base installations and facilities.

The Commander in Chief has been in close association with the Government for over two years. His position has been one of delicacy fraught with possibilities of trouble and difficulty if tact, discretion and diplomacy were not employed on both sides, but it is my great pleasure to state that the most cordial relations have been maintained and the closest working cooperation established. General MacArthur has displayed all the qualities of an able diplomat as well as those of a great Commander.

A feature of the story of the New Guinea campaign will be the genius with which air power was integrated with naval and land strength to render possible a new conception of offensive power in the realms of strategy, tactics and logistics. I vividly recall the critical stage of the

New Guinea campaign when every civil air service in Australia was suspended to provide the Commander in Chief with transport aircraft to support his operations. The incident was typical of the close cooperation existing between General MacArthur and the Government.

With relatively little loss of life and the minimum of frontal assaults by ground forces, enemy strongholds have been by-passed and their supply lines severed first by air attacks and then by naval forces. The objective of each advance has been the seizure of air fields which determine the scope and distance of the next advance. As a result, the infantry front has moved forward from the Owen Stanley Range to the northern islands of the Bismarck Archipelago. The fighter and bomber line has also leap-frogged onwards, until the Japanese mandates north of the Equator have come within the range of air bombardment from the Southwest Pacific Area.

General MacArthur has achieved the main objective laid down in his directive: To hold Australia as a base for future offensive action against Japan, and to check Japanese aggression in the Southwest Pacific Area [and then] to prepare to take the offensive.

7 MacArthur's Cloak-and-Dagger Men

IN Washington, from 1942 on, "Wild Bill" Donovan's Office of Strategic Services operatives had a fixed idea that they were arbitrarily kept out of MacArthur's Southwest Pacific Theater. Actually, MacArthur had to go along without the help of the Office of Strategic Services because he couldn't afford to wait for it. Unlike the war in Europe, the U.S. war in Asia was a "shooting war" from the start. Where the OSS in Washington had time to gather information about North Africa, about the "soft underbelly" of the Axis in the Mediterranean, and about Europe in general, long before a single landing craft or soldier was ever risked in battle, MacArthur had to improvise his intelligence from scratch with the Japanese breathing down his neck. He couldn't sit back and ransack libraries, even assuming the data was there; he had to have his reports from a 3,000-mile battle arc long before Roosevelt had even given Bill Donovan his basic directives on Europe.

At the outset of the shooting war in the Pacific, MacArthur was faced with what threatened to be insuperable intelligence obstacles. Summed up in MacArthur's Tokyo records, they were:

Worldwide lack of accurate information on Japanese strength, resources, dispositions and battle order; scanty information on terrain held or threatened by the enemy [compared to Europe, with its prolific maps, New Guinea, for example, was an uncharted wilderness]; an enemy with one of the world's most abstruse language systems, which complicated interrogation, translation and cryptanalysis; the need for immediate creation of intelligence agencies for geographical, linguistic and covert operations.

144

These problems were met and solved with a dispatch that could not have been had if MacArthur had waited for the creation of machinery in Washington. In the long advance of 2,500 miles from Papua to the Philippines, made with a record-breaking minimum of casualties, intelligence played an extremely important role. Since MacArthur proposed bypassing strong points with his own weaker forces, it was absolutely essential to know the whereabouts of the Japanese, the nature and vulnerability of their supply lines, and the chances for outguessing them in the act of flowing around them. Accurate information was the *sine qua non* of the whole planning function in leapfrog war. MacArthur's shoestring operations could not have been pushed to successful conclusion without a flood of intelligence data of every category.

The function of brains, including information-gathering brains, in the Southwest Pacific victory, was accurately appraised by Col. Masura Shinohara, of the Japanese Eighth Army staff. The Americans won, according to Colonel Shinohara, because of:

. . . air superiority; superior strategy; MacArthur's over-all offensive plan; superior weapons and superior intelligence. . . . I was amazed to find that American intelligence possessed the name, rank and unit of almost every Japanese officer in New Guinea.

Of the several branches of the intelligence service established at Brisbane, the so-called Allied Intelligence Bureau (AIB), a clandestine outfit, was easily the most picturesque. This was the organization that worked behind the Japanese lines from Singapore to Guadalcanal. Like its operations:

. . . the history of the AIB is a secret, little-publicized but highly important chapter in the story of the Southwest Pacific. From the Solomons to Borneo, from Java to the Philippines, a small adventurous group of carefully trained specialists spread a network of observers and operatives behind the enemy lines well in advance of our main body. . . . Operating in almost total isolation and normally without hope of outside support, every expedition was carried out in the face of great personal risk. If discovered by the enemy, the small parties were doomed to almost certain capture and probable death. In that event those who died quickly were fortunate. . . . Jungle-wise "coastwatchers," with tiny radio transmitter-receiver outfits, remained behind as the Japanese invasion wave swept forward. . . . From these few fearless men a powerful network of sea, air and ground spotters was developed until finally it became impossible for the enemy to make a single major move on the surface or in the sky without intelligence reports being flashed in advance to Allied forces. . . . At the conclusion of the desperate Guadalcanal campaign, Admiral Halsey publicly stated that it was probable that the allies could not have retained their hard-won initiative on Guadalcanal Island had it not been for the consistent advance radio warnings by AIB agents of impending enemy air attacks.

The coast watchers had been set up by the Royal Australian Navy even before the war broke out in Europe. They were recruited from among the hard-bitten gold miners of New Guinea, the copra traders and planters of the Solomons, the telegraph operators and administrative officials in a score of slatternly tropical ports. Credit for the initiation of this service should go to Capt. R. H. Long, director of Australian naval intelligence in Melbourne. A brilliantly intuitive man, Long was also an excessively modest sailor, and his talent for organizing clandestine intelligence has never been fully appreciated by the world at large. But it was appreciated quite early by MacArthur's G-2. Coming into Brisbane in 1942 with no clandestine network of its own outside of the Philippines, G-2 quickly recognized the value of Long's organization and expanded the early nucleus enormously. Intelligence notes of the period cover the final organizations and subdivisions:

In order to eliminate duplication of effort and tighten operational control of G-2, all activities of the various intelligence agencies in Australia concerned with clandestine or secret operations were merged under a single organization, the "Allied Intelligence Bureau," or AIB. On 6 July 1942, a GHQ directive established this organization, to "obtain and report information of the enemy, weaken the enemy by sabotage and destruction of morale, and to lend aid and assistance to local efforts to the same end in enemy occupied territories." Its field of operations was in the Southwest Pacific Area, exclusive of the continents of Tasmania and Australia. . . .

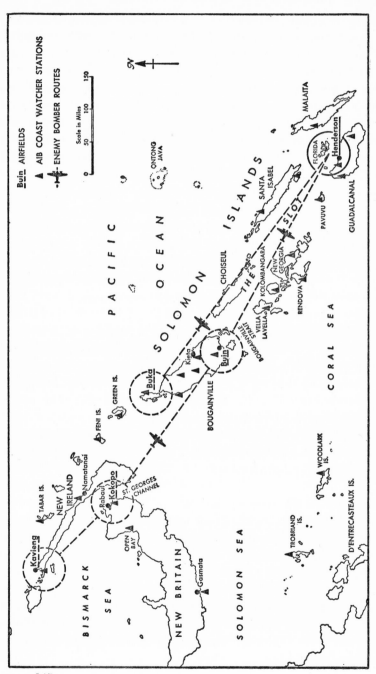

. . . It was found necessary to adjust the organizational structure on a "geographic" rather than a purely "functional" basis primarily to protect and reconcile political sovereignties. A very interesting figure emerged in the often delicate negotiations, one Mr. Van der Plaas, a former Governor of Eastern Java, related to native princes, and a top-flight diplomat. His persuasive formula was the division of the vast Southwest Pacific along colonial lines, preserving the prewar status quo. Colonel Van S. Merle-Smith, G-2 Deputy who had handled million dollar New York corporations before the war, was just the tough hombre to cut his way through tropical ambitions.

The chiefs of the various AIB sections were placed under an Australian Comptroller who, in turn, was responsible to G-2 headquarters; an American Deputy Comptroller was inserted as the Finance Officer. Thus we retained a double check upon the Bureau and its elusive international components; a coordinating staff, consisting of liaison officers from each headquarters, was named to assist the organization.

Running true to form, though ostensibly under a single directorship, each of the sub-sections attempted to remain more or less autonomous, and continuous readjustments were necessary during the lifetime of the Bureau in order to achieve centralized control.

Commander Eric Feldt, one of Long's subordinates and a very remarkable officer, modest, silent, deliberate—but with the capacity of speed in an emergency, played an important local role, directing operations in the Solomons—the so-called "Northeast Area"—from Port Moresby. The record of Feldt's sector has a direct bearing on the Guadalcanal victory. Feldt's humor is of the slightly sardonic variety; he gave his deadly serious operation the code name "Ferdinand," after the flower-loving bull:

On August 7, 1942, a relatively small force of American Marines, escorted by Australian and United States warships, landed at Guadalcanal, in the Solomons.

The AIB network in the Solomons was so organized that "coastwatchers" were able to spot Japanese flight formations from Rabaul or Kavieng. The observers were thus in a position to radio advance warnings to Guadalcanal, ranging from two hours to a minimum of 45 minutes.

Exactly four hours after the American landing, AIB agents on Buin and the Buka Passage flashed warnings that 24 Japanese torpedo bombers were en route southward. The Japs ran into a waiting trap of Allied fighter planes, in position of readiness: only one enemy plane escaped.

Early next morning, at 8:40 A.M., our observer at Buka Passage reported 45 bombers and fighters roaring overhead. By 9:10 A.M. unhurried Allied preparations had been made to crush the expected attack. That same afternoon the agent at Buin spotted more hostile aircraft flying to their doom. Allied fighters in position broke up the attack.

The Japanese lost 55 planes during the first three days after the landing. The baffled enemy was unable to mount another strike for several days, thus giving our forces invaluable time to consolidate their beachhead.

Practically the same story could be told over and over again, in other fighting areas. Prior to the landing of the Marine Division on Cape Gloucester and the 112th U.S. Cavalry Regiment on Arawe, advance air-raid warning nets were set up for the safety of our naval convoys. The MacArthur records cover these actions:

The capture of Finschafen and Satelberg, in 1943 . . . commanded the western approach to Vitiaz Strait. In order to gain unhampered control of this 60-mile-wide strategic seaway, MacArthur decided to take Cape Gloucester, on New Britain, first making a "diversion" at Arawe, about 65 miles to the south.

It was expected that Japanese fighters and bombers would fly a more or less direct route to our invasion points. Kenney's air force demanded advance warning of Japanese attack flights out of Rabaul, in order to time his air umbrella over our naval convoys.

Two months prior to the planned American invasion, the U.S. submarine *Grouper* landed 16 AIB operatives and 27 specially trained natives on New Britain. It took weeks of jungle trek for these parties to reach their stations. Local natives had been terrorized by Japanese patrols and could not be trusted; the job had to be done alone.

On the 15th December, the 112th Cavalry landed at Arawe. Within two hours over 85 Japanese dive bombers attacked Allied shipping.

Forewarned, our fighters were overhead waiting for the kill and the enemy lost heavily.

With this test of effective radio warnings, the 1st Marine Division landed at Cape Gloucester on December 26. Again AIB spotters gave advance warning of 45–60 minutes. Four enemy raids were intercepted on the first day. In two formations of 70 and 90 fighters and bombers, the Japanese lost 75 planes as against five of the Allies. Within three days it was reported that over 180 enemy planes had been knocked out.

The cordon of AIB spotters and radio stations on the Gazelle Peninsula over which all enemy formations had to fly en route to Gloucester, had played its part on New Britain exactly as on Guadalcanal.

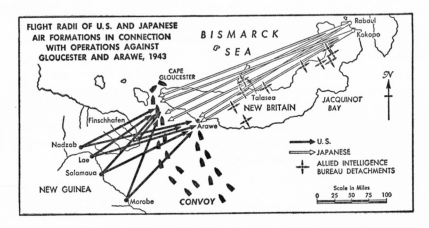

As has been seen in Chapter 6, "The Shoulders of a Penetration," Cape Gloucester and Finschafen were the preludes for the seizure of the Admiralty Islands to the north of New Guinea and to the west of Rabaul. Originally MacArthur thought he might have the Admiralties for the mere asking, for air reconnaissance over the area reported a total lack of enemy activity. For instance, Momote Airfield was reported unused; bomb craters in the runways remained unfilled, adjacent buildings seemed empty or in bad repair. From this General Kenney's men drew the inference that Momote had been completely abandoned.

G-2 flatly challenged this assumption. Its own information about the Admiralties pointed up an interesting historical example of the inherent limitations of spying from the air and "push-button" war in general. At modern speeds, aircraft simply cannot reconnoiter efficiently if the enemy chooses to use camouflage, remains stationary, or moves only under cover of darkness. In the Admiralties, the Air Force flew freely, unrestrictedly, and at treetop height. It saw little and reported less. Nevertheless, there was plenty of "enemy" in the Admiralties hidden from airplane view. Six years later, along the Yalu in Korea, fifty-three Chinese Communist divisions were to "play dead" by day. The Air Force of 1950 missed them even as Kenney's air force had missed the Japs in the Admiralties.

The MacArthur records show how standard G-2 techniques, utilizing the coast watchers, prepared the way in the Admiralties:

G-2 tabulated data over long periods of observation, based on radio intercepts, interrogation of natives from the islands, raids into enemy territory by agents of General Krueger's G-2—the whole paraphernalia of operative intelligence in motion!—and insisted blandly that the area was strongly defended and that we must be prepared to fight. Long in advance of the landing, the intelligence summaries—a sort of daily newspaper containing locator maps that showed enemy gun positions, supply traffic, assembly areas—put together a mosaic . . . until a final pattern emerged. G-2 was even in a position positively to identify the major units of the Japanese garrison, viz.:

Unit	Combat	Base	Service	Total
Elements 17th Div.	1,000			1,000
1st Ban 1st Regt	600			600
Elements 38th Div.	300			300
Oita Sea Detachment	300			300
Anti-Aircraft Bty		200		200
51st Transport Unit			800	800
51st Div. Hospital			50	50
			Aggregate	3,250

Later, after the capture of prisoners, G-2 "estimates" were entirely confirmed. Initially surprised by the landing of the 1st Cavalry, the enemy rallied promptly. That very night Japanese troops attacked with suicidal fury. Our situation became so critical that hospital personnel, mechanics, cooks and kitchen crews had to be thrown into the fight.

One Japanese group broke through within a few feet of General Chase's headquarters before it was stopped; Bill Chase led a charmed life on this particular occasion.

When the last pockets of resistance had been cleaned out several days later, G-2's "enemy forecasts" were substantiated. The Division reported officially:

". . . Air reconnaissance had indicated that not only was the airstrip unused but that there had been no noticeable activity on Los Negros Island for the preceding two weeks.

"After the battle, although the official count of their dead did not include those removed by the enemy for burial, the total was 3,280 Japanese killed and 75 captured, which almost equalled the original G-2 forecast of the garrison's size. . . ."

The techniques applied in developing the Admiralty Islands "situation map," in plotting day-by-day information about the enemy, were used again and again as the war went on. The situation maps issued for the Inchon landing in Korea were reminiscent of the Manus Island maps six years earlier.

The special Allied Intelligence Bureau organization expanded rapidly as a G-2 operating agency with inter-Allied personnel, an Australian commander, and an American deputy. Operatives were delivered by submarine or parachuted into Borneo, Timor, Java, and the Philippines; their activities ranged from collecting intelligence and spreading propaganda to outright subversion and sabotage.

The outstanding personages—American, Australian, and Dutch —in this important enterprise were the following: Brig. K. A. Wills, Brig. C. F. Rogers, Capt. R. H. Long, Col. C. G. Roberts, Col. C. S. Myers, Lt. Col. A. W. Ind, Col. E. G. Mott, Comdr. Eric Feldt, Comdr. R. Kendall, Comdr. J. C. Proud, and Lt. Col. F. Spoor, who was later to become Commander in Chief of the Netherlands East Indies forces.

Coast-watcher stations were established initially on northern New Guinea from Aitape to Samarai, along the New Guinea southern coast of Papua, and in the Torres Straits area. There were two stations on the northern coast of New Britain, one on Tabar Island, one at Muliama on New Ireland, one at Buka Passage in the Solomons, and one at Buin; all of these reported to naval intelligence officers at Port Moresby, Rabaul, Tulagi, and Villa, who relayed the information to area command at Townsville in Australia, later to Port Moresby, headquarters of Commander Feldt.

Some of the most amazing jungle treks of the war must be credited to members of the AIB section engaged in watching not only the north coast of New Guinea but in patrolling the rugged inland mountains and plateau country in order to keep tab on the movements of the Japanese as they aggressively fanned inward from the coast.

Later in the war, the Australian Army, charged with eliminating the Japanese forces still in the New Guinea area, depended heavily on AIB field intelligence, particularly for the routes of escape the defeated troops were taking. The Commanding General of the Australian forces, while mopping up in New Guinea and New Britain, reported that more than 50 per cent of his total field intelligence in that particular area came from AIB sources.

As this stalking phase of operations became established, AIB organized an infantry battalion composed of Papuan natives, many of whom had served previously on coast-watching assignments. Trained in Australia and in the field, these units led by coast-watcher personnel became strikingly efficient in tracking down, isolating, and decimating enemy units in Papua, New Britain, and the Solomons.

In mid-March 1942 Gen. Sir Thomas Blamey, the Australian Senior Commander, thought that a subversion-sabotage organization for special assignments would probably be useful. The suggestion came from London, which transferred a clever specialist, Col. E. G. Mott, who was formerly in Malaya, to assist in establishing an Australian Section of the famous British "special operations." Activation of this unit was authorized by headquarters as the "Inter-Allied Services Department." Actually an innocuous cover name, the ISD, was promptly incorporated into the Allied Intelligence Bureau in the directive of July 6, 1942.

To quote from intelligence notes of the period:

ISD came again into great prominence during 1945 when Australian headquarters was in urgent need of detailed information concerning Borneo and the islands adjacent thereto. During this period of intense activity, in preparation for landing attacks, GHQ received much of its field intelligence from operatives, most of whom had been dropped by aircraft. Over a hundred penetrations were successfully carried out. . . .

The problem of the Netherlands Sub-Section of AIB was rendered acute by the serious shortage of personnel in every branch of the remnant Dutch forces in Australia and by the fact that agents were compelled to operate in areas known to be intensely hostile. A total of 30 projects were undertaken by the Dutch Section from the middle of September 1942, through the middle of August 1945. More than one-third of these projects had to be written off as "lost or captured"; many of these instances involved only one agent rather than a whole party; nevertheless, whole parties of several individuals each did disappear in the dragnet of the Japanese "Kempei-Tai," aided and abetted by local collaborators.

On the credit side there is a record of nineteen parties having obtained considerable information, primarily of importance to the Dutch. . . .

The Netherlands Section was responsible for the development of a highly efficient radio transmitting and receiving unit, especially adapted to the needs of the agents operating in remote parts and having need for communication with GHQ through AIB; this Dutch radio set was utilized by the Philippine parties with great success later on.

The Netherlands Section, which was attached to general headquarters, was headed by Maj. F. Spoor, a very able soldier. He came to the favorable attention of his government and was promoted successively to the grade of General and finally Commander in Chief of the Dutch Colonial Forces in the Netherlands East Indies. Later he achieved the postwar pacification of the Islands in spite of surrendered Japanese arms which had found their way into the hands of Soekarno and other "patriots."

Because of subsequent political decisions that forced the Dutch out of Indonesia, Spoor's victories turned to ashes and the man died of a broken heart and broken spirit. The French, with considerably shorter tenure of office in Indo-China than the Dutch had had in Indonesia, were permitted to remain.

A very specialized unit called Secret Intelligence Australia (SIA) was organized to deal with subversion. Some of its more interesting operations were concerned with the introduction of native Moslem priests into Indonesia and elsewhere. The real purpose was to collect intelligence, but it also contributed to maintaining Islamitic solidarity to offset the current Japanese racial propaganda. For this purpose authentic "Hadjis" were imported from Cairo. The decision to use Hadjis followed upon the advice of the Rajah of Sarawak, then in Australia. General Willoughby's notes represent a glittering chip in the oriental mosaic:

The Rajah was Sir Vyner Brooks, of the picturesque British family that had carved out a bit of "empire" in the northwest corner of Borneo. The British in Melbourne were rather cool toward him. There was some talk that the "old boy" should have "stuck it" or even that he had flirted mildly with the invading Japanese. This seems silly today, when practically all the more hearty collaborators in the Pacific have since become chief magistrates, like Soekarno in Java, and the equally shifty Laurel in the Philippines. G-2 took the Rajah under its wings. He was in a quandary about his family at that time and needed air transport to the States. It seemed that his lively daughters were getting into all sorts of domestic difficulties; Hollywood is indeed no place for exotic and beauteous princesses from Borneo. Sir Vyner Brooks was horrified to learn that one of them proposed to marry a wrestler. We sent the Rajah in comfort and dignity on one of our Stateside bombers.

While in Melbourne this shrewd old man was a goldmine of expert information. He had with him his Secretary and former Minister, a sort of Grand Vizier, a Scotsman who had turned Mohammedan, a wearer of the green turban, a bonafide "Hadji," a holy man and a pilgrim. This gentleman could have stepped right out of Joseph Conrad; he might have doubled in appearance for the cadaverous villain in *Victory*. He turned out to be a cynical, brilliant personage and easily the most informed individual on the Islamic world. G-2 operatives learned from him that Islam had a most aggressive and highly organized missionary service abroad with spiritual headquarters in Cairo. They also remembered the wandering Moslem priests that were seen periodically in the Morro villages of central Mindanao.

In these days the casualty rate was high among Dutch and Australian operatives attempting to penetrate the Netherlands East Indies, Borneo and the islands to the north of Australia. The Rajah considered that the use of itinerant Moslem priests whom the natives were not likely to betray had good practical possibilities. Some difficulty was experienced in inserting these specialized agents, however, and still more in following up to obtain results of their activities. Several of them were apparently captured by the Japanese, who would not be too much impressed by green turbans; nothing was heard from them again. Others managed to obtain useful information before Allied forces occupied the islands in the Halmaheras, particularly Morotai.

Secret Intelligence Australia assisted in the development of a Celebes coast-watcher net; other parties operated in the Banda Sea area, flashing their signals to the net-control stations at Biak and Darwin. SIA communications were operated in conjunction with the efficient Netherlands net. The group succeeded in establishing five excellent information and weather-reporting stations in the hostile Java area. One operated off Soerabaja, in the west, while another covered the Sunda Straits between Java and Sumatra; three others were on perimeter islands. These stations were in operation at the war's end and, in fact, were continued for a while after the cessation of hostilities in order to check movements of Japanese renegade forces.

The whole record of the Allied Intelligence Bureau and its components is brilliant. In a single year, 155 sorties were made into enemy territory—91 by land-based aircraft, 14 by submarine or surface craft, and 50 by flying-boat; about 350,000 pounds of supplies were air-dropped or delivered to parties. Although they "worked in the shadows" and combat was definitely not one of their missions, these parties were sometimes forced to fight; over the years they killed substantial numbers of the enemy and brought in 150 high-level prisoners for interrogation. A little-advertised but calculated by-product of their silent work is found in the spectacular rescue of hundreds of Allied air, ground, or naval personnel, crash-landed or lost in enemy territory.

Hollywood made good use of the Allied Intelligence Bureau's records in the Pacific: the bright boys in berets borrowed and artfully polished such gems as Colonel Manzano's report on the silver bullion that was sunk in Manila Bay. Another popular film dealt with our rescue of missionaries in the Solomons under the noses of the Japanese who were brutally using a combination of local head-hunters and bloodhounds. The real point of that story was the split-second secret "intelligence" needed to assemble frightened and hunted people, including women and children; the timing of our coast watchers to get them to the beach; the coordination with the Navy to get them out. Hollywood ignored these vulgar items and concentrated on angelic nuns and blue-jawed naval ratings trying to cope with squalling babies. The film looked more like a brochure on the care and feeding of infants on the high seas than a narrow escape from death in unpleasant variations. Other pictures and stories have dealt with colorful "remittance men" who redeemed themselves in heroic endings—but the records of Commander Feldt and Captain Long list only a number of extremely respectable colonial magistrates, hardy local planters, and retired or active colonial police officers who were in the Australian reserves. These gallant men, who either remained in the vicinity of their plantations in the Solomons or were parachuted or submarined to their posts, led a precarious existence, always on the *qui vive*, shifting from one hilltop to another until the end of the war. Some of them were betrayed by their native carriers; indeed, the debit side of the AIB ledger is long. Many lives were lost; in carrying out 264 AIB missions, our casualties totaled 164 killed, 75 captured, and 178 missing. Personnel of the bureau earned one hundred battle awards and highest decorations. Operating in almost total isolation and normally with little hope of outside support, every expedition was carried out in the face of great personal danger. If discovered by the enemy, our parties were exposed to probable capture and. if captured, certain death; in that event, those who died quickly were fortunate.

The MacArthur records contain a specific reminder on this sinister subject: this gruesome reminder consists of film and documentation of a typical Japanese execution. The photographs were taken by a Japanese candid-camera fan, the text enlarging on the pictures was in diary form; both pictures and diary were picked up by G-2 after the Hollandia landing. The Japanese writer's style suggests the trained journalist; he gave his diary entry a sensational title, "Blood Carnival":

March 29, 1943: "All four of us—Kurokawa, Nishiguchi, Yawate and myself—assembled in front of Headquarters at 1500 Hrs. . . . The 'Tai' commander Komai, who came to the observation post today, told us personally that in accordance with the compassionate sentiments of Japanese *Bushido*, he was going to kill the prisoner himself, with his favorite sword. So we gathered to observe this. After we had waited a little more than ten minutes, the truck came along.

"The prisoner who is at the side of the guard house is given his last drink of water. The surgeon, Major Komai, and Headquarters Platoon Commander come out of the Officers Mess, wearing their military swords. The time has come. The prisoner with his arms bound and his long hair now cropped short totters forward. He probably suspects what is afoot but he is more composed than I thought he would be. Without more ado, he is put on the truck and we set out for our destination.

"I have a seat next to the surgeon. About ten guards ride with us. To the pleasant rumble of the engine, we run swiftly along the road in the growing twilight. The glowing sun has set behind the western hills. Gigantic clouds rise before us and dusk is falling all around. It will not be long now. As I picture the scene we are about to witness, my heart beats faster.

"I glance at the prisoner. He has probably resigned himself to his fate. As though saying farewell to the world, he looks about as he sits in the truck, at the hills, the sea, and seems in deep thought. I feel a surge of pity and turn my eyes away. The truck runs along the seashore now. We have left the Navy guard sector behind us and now come into the Army sector. Here and there we see sentries in the grassy fields and I thank them in my heart for their toil, as we drive on; they must have 'got it' in the bombing night before last; there were great gaping holes by the side of the road, full of water from the rain. In a little over twenty minutes, we arrive at our destination and all get off.

"Major Komai stands up and says to the prisoner: 'We are going to kill you.' When he tells the prisoner that in accordance with Japanese *Bushido* he would be killed with a Japanese sword and that he would have two or three minutes' grace, he listens with bowed head. He says a few words in a low voice. He is an officer, probably a flight lieutenant. Apparently, he wants to be killed with one stroke of the sword. I hear him say the word 'one'; the Major's face becomes tense as he replies: 'Yes.'

"Now the time has come and the prisoner is made to kneel on the bank of a bomb crater, filled with water. He is apparently resigned. The precaution is taken of surrounding him with guards with fixed bayonets, but he remains calm. He even stretches his neck out. He is a very brave man indeed. When I put myself in the prisoner's place and think that in one more minute it will be good-bye to this world, although the daily bombings have filled me with hate, ordinary human feelings make me pity him.

"The Major has drawn his favorite sword. It is the famous *masamune* sword which he has shown us at the observation station. It glitters in the light and sends a cold shiver down my spine. He taps the prisoner's neck lightly with the back of the blade, then raises it above his head with both arms and brings it down with a powerful sweep. I had been standing with muscles tensed but in that moment I closed my eyes.

"A hissing sound—it must be the sound of spurting blood, spurting from the arteries: the body falls forward. It is amazing—he has killed him with one stroke.

"The onlookers crowd forward. The head, detached from the trunk, rolls forward in front of it. The dark blood gushes out. It is all over. The head is dead white, like a doll. The savageness which I felt only a little while ago is gone, and now I feel nothing but the true compassion of Japanese *Bushido*.

"A corporal laughs: 'Well—he will be entering Nirvana now.' A seaman of the medical unit takes the surgeon's sword and, intent on paying off old scores, turns the headless body over on its back and cuts the abdomen open with one clean stroke. They are thick-skinned, these *keto* [hairy foreigner—term of opprobrium for a white man]; even the skin of their bellies is thick. Not a drop of blood comes out of the body. It is pushed into the crater at once and buried.

"Now the wind blows mournfully and I see the scene again in my mind's eye. We get on the truck again and start back. It is dark now. We get off in front of Headquarters. I say good-bye to the Major and climb up the hill with Technician Kurokawa. This will be something to remember all my life. If I ever get back alive, it will make a good story to tell; so I have written it down."

There are some revealing psychological touches here: the maudlin blend of human feeling and Japanese *Bushido*, or the code of the warrior; the involuntary undertones of oriental savagery; naïve respect and admiration for the calm manner with which the brave man died; the reference to the prisoner as he "totters forward"—obviously in physical and nervous exhaustion after having been cross-examined for several days, the effect of a third degree and worse. This is another "tale from the South Pacific"—but there is no glamour, only a barbarous and brutal death. Later on, in Korea, Americans were to encounter the same kind of savage ferocity, this time at the hands of Communist Koreans and Chinese. And there would be identical photographs of executions.

The Allied Intelligence Bureau called for a curious blend of warm human gallantry and cold-blooded technological finesse. Both elements are clearly recognizable in the story of a sensational raid into Singapore, made under the code name of "Jaywick."

After the Japanese had taken Singapore, the British feared the next objective would be India. Already the Japanese had made a naval foray into the Indian Ocean; a landing on the Indian subcontinent might start rebellion. Since Empire prestige had been practically demolished by the fall of Hong Kong and Singapore and could stand not another ounce of pressure, Lord Mountbatten cabled MacArthur from Ceylon that "something must be done to keep the Japanese Fleet out of Indian waters: H.M.'s command hoped some diversion could be staged in direction of Singapore."

MacArthur's axis of advance ran from New Guinea to the Philippines about 3,000 miles east of Malaya as the crow flies. American planes based on Australia could not handle that distance. Kenney became infuriated at the bland suggestion of "a one way trip." As for MacArthur's modest fleet, it was mainly engaged in New Guinea and Solomon Islands waters. What few submarines he could call on were already ranging the China Sea; actually, their main targets were in and around Philippine waters in general support of our Pacific operations; even if MacArthur or Nimitz could spare these expensive and vulnerable craft, there was still the problem of getting into heavily defended Singapore harbor.

To make plain its difficulty, Mountbatten's bright idea of a Singapore diversion should be examined in terms of a comparable situation

involving the United States. At the time of the Mountbatten request, Singapore was generally better defended than any port on
the East or West Coast of America. How would an enemy submarine sneak into the inner harbors of San Francisco or New York
and sink Matson Line or Cunard ships at their own docks? Mountbatten's casual recommendation entailed exactly that kind of
problem. He wanted the Japanese Southern Fleet, based on Singapore, to be frightened into immobility; the sinking of Japanese transports, tankers, or freighters at Singapore docks would do the trick.

As usual, the "buck was passed" to G-2, the whipping boy of
the staff, the garbage can for all spurious or half-baked ideas. Everything was against the Mountbatten demand, for submarines were
not available and fast seagoing craft were equally scarce. Luckily,
G-2 was more fortunate with personnel. If the Singapore diversion
were to be made a reality, the leader of the party had to be someone
who knew the harbor of Singapore, preferably a local yachtsman
familiar not only with bays, inlets, and channels but with native
boatmen. Such a specialist was found in the person of a British
officer, Lt. Col. I. Lyon of the Gordon Highlanders, who, after
some high-level negotiations, had to be "imported" from England
to do the job. This is his story, soberly told, with characteristic
British understatement:

Jaywick was the code name for a plan of attack against Japanese
shipping in Singapore Harbor. After arrangements with Australian
Naval authorities, personnel was selected from Flinders Naval Depot.
Training which continued for four months began in a special camp
near Sydney. The party consisted of four officers and ten naval ratings.

The motor vessel *Krait* selected for the trip had been brought as
deck cargo from India. This vessel had formerly been the property of
a "Japanese fishing concern in Singapore." Since there were many
ships like her, it was expected that she would not be challenged by
Japanese harbor patrols.

She was a wooden vessel of 70 ft. with very little beam, about 11
ft., which made her an uncomfortable craft in bad weather. She was
fitted with a Gardner-Diesel of about 100 h.p. Her top speed was 6½
knots and her cruising range 8,000 miles. After training was completed

and when the *Krait* was on her way up the East Coast of Australia, she developed serious engine trouble. The installation of a new engine delayed the departure of the expedition.

At 1400 September 2/1943, the *Krait* sailed for Exmouth Gulf, Western Australia, bound for the Rhio Archipelago. By nightfall she was clear of the Gulf and was steering a course that would take her about fifty miles west of a direct line between the Gulf and Lombok.

A fresh southerly breeze which had been blowing for twenty-four hours produced an unpleasant sea on the port quarter. It was the first opportunity the crew had to gauge the *Krait's* seagoing qualities in her overloaded state. Despite removal of the deck armor, she rolled heavily and was very sluggish in her recovery, on one occasion lying over until a man standing beside the wheel house found himself waist-deep in water; by the following morning, conditions had returned to normal.

The first danger area was in the vicinity of Lombok Straits, between Lombok and Bali, which was expected to be guarded by patrol vessels and aircraft. The party hoped to slip through at night, under cover of the seasonal haze. On approaching Lombok, it was very evident that far from being hazy, the weather was perfect; the leader decided therefore to ignore the threat of air reconnaissance, to rely upon the Japanese "silhouette" of his ship, and to make a direct approach.

On September 8, in condition of perfect visibility, *Krait* approached to within twenty miles of Palau-Nusau-Besar Island at the southern entrance of the Straits, without sighting any enemy activity. On entering the Straits, *Krait* experienced the exceptionally strong south-flowing tidal stream of those waters and for some hours her progress was negligible. In the late evening, she took four hours to pass the four mile coast line of Nusau-Besar; under Dutch rule this island had been almost uninhabited, except for a settlement in the northwestern corner. It seemed now, however, to be a center of activity, numerous controlled fires and fixed and moving lights being observed. During the night with the northbound tide, the vessel made good progress. By 1000 Hrs. the seasonal haze developed and under cover of this, the *Krait* skipped out into the Java Sea on a course to take her north of the Kangeon group.

The passage of the Lombok Straits was the first test of the protection afforded by the *Krait*. Her outward appearance was that of a normal Japanese fishing craft; to heighten the disguise, the members of the

American troops
landing on
New Guinea

The conference in Hawaii: President Roosevelt, General MacArthur, and Admirals Leahy and Nimitz (US Navy Photo)

En route to Leyte: Generals Kenney and Sutherland, President Osmena, General Mac-Arthur, and Colonel Romulo (US Army Signal Corps)

Above: Wading ashore at Leyte   *Below:* General MacArthur
with General Krueger

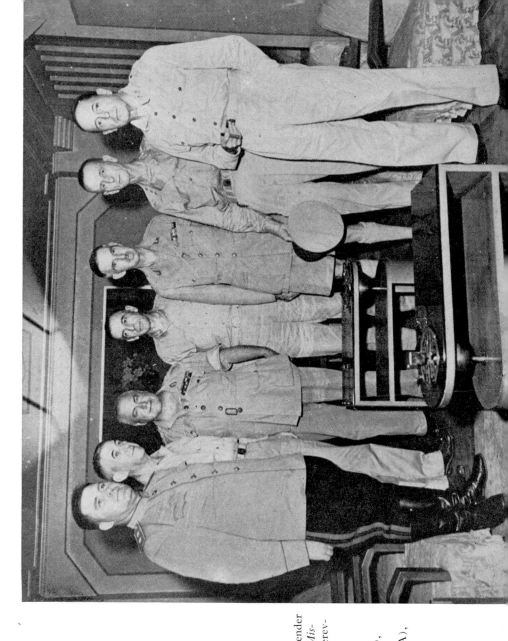

Awaiting the Surrender aboard the USS *Missouri*: Generals Derevyanko (USSR), Krueger (USA), Blamey (RAA), Sutherland (USA), Percival (UK), Wainwright (USA), and MacArthur

Above: Japanese troops, repatriated from the South Seas area, carrying the ashes of dead comrades *Below:* Flotsam of war: displaced Japanese civilians (US Army Signal Corps)

At Inchon: General MacArthur with Marine troops (by *Life* Photographer Carl Mydans © TIME, Inc.)

Restoring the capital of Korea to Syngman Rhee: Generals Hickey, MacArthur, Almond, Walker, and Barr with President Rhee and Ambassador Muccio (US Army Photo)

Above: Press conference in Korea: Generals MacArthur, Whitney, and Ridgway (US Army Photo) *Below:* Flying over the Yalu: Generals MacArthur, Wright, and Stratemeyer (US Army Photo)

On Formosa: Generals Willoughby, Almond, Stratemeyer, and MacArthur with Generalissimo and Madame Chiang Kai-shek (US Army Photo)

Japanese civilians bidding good-by to MacArthur (US Army Photo)

MacArthur leaves Japan (US Army Photo)

party had dyed their bodies and dressed as natives; after this test, "Jay-wick" company felt reasonably secure in their disguise. . . .

Through the Java Sea, the voyage was dull and uneventful. Some Macassar "prahus" were seen on easterly and westerly courses, but were avoided. The course was set for Tamiang Straits and the coast of Dutch Borneo. As they were trying to pick up land in the early hours of September 16, they sighted their first shipping: a large tanker passed a quarter of a mile ahead on a northerly course; she was blacked out and gave no sign of having sighted the *Krait*.

Sailing through the Straits, they made for Pompong Island as a possible transshipment area. A reconnaissance showed, however, that neither Pompong nor any of the adjacent islands were suitable, so it was decided to investigate some of the islands of the Rhio Archipelago which lies between Pompong and Singapore itself. While reconnoitering Bengku Island, a low flying float-plane passed closely by but took no notice of the party.

Events had led to the conclusion that peacetime conditions prevailed around Singapore and that the safest role for the *Krait* was to rely on her disguise without any attempt at further deception, taking care to avoid all contact with natives; the cumulative effect of native gossip was considered a far greater risk than were casual enemy patrols. It was decided, therefore, that the canoeists be landed the following night and that the *Krait* return to the coast of Dutch Borneo to fill in the time.

After dark, much enemy activity in the form of searchlights, float-planes and transport aircraft made it obvious that they were in a very active area. Searchlights were showing from Chompa Island, fifteen miles southwest of Pompong. It was obvious that the formerly unde-fended Lingga Group now contained a naval aviation base; this em-phasized more than ever the necessity to off-load the expedition.

The mast was lowered to decrease the vessel's visibility, but while they were stowing the rigging and gear, some natives in a canoe were seen approaching. *Krait* was gotten under way immediately and headed north at slow speed. To kill time, she sailed on this course to the Petong Group and then eastward to Galang Bahru. Two miles from shore they sighted a new building with an observation tower alongside it. *Krait* apparently aroused no suspicion, but they cautiously altered the course until heading as though bound from Sumatra to Singapore. Not know-ing whether they had been reported at the observation post, they were committed to maintaining their course for the remaining hours of day-light.

North of Galang Bahru lies the island of Pulau Panjang. Previously passing along its western shore, they had noticed some sandy coves and no signs of habitation.

Shortly before dark, they were five miles north of Panjang when a launch was sighted approaching *Krait*. The crew stood to action stations, but the launch passed them about one mile distant and evinced no interest. By nightfall, *Krait* was in the entrance to the Bulan Strait and only twenty miles from Singapore, the lights of which could be seen reflected in the clouds. Certain that they could no longer be seen, the engine was silenced, and *Krait* headed towards Panjang.

A suitable anchorage was found and by 0500 Hrs. on the 18th all operational gear and personnel, together with stores, food and water for one month, had been landed. *Krait* thereupon weighed anchor and sailed for Borneo with instructions to rendezvous at Pompong Island between the hours of dusk and dawn, on the night of October 1/2.

On arrival at the Panjang base, "Jaywick" had been able to ensure only that there was cover and no sign of habitation. At dawn a more extensive reconnaissance showed that there was a village about a quarter of a mile away on the other side of the island, but there was no sign of any track leading to Otters Bay, where they had made their first camp. The stores were carried back into the jungle and camp was pitched beside a waterhole; by noon, reserves of food had been cached in a cliff face. On returning to camp, they found that an army of hermit crabs had effectively obliterated their tracks in the sand. A sentry posted for observation reported the usual activities of small junks, fishing craft and aircraft.

On the 20th, stores and equipment were checked in preparation for starting at dawn. Departure was delayed by the passage of a 70 ft. patrol launch, a mile to seaward of the base; on the two previous nights, the noise of her exhaust had been heard at regular intervals.

The canoes were loaded with food and water for one week; with operational stores and men, the cargo's total weight was approximately 700 lbs.; with such a load, the canoes sat low in the water and were very sluggish. At dusk 20 Sept./43, the party set off in close arrowhead formation, Lt. Davidson navigating.

By midnight, having covered a distance of ten miles, they selected a

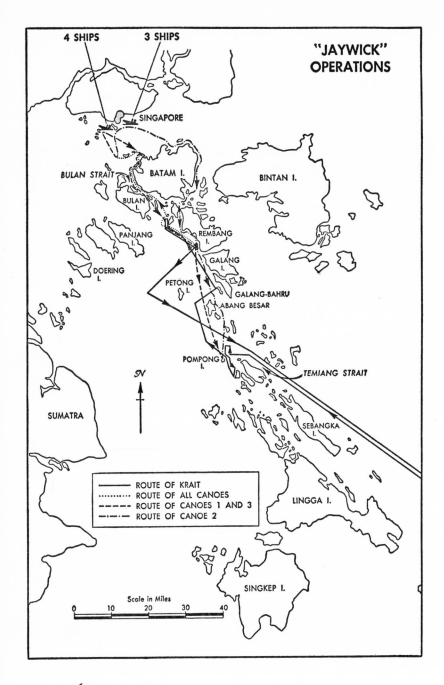

4 SHIPS   3 SHIPS

"JAYWICK"
OPERATIONS

SINGAPORE

BULAN STRAIT   BATAM I.   BINTAN I.

BULAN
I.

PANJANG
I.   REMBANG
I.

DOERING
I.   GALANG
I.

PETONG
I.   GALANG-BAHRU

ABANG BESAR

POMPONG
I.   TEMIANG STRAIT

𝒩

SUMATRA

SEBANGKA
I.

ROUTE OF KRAIT
ROUTE OF ALL CANOES
ROUTE OF CANOES 1 AND 3
ROUTE OF CANOE 2

LINGGA I.

Scale in Miles
0   10   20   30   40

SINGKEP I.

camping place at Pulau Bulat; the rest of the night and the following day were spent here observing the passage of small craft in and out of the Straits. At dusk Sept. 21, the canoes paddled up Bulan Straits, but owing to constant alerts, poor progress was made. They were obliged to shelter in a sandfly infested swamp to avoid being caught in daylight. It was a bad hideout. The party was exactly opposite a village, only 300 yards away, on the Island of Boyan. They spent a most uncomfortable day.

On the evening of Sept. 22, excellent progress was made. . . . The canoes arrived at Pulau Dongas about midnight, the island chosen for their forward observation post, about eight miles south-southeast of Singapore harbor. It was jungle covered with an extensive swamp on the south side; it was uninhabited and had only one landing place, a narrow inlet with a sandy cove at its head; a sand pit ran back into the swamp providing facility for concealment and some comfort. Daylight reconnaissance revealed an excellent observation point on high ground, and drinking water was available in a disused well.

It was possible to see into Keppel harbor, the Roads and Examination anchorage. In Singapore, there was no blackout and the lights of cars driving down Beach road could be clearly seen. There were no harbor or navigation lights burning, and all ships were stationary. In the day, there was much movement of shipping in the roads. During five days of observation, there was at no time less than 100,000 tons of shipping in the area, and the freedom of movement enjoyed by medium draught native craft showed that no minefields had been laid; it was decided to wait until there was a considerable concentration of shipping in one place before carrying out the attack.

During the afternoon of Sept. 24, a concentration totaling 65,000 tons assembled in the roads opposite Dongas. It was realized that unfavorable tides would render an attack extremely difficult, but the target was so tempting that it seemed imperative to try. At 2000 Hrs. the canoes proceeded toward the target area. No patrols were encountered. A weak searchlight from the direction of the city, probably situated on the Cathay Building, cast its beams toward the canoes and remained stationary for about 30 seconds; apparently the canoes were not observed, as nothing further happened.

As the party approached the target, the current increased in strength. It soon became obvious that the canoes could not battle against it and at 0100 Hrs. the attack was abandoned. It was decided to return to Dongas and await more favorable conditions. Canoes 2 and 3 managed to reach Dongas before daybreak. Colonel Lyon's canoe, however, was taken eastward by the current; to avoid detection, the crew hid among some boulders in the swamp; as it rained all the time, they spent a most miserable day. They rejoined the party at dark.

As it appeared that weather and tides unfavorable for an attack would continue for a few days, Lt. Davidson planned a move to an alternate hideout, from which an attack could be launched the following night under more favorable conditions. His prompt decision was a vital factor in the ultimate success of the expedition. On the night of Sept. 25, the party moved westward to Pulau Subar, a small island overlooking the Examination anchorage; the island was waterless and had no beach but provided an excellent vantage point for observation.

During the afternoon of Sept. 26, targets were selected and assigned. By 1900 Hrs. the canoes were loaded and the party embarked for the second attack; target areas were as follows: Examination anchorage— Col. Lyon; Keppel Harbor and the Roads—Lt. Davidson; and Pulau Bukum Wharf—Lt. Page. Lyon and Page decided to remain together during the approach. They paddled at an easy pace, making good progress on the cross-tide, pausing only when the Blakang Mati searchlight shone uncomfortably close to them; at 2130 Hrs. they parted company.

Col. Lyon arrived in his target area about 2230 Hrs. to find all shipping, except tankers, completely blacked out and invisible against a background of hills. When his time limit was almost exhausted, Lyon decided to attack a tanker, two of which were recognizable by their red riding lights. He made a direct approach from astern and placed two "limpets," magnetized time bombs, abreast the engine room, and one on the propeller shaft. With their task only half completed, Lyon's attention was called to a man who was watching them intently from a port hole ten feet above. The man continued to look in their direction until just before they left the ship, when he withdrew his head and lighted his bedside lamp. Apparently he took no action. The task completed, the canoes set off on the twelve mile journey to Dongas, which was reached at 5015 Hrs.

After leaving Col. Lyon, Lt. Page in canoe No. 3 headed toward . . . the wharves at Pulau Bukum, which he reached at 2200 Hrs. He examined the whole length of the wharves, finding only one suitable target, a freighter of the Maru class; a large tanker was tied up and fully laden; the wharves were brightly lighted and a sentry was stationed near the bows of the tanker.

By 2300 Hrs. the tide had turned and was running to the east. The first target was attacked from the stern; with a following tide, Davidson paddled along Keppel harbor towards the second target, a modern freighter. Charges were placed on this vessel and, continuing, they attacked their third target, an old freighter identified later as either the *Yamagata* or the *Nagano Maru.* From this point Lt. Page returned to Dongas, which was reached at 0445 Hrs.

As regards Lt. Davidson, he reached his target area against the flood-tide. Keeping to the boat channel, the tripod pilons of Keppel harbor boom were picked up. A tug, burning navigation lights and found to the south of Blakang Mati, nearly ran them down but they were not sighted. At the Tanjong Pagar end, they found the boom gate open and no boom vessel in attendance. At the main wharf there was no shipping, and that in the Empire docks was too brilliantly lighted. They turned back and headed for the Roads. There were many excellent targets. Three of the largest cargo vessels were selected for the attack. They were 5/600 "engine aft" cargo vessels; one was later identified as the "Taiyo Maru." Each ship was attacked from the port side away from Singapore's lights. After attaching the charges, they left the Roads at 0115 Hrs.

Meanwhile the crews of canoes 1 and 3 had reunited at Dongas on Sept. 27 and set up an observation post to observe the results of the attack; between 0510 and 0550 Hrs. a total of seven explosions were heard, indicating that all attacks had been effective. As the sun rose, the Examination anchorage could be clearly observed. One ship was seen sunk by the stern with her bows protruding from the water. A tanker was burning fiercely and belching forth thick black smoke which almost entirely covered the area; owing to haze and smoke, no other results could be seen.

Fifteen minutes after the first explosion, ship sirens started and after another fifteen minutes Singapore and Sambu were blacked out. At dawn, ships were seen to be under weigh and aimlessly cruising about. After the first confusion in which bedlam reigned with a vengeance, there was considerable activity of small harbor craft in the target areas and motor launches patrolled the north coast of Batam Island. Air searches were made continuously throughout the day.

After observing results during the 27th, canoes 1 and 3 moved off at dusk to the rendezvous at Pompong. Arriving at the north entrance to Bulan Straits, they saw a small ship lying at anchor but drifted past it on the tide. They were all very tired and decided to make camp at the first suitable location. They found an excellent hideout in what turned out to be a Chinese graveyard. On the night of Sept. 28, they continued their journey to Bulat without incident, thence to Otters Bay, where they arrived in the midst of a violent storm in the early hours of the 30th.

Heavy cloud banks to the west indicated that there would be another storm; to risk a day passage of 28 miles was a very serious decision, but on the morning of Oct. 1 they moved on, paddling all day against a head wind. Several aircraft flew overhead without taking any interest in them; they must also have been clearly visible to the lookout at Ngoel. However, they made Pulau Torte without incident; they rested for an hour and then covered the 16-mile journey to Pompong. They reached the island at 0300 Hrs. and circumnavigated the whole island in search of *Krait;* there was no trace of her in the anchorage.

They slept on the beach until dawn, when they stowed the canoes in the jungle. While they were doing this, they saw the *Krait* about two miles away heading down Temiang Straits. So great had been their fatigue on the previous night, that they had paddled to and fro in the anchorage without being able to see the ship. Searching the island, they found traces of a newly vacated camp site. It seemed probable that Lt. Davidson had succeeded in keeping the rendezvous and that *Krait,* aware of the adverse weather conditions of the two previous nights, would return later; meanwhile they promptly organized themselves for a stay of several weeks. Page started to build a hut, while Lyon contacted some friendly Malays who promised to supply the party with fish and vegetables as long as they cared to stay on the island. At this time the party intended to seize a native vessel and sail to India on the change of the monsoon.

Their problem was solved, however, by the return of the faithful *Krait* at 22 Hrs. on Oct. 3. They were immediately taken aboard and the vessel sailed for Australia.

The return voyage through the Java Seas was uneventful. On Oct. 11 they entered Lombok Straits. They had a feeling of supreme confidence, which was rudely shaken at midnight by the appearance of a Japanese patrol vessel. However, *Krait* was not challenged. By dawn, they had passed the Straits and were out of sight of land on a course for Exmouth Gulf, which was reached on Oct. 19.

The cruise had occupied 48 days, during which 4,000 miles of enemy waters had been traversed without casualties or mishaps.

Damages resulting from the "Jaywick" raid aggregated between 36/40,000 tons, with six freighters of 4/500 tons sunk or damaged, and one tanker of 10,000 damaged and on fire. The Japanese Southern Fleet took strenuous local precautions thereafter and abstained from any further penetration into the Indian Ocean. . . .

There is a sad sequel to this brilliant exploit. The threat against Singapore had to be continuous and not a "one-shot" affair; Mountbatten's and MacArthur's interests coincided this time to keep the Japanese Fleet locally occupied, since in 1944 the Americans were already committed to operations in the direction of the Philippines. "Rimau," the code name for the second expedition into Singapore Harbor, came naturally under the direction of the intrepid Lyon, who had led "Jaywick" to such a successful conclusion. G-2 was uneasy—a professional who firmly believed in "luck" also believed in not crowding it.

On the second trip, mistaking a native police craft for a Japanese patrol boat, Lyon's party opened fire and killed all the natives in the approaching boat. Security was lost and the mission was abandoned. The party split immediately for a later rendezvous, but the manhunt was on; the Jap was always good at this sort of thing. The party was tracked down and intercepted on Sole Island, the rendezvous point.

All members were lost; the three officers, including Colonel Lyon, were killed in action; eleven members were captured and taken to Singapore, where they were tried before a makeshift court-martial, sentenced to death, and beheaded.

There are nine members of the party still unaccounted for; nobody has ever been able to determine their fate.

8 The Conquest of New Guinea

SIX hours after the first assault wave had gone ashore on Los Negros, one of the Admiralty Islands, at the tag end of February 1944, MacArthur landed to survey the situation. He liked what he saw. The Japanese, who were set to defend important Seeadler Harbor, had been caught with their big guns facing the wrong way, and they had lost a strategic airstrip in the preliminary fighting. "Hold what you have taken," MacArthur said to Gen. William C. Chase, "no matter against what odds. You have your teeth in him now—don't let go."

Assured of the victory in the Admiralties, which practically isolated the big Japanese base to the east at Rabaul, MacArthur returned to New Guinea. "The cork," as he put it, "was in the bottle." On March 1, 1944, he reported:

We have landed in the Admiralty Islands which stand at the northern entrance to the Bismarck Sea almost due south of Guam and 1,300 miles from the Philippines. . . . This marks a final stage in the great swinging move pivoting on New Guinea which has been the basic purpose of the operations initiated on June 29, 1943, when the Southwest Pacific Area and South Pacific Area were united under General MacArthur's command. The axis of advance has thereby been changed from the north to the west. This relieves our supply line of the constant threat of flank attack which has been present since the beginning of the Papuan campaign. This line, previously so precariously exposed, is now firmly secured not only by air coverage, but by our own front to which it is perpendicular. The operation has been a delicate one and its final success lays a strategically firm foundation for the future.

171

Tactically it tightens the blockade of the enemy's remaining bases. Their supply lines are definitely and conclusively severed, and only a minimum of blockade running, by submarine and individual surface craft, is now possible. In addition to the troops trapped in the Solomons, some fifty thousand of the enemy, largely in New Britain and at Rabaul, are now inclosed. Their situation has become precarious and their ultimate fate is certain under blockade, bombardment and the increasing pressure of besieging ground forces. The end of the Bismarck Campaign is now clearly in sight with a minimum of loss to ourselves.

The Japanese, realizing they were about to suffer an irreparable disaster, reacted with an almost foolhardy violence. Fortunately, General Chase's forces, which had already been reinforced, were set for it. The preinvasion air reconnaissance of Manus and Los Negros Islands in the Admiralties had shown bomb-cratered Japanese airstrips, dilapidated installations, no anti-air activity, and few signs of Japanese garrison life. But the atmosphere of desertion was merely a come-on: actually, as G-2 interceptions and Allied Intelligence Bureau agent reports showed, there were thousands of Japanese hidden in the bush. Finally, an enemy document captured on March 2 had revealed the Japanese plans for a series of banzai charges on the night of March 3. As a result of all the forewarnings, General Chase was able to stand on the alert with his positions fully prepared. A staff notation covers the action of the night of March 3:

Wave after wave of tough Japanese infantry came pouring through the darkness. . . . When those in front were mowed down by mines and machine gun fire, the others rushed on undaunted over the bodies of their comrades only to be cut down in turn. During the course of these suicidal "banzai" charges, the enemy resorted to wily and fanciful tactics. Japanese, who had somehow managed to learn the names of Allied platoon leaders, tried to trick them into misdirecting or ceasing their fire by interpolating false orders in perfect English into tapped telephone wires. One column of enemy troops came marching forward, singing, for no apparent reason, "Deep in the Heart of Texas." Bayonets were affixed to five-foot poles and used as spears by the Japanese as their ammunition gave out. Bandages were discovered tied around their arms at pressure points, presumably to provide a ready tourniquet which would permit them to continue fighting should they lose the use of either hand.

By the end of the bloody night the Japanese dead littered the field in front of Momote Airfield.

G-2 summed up the Admiralties campaign as follows:

With both of the enemy's flanks rolled back or immobilized, with the XVIII Army in full retreat and the Eighth area Army emasculated in Rabaul, the drive on the Admiralties, in a classical breakthrough operation was next in order. A logistical and strategical trap closing upon enemy forces previously by-passed in the Solomons and subsequently again in the Bismarcks was envisaged. The Japanese position on the principal Admiralty Islands of Manus and Los Negros was by then growing precarious. Our air attrition of his sea supply lanes had prevented influx of sufficient stores to maintain an active defensive and reinforcement of the Admiralties in the time to affect an imminent operation was not deemed probable. Dependent upon submarine supply runs and parachute dropping for maintenance, the enemy on Negros and Manus nervously watched and waited for a blow he knew not where.

Slight opposition to our initial landings at Haynes Harbor indicated not only that tactical surprise had again been achieved, but again demonstrated the usual underestimation of his opponent that had become a Japanese military characteristic. Every subsequent direct enemy assault was repulsed, even though enemy elements participating in the defense of Manus were fresh units of the 229th Infantry, not previously committed to combat. The enemy was again pursuing his traditional dissipation of strength through indecisive partial commitment of reserves. Each succeeding offensive blow neutralized enemy mobility and forced hasty occupation of scattered local defenses. We applied the tactic of relentless pursuit to prevent the enemy from regaining his balance. The reduction of enemy opposition to isolated pockets is graphically reflected in an entry dated 22 March 1944, translated from the inevitable Japanese diary recovered during the campaign.

ADMIRALTIES

1 Feb 44: "Boarded destroyer Akikaze. 2300 hours arrived at Manus."

3 Feb 44: "Received half of the usual rations. To my surprise the enemy has air superiority over this area."

13 Feb 44: "Air raid. A considerable number of bombs was dropped. Our airplanes did not appear. Heard that we would launch an offensive in Mar. I firmly believed this would happen."

19 Mar 44: "Arrived at our positions in the afternoon. Today enemy mortar fire was light. It is 20 days since the enemy landed at Hyane Air Field. What tactical action will our army take? Will we die a heroic death, or will the Japanese Army begin an attack in the near future? Enemy planes fly overhead every day without hindrance. We worked on our positions."

22 Mar 44: "Today also our troops, to say nothing of our airplanes, did not come. Those of us who are healthy are daily continuing a last counterattack under enemy mortar fire. It is discouraging to think of how much ammunition and provisions remain. I am tired in mind and body due to lack of nourishment on morning duty. The only thing I wish is not to turn this island over to the enemy. I pray the gods that reinforcements will come even one day sooner, so that we may take the offensive."

23 Mar 44: "We meet an honorable death, and our names will be glorious, but still I feel some regret. The lives of the 300 of us will only last a few days longer. Our orders have returned to what they were to start with, and we set out on the withdrawal of Lorengau."

1 Apr 44: "Arrived at a native hut. According to a communication we received, our forces at Lorengau can no longer help withdrawing. From now on, we can only live as the natives do."

The circle around Rabaul was closed by further landings, virtually unopposed, on Emirau and Elomusao Islands; and our surrounding of enemy remnants on Manus and Los Negros sealed the fate of the Japanese garrisons in the Bismarcks.

To MacArthur, victory in the Admiralties meant the last knot in the noose around Rabaul had been pulled tight. He reacted at once with the idea of the bold maneuver to leap 500 miles up the New Guinea coast to Hollandia—a move that would not only bring him to within 800 miles of the Philippines, but would also trap some 40,-000 Japanese troops in a strong Allied vise. On March 5, just five days after his return from Los Negros to New Guinea, MacArthur sent his daring Hollandia plan to the Joint Chiefs of Staff in Washington:

Recent seizure of a foothold in the Admiralties which will shortly be followed by complete occupation presents an immediate opportunity for rapid exploitation along the north coast of New Guinea. To this end I propose to make the Hollandia area instead of Hansa Bay my next objective, capturing the air fields and base in that vicinity for further support of operations toward the Philippines. The enemy has concentrated the mass of his ground forces forward in the Madang-Wewak area, leaving relatively weak forces in the Hollandia Bay area. He is attempting to concentrate land-based air forces in the area of western New Guinea and is developing additional fields to consolidate this area into a bulwark of air defense. SWPA land and air forces are disposed favorably to launch a two division reinforced assault against the objective. . . . I propose . . . an assault on Hollandia. . . . For this purpose it will be necessary to retain that part of the naval reinforcements allocated from Central Pacific . . . for the Kavieng-Admiralties but which were not included in the Hansa Bay allocation for a short additional period. It will also be necessary to continue the operation of naval forces in the theater of SWPA until Hollandia is secured. I request prompt approval. Admiral Halsey concurs. Establishment of our forces in this area will have wide implications. It will hopelessly isolate some 40,000 of the enemy ground forces along the New Guinea coast, will place in our hands airdromes from which our land-based air forces can dominate the Vogelkop [at the western end of New Guinea], and hasten the advance westward by several months.

Hollandia was, in many respects, the crucial move of the Pacific war, as important to the wind-up in New Guinea as Leyte was to the conquest of the Philippines. Everything came together to make Hollandia possible: the breaking of Japanese codes which showed it to be weakly held, the fact that the Japanese were caught short during a period in which they were shifting their troops and changing their New Guinea command, the speed of General Chase's antecedent victory in the Admiralties, and the big carrier strike at Truk in February of 1944, which showed a surprising Japanese weakness in the Caroline Islands and a consequent lack of menace to MacArthur and Halsey on their right flank. Since the ninepins were at last falling down all over the Central and Southwestern Pacific, the Joint Chiefs couldn't very well say "no" to Hollandia. The sudden "yes" that was accorded MacArthur on his big New Guinea leapfrogging proposition came, however, as the culmination of a reversal of attitude, for always, up to March 1944, the Navy and the Army Air Force had carried their arguments with the Joint Chiefs for the priority of the Central Pacific.

The Navy and MacArthur had debated this question of priority in meeting after meeting. In his Reno I Plan (February 25, 1943), MacArthur had objected that a progressive conquest of the Caroline Islands in the Central Pacific would have to be undertaken without land-based air support. It would necessarily entail costly amphibious frontal assaults on small islands, and be "time consuming and expensive in naval power and shipping." The Navy countered with its own arguments: MacArthur's route along New Guinea to Mindanao, Luzon, Formosa, and Japan was roundabout, and would require more ships, aircraft, men, and time. Besides, New Guinea was a pesthole of disease, whereas the Caroline and Mariana Islands were swept by the trade winds and so were relatively hygienic. Most compelling argument of all with the Navy was its hope that an attack through the Central Pacific would bring the Japanese fleet out of hiding, to be defeated by Nimitz's forces in a day.

With Admiral King and the Army Air Force both arguing for a quick seizure of the Mariana Islands and a base on the China coast in order to put the new B-29 bombers over Tokyo in the shortest possible amount of time, MacArthur had two services against him whenever he stressed his own conception of the "arrow-straight" line from New Guinea to Luzon. To MacArthur it seemed that nothing would so shake the Japanese Empire as the disruption of its supply lines from Singapore and the Indies—and what better way to smash these supply lines than to get a straddle across them from the Philippines?

The Joint Chiefs listened unconvinced when MacArthur cabled Washington in February of 1944:

. . . there are now large forces in the Pacific which would place us in the Philippines in *December* if the forces were employed in effective combination. . . . All available ground, air and assault forces in the Pacific should be combined in a drive along the New Guinea–Mindanao axis, supported by the main Fleet. . . . I propose that on completion of operations in the Marshalls, the maximum force from *all sources in the Pacific* be concentrated in my drive up the New Guinea coast, to be coordinated with a Central Pacific operation against the Palaus and the support by combatant elements of the Pacific Fleet with orders to contain or destroy the Japanese Fleet. Time presses. . . .

But if the Joint Chiefs could not be won over to MacArthur's strategic conception by verbal logic, they were soon to be persuaded by the sheer force of practical considerations. The facts of the situation were on his side. In the first place, the rapidity of his movement into the Admiralties put his flank well ahead of the Navy's frontal movement in the Central Pacific. Secondly, the Joint Chiefs knew that there was no physical way of transferring MacArthur's growingly important Australian-American forces to the Central Pacific Theater in time to make use of them. They were already in New Guinea and moving westward, and the shipping did not exist in sufficient quantity to transport them to staging areas in the Marshall and Caroline Islands. Moreover, any diminution of pressure in New Guinea would allow the Japanese to flow back into the Rabaul area in full strength. This would endanger the American Navy from the south; it would also serve to dismay and anger the entire Australian continent.

Confronted with these interacting military and political realities, the Joint Chiefs were forced to push both the Central Pacific and the Southwest Pacific campaigns together within the limits of Allied means. And priority, in the nature of things, would eventually go to the theater that made the most capital with what it had.

This was all that MacArthur needed. With the Admiralties the camel got his nose under the tent; after Hollandia, the camel moved in.

For Hollandia MacArthur finally had his command and his troops set and in well-oiled working order. The 7th Amphibious Force, under Admiral Dan ("the amphibious man") Barbey, had been trained to the pitch. The 2d Engineer Special Brigade, the pioneer amphibious force in the Southwest Pacific Area, had the invaluable experience of their "starved" days at Lae and Finschafen behind them. And the over-all command structure of the SWPA was finally to MacArthur's liking: he described his headquarters of the period as a real integration of the three arms, a real "unity of the services":

Naval and Air commanders and their staffs are in the same building with General Headquarters. The land commander and his staff are nearby.

These commanders confer frequently with the C in C. In addition to their complete functions as commanders, they operate, in effect, as a planning staff to the Commander-in-Chief. Personal relationships and physical location of subordinate Headquarters make possible a constant daily participation of the staffs in all details of planning and operations.

General Headquarters is . . . [an organ] for planning and executing operations demanding effective combination of land, sea and air power. General Headquarters has successfully developed an attitude that is without service bias. It is only the determination of General Headquarters that it shall not act as the Headquarters of a single service that will produce the unanimity of action and singleness of purpose that is essential for the successful conduct of combined operations. . . .

Hollandia involved the most intricate series of cross-plays between Planning, Intelligence, and the other "Gs" of MacArthur's staff. Since the concept of leapfrogging involved leaving some 125,-000 Japanese troops at Rabaul (as the count after 1945 disclosed), any mistake in estimating Japanese ability to move or reinforce or supply these "behind-the-lines" troops might have been fatal. Steve Chamberlin's G-3 planning had to count on keeping the bypassed Japanese off balance and under constant interdiction lest they become a menace in MacArthur's own rear. Matters were further complicated by the fact that the naval forces on loan from Nimitz were "in" for Hollandia on a strictly limited basis: Nimitz refused to allow his large carriers to remain in New Guinea coastal waters for more than four days after D-day, for he was afraid of Japanese reprisals from ground air bases in the Indies. Since MacArthur's own land-based fighter planes couldn't reach Hollandia from the Fin-

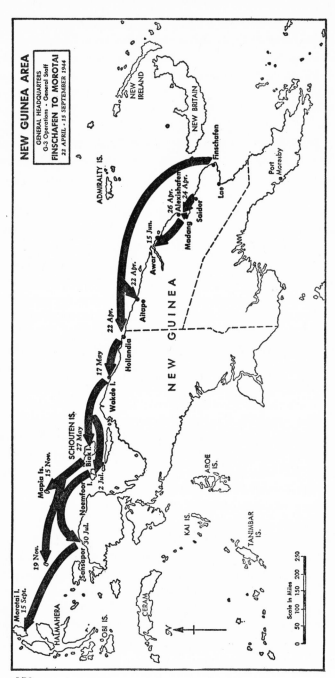

NEW GUINEA AREA

GENERAL HEADQUARTERS
G-3 Operations - General Staff
FINSCHAFEN TO MOROTAI
22 APRIL - 15 SEPTEMBER 1944

179

schafen area of the eastern New Guinea coast, this interposed an extra planning problem: simultaneously with the landings at Hollandia there would have to be an "intermediate" seizure of the Aitape air strip between Hollandia and Finschafen. This would not only yield a base for fighter-plane protection of the Hollandia Task Force "Reckless" under General Eichelberger, it would also put Allied soldiers between Hollandia and the trapped Japanese Eighteenth Army under General Adachi. MacArthur regarded the Aitape landing as vital insurance, for aside from Admiral Barbey's local SWPA amphibious units, he had no control over the American warships. The carriers of Admiral Mitscher's task force retained their option to chase the Japanese Fleet if it should be encountered—the very same sort of option that almost precipitated a disaster when Halsey was to exercise it some months later at Leyte.

The problems of a divided command never became crucial at Hollandia because everything went off with clockwork precision. For the first time in the New Guinea Theater MacArthur had proper landing craft—LSTs, LCIs, Australian-built "beach sleds," and amphibious "alligators" for crawling over jagged coral. But most important of all, he had foreknowledge of everything the Japanese were doing.

Quite early in the Hollandia planning, intelligence entered the picture in one of its most hush-hush phases: cryptanalysis, or the decoding of intercepts of enemy radio messages. This material was furnished by a secret organization, the "Central Bureau" under the able direction of Spencer Akin, MacArthur's signal officer. It proved as decisive at Hollandia as the German interception of the Russian General Samsonov's radio traffic had proved at the Battle of Tannenberg in 1914. Radio intercepts in February of 1944 showed that the Japanese were strengthening their bases at Hansa Bay, a good harbor protected by high headlands, and at Wewak. A February 28 intercept revealed Japanese major-unit locations by divisions; it also revealed Japanese estimates of Allied intentions. Knowledge of these two factors enabled G-2 to suggest a comprehensive deception plan to MacArthur:

Your attention is invited to the probable Japanese plan of defense of the Madang-Wewak Sector of the New Guinea coast. The Japanese plan suggests an attractive opportunity for the use of deception in connection with our Hollandia invasion. The enemy expects an Allied thrust against the Madang–Hansa Bay area and has disposed three (3) divisions for mobile defense, to trap our landings in vicinity of Ulingan.

We recommend measures designed to confirm his estimates and focus his attention south of the Sepik River and away from our objective [Hollandia].

a. Frequent aerial reconnaissance over the Ulingan area.

b. An Allied feint in the Ulingan area, in advance of the Hollandia operations, may influence the enemy to commence displacement of reserves to that area; it may induce him to use the 20th and 51st Divisions rather than the 40th, in the south. Enemy air reinforcements, based on Hollandia and Wewak, are poised for intervention. Thus a fake landing should draw the enemy forward.

Recognizing the validity of the intercepts and the G-2 interpretation, MacArthur ordered the execution of deceptive measures on a big scale. Kenney's air force intensified its attacks on Madang and Wewak. Dummy parachutes were dropped in the Hansa Bay area. Increased reconnaissance flights were sent out on conspicuous mapping and photographic missions. The Navy staged torpedo-boat raids on selected coastal spots. Empty rubber landing boats, suggestive of disembarked intelligence parties, were spotted along the shore. Allied Intelligence Bureau parties from the interior converged openly toward the coast, making certain that native "fuzzies" would spot them. Some of these natives were paid by the AIB and managed to collect from the Japanese as well.

While radio intercepts worked well for MacArthur in the Hollandia show, the Intelligence Bureau's agents were on the whole unlucky. As usual, penetration parties had been launched far ahead of operations. An overland party, code name "Whiting," traveled 514 miles by trek and 225 miles on jungle waterways toward Hollandia, only to be ambushed by a Japanese patrol. A more direct approach to Hollandia was made by Captain Harris, an Australian. His story is contained in the G-2 files:

The party embarked on a U.S. submarine at Finschafen and proceeded to Tanahmerah, arriving off this point in the night of March 23.

Periscope reconnaissance selected a likely looking beach area. Disembarking in darkness, the party attempted to land in rubber boats. There was a slight groundswell and the tide was ebbing. The swell running steeply over an unobserved reef, about 150 yards offshore, capsized the boats. Harris scrambled ashore. The natives in the party salvaged some equipment, including a damaged radio set.

Ashore, there were indications that Japanese were afoot. The party moved inland and camped for the night near a native village. Apparently, they were seen. A Japanese patrol set out for Dépapré and intercepted the party. Captain Harris and two Australian soldiers who were in the lead drew fire upon themselves deliberately, to give the rest a chance to scatter into the brush. The two soldiers were killed instantly. Harris was seriously wounded. The Japanese attempted to interrogate him; when he refused to answer, the infuriated Japanese bayonetted him. There were five survivors who later made their way into the Allied lines, after the landing.

During March and April Kenney's B-25s blasted the Japanese airfields at Hansa Bay, Wewak, and Hollandia indiscriminately. Thus the Japanese could attach no especial significance to Hollandia. Nevertheless, the April 3 air raid on Hollandia proved particularly punishing. As MacArthur described it:

In the heaviest attack so far made on this enemy base, our escorted heavy units followed by medium and attack planes at minimum altitude, dropped 400 tons of bombs and expended 275,000 rounds of ammunition on the three airdromes . . . the runways were left unserviceable, and equipment and installations heavily damaged. . . . In the air we destroyed 26 intercepting enemy fighters for the loss of one plane. The enemy's strong air reserves built up in this area have been destroyed at negligible cost to us. Of the 288 planes present in this area on March 30 all have been demolished or irreparably damaged.

On April 21 the Allied amphibious invasion force, which had sailed north around the Admiralties for purposes of deception, turned to the west. The intercept of the Japanese "estimate" of its destination read as follows:

. . . the signs of an enemy plan to make a new landing in the New Guinea area are clear. The greatest probability is a landing between Madang and Hansa. A landing in the Wewak sector is next in probability in the light of recent bombings of Hansa, the naval bombardment of Wewak, reconnaissance and leaflet drops. It is also possible that the enemy will land in the Hollandia sector; however, since there was no reconnaissance carried out by submarines, destroyers or other means, the probability of a landing in this sector is thought to be minor. . . .

Until the huge Allied naval convoy actually sailed past Wewak, the enemy had no notion of where to commit himself for defense. Consequently, the landings in the Hollandia region caught the Japanese completely off balance.

Questioned after the war, Japanese commanders who served in western New Guinea all spoke of the surprise:

"The Allied invasion of Hollandia and Aitape was a complete surprise to us," said Lt. Gen. Jo Iimura, Commander of the Second Area Army. "Although after considering the past operational tactics of the enemy, we were confident that the Allies would eventually attack Hollandia, we rather believed they would attempt to acquire an important position somewhere east of Aitape, prior to an invasion of either Aitape or Hollandia. Because we misjudged the time of the Allied invasion on Hollandia and Aitape, we were neither able to reinforce nor send war supplies to their defending units." According to Lt. Col. Nobuo Kitamori, Staff Officer of the Second Area Army, the attack on Hollandia "was not a complete surprise in that we expected the enemy to come some time or other because it was such an important place. However, we did not think that the attack would come when it did. The morning that we found out that the Allies were going to come to Hollandia, they were already in the harbor with their transports and battleships. In that sense it certainly was a surprise." Colonel Kazuo Horiba, Staff Officer of the Southern Army, said: "It was a surprise attack as far as operations go, but not so strategically. We had planned on the fact the enemy was coming, but it was a surprise when the enemy came when he did, far before the time we expected and our defense preparations were not completed."

From the standpoint of surprise, the maneuver was an almost exact parallel of the one repeated years later at Inchon in Korea. It also offered the picture of a planned "double envelopment" of the Japanese at Hollandia that could virtually be superimposed on Hannibal's famous double envelopment at Cannae.

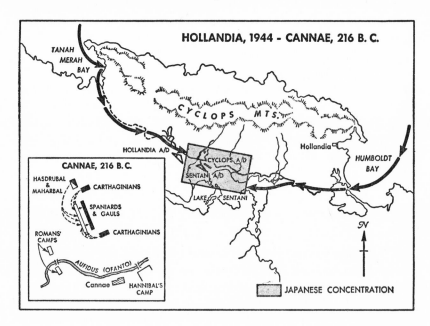

The G-2 paper suggesting the Cannae parallel runs as follows:

It was defensive strategy for the Japanese XVIII Army to extricate itself from the untenable Madang-Alexishafen sector; it withdrew what ranks it could muster beyond Hansa Bay, put the Sepik River behind, and concentrated on the defensive development of its base at Wewak. Its new boundary ran just west of Hollandia, with relatively thinly held coastal garrisons guarding its lines of communication between there and Wewak. The enemy relied on distance transmuted into time to delay any Allied frontal drive on this new defensive sector.

But having again forced his Japanese opponent to set up the draughts for a double jump, General MacArthur rendered that time factor a Pyrrhic advantage by refusing a frontal Wewak engagement. After a delusive feint at Wewak, he struck a massive amphibious blow 500 miles forward of our most advanced base. The western arm of this attack executed a double envelopment in the grand manner of Hannibal at Cannae, captured the Hollandia triad of airdromes in three days, together with the important Sentani Lake region between Tanahmerah and Humboldt Bays. The error in enemy intelligence forecasting a frontal attack on Wewak caused reinforcements to be shifted to that area, leaving Hollandia poorly defended; no resistance was met at Tanahmerah Bay, and opposition encountered at Humboldt Bay was slight.

The Allied forces went ashore in the Hollandia area in two groups about thirty miles apart. One group landed at Humboldt Bay, at the east end of a coastal range known as the Cyclops Mountains. The other group landed at Tanahmerah Bay, at the west end of the Cyclops. The surprise was so complete at both points that Allied casualties were almost negligible. The dumfounded Japanese—some 15,000, mostly lightly armed service troops—faded rapidly into the jungle. A G-2 summary of the time describes them as deserting

. . . uneaten breakfasts and hastily [taking] to the surrounding mountains. The subsequent starved and aimless wanderings of those miserable remnants, the sporadic finding by patrols of their emaciated cadavers green from gangrene and a diet of grass, is a sinister index to the complete strategical isolation and cheap acquisition of this vital advanced base.

Diaries found on the Japanese corpses helped G-2 to piece together the grisly story:

22 Apr 44: "Resigned to death, I entered the muddy jungle. Enemy airplanes are flying overhead. I am hungry and am beginning to become alarmed about the situation. I plunged through the jungle because I believe it is dangerous to remain here. The vast expanse of the jungle cannot be expressed in words."

2 May 44: "At a small creek. There is no end to this life. We are still roaming aimlessly on the 13th day. Perhaps this is part of our fate. We hoped that we would meet our commander and his amiable staff. We are beginning to hate everything in this world. We live each day sympathizing with one another. At times, we see someone in our group shedding tears."

24 May 44: ". . . The jungle is everywhere, and there is absolutely no water in this area. We must reach Kotabaru or we will all die."

26 May 44: "In the wilderness. As we proceeded further we met our troops. This force was retreating from Aitape. They were shouldering rice which they stole from Kotabaru supply depot. I heard the news from the commanding officer. It was terrifying news. They had marched ahead with the men falling dead one by one."

MacArthur came up from Brisbane to join the invasion convoy the day before D-day at Tanahmerah. As a gesture of his certainty that all would go off according to plan, he brought the makings for ice-cream sodas, which were consumed with relish by the high command before he went ashore with General Krueger and General Eichelberger. There was stiffer Japanese resistance as the Allied double-envelopment invasion prongs cut inland from the two ends of the Cyclops range to seize the air strips along Lake Sentani, to the south of the mountains. But the Japanese failed to exploit the Cyclops defiles, and four days after the landings the Sentani, Cyclops, and Hollandia airdromes, along with the Tami air strip lying on the coastal flat to the east of Humboldt Bay, had all been secured. Meanwhile the "insurance" invasion of Aitape, a hundred miles to the east of Hollandia, had developed little opposition: the Aitape airfield was quickly won.

MacArthur emphasized the strategic importance of Hollandia after his return to Brisbane:

The operation throws a loop of envelopment around the enemy's 18th Army, dispersed along the coast of New Guinea in the Madang, Alixshafen, Hansa Bay, Wewak sectors, similar to the Solomons and Bismarck loops of envelopment. To the east are the Australians and Americans; to the west the Americans; to the north the sea controlled by our Allied naval forces; to the south untraversed jungle mountain ranges; and over all our Allied air mastery. The enemy army is now completely isolated. With its communication and supply lines severed, its condition becomes similar to that of the beleaguered . . . armies in the Bismarck and Solomon archipelagos. Its present strength is estimated at 60,000. The total remaining forces . . . are estimated at 140,-000: 50,000 in New Britain, 10,000 in New Ireland, 20,000 in Bougainville, and 60,000 in New Guinea. Since the start of the campaign they have lost 110,000 men, 44 per cent of their original strength of a quarter of a million, and the remainder is now neutralized and strategically impotent. . . . His invested garrisons can be expected to strike desperately to free themselves . . . but their ultimate fate is now certain. Their situation reverses Bataan. The present operation when completed frees British New Guinea from enemy control, and is the first recapture of Dutch territory in the war.

The Japanese had been in the course of preparing Hollandia as a big supply depot: the Allies captured 600 supply dumps, including hills of rice, great saki and beer caches, and large amounts of quinine. Hard on the seizure of the area—which Gen. George Marshall called "a model of strategic and tactical maneuver"—Pat Casey proceeded to turn Hollandia into a great supply base and staging area for the subsequent reach into the Philippines. The engineers worked desperately to build

. . . docks, a 900-foot channel through the coral reef at Dépapré, the completion and improvement of the roadnet, the rapid . . . improvement of captured airdromes, water supply facilities, and fuel pipe lines. As roads improved and building materials became available, emphasis shifted to the construction of hospitals, camps, headquarters areas and warehouses. . . .

The construction was so rapid that it gave rise to legends, in particular the legend of a "million-dollar mansion" on dreamy Lake Sentani for MacArthur. Curious about the "million-dollar mansion," "Pappy" Gunn, the individualist aviator, dropped in at Hollandia for a look-see. He found nothing more substantial than a

. . . neat looking structure of rough lumber . . . it wasn't a mansion by any means. We had had to live in such dilapidated places . . . that anything looked good to us. A tin roof looked wonderful.

The "neat looking structure of rough lumber" became MacArthur's advanced headquarters for planning the final details of the Philippine invasion. Actually, though "Pappy" Gunn overlooked the architectural underpinnings, the headquarters consisted of three

prefabricated houses joined together. The structure was jointly occupied by MacArthur and members of his staff, and besides the living
quarters there were a staff dining room, a conference room, and
office space for MacArthur and Sutherland. Convinced at last that
he was leaving Australia and his Lennon's Hotel quarters in Brisbane
behind him for good, MacArthur moved some furniture and rugs
to the "mansion" on Lake Sentani. With carpets inside and the deep,
dreamy blue of the lake outside, the place was quite "livable"—a
quality that soon gave rise to the gossip that MacArthur was doing
well for himself. The gossips overlooked the fact that it was the
gorgeous tropical scenery that provided nine-tenths of the "plush"
at Lake Sentani. All of MacArthur's officers—Eichelberger, Kenney,
Admiral Kinkaid, to name a few—loved the place, and many of
them have left written testimony to its charms.

The successful surprise at Hollandia was capitalized almost immediately by a series of pushes toward the Vogelkop at the extreme
western end of New Guinea. Wakde Island, Biak, Noemfoor,
Sansapor—these were some of the engagements which put Mac-
Arthur's forces in control of all New Guinea and provided the air
strips necessary to cover the advance to the islands of Morotai and
Halmahera, from which Mindanao in the Philippines could be
reached under an air umbrella.

The Japanese resisted strongly, particularly at the island of Biak,
where they holed up in caves. To quote MacArthur's Tokyo records:

This island, 200 miles west of Wakde, possessed one of the two
remaining major groups of enemy airdromes between Hollandia and
Halmahera and therefore constituted a valuable military asset to the
Allied scheme of operations. On 27 May, just one week after the last
enemy guns were silenced on Wakde, the 41st Division, less the 163rd
Regimental Combat Team, made the first assault at Bosnek, on southern
Biak. Its immediate objectives were the three airdromes at Mokmer,
Borokoe, and Sorido near the southwest coast.

Initial opposition was relatively light and the landing force began an
advance inland toward the air fields. General MacArthur described the
landing operation and its strategic value as follows:

"We have landed on Biak Island. . . . The capture of this stronghold will give us command domination of Dutch New Guinea except

for isolated enemy positions. For strategic purposes this marks the practical end of the New Guinea campaign. The final stage has also been reached in the offensive initiated in this theater on 29 June 1943, by the combined forces of the Southwest Pacific and South Pacific Areas. It has resulted in the reconquest or neutralization of the Solomons, the Bismarcks, the Admiralties, and New Guinea. From the forward point reached by the Japanese we have advanced our front approximately 1,800 statute miles westward and approximately 700 miles to the north. . . . Compared with the enemy our offensive employed only modest forces and through the maximum use of maneuver and surprise has incurred only light losses. The operations have effected a strategic penetration of the conquered empire Japan was attempting to consolidate in the Southwest Pacific and have secured bases of departure for the advance to its vital areas in the Philippines and the Netherlands East Indies."

The slight opposition to the beach landings, however, was little indication of the bitter struggle to follow, for "the Japanese defense of Biak," as General Eichelberger's report described it, "was based on brilliant appreciation and use of the terrain." In this instance, the enemy had purposely withheld his main forces until the United States troops had advanced to the rugged terrain beyond the beaches. Then, from the dominating cliffs and caves overlooking the moving Allied columns, the Japanese launched a savage counterattack and, aided by 5-ton tanks, succeeded in driving a block between the beachhead and invading forces. Enemy frontal pressure increased considerably and a temporary retirement and regrouping was necessary.

The situation remained critical until the remainder of the 41st Division could be brought in from Wakde to bolster the United States positions. Thus strengthened, the 41st Division renewed its drive toward Mokmer at dawn on 2 June and, after several days of severe and violent fighting, seized the important airdrome at Mokmer on 7 June. Even then, the struggle continued unabated as the Japanese poured a heavy fire into the newly established air field positions. It was another week before the strip could be brought into use. Additional United States reinforcements were sent in and, despite the enemy's fierce and valiant attempts to hold the remaining air fields at Sorido and Borokoe, the two strips were finally wrested from the Japanese. Effective resistance on Biak had been overcome by 21 June, although the Japanese continued sporadic nuisance raids until the end of July. Mopping up operations continued with amphibious shore-to-shore landings in August at Korim Bay, Wardo, and Warsa Bay. Other landings on Soepiori Island in September brought the campaign to a close. The figure of over 6,000 enemy killed by 30 September indicates the tenacity with which the Japanese fought to keep Biak from falling to the Allies.

But the most dangerous Japanese opposition in the immediate period after Hollandia came not from the troops in front of Mac-Arthur but from those trapped far to the rear. The Japanese General Adachi, commander of the once powerful Eighteenth Army, brooded for two months at Wewak, his escape routes cut to the north and west. Faced with the ultimate starvation and disintegration of his forces, Adachi decided on a blind attempt to break through the Allied lines at Aitape. In an exhortation to his soldiers Adachi said:

I cannot find any means nor method which will solve this situation strategically or technically. Therefore, I intend to overcome this by relying on our Japanese *Bushido*. . . . I am determined to destroy the enemy at Aitape by attacking him ruthlessly with the concentration of our entire force in that area. . . . This will be our final opportunity to employ our entire strength to annihilate the enemy. . . . Make the supreme sacrifice, display the spirit of the Imperial Army.

Fortunately, General Adachi's plans were already in MacArthur's possession before they had reached fruition. Intercepts, captured documents, Nisei interrogation of captured troops, PT-boat and air reconnaissance, and intelligence from native sources, all combined to give the Eighteenth Army's intentions away. When the *Bushido* attacks on the Allies at Aitape started, Adachi found not merely a regiment in front of him but a far stronger force.

The Japanese Army's failure to breach the Aitape barrier had its preamble in the systematic destruction of its lines of communication through the combined operations of our naval surface craft, aerial bombing and strafing attacks. Sinking of a constantly dwindling number of supply barges, the destruction by direct hits on truck columns, roads and bridges, and the firing of supply dumps forced the enemy to adopt starvation rations. His main supply dumps and barge relay points were ceaselessly bombed and strafed; his consequent losses of supplies and personnel present an irrefutable picture of attrition and disaster, an integral factor of the Eighteenth Army's final defeat.

From captured Japanese diaries comes further evidence of the effectiveness of the action:

26 June 44: ". . . men began to use jungle plants for food. Regt did not send any rations detail to the rear for replenishment. . . . Fighting spirit had left the men."

8–12 July 44: ". . . so far only three sacks of rice, hardtack for 180 meals and two crates of emergency rations have been received."

5 Jul 44: "I saw white bones of our comrades of 20 Div strewn here and there."

The success of the entire Hollandia-Aitape campaign was celebrated by a G-2 "clarification" paper comparing the "maneuver of New Guinea" with the Battle of Eylau (1807):

Another historical parallel between New Guinea and Eylau is irresistible. Both Eylau and New Guinea were planned maneuvers extending over a period of time.

Napoleon's concept of maneuver and his concept of battle were intellectually and tactically related. Napoleon himself remarked on this inter-relation: "In the difficult art of war, the system of battle is already conceived in the system of operations, of the Campaign, as a whole; this is ordinarily not understood."

This though is as applicable today as it was a hundred and fifty years ago; it applies especially to the control of large units, army, corps, and divisions. The disposition of such units is not easily changed. A platoon commander may change his mind and his small unit will react quickly; but that is not practicable with large units.

The initial dispositions of large units must conform to a master plan, culminating in maneuver, and therein lies the enormous personal responsibility of the commander: the necessity for anticipation. That anticipation increases in direct ratio with an increase in the size of his unit. The Brigade commander ordinarily will not have to think beyond

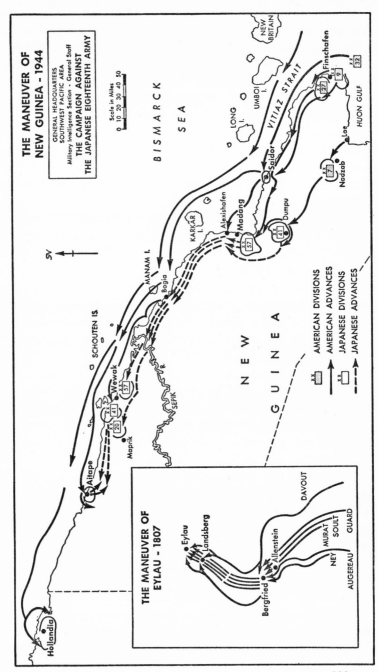

THE MANEUVER OF
NEW GUINEA - 1944

GENERAL HEADQUARTERS
SOUTHWEST PACIFIC AREA
Military Intelligence Section - General Staff
THE CAMPAIGN AGAINST
THE JAPANESE EIGHTEENTH ARMY

Scale in Miles
0 10 20 30 40 50

BISMARCK

SEA

NEW BRITAIN

VITIAZ STRAIT

Finschafen

HUON GULF

Lae

Nadzab

Saidor

Dumpu

Alexishafen
Madang

KARKAR I.

UMBOI I.

LONG I.

MANAM I.

Bogia

SCHOUTEN IS.

Wewak

Maprik

SEPIK R.

Aitape

Hollandia

NEW

GUINEA

AMERICAN DIVISIONS
AMERICAN ADVANCES
JAPANESE DIVISIONS
JAPANESE ADVANCES

THE MANEUVER OF
EYLAU - 1807

Eylau
Landsberg

Bergfried

Allenstein

DAVOUT

MURAT
SOULT
GUARD

NEY

AUGEREAU

the local combat zone, a zone limited by the effect of fire. The division commander may have to enlarge this to a radius of action of one or two days; the Corps increasingly so, and the Army to a radius of action comprising a theater of war. The advent of the Air army has increased the range and speed of anticipation and forward planning.

On the battlefield of Eylau, Napoleon brought about a double envelopment, in conjunction with a frontal attack. If one examines critically the march-graph of the Imperial Army, it is apparent that a speculative initial idea governed the movements of the army and dictated the general march dispositions: central columns to fix and contain the enemy, and flank columns to close in on the enemy as soon as he had been fixed by the central mass.

One can readily see the suppleness of this system and this formation. The maneuver idea is independent of the zone or area in which it will be executed: whether the battlefield be Bergfried, Landsberg or Eylau, there is still a frontal attack aided by two flank attacks.

In such a situation, the enemy may either turn and fight or try to escape. The "central mass" moves on him, while "flank detachments" intercept alternate lines of retreat or withdrawal. When the mass gains contact, it engages the enemy and pins him down while the flank detachments close in to decide the issue.

In the modern situation, the central columns to fix and contain the Jap in retreat were furnished by the Australians, pressing on land via Madang toward the Sepik River. The flank columns, to intercept and close in on the enemy, were represented by American sea-borne Divisions and the incessant "aerial envelopment" by bombardment aviation; whether the battlefield be Saidor, Madang, Wewak, or Aitape, there would still be a frontal attack, aided by flank attacks. Ultimately, the enemy was cut off completely by our Hollandia-Aitape landings.

Aitape became a forward covering position for the airdrome area of Hollandia.

The Jap XVIIIth Army, isolated, hemmed in by air, sea, and land, made a gallant gesture. They dragged their positions forward painfully, only to collide with American positions along the Driniumor River. Skirmishes: tentative piercing of lines, here and there, finally the basic maneuver, and envelopment of the American south flank—like Leuthen (1757), analogous to Tarleton's maneuver at the Cowpens, 1781. The Americans instantly set in motion a counter envelopment, in the rear of the Jap movement; this corresponds entirely to the envelopment by Washington's Cavalry at the Cowpens.

The blueprint of war is very constant; the high company of military commanders, through centuries, is a distinguished fraternal order and their workmanship is of a single pattern. Continuity of design is an essential element of MacArthur's strategy.

The defeat of the Japanese on the bloody Driniumor snuffed out the last flickering hopes of a stand against MacArthur in New Guinea. To quote MacArthur's Tokyo records on the significance of New Guinea:

Control of the entire stretch of coastline from Milne Bay to the Vogelkop Peninsula was now firmly in Allied hands. In less than thirteen months, General MacArthur's forces, boring through layer after layer of Japan's outer defense perimeter, had moved 1,300 miles closer to the core of her island empire. The thousands of Japanese troops they had pocketed and cut off from outside aid had lost all ability to interfere seriously with Allied operational plans. When queried as to the immediate disposition of these isolated enemy segments, General MacArthur recommended that they be ignored until the main task was accomplished:

"The enemy garrisons which have been bypassed in the Solomons and New Guinea represent no menace to current or future operations. Their capacity for organized offensive effort has passed. The various processes of attrition will eventually account for their final disposition. The actual time of their destruction is of little or no importance and their influence as a contributing factor to the war is already negligible. The actual process of their immediate destruction by assault methods would unquestionably involve heavy loss of life without adequate compensating strategic advantages. The present allotment of shipping and assault craft would not permit such operations except at the expense of those which are now scheduled. . . ."

Since New Guinea was largely a roadless, even a trackless, land, the battle for its coastal villages was a continual struggle with the Japanese for supremacy offshore. To quote from MacArthur's Tokyo records again:

The battle against enemy shipping was another significant feature of the New Guinea Campaign. The wholesale destruction by our planes, submarines, and PT boats of enemy coastal vessels, transports, barges, schooners, and sailing craft in the Southwest Pacific Area gradually paralyzed enemy efforts to supply, reinforce, or evacuate the remnants of his armies cut off in New Guinea, New Britain, New Ireland, and the Solomons. More than 5,000 of these craft were destroyed. After the conclusion of the fighting in the Buna-Lae area and the Solomons, the Japanese were reluctant to risk major naval units, and as a result of their heavy losses in cargo ships and transports they were forced to devise a new supply technique. . . . Accordingly, the enemy's most ambitious efforts along these lines were directed to a greatly expanded use of barge traffic. . . .

When the enemy's use of small craft for transportation and supply purposes began to assume serious dimensions, the Allies found it imperative to develop effective counter tactics. The answer lay in a coordinated, intensive employment of PT boats, Catalinas, and low-flying planes. This combination destroyed the enemy's small craft much faster than they could be rebuilt. The Japanese reacted by emplacing scores of heavy caliber shore batteries to cover their lugger and barge movements. These measures proved ineffective against the fast striking PT boats and planes, however, and the Japanese were forced to abandon daylight traffic almost entirely. Attempts were thereafter confined to movement by night as their barges, restricted by the darkness, crept furtively from cove to cove under cover of elaborate camouflage and security measures. This almost complete interdiction of all water-borne reinforcement was a major factor in the enemy's defeat in New Guinea and demonstrated again the resourceful capabilities of the Allied forces in countering each new threat as it arose.

Meanwhile, as the Japanese barges were being wiped out, MacArthur's men had their own troubles in assembling enough transports to wage amphibious war. To quote from MacArthur's Tokyo records:

The lack of adequate and suitable water transportation with which to concentrate troops in staging areas and take them into combat at times considerably hampered the planning of operations. Amphibious

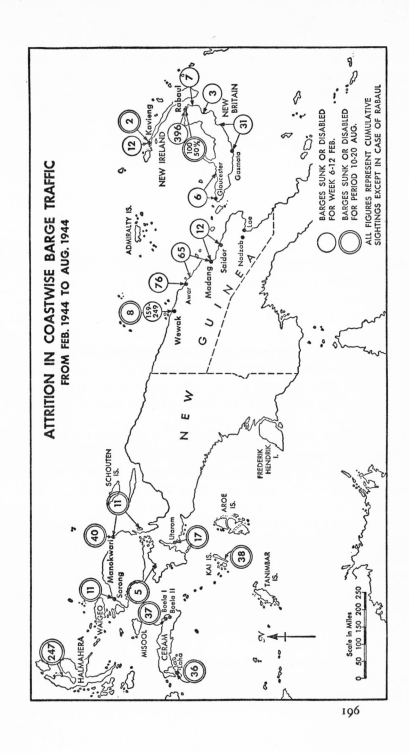

ATTRITION IN COASTWISE BARGE TRAFFIC

FROM FEB. 1944 TO AUG. 1944

BARGES SUNK OR DISABLED FOR WEEK 6-12 FEB.

BARGES SUNK OR DISABLED FOR PERIOD 10-20 AUG.

ALL FIGURES REPRESENT CUMULATIVE SIGHTINGS EXCEPT IN CASE OF RABAUL

landing craft were always critically short and liberty type ships had to be used as troop transports, both for assembling troops and for moving supporting elements into objective areas. Such cargo vessels were altered to add necessary facilities by the construction of crude accommodations on deck. Movements of troops in the tropical areas of the Southwest Pacific were accomplished in a manner which would have been utterly impossible in less temperate climates.

G-2's own record of the struggle for the coastal sea lanes along New Guinea is contained in a paper called "Action on the Sea":

The strategy of amphibious envelopment, obviating the delays and losses of jungle campaigns, rendered the otherwise ponderous barrier of North New Guinea a springboard toward the Philippines. . . .

Landings were of variegated character, dictated by strategic location rather than by sympathetic terrain. Some assault waves waded ashore on ideal beaches; others floundered across wicked, wide, drying coral reefs; assault craft would hit the beach fluently in the first echelon yesterday; today it would be rubber boats; tomorrow, armored amphibious tractors. But everywhere, their progress was thunderously preceded by the preparatory interdiction fires laid down by Army and Naval Aviation, light naval craft from close inshore, and the terrific thunder bolt of heavy Naval artillery.

Allied cruisers and destroyers covered the assault forces by preparatory bombardments which disrupted the enemy's coastal defenses and shore batteries and in many cases, as at Tanahmerah Bay, Hollandia, Gloucester and Arawe, demoralized and drove his troops inland. As H-hour approached, the tremendous firepower of every available warship, from cruiser to torpedo boat, would be concentrated on the landing beaches; and, after the first elements were ashore, destroyers and smaller craft running close inshore blasted pin-pointed targets. Cruisers and destroyers discharged a further, equally important responsibility to block sea approaches to the landing areas, preventing interference with landing operations and enemy reinforcement by sea; this protection was invaluable. . . .

During that entire period, allied torpedo boats continued close-in operations against enemy barge traffic and supply areas. Torpedo boats based at Aitape operated with aircraft and destroyers to attack enemy positions, bivouac areas, trucks on coastal roads, and barges, from Yakamul to Wewak and supported ground operations east of the Driniumor River by protecting the north flank of our ground forces.

In early 1944 the enemy was employing many barges to distribute supplies to the Bismarcks and in the area from Wewak to Saidor, the area to the west of Wewak being supplied, at this time, by ocean-going vessels. The largest concentrations of these small craft were at Rabaul (396 sighted at one time), and at Wewak (159–249 sighted during a week). Though harassed by Allied aircraft during daylight, at this time the enemy's barge system was functioning rather efficiently. The effect of Allied advances and the establishment of torpedo boat bases in forward areas from which PTs could patrol the coastlines deep into enemy territory, is shown by the record of sightings for a 10-day period in August; barges at Rabaul reduced to 100, fifty of which were believed to be unserviceable. In Wewak only a negligible number of craft remained; barge traffic to the east of the Vogelkop had ceased. The enemy's attempt to protect these barge lanes by emplacing many shore batteries along the routes was insufficient materially to change the final outcome.

The persistence of our offensive over the sea areas has resulted in a tremendous cumulative score. In the Southwest Pacific from April 1942 and in the Solomons area from 29 June 1943 until 26 May 1944, Air and Navy destroyed 374 warships, 2,435 barges and other small craft, and 973,250 tons of merchant vessels. It is understandable that the enemy's seaborne supply has become less daring, more wary, and addicted to the cover of night when he approaches the boundaries of our blockade; but the periodic extension of those boundaries is furnishing us with more targets whose exploitation will continue.

An important contribution of Navy Air elements in areas south of the Philippines must not be overlooked. Naval Air activity there has revolved principally around the mission of Catalina (PBY) squadrons, which not only include patrols in various enemy sea lanes, but also engagements with convoy traffic. Reports covering a recent three-month period reveal bombing Catalinas sent over 100,000 tons of merchant shipping to the bottom; damaged more than 50,000 tons; sank and damaged several submarines, and scored hits on a dozen Jap warships, including destroyers and light and heavy cruisers. In view of the limited number of planes involved, this record is unquestionably outstanding in the annals of world aviation.

The relative absence of interference by major enemy Fleet units with our advances has made possible a rate of progress that could not otherwise have been achieved with the limited forces at hand. This favorable factor may largely be attributed to the enemy's tremendous and increasing losses of ships, war cargo and men, to the diminishment in this and other areas from time to time of his total naval forces, and to his preoccupation with the activities, actual and threatened, of our Central Pacific Naval forces, and the constant harassing by the Army Air Force.

Diary entries, from captured Japanese diaries, Wakde area:

"Wakde Air Field was bombed and put out of commission, while every airplane was destroyed. Sewar Air Field was also raided and the airplanes were destroyed. The American air force has definite air supremacy. Sarmi Hq has been greatly damaged. A 3,000 ton freighter which was in Sarmi Harbor was hit by three bombs and sank. Rations (Div's one-year rations), which were piled up, were almost completely burnt by an incendiary bomb. Heard that many men were killed or missing. Total number of airplanes for today was 300. Some were shot down but it is nothing compared to the damage our forces received."

26 May 44: "The rain is cold and there is nothing to eat."

27 May 44: "The present strength of my platoon is 16. Am trying hard to get rations."

25 Jun 44: "Under the existing situation, we are helpless. 'Let us be the guardian spirits of the Empire,' said one Sgt . . . before he killed himself. There were about thirty of us wounded soldiers left in the cave. Those who could move assisted others. They all shouted 'Long live the Emperor' before leaving this world. My friend Nagasaka stabbed his throat with a knife, but he did not succeed in killing himself. I finally decided to assist him so that he could rest in peace. I stabbed my own brother in arms. Who could understand my horrible predicament? I still have two hand grenades; one to destroy myself, and one for the enemy. I don't know whether or not my rations will last till we are rescued. I determined to kill myself before I lose the power to pull the grenade pin. I want to restore my health so that I can die on the battlefront and follow Nagasaka."

25 Jun 44: "Long live the Emperor!

"Father and mother, please forgive me for dying before you do. I

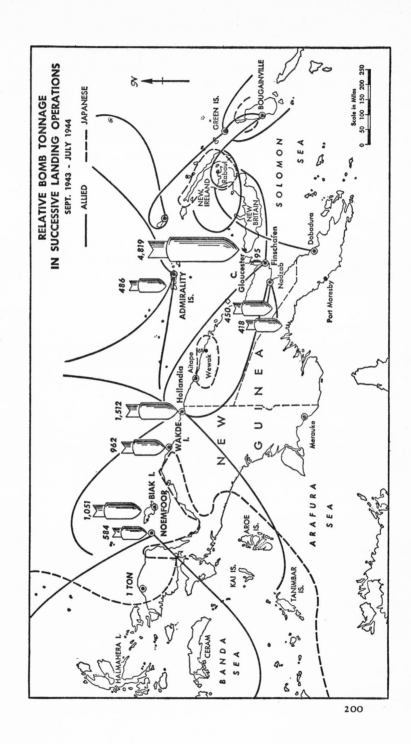

RELATIVE BOMB TONNAGE
IN SUCCESSIVE LANDING OPERATIONS

SEPT. 1943 - JULY 1944

ALLIED ———
JAPANESE ----

hope that you will be able to live the rest of your lives in peace. I wish you good health. I have done my duty to my country. My dearest parents, I am committing suicide with a hand grenade, my ashes will not reach you."

Mastery of the tremendous distance involved needs no review; nor does the encircling destruction of island bases and the forced inland withdrawal of neutralized mainland garrison require elaboration. The essence of each operation in this phase was succinctly distilled by the General himself into a single phrase, following the Morotai landings: "They may have the bottle, but I hold the stopper."

Establishment of the Cape Sansapor beachhead, however, had more significant reverberations than just the acquisition of another airdrome. The II Jap Army Commander's early decision to withdraw elements of the 35th and 36th Divisions as well as his own headquarters indicated a realization of the general effect on his forces of our westward drive. . . . Therefore, he decided to withdraw the remaining elements of the 36th Division from Manokwari in order to consolidate a comparatively strong force at Sorong. . . . Meanwhile, the enemy troops on the Vogelkop, then engaged in a coastal trek to the west, had one important line of withdrawal severed when we established ourselves astride his barge and overland route at Sansapor.

The seizure of Noemfoor, the elimination of the Biak garrison, and the establishment and consolidation of our Sansapor-Mar beachheads also exposed the flank of the neighboring enemy army, rendering its forward positions precarious. . . .

With the XVII, VIII, XVIII, II, and XIX Japanese Armies either destroyed, put to flight or impotently dislocated, a new axis of advance through the Moluccas secure, the return to Manila was paved. . . .

Conclusion: From the enemy viewpoint, the situation forces strategic withdrawal of the major portion of his air strength, probably to the line Ceram-Halmahera-Philippines. . . . .

Restricted by shrinking and neutralized air base facilities, smothered by our air superiority, the enemy's air services were now in full retreat. The Sarmi-Wakde-Biak blows fell with hammerlike regularity. Air opposition was negligible.

Our Cape Sansapor seizure was unopposed in the air. The absence of even a strong air threat-in-being was commented on in a daily G-2 summary:

There is no practical application of air power by the enemy in the forward area. Again he has failed to react initially with his aircraft against a further Allied advance upon New Guinea, at Cape Sansapor. . . . From this strength it is probable that the enemy has less than 100 effective aircraft for immediate operations against us. Hence, for the first time in SWPA, the enemy has not reserved a strong and poised threat-in-being. It may be predicted that the enemy, by design, is maintaining no real air facility other than the secondary capability to utilize inter-linked air bases over which he might employ his distant air strength based in the Philippines.

The end of the New Guinea campaign is covered by MacArthur's Tokyo records:

The Allies quickly developed their newly captured territory for immediate use. A major heavy bomber base was constructed on Biak, and fighters and medium bombers were stationed on Wakde, Noemfoor and at Sansapor. From these bases the Far Eastern Air Force was to strike during the next few months at Japanese positions in Ceram, Celebes, Halmahera, Dutch Borneo, Java and the Palaus in preparation for the assault against the Philippines. In the meantime, the Royal Australian Air Force Command was to interdict the Arafura, Banda and Ceram Seas and adjacent land areas thus protecting General MacArthur's southern flank.

G-2 also took a look ahead in a summary drawn up on the eve of the Philippine invasion:

The enemy's forward air strength now comprises all aircraft based in the Philippines, his tactical air reserve, air craft from his concentrations in Formosa, the South China Coast and the Nansei Islands; his strategic air reserve, concentrated in the Empire and dispersed through China, SE Asia and Manchuria.

Exposure of all the Philippines to massed carrier air attack has resulted in a makeshift program of feverish airdrome building, hampered by an increasingly hostile civil population. The large Clark Field–Manila bases, depot installations, training cadres, assembly and repair facilities and the bulk of his stored aviation gasoline are installations found normally far to the rear of forward air operations. They stand now squarely in the forward area, insecure and exposed to the full weight of all our preparatory counter air force operations.

Only if the enemy's aircraft production program is successful will the combined Jap Army-Navy Air Services be able to increase in effectiveness as we near the heartland. Lack of time will probably result in a Jap loss of the air battle for the Philippines.

The date of this estimate was Sept. 1, 1944. By Sept. 25 Admiral Halsey turned in a stupendous box-score in his successive strikes in the Philippines:

". . . Total box-score for 3rd Fleet now stands at 380 enemy planes shot down, 598 destroyed on ground, probables not included; 122 classified ships and 61 small craft sunk. 137 classified ships and 109 small craft damaged including those probably sunk. Extensive damage to aviation and maritime facilities and installations. Hope to pass the 1,000 plane mark and add some shipping after today's strike on the Visayas. . . . Nothing on the screen but Hedy Lamarr. . . ."

Things were already shaping up for Leyte in the summer of 1944, although MacArthur himself had not yet decided that Leyte would be a better point of entry into the Philippines than Mindanao. The seizure in September of the island of Morotai between New Guinea and the Philippines made Mindanao a logical jump, for it could have been made under cover of land-based bombers. But with each success the Allies were emboldened to take longer calculated risks. MacArthur now had two armies ready for the Philippines—the Sixth under Krueger and the newly created Eighth under Eichelberger. He had a corollary Navy component—Admiral T. C. Kinkaid's Seventh Fleet, which was under his control. And he was coming to trust the vigor and dash of "Bull" Halsey's Third Fleet, even though Halsey remained an autonomous figure under Nimitz.

As the battle for Morotai Island was unfolding, MacArthur took a look ahead. He said:

We now dominate the Moluccas. I rejoice that it has been done with so little loss. Our campaign is entering upon its decisive stage. Japanese ground troops still fight with the greatest tenacity. . . . Their officer corps, however, deteriorates as you go up the scale. It is fundamentally based upon a caste and feudal system and does not represent strict professional merit. Therein lies Japan's weakness. . . . Gripped inexorably by a military hierarchy, that hierarchy is now failing the nation. It has neither the imagination or the foresighted ability to organize Japanese resources for a total war. Defeat now stares Japan in the face. . . . When public opinion realizes that its generals and admirals have failed in the field of actual combat and campaign, the revulsion produced in Japanese thought will be terrific. Therein lies a basis for ultimate hope that the Japanese citizen will cease his almost idolatrous worship of the military [which] failed him. . . . That failure may mark the beginning of a new and ultimately happier era for him; his hour of decision is close at hand.

This forecast of the peace came almost a year before the *Missouri* sailed into Tokyo Bay. But it was soundly based on what had already happened in New Guinea. MacArthur had lived through lean days, and he knew what could be done with a few good men under imaginative leadership against comparatively large numbers of poorly led Japanese. His balance sheet in New Guinea was that of a great military economist. The statistics of comparative Japanese and American casualties in the New Guinea actions after the first bloody days of Buna and Sanananda speak for themselves. The campaign from Finschafen to the Vogelkop, from the winter of 1943 to the summer of 1944, represents a striking ratio in killed in favor of the Americans—the payoff for the system of bypassing frontal resistance, the tactical benefits of the envelopment:

Battle Areas	American Losses	Japanese Losses	Ratios
Arawe-Gloucester	472	4,914	1 : 10
Saidor	55	1,275	1 : 23
Admiralties	155	4,143	1 : 27
Hollandia	87	4,441	1 : 51
Aitape	440	3,370	1 : 19
Wakde	646	3,899	1 : 6
Biak	524	5,093	1 : 10
Noemfoor	63	2,328	1 : 37
Sansapor	2	374	1 : 187

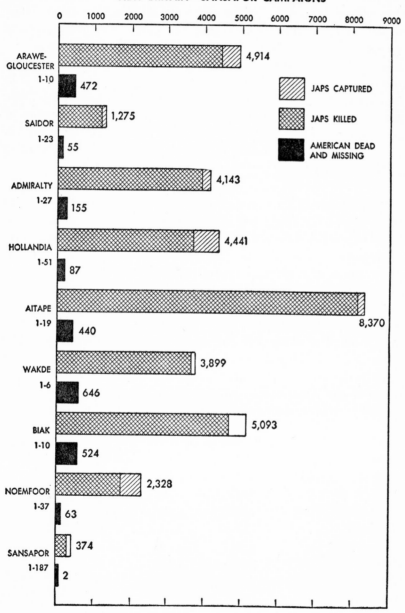

COMPARATIVE CASUALTIES
NEW BRITAIN - SANSAPOR CAMPAIGNS

JAPS CAPTURED

JAPS KILLED

AMERICAN DEAD
AND MISSING

ARAWE-
GLOUCESTER
1-10
4,914
472

SAIDOR
1-23
1,275
55

ADMIRALTY
1-27
4,143
155

HOLLANDIA
1-51
4,441
87

AITAPE
1-19
8,370
440

WAKDE
1-6
3,899
646

BIAK
1-10
5,093
524

NOEMFOOR
1-37
2,328
63

SANSAPOR
1-187
374
2

205

Even if the wounded in all degrees are included in American military expenditures for New Guinea, the total of casualties from 1942 to the summer of 1944 comes to 16,278 men and 2,479 officers —which was not much above the price paid for a single island in the Central Pacific—for example, Saipan.

With reference to August 13, coincidental with the operations of Aitape and Guam, MacArthur's staff was struck by the allocation of space in a typical Australian newspaper: five columns for France, Russia, and Italy—in fact, the entire front page—then one column for the Pacific, with easily one-third devoted to Guam; nothing at all was said about Aitape. Yet the tactical structure of these battles, though widely separated, show comparable similarities—though in reverse: on Guam, the Americans had to attack; on Aitape, MacArthur forced the Japanese to attack, on his own terms. The tally of losses reflects the efficacy of the maneuver:

Locality	Troops	Japanese Losses	American Losses
Aitape-Hollandia	41 & 20 Jap. Div.	8,370	1,527
Guam-Apra	3 Mar & 77 U.S. Div.	7,893	6,291

To military technicians who know that war is a form of bookkeeping in flesh and blood, in payments that are final with a white cross as signature, it is obvious that MacArthur was an excellent bookkeeper in every category of military accounts: men, equipment, and supplies. Applying the yardstick of comparison expressed in terms of shipments from U.S. ports to overseas theaters, MacArthur's ability to "make-do" becomes particularly obvious. While MacArthur had about 12 per cent of all troops abroad in 1943, he received less than 9 per cent of supplies sent overseas from America. In comparison with tonnage shipped to North Africa, he received only one-sixth, although on June 30, 1943, he had half the troop total reported in Africa. In three months North Africa received more than the Southwest Pacific received in an entire year; this same discriminatory ratio generally operated in favor of the European Theater.

Supplies shipped from the United States were seldom available in the front-line theaters until ninety days after shipment. The real measure of supplies available in 1943 was the sum of the last quarter of 1942 and the first nine months of 1943. In that period MacArthur received only five tons per man, while Africa received fifteen tons per man. (This vital point has already been graphically presented on p. 75.)

The table on general cargo and supply shipments for troops in combat was viewed rather sourly by the MacArthur staff against the background of a contemporaneous statistical item, namely, the shipments of civilian supplies to Italy. It is a stunning example of American altruism that an alien enemy, in defeat, should receive for civilian aid supply shipments in a single year that compare favorably to what was being sent to Pacific theaters for the conduct of military operations.

The Department of State Radio News Bulletin 239, October 4, 1944, gave the astonishing details:

. . . measures are now being taken to provide Italy with supplies during the forthcoming winter . . . a delegation of supply officers has been called from Italy to Washington . . . 150,000 tons of wheat and flour are now scheduled for shipment . . . it is planned to send 1,700 additional trucks to Italy . . . since the beginning of the Sicily campaign to the end of this year, 2,300,000 long tons of civilian supplies have been shipped to Italy; of this total, 1,107,000 tons were food and the balance consisted of coal, fertilizer, seeds, medical and sanitary supplies and clothing . . . in addition, preparations are under way to supply substantial quantities of generating equipment . . . to furnish electricity to essential industries and public utilities in Central Italy, which have been brought to a standstill . . . by doing these things, this country is serving the military aims and objectives of the United Nations . . . engaged in the final overthrow of Germany and Japan.

From the viewpoint of humanitarian generosity, this tonnage for relief of civilians was a noble act. Viewing war as a business, however, MacArthur's men, still fighting at the time, resented the supplies that went to enemy civilians in Italy.

With all the drawbacks interposed by European priorities, however, the combined economic systems of America and Australia produced enough to tip the balance against the Japanese in 1944.

Using what he had with great fluidity and flexibility, avoiding the costly frontal battles of the World War I type, MacArthur was ready for the Philippine invasion long before anyone would have deemed it possible in 1942. The seizure of Hollandia was a long time in the making, but once accomplished it speeded up Morotai, which in turn speeded up Leyte. The end in Tokyo Bay, once far over the horizon, was now less than a year away.

9 The Guerrilla Movement in the Philippines

FROM the day of his confident parting message to the Filipinos, "I shall return," no deviation from MacArthur's single-minded plan is discernible. Every battle action in New Guinea, every air raid on Rabaul or PT-boat attack on Japanese barges in the Bismarck Sea, was a mere preliminary for the reconquest of the Philippines. In the field of intelligence, the development of the Philippines guerrilla movement over the years was a calculated prerequisite for Mac-Arthur's return. The Philippines "underground" was in position to assist MacArthur's landing forces on Mindanao, Leyte, or Luzon. Information direct from the Philippines ranged from "inside" government dope (furnished by Manuel Roxas, who had "cover" as a collaborator) to the guest lists of the Manila Hotel—an infallible clue to high-level Japanese military or naval conferences.

With the preferential publicity for the European Theater, the French "maquis" was built into a fabulous figure. But just as impressive as the maquis was the rise of the Filipinos against the Japanese invader. Indeed, the resistance movement in the Philippines involved dangers even greater than those incurred in flaunting the Nazi Gestapo. The Japanese practiced terrorism with the bland efficiency of a long Oriental tradition; and in the Far Pacific there were no convenient Swiss or Spanish frontiers over which to escape.

After their initial and hopelessly abortive efforts to draw the Philippines into the "Greater East Asia Co-Prosperity Sphere" through intensive propaganda, quisling emissaries, promises of immunity, and outright bribery and subversion, the nervously apprehensive Japanese invaders turned sullen and savage. Wholesale arrests, torture killings, and punitive expeditions that wiped out whole villages became the order of the day. The firing squad of the Western world varied here with Oriental beheadings; sometimes the nervous executioner, a local amateur using a priceless heirloom sword, missed by a few inches. It is against this background of mortal peril and calculated savagery that the Filipino resistance movement must be appraised.

After General MacArthur's Staff arrived in Australia in March 1942, radio contact was maintained with Corregidor for a short time. With the surrender on Corregidor, all communication with the Philippines was cut off except for a radio station operated by Lt. Col. Guillermo Nakar, PA, who was leading an unsurrendered group of Filipinos and Americans in the province of Nueva Ecija. The last message received from Nakar was dated August 22, 1942. He was captured early in September 1942 and was executed in Ft. Santiago.

The first direct personal information from the Philippines was brought by Capt. William L. Osborne and Capt. Damon J. Gause, who escaped from Corregidor after the surrender and more or less drifted to Australia by way of Palawan, North Borneo, Tawi Tawi, and Macassar Strait—an astonishing bit of navigation.

An almost parallel feat was accomplished by Captain Frank H. Young, a messenger of Col. Claude Thorpe, a guerrilla leader of remnant groups in central Luzon. Young left in July and traveled via the Bicols, Samar, Leyte, Cebu, and Negros to Panay; there he joined Albert Klestadt, a German civilian, and came to Australia via Zamboanga. As did Osborne and Gause, they brought important and lucid information of the enemy and guerrilla activity in the areas through which they had passed.

While the total information on the Philippines accumulated to this time was not impressive, the interrogation of these escapees confirmed the existence of guerrilla organizations throughout the Islands. Leading personalities had not yet been clearly identified. However, several radio contacts were being established with the Philippine guerrillas at this time, and it was already clear that loyal organizations were forming everywhere and that in many places friendly persons could be contacted. For instance, Station KFS (San Francisco), in November 1942, intercepted radio calls from Major Praeger, a guerrilla commander in northern Luzon, operating Station WYY. Although this early radio contact with the Philippines was limited to a few messages—only twenty-two were received in December 1942—the number began to increase through 1943 and 1944, reaching a peak of 3,700 at the time of the landings in Luzon in January 1944.

The chief problem immediately confronting intelligence penetration was the lack of knowledge of the Japanese police and counter-espionage methods, the coverage and the extent of their subversion of Filipinos. The ultimate development of "puppet" government was already anticipated. This dictated caution. However, initial fragments of information gave a decisive impulse to the immediate planning for Intelligence penetration of the Islands. The groundwork was started in earnest.

G-2 developed a Philippine sub-section, as a miniature branch concerned solely with Philippine intelligence, in contrast with the broad general interests and activities of its parent organization. Information of all sorts was processed and disseminated in great volume; many intelligence-penetration parties were briefed, and advice on policies was prepared; this state of expanded production lasted until after the Leyte landing in October 1944; thereafter the section's activities steadily decreased.

Realizing also the great potentialities of the resistance movement, headquarters began to guide the guerrilla efforts so that their reports became of increasing value. General instruction laid stress on information of strategic character: enemy identification; land, sea, and air movements; enemy activities and dispositions; captured documents, etc.

One outstanding contribution of the Philippine Section was the comprehensive reference files to which additions were constantly made; its monographs on the guerrilla resistance movement became standard; in 1948 they were still consulted by American and Philippine authorities dealing with the official recognition of guerrillas—although the information therein did not apparently curb the postwar evil of "bandwagon" jumping, in which literally thousands claimed guerrilla status and collected back pay on it.

In the wake of military conquest by foreign invaders, there have been great historical "resistance movements" within oppressed popu-

C O N F I D E N T I A L

Philippine Intelligence Guide

lations; a famous instance is that of the Tyrolese rising against Napoleon. These movements have one thing in common: they are usually suppressed with ruthless savagery.

Fighting "underground" has commonly earned a one-way ticket to the firing squad or the gallows, usually via the torture chamber. The historical pattern has been consistent. The Tyrolese patriot Andreas Hofer was executed at Mantua. Spanish patriots fell before the French firing squads at Cordova and Saragossa. World War I rang with the echoes of rifle volleys, with a blindfolded victim standing forlornly against a brick wall or tied to a telephone pole. It was left to World War II, however, to exceed any previous war in calculated terrorism. In the Pacific war, gloomy Ft. Santiago in Manila, heritage of sixteenth-century Spain and erstwhile MacArthur headquarters, became the execution chamber of the Japanese Kempei-tai, the ruthless secret military police.

The American public usually conceives of the fighting in the Philippines as primarily consisting of defensive operations against the initial Japanese invasion of 1941, and the American return invasion of 1944; the widespread guerrilla operations and the extensive American intelligence penetration of the Philippines, in the intervening years, are not generally known.

The spirit of resistance of the Filipinos is reflected in one of the most remarkable wartime documents of the period. Tomas Confesor, prewar governor of Panay, also headed the free civil government during the Japanese occupation. Considerable local pressure was exerted by quisling politicians to induce Confesor to collaborate with the Japanese. In 1943 he wrote a stinging letter of rebuke to one of these quisling Filipinos:

There is a total war in which the issues between the warring parties are less concerned with territorial questions but more with forms of government, ways of life, and those that affect even the very thoughts, feelings and sentiments of every man. In other words, the question at stake with respect to the Philippines is not whether Japan or the United States should possess it but more fundamentally it is: what system of government would stand here and what ways of life, system of social organizations and code for morals should govern our existence. . . .

You may not agree with me but the truth is that the present war is a blessing in disguise to our people and that the burden it imposes and the hardships it has brought upon us are a test of our character to determine the sincerity of our convictions and the integrity of our souls. In other words, this war has placed us in the crucible to assay the metal in our being. For as a people, we have been living during the last forty years under a regime of justice and liberty regulated only by universally accepted principles of constitutional governments. We have come to enjoy personal privileges and civil liberties without much struggle, without undergoing any pain to attain them. They were practically a gift from a generous and magnanimous people—the people of the United States of America. Now that Japan is attempting to destroy those liberties, should we not exert any effort to defend them? Should we not be willing to suffer for their defense? If our people are undergoing hardships now, we are doing it gladly, it is because we are willing to pay the price for those constitutional liberties and privileges. You cannot become wealthy by honest means without sweating heavily. You very well know that the principles of democracy and democratic institutions were brought to life through bloodshed and fire. If we sincerely believe in those principles and institutions, as we who are resisting Japan do, we should contribute to the utmost of our capacity to the cost of its maintenance to save them from destruction and annihilation and such contribution should be in terms of painful sacrifices, the same currency that other peoples paid for those principles. . . .

By mid-1942 guerrilla units had sprung up in all parts of the Islands. Effective steps were taken promptly to reach these isolated centers of resistance and to furnish them substantial supplies, equipment, command direction, and—perhaps equally important—moral support. Intelligence parties were initially organized, trained, and dispatched from Australia through the G-2 Allied Intelligence Bureau (1942–1943); later on the penetration of the Philippines was handled by an autonomous organization, the Philippine Regional Section, or PRS (1943–1944).

This PRS brought Gen. Courtney Whitney, MacArthur's trusted personal adviser, on the stage of history. A prominent Manila lawyer, thoroughly familiar with prewar conditions and personalities in the Islands, this brilliant executive gave PRS his undivided attention. It was Whitney who developed an efficient supply and delivery service which utilized the cargo submarine. Lt. Comdr. "Chick" Parsons of the Luzon Stevedore Company, Manila, handled the supply runs for Whitney and made several landings himself. Parsons has recorded his experiences in a book that describes vividly the hazardous landings of submarines on split-second schedules, never quite certain that Japanese patrols were not waiting at the rendezvous with depth charges. There is a glimpse of how a passenger feels in the report of Major Cruz, offered later on in this chapter.

The Philippine Regional Section cargo service became the lifeline of the resistance movement. When Macario Peralta, one of the most aggressive guerrilla commanders, was begging for supplies to Panay early in 1943, he closed a message with the words: "Still hoping the grass arrives before the horse dies." Because of PRS the horse recovered and kicked lustily until the end of the war. Radio transmitters, cyphers, and technical personnel, as well as munitions, were smuggled into the Islands in ever increasing numbers; a widespread intelligence and coast-watcher net developed simultaneously with the guerrilla movement.

Quite early in the game a problem of jurisdiction between guerrilla commands arose: the guerrilla leaders were individualists and bound to clash. General MacArthur made his usual sharp decision: he revived the prewar territorial division of the Philippine Army and appointed or "recognized" the de facto leaders. Since they were either American or Filipino Army officers, they fell in readily with the old-time "command areas." Some leaders dropped by the wayside; others were relieved; some emerged as really strong men, as leaders will always emerge in time of stress and disaster. The names of Peralta, Abcede, Kangleon, and Fertig will hold their historical niche.

Guerrilla intelligence reports were always of value because of their richness and variety. Contacts ranged all the way up the economic and social scale, from dock laborers unloading Japanese ships and mechanics working at Japanese airfields, to General Roxas, who had numerous pipelines to the highest Japanese councils and the "puppet" regime in Manila. Overlapping coverage of various guerrilla nets and the parallel reports by separate penetration-parties nets enabled MacArthur's G-2 to cross-check the reliability of information. Intelligence of all sorts continued to reach Headquarters until our own invasion of the Philippines. When American forces landed on Leyte in October 1944, the intelligence groups, radio nets, coast-watcher stations, etc., could claim substantial credit for their contributions to the success of the campaign. After the Sixth and the Eighth Armies took the field, the story of these nets, as well as the achievements of the guerrilla bands in the actual fighting, became a part of the history of these two armies.

The pioneer AIB trip into the Philippines was made by Capt. J. A. Villamor, a Filipino aviator who had won early distinction in air combat in the Corregidor fighting. His mission was standard:

1. Establish a net for military intelligence and secret services throughout the Islands.

2. Establish a chain of communication, both local and to Australia.

3. Establish an eventual escape route to accommodate evacuation of selected individuals in the interest of future planning.

4. Develop an organization for covert subversive activities and propaganda for use at the appropriate time.

5. Locate and contact individuals known to be loyal.

6. Establish the rudiments of the net, to be formulated upon the "cell" system for mutual protection.

7. Establish a radio transmitter for contacting Darwin on matters of transportation rendezvous only.

Villamor left for the Islands on December 27, 1942, on the U.S. Submarine *Gudgeon*. Radio contact with the party was established one month later on January 26, 1943. Villamor's character as a national hero "boomeranged" on his position as a secret observer, since he was enthusiastically recognized wherever he went; he consequently took refuge in a very secret retreat and directed the organization of his nets from that point. This was progressing rather successfully considering the heavy hand of the Japanese: within sixty days contacts had been made with the principal islands; key personnel were being trained and communication channels established. Some of these original contacts continued to play an important part as late as October 1944 in our major Philippine landings.

The first half of the year 1944 saw a marked speed-up in the activities of the Philippine Regional Section. The number of sub-

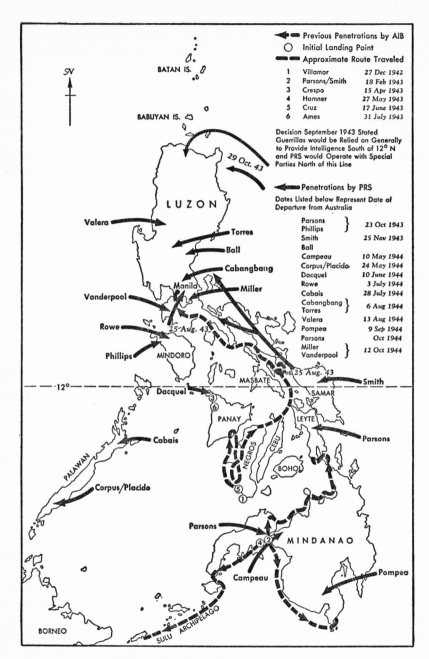

AIB and PRS Intelligence penetrations

marine-borne parties was increased and the tonnage of transported materials considerably augmented. In January supplies were landed on Panay and Negros; in February, on Tawi Tawi and Mindanao. The month of May was a particularly active one. A large party of specially trained agents was dispatched to Colonel Smith on Samar and another to Colonel Fertig on Mindanao. Additional quantities of supplies were brought into this latter island for distribution to the north. During May, too, the first agents were sent to the island of Palawan. In June a party with complete equipment for transmission of weather information was sent to Negros.

While an expensive machine was being set in motion to get into the Islands and ultimately into Manila, there were some competent people already "inside" trying to get out. Colonel Manzano, an engineer officer with the old Philippines Division, a veteran outfit of distinction, became a prisoner of war when Corregidor fell. With other Filipino officers and men he was paroled from the deathtrap of Camp O'Donnell "on account of sickness"; the Japanese were generous that way and sent people "home to die." Manzano, however, chose to recover and got in touch with a trusted assistant, Lt. Osmundo Mondonedo, Philippines Army, for the purpose of establishing contacts with the "underground" and developing an intelligence or sabotage unit.

Manzano covered Manila, while Mondonedo operated from Los Banos, Laguna. By the middle of 1943, Manzano had satisfactory relations with an odd assortment of Luzon organizations that grew jungle-wise in an atmosphere of Japanese terror. He played around with the "Free Philippines," a sort of clearing house of local guerrilla activities; he examined the "Hukbalahap," a radical, Communist tainted outfit which professed to be anti-Japanese and might possibly become useful. He was in touch with Major Ramsey, who headed the "East Central Luzon Guerrilla Area," with Anderson's guerrilla group, with Terry Hunter's "ROTC Guerrillas," with Colonel Enriquez, with Col. Hugh Straughn, and with the picturesque Marking and the equally picturesque Yay Panlillio. Wherever he could safely get in, he established contact with independent formations, of fluid life and character, not to mention a few remnant Spanish republicans.

Manzano's group paid a heavy price for their service. Manzano himself was implicated in the Elizalde-Ozamis-Pirovano trial, but managed to escape. His wife was arrested and kept four months in Ft. Santiago; fortunately she knew very little about her husband's private affairs. The following were killed: Ramon Amusategui, secretary of the "Ahorro Insular," a building and loan association; Mr. Duggleby of the Benguet Mines; Sergeant Ortega, 14th Engineers; Mr. Rafael Roces, member of the "Free Philippines"; Maj. Robert Lothrop, U.S. prisoner at Ft. Mills; Mr. Jose Oriol; Mr. Antonio Bautista; Senator Jose Ozamis; and Brig. Gen. Vicente Lim, PA.

It was a foregone conclusion that Manzano would drift eventually into a particular high-level group that was dissatisfied with the "puppet" government and hated the Japanese conqueror—the group around Brigadier General Roxas, later to become the President of the Republic. Roxas was with MacArthur in Corregidor but remained in the Islands on MacArthur's instructions. A top-flight politician with great influence and popular appeal, he was wooed ardently by Laurel and his collaborationist crowd. All sorts of pressures and threats were exercised to get him to accept a position under the Japanese. He managed to avoid this damaging official entanglement under some pretext or other, usually "failing health," though he played with his life; the temper of the Japanese was getting short and the dungeons of Ft. Santiago held many distinguished victims. Roxas became a natural center of information, or refuge, for all those in the twilight zone of the resistance movement. When MacArthur finally sent Maj. Emigdio Cruz in to Manila, as the personal emissary of President Quezon, it was with the idea of getting in touch with Roxas and other former associates of Quezon in order to clarify the many confused stories that were coming out of Luzon.

Here enters one Franco Vera Reyes, citizen-at-large of Manila. When the Japs entered the city, he was doing a stretch in Bilibid, the local penitentiary, for larceny and forgery. At odd moments he had worked as a broker's clerk—but never for long. There are some disreputable suburbs of Manila in which Western and Oriental crime merge to produce a fantastic Hollywood atmosphere: Mr. Reyes was well known hereabouts, in what Hollywood might describe as dens of vice. The Japanese secret police, with most thorough training in the dockyards of Shanghai and Yokohama, were completely at home in this exotic underworld. They were also very efficient in the use of stool pigeons and informers, and their discipline of these shady characters was most effective. The local jailbirds and hop-heads became immediately available to the Japanese police. Mr. Reyes obtained his freedom from jail after certain discreet negotiations in which a bundle of "mickey mouse" money on one side, and a loaded gun on the other, left practically no choice for a gentleman of Mr. Reyes's persuasion.

Mr. Reyes then began to operate. He frequented the night spots that were doing a rather gloomy business, having more money to spend than he ever dreamed of. He developed a following of sorts, let himself be known as an Allied Intelligence Bureau operator.

Manila was desperate for authentic contacts with the outer world, the almost forgotten world of American *laissez faire* and American gadgets and luxuries: the Manila citizens were tired of Japanese "austerity" and requisitions and cheap "mickey mouse" money. MacArthur's G-2 decided about that time to make this cheap money even cheaper, and experts of the United States Mint had duplicated, even "aged," the Japanese-printed Philippines occupation peso.

When Reyes got into the confidence of Senator Ozamis, who was in the Roxas group, he struck pay dirt. Manzano, however, was not quite satisfied. Reyes had also approached him; he made a luncheon appointment with Manzano at Tom's "Dixie Kitchen." That famous old landmark in Manila was able to do business as usual; Tom, though American, was not seriously molested by the Japanese. It must have been Tom's "Southern" cooking and the old smoothy's disarming ways. Anyhow, the Japanese were *bon vivants*, especially when it cost practically nothing. Manzano posted a few ex-constabularies who knew the prewar criminal world, a sort of informal police line-up. When luncheon was over, they brought the bad news; they identified Reyes as a Japanese stool pigeon. Manzano had barely time enough to warn Ozamis, who did not want to believe him.

The story of how Reyes exposed some top-level key resistance men was filled in after the war by another member of the Roxas group, Manuel Elizalde, whose brother Juan was executed by the Japanese as a result of Reyes's double-dealing. According to Manuel Elizalde:

Reyes managed to get an introduction to a group of American women who were in a hospital outside the St. Tomas Internment Camp. At least some of the ladies must have given Reyes an unusual degree of confidence. At the end of 1943, Senator Ozamis [viewed with suspicion by the Japanese] had made a trip to Mindanao where he contacted some guerrilla leaders who were in touch with Australia. Ozamis brought with him some letters, including personal photos, for delivery to certain Manila residents. When this correspondence was shown to members of Roxas' group, it was decided to destroy everything, since the danger of compromise was obvious. Possibly, the soft heart of one or the other of this group led him to deliver some of these letters. Reyes got wind of this and wasted no time in notifying the Kempei-Tai.

The subsequent arrests were made in the swift and terrible Japanese fashion. First the ladies were arrested, followed by their husbands. Ozamis, Juan Elizalde and Pirovano were pulled in; the dragnet expanded to reach for Virgilio Lobregadt, T. Grupe, Enrique Santamaria, J. Corominas, H. Menzies, and even the Roxas brothers. Juan Elizalde, a first-class polo player in his lighter moments, was also a first-class sportsman: he tried to take entire personal responsibility in order to save the others. He failed in his gallant attempt and he, with many in his group, was executed.

From this point on Mr. Reyes's life became very complicated. The word was out; every guerrilla was looking for him. He was reported killed shortly thereafter. The Japanese regarded his disappearance with amiable indifference; when their protégés became useless, they were even willing to help things along.

Manzano's exposure of Reyes had come too late to save Juan Elizalde and some of the others. Moreover General Roxas had been compromised by Reyes, and he had every reason to become restless. Any night the crash of a rifle butt might reverberate against his door, with a truck waiting and a Japanese lieutenant waving his pistol around and reading an order for his arrest. Fearful of the future, Roxas decided to send a special emissary to Australia—and picked Manzano for the trip.

While Manzano was trying to get out of Manila and the Islands, another man was trying to get in. This man was Dr. Emigidio Cruz, a Philippine Army surgeon who was serving with Quezon in Washington as an aide, in addition to being one of his doctors.

While information from Luzon was improving all the time both in volume and quality, real "inside stuff" from Manila was erratic and did not always sound authentic. President Quezon was particularly concerned about news of Laurel's collaboration with the Japanese high command. It was important to get someone inside Manila with sufficient prestige to reach into the highest government level—to Roxas, Alunan, Vargas, and other Quezon associates—for the real story. The Filipino politicians around Malacanan Palace were not likely to talk to an ordinary agent; with the execution of Ozamis and Juan Elizalde, the official honeymoon was over. But there was an excellent chance that the Manila crowd would talk to Dr. Cruz; in any event, they were not likely to betray him.

The trip nevertheless represented a terrible risk; the chances of capture en route were ten to one. It was a conspicuously gallant effort—and the wonder is that it succeeded completely. Major Cruz told his own story in a special report:

I left the submarine base at Perth, Australia, on board the U.S.S. *Thresher*. When I got aboard the submarine and found several tons of arms and ammunition consigned to the guerrillas on Negros, I felt elated and encouraged. The *Thresher* was on regular combat patrol; I was only an incidental passenger, but the officers soon made me feel at home.

On the fourth day of our trip, we gave chase to a Japanese convoy of three tankers and a destroyer. The fourth torpedo hit one of the tankers and we crash-dived. We stayed under water for about eighteen hours hearing and feeling the concussion of the depth charges. By the time we reached Philippine waters, we had sunk three tankers and one Japanese destroyer.

On July 6, 1943, we received radio instructions from [Whitney] Australia that I was to land on the southwestern shore of the Island of Negros. On the morning of July 9, scanning the western shore of Negros through the periscope, the skipper saw a Japanese cruiser patrolling the very point where I was going to land. We laid low and waited until dark. At about seven that evening, the coast was clear and I saw the familiar sight of a Filipino sailboat. We made contact with the guerrillas and unloaded the seven tons of ammunition in the record time of forty-five minutes. . . .

On the third day after my arrival, the Japanese made a surprise raid on the place of my landing. They captured a considerable amount of the arms and ammunition I came with. . . . During this period of delay I occupied myself with treating and curing the sick who were in a very miserable condition, including the wife of Villamor himself, who was suffering from advanced anemia, secondary to malaria.

One day Villamor told me that he thought it was not safe for me to go to Manila. "Even among the guerrillas there are some who know your true identity," he said. . . .

My plan was to ask the help of Colonel Peralta or Governor Alfredo Montelibano, who was hiding in the northern sector of the island. I also appealed to Colonel Abcede, who was then District Commander of the Negros guerrillas. He not only gave me a guide but provided me with an escort; only three reached with me the hiding place of Governor Montelibano at the top of the Caloan volcano.

I had been with Governor Montelibano five days when the Japanese raided us and drove us deeper into the jungle. The guerrillas fought the Japanese for three days and gave a good account of themselves, killing more than sixty of the enemy, with three wounded on the guerrilla side; the new arms and ammunition I brought had their baptism.

Through one of the guerrillas I learned that a friend, Major Roberto, was in the neighboring hills. By a stroke of luck he had at that time a crew of five men from Sorsogon who had been stranded in Negros and who were anxious to go back to their families. We took the risk and went through the enemy cordon; after refitting a small sailboat, we left the shores of Cadiz for Luzon.

My crew were all from Sorsogon; they spoke nothing but Bicol, which I had to learn. During my stay in Negros, I had learned to speak the Visayan dialect, a fact which pulled me out of many tight spots.

I loaded my ship with dried fish and chickens and posed as a trader; ordinarily the trip should take only seven days; this time it took fifteen, eluding the Japanese patrol boats and stopping on several islands to dispose of and replenish my goods. On one of those inter-island trips I was becalmed in the middle of the sea and was overtaken by a Japanese patrol boat. They searched us and the boat suspiciously. When they learned that I came from Negros, they brought out a Visayan interpreter. This Visayan asked questions about Major Cruz, the "bandit" who had brought arms to Negros. I answered in Visayan, saying that I did not know anything and that I was just a merchant; then I overheard the interpreter say: "He is no Tagalog, he is a Visayan." Then it occurred to me that they were looking for a Tagalog; from then on I became very chatty with my crew and tried to learn more of the Bicol dialect; by the time we reached the Island of Galintaan, I was able to pass as a Bicolano. I paid off my crew in this Island of Calintaan and, unknown to them, I crossed the Straits of Sorsogon that same night.

I felt more confident as I set foot on Luzon soil. I assumed the name of Emilio C. Conde and entered the town of Matnog. I was lucky enough to win the confidence of a young man from Matnog named Arturo Almasan, who served as guide and companion in all my trips in the Bicol region and Manila.

I proceeded to Magdalena, a coastal town, controlled by the Japanese. The town mayor, a Japanese old-timer named Daito, was quite friendly. I was able to convince him that I was an old-timer like himself. He sold me a local residence certificate, necessary for travel, for two hundred Japanese pesos. Armed with this paper I went back to the town of Matnog as it was the best place to get transportation for Lucena and Manila. . . . When I got into the place, the sailboat of a Chinese merchant, Tiong Hing, was getting ready to sail for Lucena, Tayabas. Somehow the Chinese sensed that I was connected with the "underground," but after a little persuasion, he agreed to take me along.

That evening a group of eight men under the lead of an American mestizo named Johnson came over to the house where I was hiding and demanded an explanation of my presence in town. Johnson accused me of being a Japanese spy. He made me carry a shovel and said that he was going to show me how they dealt with Japanese spies in this place. After a few minutes' silence, with my feet getting heavier with each step, I asked if he was going to kill a "Bataan boy" without even hearing what I had to say. The word Bataan worked like magic on him. He turned around and asked with surprise: "Are you from Bataan? I fought in Bataan, too," he continued without waiting for me to answer. He ordered his men to go back to the house, and the two of us walked slowly behind. He did most of the talking, enthusiastically narrating his dramatic escape after the surrender. . . .

Making arrangements with the Chinese merchant to pick me up

at the neighboring barrio, I left that same night. . . . Our first stop was Bulan, a Japanese naval base. There were no ships in view in the bay except for two small launches and two submarines; it looked more like a patrol boat-pool than a naval base. We were met at the pier by a Japanese constabulary and were subjected to a comparatively light inspection and questioning. Then everybody was told to go ashore, with an escort of two Japanese guards with fixed bayonets. It was October 14, 1943, but nobody knew what was going on until we were told that it was the inauguration of the Japanese "Puppet" Philippine Independence. We were marched to the Plaza and were required to bow to every Japanese sentinel. The Plaza was packed with men, women and children. The atmosphere was tense with fear and sad foreboding. Every number in the program was applauded mechanically, not enthusiastically. After the program, three shouts of "Banzai" gave the signal to disperse.

I was on my way to the boat when I was hailed by a man on a bicycle, shouting: "Cruz, Cruz. I am very glad to see you. When did you come? How is everything with you?" Before I could utter a word, my hands were shaken violently by my old classmate Dr. Castro. I don't remember exactly how I got rid of him, but I certainly did it quickly. I lost no time in getting back to the boat and stayed there most of the time.

The next day we set sail for Lucena. We had been sailing for two days when we met a Japanese patrol boat near Tablas Island. I bundled together all the personal letters of President Quezon, weighted them with a small stone, and threw them into the sea. The Japanese boarded our ship and all of us were made to kneel on the outriggers. They searched the boat carefully; then they asked where we were going. Our pilot said Lucena and showed the Japanese pass for the boat. With the help of two fat hens, we were allowed to proceed on our way.

It was low tide when we entered Lucena Bay. . . .

I stayed in the New Banshaw Hotel, in Lucena. The officers of the Japanese garrison ate their meals at the hotel. I learned from the manager that the Japanese were fond of shrimps. Early one morning I went down to the barrio and bought all the eggs and shrimps in the place, and sold them to the Japanese soldiers, but keeping some of the best shrimps. I had the shrimps cooked the way the Japanese like and asked the hotel manager to invite the officers to be my guests that noon; we had a hearty luncheon complete with Japanese beer. After a few more days trading with the Japanese, we became quite friendly and I was invited to visit the Japanese garrison. The captain of the garrison, Captain Ando, gave me a letter of recommendation when I told him that I wanted to sell chickens and eggs in Manila.

On October 22, 1943, I boarded a train from Lucena to Manila. With my basket of chickens I got off at the Blumentritt railroad station. I went directly to the house of my sister-in-law in Sampaloc, Manila. After the first shock of my sudden appearance, my sister-in-law and her husband, Judge Antonio Cuyugan, told me that my wife was in the city, that we would have to be careful because the Japanese had made several inquiries about me in that house and also in Arayat, my home town.

My wife was shocked, too, when she saw me, but after praying for a few minutes to the Image of our Holy Virgin, she became composed. She was speechless, keeping a tight hold on me and trying to convince herself that I was not a product of her imagination. She then told me of the horrible things that the Japanese had been doing; the wanton and indiscriminate killings of men, women and children and destruction of property. She described her terrible experiences in the mountains, where she took our six children to escape Japanese atrocities. She had been questioned about me several times by the Japanese. Her only answer was that I had been killed in Bataan. . . .

I met General Roxas at night in a house at 893 Lepanto Street, Manila. I transmitted the messages of President Quezon; his faith and confidence in the integrity, loyalty and patriotism of Roxas and other leaders of the Philippines, and how he had singled out Roxas as the only man in whose abilities, courage and patriotism he could entrust the destiny of his country and the strong desire of the President that Roxas should join him in Washington, D.C. I also asked General Roxas for information regarding the reactions of other Filipino leaders and the people in general towards Quezon's departure to the United States, the present attitude of the government leaders and the people in general towards the United States and Japan. . . . I also told Roxas of MacArthur's instructions for the underground to lie low and refrain from indiscreet killings of Japanese and Japanese spies, to avoid painful retaliations.

I asked General Roxas' opinion on whether or not Vice President Osmena should succeed Quezon at the expiration of the latter's term of office. General Roxas said that in his opinion the President should continue in office, regardless of the constitution, because the expediency of war needed his services. General Roxas said that he appreciated the high regard President Quezon had for him, but declined to go to Washington, at that time, because he had very important work to do; he was the only one in a position to advise the underground and to stop them from manifesting their intense hatred for the Japanese. . . . He further added that he had an understanding with General Francisco that in case there would be conscription of Filipinos into the Japanese Army, loyal Filipinos would be placed in key positions so that they could turn the whole conscripted army against the Japanese. General Roxas also said that he had connections with several guerrilla leaders. . . . He told me that there were at that time 120,000 Japanese soldiers in Batangas, Cavite, Bataan, Manila, Pampanga, Tarlac and Pangasinan. "All indications show that they will try to hold Manila," he said. "Tell the President and General MacArthur that there is no doubt about the loyalty of the Filipinos, including those who are holding positions in the government. It can be safely stated that 95% of the entire Filipino people are loyal to America and the leadership of President Quezon."

He wanted to get out of the Islands later on and told me to request General MacArthur to get him out one month before the expected invasion. I later transmitted all this to General MacArthur and President Quezon. Roxas warned me not to stay more than a few days in the city, because the Japanese knew already of my arrival in the Philippines via submarine and it would only be a question of time before they would start looking for me in Manila.

The next day I met Speaker Yulo, Secretary Rafael Alunan, Ramon and Amado Arraneta. . . . I transmitted President Quezon's message and asked information which the President required. All of them wanted the President to continue, except Alunan, who thought that the constitution should be respected. Mr. Yulo wanted more advice from some older men, so he asked me to see him again the next day. . . .

The next day I met with Colonel Rafael Jalandoni. He was working as a clerk in Malacanan, compiling the census of Filipino war prisoners. He reported that 43,000 Filipino officers and men reached O'Donnell alive; 29,000 of them died in the camp. He could not tell how many more died after they were sent home. He assured me that all the Bataan boys were loyal and anxious to take up arms against the enemy, despite their harrowing experiences. He was living miserably with his wife and daughter; the forty pesos a month he was receiving were not even enough to buy a sack of camotes. My younger brother, Rafael Cruz, said that he found Jalandoni and his family living in a small, dilapidated hut. In spite of this misery, he refused to accept many lucrative jobs offered to him, including the office of aide-de-camp to Vargas and then to Laurel. For his oft repeated refusal he was suspected and closely watched.

That night my brother Rafael contacted Mr. Jose Razon to find out where I could meet him. Mr. Razon set the time for seven-thirty in the same old Quiapo Church. I had a hard time eluding the people I knew. Razon and Amado Arraneta came twenty minutes late. They were delayed because of a bundle which General Roxas wanted me to take to the United States. I found out that the bundle comprised a complete set of the "Philippine Gazette," containing the reports and records of all the Bureaus and Departments of the Philippine Government, including the speeches of the government officials. . . .

I met Speaker Yulo for the second time. . . . Yulo advised me to get out of the city as soon as possible, because many people already knew of my presence in Manila and it would be only a matter of days before the Japanese learned about it. In spite of these things, I made other attempts to see Vargas. Disguised as a vegetable seller, I entered the Vargas garden to see him and let him see me, but there were Japanese soldiers in his garden. By that time my supply of Japanese money was running low. I requested Mr. Yulo to give me 2,000 pesos; the money was delivered to me at San Sebastian Church by the Arranetas. Ramon had a pass to go in and out of the prison and concentration camps. He said that in Muntinglupa prison, there were about 10,000 prisoners, all Filipinos and mostly political prisoners; they were miserably treated and practically starved. The American civilians in Santo Tomas University were better off because food and money could be smuggled in to them. The American prisoners in the Port Area were in the worst condition, sick and emaciated beyond recognition. He also informed me that the Japanese were constructing wooden barges . . . at the rate of seven a day and that Japanese war tanks were being assembled. . . .

I contacted General Lim in the Philippine General Hospital. He and Roxas were the only two who had not yet signed the oath of allegiance to Japan. General Lim succeeded in pretending to be more sick than he really was and was only waiting for a chance to escape and join the guerrillas. I stayed in the city several more days, contacting some of the other men I was ordered to contact. . . .

I found the morale of the people very high. . . . The people in general recognize only one lawfully constituted government, the Commonwealth Government headed by President Quezon. They refer to President Quezon's name with respect and love, in contrast to the mockery and derision with which they refer to the Japanese-sponsored Philippine Republic and to President Jose Laurel. In Manila and neighboring provinces people refer to the Philippine Independence granted by Japan as *Vals Wals*, a contraction of the Tagalog phrase *Vale Wala*, meaning "worth nothing." During the inauguration of [the] so-called Philippine Republic big posters carrying the Spanish phrase *Aqui No Duran Laureles* were seen in many public places in Manila and provinces. That phrase, composed of the names of Benigno *Aquino*, Pio *Duran*, Jose *Laurel*, means "here no Laurels will last." That phrase expresses aptly the hatred of the people towards all Japanese sympathizers.

The true and loyal Filipino leaders are: Manuel Roxas, Jose Yulo, Rafael Alunan, Quintin Paredes, Vincente Madrigal, Ramon Fernandez, Eulogio Rodriguez Sr., Eulogio Rodriguez Jr., former Chief Justice Ramon Avancena, all the Justices of the Supreme Court, Generals Lim, Capimpin, Segundo, and Francisco.

Many guerrilla units and sympathizers are working inside Manila and are instrumental in the killing of many Japanese spies and puppets. . . . In Manila and neighboring provinces Prof. Lava, formerly of the U.P., organized a band called HucBaLaJap, meaning *Hukbong laban sa Japon*, a Tagalog phrase for *Army against the Japs*. This unit has more than three thousand members who consist mostly of Communists from Pampanga, Nueva Ecija, Tarlac and Laguna. . . .

General Roxas is also organizing a contact network between Manila and the provinces of Luzon, Visayas and Mindanao. Many of the Bataan ex-soldiers are wise to the part that is being played by Gen. Roxas and are rallying behind him. He expressed the desire to leave the Islands as soon as his work has been accomplished, preferably one or two months before we make the landings. He is also of the opinion that a premature appearance of American planes in Manila and Luzon will cause a general demonstration of hostility against the Japanese and may lead to terrible Japanese retaliations . . .

With the "Official Gazette" given me by General Roxas hidden in the bottom of a bamboo trunk and covered by boxes of cigars, hand-bags and wooden shoes, I left the city for Lucena by train. I left Lucena in a small sailboat on November 8, 1943, bound for Negros. A typhoon overtook us and we were stranded on the Island of Gigantangan, Leyte. On this Island I wrote my message in longhand and sent it to Colonel Peralta by courier, to be transmitted to Australia. I arrived on the northern tip of Negros on the night of December 3, 1943. From Cadiz I sent another message, which was relayed to Australia by radio through Colonel Edwin Andrews. On February 12, 1944, I was picked up by the submarine *Narwhal*. . . .

Cruz got back to the States, to his President and the luxury of the Shoreham Hotel. As it affects General Roxas, the Cruz story is a

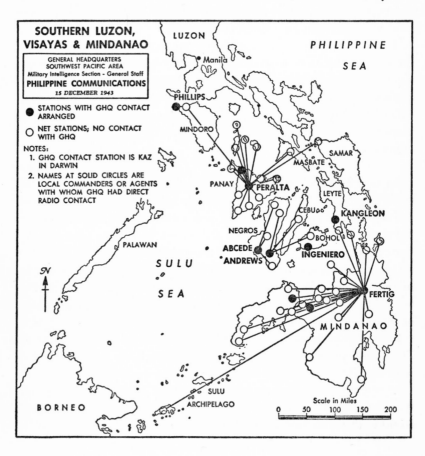

complete refutation of the charge that MacArthur was dealing with a "collaborator" when he kept Roxas in power after 1945. Roxas was "our" man all the time.

There were other raids into Japanese territory by other intrepid men. With the invasion of the Philippines just around the corner, Whitney's directives to the guerrillas wove their activities into the pattern of our landings.

Chick Parsons was dispatched to Leyte to alert Kangleon and to coordinate guerrilla sabotage, to clear the landing beaches and arrange for increased intelligence of Japanese dispositions. It was a great test of guerrilla organization and discipline, to hang on to villages along the landing beaches until H-hour, in a casual manner that would not give the show away to the nervous Japanese garrisons, and then to fade into the country as the first silhouettes of American warships appeared in Leyte Gulf.

The enormous volume of valuable military information sent by the guerrilla units to general headquarters constituted as important a contribution as their direct combat efforts. Perhaps the best—and certainly the most authentic—recapitulation of the rise of the guerrilla movement and the role it played in the liberation was given by General MacArthur himself. This is what he said shortly after the landing in Leyte:

As our forces of liberation roll forward the splendid aid we are receiving from guerrilla units throughout the immediate objective area and adjacent islands causes me at this time to pay public tribute to those great patriots both Filipino and American who had led and supported the resistance movement in the Philippines since the dark days of 1942. These inadequately armed patriots have fought the enemy for more than two years. Most are Filipinos but among these are a number of Americans who never surrendered, who escaped from prison camps, or who were sent in to carry out specific missions. . . .

In [the resistance] I recognized the spontaneous movement of the Filipino people to resist the shackles with which the enemy sought to bind them both physically and spiritually. I saw a people in one of the most tragic hours of human history, bereft of all reason for hope and without material support, endeavoring, despite the stern realities confronting them, to hold aloft the flaming torch of liberty. . . .

10 Leyte: MacArthur Beyond His Air Cover

EVER since Buna, which first established the Allies on the northern side of New Guinea in early 1943, MacArthur kept his planning staff busy with "Reno," a master plan for winning the war in the Far East. Reno underwent several sharp modifications, becoming Reno II, III, IV, and V as the Allies leapfrogged along New Guinea to the west. But one premise controlled Reno in all its phases—the premise that seizure of the Philippines would sever the main south-north artery of supply to Japanese factories and thus end the war with a minimum of loss and risk.

In all the various implementations of Reno, MacArthur stuck to one other basic premise: that the jump to the Philippines should take place under cover of his own land-based bombers. This meant a landing on Mindanao, covered by Kenney's air force from Morotai in the Halmaheras, the archipelago which is 300 miles across the Celebes Sea from the Philippines. There were other good reasons for landing on Mindanao—the island was large, it was lightly held, and Col. Wendell Fertig's local guerrilla forces were well-organized and active. But the controlling reason for choosing it was the safe assurance of air-cover for the invasion troops.

To the U.S. Navy, however, the Philippines seemed a distraction from the Navy's own Central Pacific axis of advance. And in mid-1944, after the great carrier raids on Palau and Truk and the capture of Saipan by the Marines, the Navy pressed upon the White House with its plan for bypassing the Philippines entirely in favor of a landing on Formosa.

When he had received an intimation of this plan from Admiral Nimitz in early 1944, MacArthur had reacted instantaneously against it. Nimitz's version of his March 25–27 meeting with MacArthur in Brisbane is contained in a letter to Admiral King: "Everything was lovely and harmonious until the last day of our conference when I called attention to the last part of the . . . directive which required of him and me to prepare alternate plans for moving faster and along shorter routes towards the Luzon-Formosa-China triangle . . . he [MacArthur] then blew up and made an oration of some length on the impossibility of bypassing the Philippines, his sacred obligations there—redemption of the 17 million people—blood on his soul—deserted by the American people, etc., etc. . . ."

The imputation of emotionalism contained in Nimitz's report to King will hardly survive a realistic look at the map of the Pacific. As MacArthur so soundly perceived, the Philippines represented too large and powerful a land mass to be bypassed with any assurance of safety, and Formosa itself offered a paucity of good landing beaches. But more importantly, the Formosa plan seemed a "Solomonic" notion, taken without regard for the infant—in this case the feelings of 17,000,000 Filipino allies who would continue to play an important political role in Asia after the war had been won. MacArthur kept urging his own views on the War Department by cable, but the Navy had the more effective representation in Washington, where it was within telephone call of the "sailor" President.

Without warning or explanation, the General received a summons in June to confer with the President at Pearl Harbor. He left his post promptly and took only one aide, Gen. Bonner Fellers, along. He was emphatically not informed that the purpose of the meeting involved a full-dress argument of retaking the Philippines vis-à-vis Formosa. The Navy team, playing on its home grounds, had easily available a tremendous paraphernalia of maps, statistics, and other visual aids. MacArthur had only his personality, his prodigious memory, and a complete grasp of tactical and strategical realities.

Upon his return to Australia, MacArthur described the Pearl Harbor meeting to his staff in some detail:

President Roosevelt stated the general purpose of the Conference was to determine the next phase of action against Japan. One plan was to attack Formosa and by-pass the Philippines. The other was to liberate the Philippines and by-pass Formosa.

Admiral Nimitz favored and presented the first plan. I favored the second, based not only on strategic but psychological grounds. Militarily, I felt and stated that if I could secure the Philippines it would enable us to clamp an air and naval blockade on the flow of all supplies from the south to Japan and thus, by paralyzing her industries, force her to early capitulation. Psychologically, I argued that it was not only a moral obligation to release this friendly possession from the enemy now that it had become possible, but that to fail to do so would not be understandable to the Oriental mind.

In Japan, I held that it would be symbolical to all that Japan had failed and was doomed. Not to do so, moreover, would result in death to the thousands of prisoners, including American women, children and men civilians held in Philippine concentration camps.

To by-pass isolated islands was one thing, but to leave in your rear such a large enemy concentration supported by an entire country's resources such as the Philippines involved serious and unnecessary risks. I assured the President I felt confident of success if he adopted the plan. Admiral Leahy seemed to support what I said.

The President accepted my recommendations and approved the Philippines plan.

MacArthur, who not only believed in but practiced "unity of the services," had this to say of the Navy:

I spoke of the high esteem and extraordinary admiration I felt for Admiral Nimitz and his naval associates, but I argued against the naval concept of frontal assault against the strongly held island positions of the enemy in the Western Pacific such as Saipan, Iwo Jima and Okinawa. I felt our losses would be far too heavy for the benefits to be gained by seizing these outposts. They were not essential to the enemy's defeat and by cutting them off from supplies they could be easily reduced and their effectiveness completely neutralized with negligible loss to ourselves. They were not in themselves possessed of sufficient resources to act as main bases in our advance.

Likewise I felt that Formosa with a hostile population might prove doubtful to serve as a base of attack against Japan itself. I was also critical of what I regarded as a major blunder in originally abandoning all effort to relieve the Philippines. I stated that had we had the will to do so, we could have opened the way to reinforce Bataan and Corregidor garrisons and probably not only saved the Philippines but thereby stopped the enemy's advance eastward toward New Guinea and Australia. I felt that to sacrifice the Philippines a second time would not be condoned or forgiven.

I was shocked at the personal appearance of President Roosevelt. I had not seen him for a number of years and he had failed immeasurably. I predict that he will be dead within the year.

Actually, the President died ten months later. How true also was General MacArthur's estimate of the slaughter our forces were to sustain in the various island attacks in the Marianas and Ryukus, and how indifferent was their contribution to the final victory in proportion to the sacrifice and effort expended in their capture.

President Roosevelt and General MacArthur were old friends, the General having served for three years as his Army Chief of Staff. Despite their many differences with reference to national policy, each man held the other in high esteem. It has been often told how the President frequently brought up matters to the General, when he was Chief of Staff, having nothing to do with military affairs. When MacArthur seemed puzzled, the President said: "Douglas, I don't bring these questions up for your advice but for your reactions. To me, you are the symbol of the conscience of the American people." This silenced the General.

MacArthur did not present anything new to Roosevelt at the Pearl Harbor meeting. He had already stated his case to the War Department:

. . . purely military considerations demand the reoccupation of the Philippines in order to cut the enemy's communications to the south and secure a base for further advance. Even if this were not the case, it would be necessary to reoccupy the Islands. It is American territory where our unsupported forces were destroyed by the enemy. Practically all of the 17,000,000 Filipinos remain loyal to the United States and are undergoing the greatest privations and sufferings because we have not been able to support or succor them; we have a great national obligation to discharge. I feel that a decision to eliminate the relief of the Philippines would cause extremely adverse reactions among the citizens of the United States. The American people, I am sure, would acknowledge this obligation.

The Pearl Harbor conference finally settled the issue between MacArthur and the Navy, and a landing on Mindanao was ordered forthwith. Having carried the day with the President, MacArthur set his staff to work on a complete plan for the reconquest of the Islands under the new code name "Musketeer," which took off from Reno V. This was developed in three objective phases—Musketeer I for Mindanao, Musketeer II for Leyte, and Musketeer III for Luzon. The planning called for a prodigious dovetailing of preparations, since the staging would have to come from West Coast American ports and the islands of the Central Pacific as well as from all along the New Guinea coast. Maps were prepared; terrain studies were made ready for the troops; the garnering of information from the guerrilla network was coordinated with the findings of the Allied Geographical Section detailing airfields, landing beaches, and roads. And, to support the assault forces, a special Army Service Command was set up under Pat Casey.

In giving air support for the operations against Morotai in the Halmaheras, which brought MacArthur within easy reach of the Philippines, the carrier-borne aircraft of Admiral Halsey's Third Fleet hit many Mindanao airfields. To Halsey's surprise, Japanese response seemed weak. Further probing disclosed that Kenney's bombers operating out of New Guinea had caused severe damage to Japanese air installations on Mindanao. This encouraged Halsey to push his carriers northward on September 9–12 to raid the Visayas, the islands of the central Philippines. Again the enemy response was relatively feeble. While the possibility could not be discounted that Japanese planes could be staged-in to Philippine fields from Formosa or Japan itself in the event of a major move by the Americans, Halsey leaped to a conclusion: Mindanao might be bypassed in favor of a Leyte landing. Accordingly, he shot a message to Nimitz on September 13 in Hawaii. Nimitz quickly forwarded the dispatch to Quebec, where the Joint Chiefs of Staff happened to be sitting with Roosevelt and Churchill. Halsey's suggestions were several: one was to call off the projected assault on Yap for the moment, another was to advance the target date for the Philippines and to hit at Leyte in October.

Knowing that MacArthur was wrapped up in "Musketeer," which presumably had Mindanao as its major concern, General Marshall hesitated; planning could not normally be switched overnight. But when Marshall queried MacArthur, he got back a quick answer: "I am prepared to move immediately on Leyte, with target date of October 20th. . . ." Musketeer II had taken care of the planning already.

The sequence of events leading up to Leyte has been described by General Marshall:

MacArthur . . . advised us that he was already prepared to shift his plans. . . . It was a remarkable administrative achievement. The message from MacArthur arrived at Quebec at night, while [we] were being entertained at a formal dinner by Canadian officers . . . we left the table for a conference. Having the utmost confidence in General MacArthur, Admiral Nimitz and Admiral Halsey, it was not a difficult decision to make. Within ninety minutes after the signal had been received in Quebec, General MacArthur and Admiral Nimitz had received their instructions to execute the Leyte operation on 20 October, abandoning the three previously approved intermediate landings.

Roosevelt's own commendation of MacArthur's flexibility came in due course in a State of the Union message:

. . . within the space of twenty-four hours, a major change of plans was accomplished which involved Army and Navy Forces from two different theatres of operations—a change which hastened the liberation of the Philippines and the final day of victory—a change which saved lives which would have been expended in the capture of islands which are now neutralized far behind our lines.

This Rooseveltian summary happened to be a capsule appraisal of MacArthur's lifesaving system of the flank maneuver as compared to the expensive frontal collisions involved in Central Pacific "island hopping."

The switch from Mindanao to Leyte was a great idea for which Halsey and the MacArthur planners of Musketeer II can share the credit. By thrusting into the Visayas, the large central archipelago of the Philippines, MacArthur put himself in a position to roll up both flanks of the Japanese occupation forces. But before Leyte could be exploited, MacArthur's men had to fight with a desperation they had not known since Buna. It was a struggle which narrowly skirted disaster as the Japanese, making a belated decision once the American intentions were known, threw everything they had—army, air force, even the mysterious monster battleships, the 64,000-ton *Yamato* and *Musashi*—into the fight. The Japanese knew Leyte was "it." As Lt. Gen. Shuichi Miyazaki, G-3 Japanese Imperial General Headquarters, put it:

. . . viewed from the standpoint of political and operational strategy, holding the Philippines was the one essential. . . . With the loss of these islands, Japanese communications with the Southern region would be severely threatened. The loss of the Philippines would greatly affect civilian morale in Japan. The islands were essential as a strategic base for the enemy advance on Japan. After their recapture, the advantage would be two to one in favor of the Americans.

Leyte began favorably enough on October 17 with the seizure, amidst cyclonic storms and heavy seas, of the small islands which guarded the eastern approaches to Leyte Gulf. Then, on October 20, came the great day—the massing off the Leyte beaches of the largest fleet of transports, assault craft, and warships ever concentrated in the Pacific. The main landings came at ten in the morning on an 18-mile front, with corps abreast, the X Corps to the north and the XXIV in the south. The landing beaches had been softened by two days of air and naval bombardment. The MacArthur records contain a reference to the Japanese sector commander, General Tomochika, and what happened to his troops:

. . . the 16th Division Artillery Regiment, along the first line of defense, was subjected to a severe naval bombardment which destroyed a great number of its field pieces. Radio telegraphic communications within the Regiment, with the 35th Corps and the 14th Army in Manila, were disrupted [and never re-established]. Direct liaison with smaller units of the Division was no longer effective.

Close behind the troops, in a drenching tropical downpour, MacArthur strode ashore on a muddy beach near the town of Palo. Following him from an LST came little Col. Carlos Romulo, the Filipino patriot who had been the Voice of Freedom on Corregidor and the last escapee from Bataan. Recalling the day at a later date, Romulo said jocularly:

The newspapers reported that I was right behind him. Little did they realize that I nearly drowned. There was the tall MacArthur, with the waters reaching up to his knees, and behind him there was little Romulo, trying to keep his head above water.

This relaxed mood of Romulo's was something distinctly after the fact. On that particular October 20 of the landing at Leyte, MacArthur struck a gravely exalted note that evoked a kindred response throughout every part of the islands. To millions of waiting Filipinos he spoke over a portable radio transmitter:

This is the Voice of Freedom, General MacArthur speaking. . . . I have returned. By the grace of Almighty God, our forces stand again on Philippine soil. . . . At my side is your President, Sergio Osmena, worthy successor of that great patriot, Manuel Quezon. . . . The seat of your Government is now therefore firmly re-established on Philippine soil.

The hour of your redemption is here. Your patriots have demonstrated an unswerving and resolute devotion to the principles of freedom that challenges the best that is written on the pages of human history. I now call upon your supreme effort that the enemy may know from the temper of an aroused and outraged people within, that he has a force there to contend with no less violent than is the force committed from without.

Rally to me. Let the indomitable spirit of Bataan and Corregidor lead on. As the lines of battle roll forward to bring you within the zone of operations, rise and strike! For future generations of your sons and daughters, strike! In the name of your sacred dead, strike! Let no heart be faint. Let every arm be steeled. The guidance of Divine God points the way. Follow in His name to the Holy Grail of righteous victory!

Even while he was urging the Filipinos to rise and strike, MacArthur was concerned lest his own forces bring unnecessary hardships to the faithful islanders. To his own air and naval commanders he issued a warning note:

One of the purposes of the Philippine campaign is to liberate the Filipinos; they will not understand liberation if accomplished by indiscriminate destruction of their homes, their civilization and their lives. Humanity and our moral standing throughout the Far East dictate that destruction of lives and property in the Philippines be held to a minimum, compatible with the assurance of a successful campaign.

MacArthur was even more apprehensive of the danger inherent in the military taking over civil administration. He warned the War Department:

It is essential in any plans for the control of civil affairs that the measure of freedom and liberty given to the Filipino people be at least comparable to that enjoyed under the Commonwealth Government before the war. It would be a matter of gravest concern if restrictions were imposed. If any impressions were created that the United States is curtailing rather than expanding liberties, the most unfortunate repercussions might be expected. . . . I repeat, utmost care should be taken that an imperialistic attitude not be introduced into the situation under the guise of military necessity. This would be entirely alien to the spirit of recent legislation passed by the Congress.

So the struggle for Leyte began under the best of humanitarian auspices as far as a free Filipino Commonwealth was concerned. During the first day's fighting on Leyte the 1st Cavalry Division, supported by tanks, seized Tacloban Airfield, the most important early objective. While the Japanese had anticipated the landings to the south at Dulag, they were not prepared for a direct assault on Tacloban; indeed, they felt so secure in this region that they had even located their Division headquarters there. General Tomochika said:

We had misestimated the location of the initial enemy landings and consequently our defense in the area was very weak. We had estimated that there was a greater possibility of an enemy landing in the Dulag area since it was at the entrance to Leyte Gulf, instead of at Tacloban which was almost at the upper extreme end of the Gulf. The strategy employed by the enemy in landing at our weak spots can be attributed to the splendid intelligence system of the enemy, aided at times by the guerrilla agents [Whitney's] who had infiltrated into our lines and had sent out vital information concerning our troops' dispositions.

While Tacloban, with its important airfield, was being nailed down by the 1st Cavalry Division, the 24th Division seized Hill 522, a strategic height dominating the whole landing-beach area near Palo, the town of MacArthur's "return." To quote from the General's Tokyo records:

As this hill commanded both the highway system and the beaches, the Japanese had fortified it with trenches, caves, and cleverly concealed emplacements that would offer serious opposition to an attacking force. A slight but serious miscalculation on the part of the enemy, however, enabled the 24th Division to seize the hill with a minimum of loss. The severity of the naval, air and artillery bombardment had forced the Japanese to leave their guns and take temporary refuge in the safer ground below. As soon as the shelling stopped, they began their move back up the slopes to reoccupy their commanding positions and open fire on the advancing Americans. They were too late. So swift was the progress of the invading forces, that troops of the 24th Division were already on the crest of the hill to meet and destroy the returning enemy.

In personal command of the landings, MacArthur summarized the initial accomplishment of the invasion:

In a major amphibious operation we have seized the eastern coast of Leyte Island in the Philippines, 600 miles north of Morotai and 2,500 miles from Milne Bay from whence our offensive started almost 24 months ago. . . . The strategic result of capturing the Philippines will be decisive. The enemy's so-called Greater East Asia Co-Prosperity

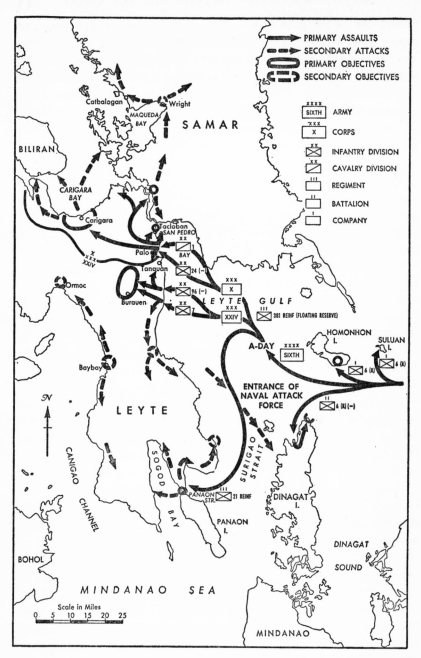

PRIMARY ASSAULTS
SECONDARY ATTACKS
PRIMARY OBJECTIVES
SECONDARY OBJECTIVES

SIXTH — ARMY
X — CORPS
— INFANTRY DIVISION
— CAVALRY DIVISION
— REGIMENT
— BATTALION
— COMPANY

Catbalogan
Wright
MAQUEDA BAY
SAMAR
BILIRAN
CARIGARA BAY
Carigara
Tacloban
SAN PEDRO
BAY
Palo
1
XXIV
Tanauan
24 (−)
96 (−)
X
Buraven
7
LEYTE GULF
XXIV
381 REINF (FLOATING RESERVE)
Ormoc
HOMONHON I.
SULUAN I.
A-DAY
SIXTH
6 (R)
6 (R)
Baybay
ENTRANCE OF NAVAL ATTACK FORCE
6 (R) (−)
N
LEYTE
CANIGAO CHANNEL
SOGOD BAY
SURIGAO STRAIT
DINAGAT I.
PANAON STR.
21 REINF
PANAON I.
DINAGAT SOUND
BOHOL
MINDANAO SEA
DINAGAT
Scale in Miles
0 5 10 15 20 25
MINDANAO

The Leyte assault

Sphere will be cut in two. . . . The great flow of transportation and supply upon which Japan's vital war industry depends will be cut as will the counter supply of his forces to the south. A half million men will be cut off without hope of support and with ultimate destruction at the leisure of the Allies a certainty . . . the defensive line of the Japanese which extends along the coast of Asia from the Japan islands . . . to Singapore and Burma will be pierced at the center, permitting an envelopment to the south and to the north.

While the Americans on Leyte were rushing to put Tacloban Airfield into shape and widening their Dulag beachhead to include another air strip, the Japanese General Staff was preparing to stake its whole remaining power on a gigantic gamble to throw Mac-Arthur out of the Philippines. Brilliantly conceived and immense in scope, the Japanese plan was to deliver a crippling attack against the U.S. Navy and to isolate and destroy MacArthur at his beachheads. The Japanese were willing to risk their entire fleet to bring their cruisers and battleships within target range of MacArthur's supply transports clustered thickly in Leyte Gulf. Admiral Soemu Toyoda, Commander in Chief of the Combined Japanese Fleet, was entirely aware of the chances he was taking:

. . . without the participation of the Combined Fleet, there was no possibility of the land-based forces in the Philippines having any chance against [the Americans]. It was decided to take the gamble and send the whole Fleet. If things went well, we might obtain unexpectedly good results; if the worst should happen, there was the chance that we would lose the entire fleet. . . . Should we lose in the Philippines, the shipping lanes to the south would be completely cut off so that the Fleet could not obtain its fuel supply. If it should remain in southern waters it could not receive supplies of arms and ammunition.

Long before the actual battle for Leyte Gulf, evidence began to accumulate in intelligence channels that defined the dispositions of the bulk of the Japanese Navy. The earliest information came with the capture of the "Z" operations orders of the Japanese Combined Fleet on March 8, 1944. From then on all Japanese ship movements were kept under close surveillance. As early as October 16 the heaviest concentration of Japanese fleet units was spotted in the Singapore-Brunei area; the remainder of the ships were in Japanese home waters and at Formosa. By way of intercepts MacArthur's G-2 had some knowledge of Japanese plans for combined inter-dependent Army, Navy and Air actions under the code name of "Sho" Operations. Sho I applied to the Philippines; Sho II to Formosa, the Ryukus, and Kyushu. The main theme of the Sho planning was to bring the various forces of the Japanese fleet from Singapore, Formosa, and the Japanese Inland Sea to bear simultaneously against any American landing flotilla. This called for Nelsonian naval maneuvering from distant quarters of the compass, all timed to coincide with intensified air attacks and ground reinforcements to wipe out American beachheads.

Sho I was activated on October 18, two days before the American landings on Leyte. Details of the Japanese plan were diagnosed in part during the first week in October; and as D-Day approached the MacArthur staff journals contained daily intercepts of the Sho planning progress.

October 14: A Japanese naval force consisting of Admiral Shima's minor units, was to sortie from the Inland Sea at 2400 hrs.

October 15: A U.S. submarine sighted Shima's force on a southeasterly course, just off Bungo Channel at 8 A.M.

October 16: A force of major units under Admiral Takeo Kurita, in the Singapore area, was preparing for a future sortie.

October 20: A Japanese 10,000-ton tanker, a repair ship and a coastal defense vessel were en route to Coron Bay.

October 22: Admiral Ozawa's carrier force was at sea in the Formosa area moving probably toward the P.I.

With this background of "special intelligence" (gleaned from intercepts, submarines, and air spotters), the coast watchers and certain "picket" submarines were alerted. On October 22 three large Japanese warships were reported in Palawan Passage to the west of the Philippines on a northern course. On the 23d the submarine *Darter* sighted "three probable battleships" on the same course. The U.S.S. *Bream* sighted more units the same day and launched a torpedo attack. The U.S.S. *Dace*, assigned to cover Balabac Strait between Borneo and Palawan, reported a force of eleven ships, including battleships. It, too, launched a torpedo attack. These were the first actual blows struck at sea in the battle for Leyte Gulf.

On October 24 the various pieces of the Japanese naval puzzle were falling into place. Early that morning continuous submarine sightings were reported from Palawan Passage—a major grouping of fifteen to twenty ships. A few hours later the submarines *Angler* and *Guitarro* reported this force heading south through Mindoro Strait; this fleet, designated thereafter by our side as Kurita's "Central Force," contained the monster battleships *Yamato* and *Musashi*; by its course around Mindoro it seemed destined for San Bernardino Strait, to the north of Leyte and Samar.

On the same day, American aircraft sighted a second enemy fleet off Cagayan Island, on a course which suggested entry into the Mindanao Sea and subsequent debouchment into Leyte Gulf via Surigao Strait. This "Southern Force," under Admiral Nishimura, showed enough strength in battleships and cruisers to mark it as a major task formation. Admiral Shima's smaller group followed Nishimura's force some fifty miles astern.

From the number and types of enemy warships moving through Philippine waters, it was apparent to MacArthur that the Japanese were launched on a full-scale pincer operation swinging around Leyte at both ends to destroy him. His G-2 estimated the enemy's capabilities at the time:

. . . a Japanese task force in the Sulu Sea, heading for the Mindanao Sea, presumably either to bring reinforcements to Leyte or make a surface attack through Surigao Strait against the southern flank of our supply line.

. . . Two forces sighted at noon on a southeast course in the Sibuyan Sea. It is considered possible that this force may proceed through San Bernardino Straits to attack our Leyte position from the north.

. . . no carriers have been reported in either of these sightings, leaving the enemy the capability of bringing his carriers down the east coast of Luzon to support the possible attacks of his converging forces in the Leyte Area.

However, it is considered probable that the carriers [are] deployed in the vicinity of Mindoro, in order that their planes may strike across the Central Philippines, possibly staging through shore bases in the Visayas. . . .

This "estimate" proved to be generally—and unfortunately—correct; MacArthur's staff did not "spot" the Japanese carriers correctly (they were off to the north in the Philippine Sea), but the employment of their planes, which flew from land bases, was soon to be felt in the anticipated way.

In the looming fight for Leyte, MacArthur's position was a strangely uncomfortable one. Throughout his campaign in New Guinea, every advance of Krueger's Sixth Army, or the so-called "Alamo Force," had been predicated on securing air bases at intervals of 300 miles, from which further advances could be made under a guaranteed air umbrella. Now, for the first time, the General was compelled to send his troops into a landing area without the protection of his own controlled air coverage.

MacArthur understood the inherent dangers perfectly. While still afloat off the landing beaches he was stunned by a tentative request of Halsey's regarding the possible withdrawal of fleet units from the Leyte operations. Said Halsey:

My present operations to meet the threat of enemy fleet forces are somewhat restricted by necessity of covering your transports and other overseas movements. Request early advice regarding withdrawal of such units to safe positions, which will permit me to execute orderly rearming program for my groups and allow further offensive operations. . . .

Within minutes a reply to Halsey crackled through the night; it defined the problem and it forecast what was about to happen very shortly:

The basic plan for this operation in which for the first time I have moved beyond my own land-based air cover was predicated upon full support by the Third Fleet. Such cover is being expedited by every possible measure, but until accomplished our mass of shipping is subject to enemy air and surface raiding during this critical period. Consider your mission to cover this operation is essential and paramount. . . .

As MacArthur's G-2 commented on Oct. 22, before a shot had been fired:

> There is no question that the Leyte position is vulnerable to the extent of U.S. Fleet availability; it is essential that its presence is continuous in adjacent waters, east of the Philippines, to interpose continuously between our land operations and possible enemy fleet intervention—which is essentially the primary mission of our Fleet. . . .

When the pattern of the Japanese naval pincer movement through the straits of San Bernardino to the north and Surigao to the south became plain, Admiral Kinkaid dispatched almost the whole of his Seventh Fleet gunnery and torpedo force to Surigao under Rear Admiral J. B. Oldendorf. The battleships at Oldendorf's command were the so-called "Old Battleships"—the ghosts that had risen to life from the mud at Pearl Harbor. (Halsey, to the north, had the more modern battleships.) Disposing his antique battlewagons—the *Pennsylvania*, the *California*, the *Tennessee*, the *Mississippi*, the *Maryland*, and the *West Virginia*—to form the horizontal bar of a "T" of vast fire power, which the enemy coming through Surigao was forced to approach vertically, Oldendorf prepared his ambush.

It worked perfectly. The Japanese Admiral Nishimura steamed blindly ahead, past PT-boat attacks and a destroyer torpedo attack from off his port bows. Coming out at Surigao's exit into Leyte Gulf, Nishimura ran head-on into the Old Battleships, which opened fire at 21,000 yards. Within a matter of minutes Nishimura's fleet was crippled; the Admiral himself went down with his flagship, the *Yamashiro*. Only one destroyer, the *Shigura*, survived the American torpedos and armor-piercing shells. Admiral Shima, who had been trailing the Japanese Southern Force, could see the flare of gunfire in the distance. After brief blinker contact with the single surviving destroyer, he turned tail and ran for Coron Bay.

The battle for Surigao Strait had ended; there could be no further threat to MacArthur's landing forces from the south. Kinkaid, who was subject to MacArthur's order, had performed his mission with precision and effectiveness.

The story was not the same up north, where free passage through San Bernardino Strait was a pivotal point of the enemy's strategy to

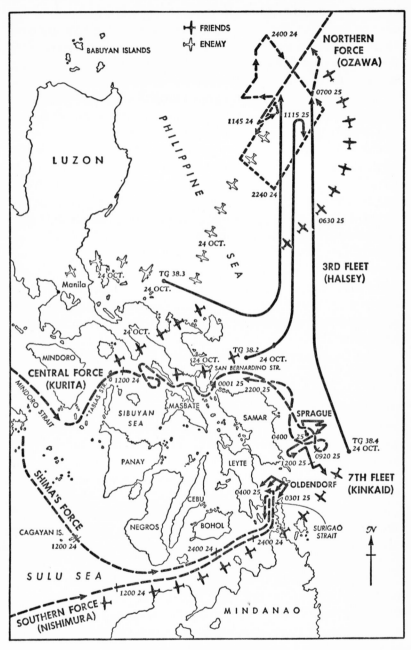

Navy battle for Leyte Gulf

get into Leyte Gulf. Through the morning and afternoon of October 24 Kurita's Central Force, the strongest of the Japanese naval groupings, pushed on through the narrow, reef-filled waters of the Sibuyan Sea. Planes from Halsey's Third Fleet carriers kept hammering him. They made an important strike on the *Musashi*, displacing about 75,000 tons and armed with the heaviest guns afloat. The Japanese Navy had kept details of design of these super-battleships a close secret for years—a remarkable example of security discipline. At 8:10 A.M., Halsey's scout planes spotted Kurita's ships and at 10:25 A.M. American carrier craft swept in for bombing attacks. This was repeated at intervals of about two hours. Badly hit at 1315 hours, the huge ship fell astern of the fleet formation. She remained afloat until 1935 hours when she sank. Besides the loss of the *Musashi*, the Japanese Central Force suffered other damage; the *Yamato*, sister ship of the *Musashi*, was hit; a heavy cruiser was crippled. Kurita, who was operating without air cover, prudently reversed his course. Overoptimistic American pilots reported this reversal as a "retirement"—but Kurita crossed them up after their departure by turning around again and heading once more for San Bernardino Strait.

Misled by his airmen, Halsey apparently eliminated Kurita's Central Force from his calculations and concentrated on reports that a big Japanese carrier force was moving through the Philippine Sea from Luzon. This was Admiral Ozawa's force. Actually, Ozawa had virtually denuded himself of planes; he had sent them to Luzon to operate from shore bases. The Ozawa carrier fleet had only one mission—to decoy the most powerful units of the U.S. Fleet from the Leyte area. To carry out his mission Ozawa was ordered to risk his own destruction.

Falling for the Japanese decoy, "Bull" Halsey pulled his three complete task groups together for a run to the north to intercept Ozawa. As he later explained his action:

1. I could guard San Bernardino with my whole fleet and wait for the Northern Force to strike me. Rejected. It yielded to the enemy the double initiative of his carriers and his fields on Luzon and would allow him to use them unmolested. 2. I could guard San Bernardino with TF 34 while I struck the Northern Force with my carriers. Re-

jected. The enemy's potential surface and air strength forbade half-measures; if his shore-based planes joined his carrier planes, together they might inflict far more damage on my half fleets separately than they could inflict on the fleet intact. 3. I could leave San Bernardino unguarded and strike the Northern Force with my whole fleet. Accepted. It preserved my fleet's integrity, it left the initiative with me, and it promised the greatest possibility of surprise. Even if the Central Force meanwhile penetrated San Bernardino and headed for Leyte Gulf, it could hope only to harry the landing operation.

Halsey's move to the north with all his ships—the "battle of Bull's Run"—left San Bernardino Strait wide open. It was to be more than "harrying," in Halsey's optimistic forecast. Kurita slipped through the darkness of San Bernardino in a remarkable feat of high-speed navigation. By midnight he had emerged into the Philippine Sea. Despite the loss of the *Musashi* he still had a formidable force of four battleships, six heavy cruisers, two light cruisers, and eleven destroyers.

Between this on-coming force and MacArthur's landing craft there stood only the "baby" or "jeep" carriers under Admiral Thomas L. Sprague. The most advanced "jeep" group, the one which collided with Kurita, was commanded by another Sprague, Rear Admiral Clifton A. F. Sprague. Becoming uneasy about San Bernardino Strait in the dark hours of the morning, MacArthur prodded Admiral Kinkaid to locate Halsey. At 0412 hours the vital question was asked: "Is Task Force 34 guarding San Bernardino Strait?" The answer, in the negative, was not sent until 0704 hours. By this time the first salvos from Kurita's ships were sounding across the waters off Samar, to the northeast of Leyte.

It was an ominous situation, and all the portents were of disaster. Should the enemy reach Leyte Gulf, his big guns could pulverize any of the transports and supply ships still waiting to unload or standing about. Halsey was almost 300 miles away in hot pursuit of a group of planeless Japanese carriers. The Old Battleships, still far to the south, had used up their armor-piercing ammunition. On shore, MacArthur was powerless; his staff was frantic. The final blow came when a pilot announced a large enemy surface group closing in on our jeep carriers at a speed of 30 knots. At 0658 hours the 18-

inch guns of the *Yamato* opened fire—the heaviest caliber fire ever encountered by U.S. naval vessels. Clifton Sprague's light carriers were straddled with dye-marked salvos that bracketed their targets with red, green, yellow, and blue splashes. Along with the surface attacks, Japanese shore-based air units launched the first great kamikaze, or suicide, strikes. In his extremity Kinkaid sent Halsey another frantic message: "Urgently needed fast battleships Leyte Gulf at once."

Clifton Sprague's escort carriers tried all the tricks of sea fighting to minimize the heavy Japanese fire. Destroyers closed in to suicidal range and fired 5-inch guns and torpedoes at cruisers and battleships. Thick smoke screens were laid down; refuges were sought in tropical squalls of rain. Pilots in the air fought to ammunition exhaustion —and when they saw their carrier decks torn open or their ships foundering they made forced landings on the already overcrowded Tacloban air strip. Many of them had to ditch their planes in the sea.

While the fight was going on, Kinkaid sent message after message to Halsey: "Under attack by cruisers and battleships . . . request immediate air strikes," and (this time in the clear) "Where is Lee? Send Lee." (Lee was Halsey's battleship commander.) Following the whole fight at an agonizing distance in Hawaii, Nimitz capped it all by a rhetorical dispatch: "The whole world wants to know where is Task Force 34."

With the escort carriers *Saint Lo* and *Gambier Bay*, the destroyers *Johnston* and *Hoel* and the destroyer escort *S. B. Roberts* sunk, it looked as if the whole U.S. escort carrier and transport fleets were doomed. But just at this moment, as if by a miracle, the Japanese Admiral Kurita suddenly and inexplicably broke off the engagement. Admiral Clifton Sprague summed it up a few days later:

. . . the failure of the enemy main body and encircling light forces to completely wipe out all vessels of this Task Unit can be attributed to our successful smoke screen, our torpedo counterattack . . . and the definite partiality of Almighty God.

The successive dispatches from Kinkaid and Nimitz finally forced Halsey to turn most of his fleet southward toward Leyte. But he was not to fire a shot. Kurita managed to slip back through San Bernardino Strait and make good his escape.

Admiral Halsey's dispatch on the day of the jeep carriers' agony contrasts with Admiral Sprague's humble words about God's "partiality":

To prevent any misunderstanding concerning recent Third Fleet operations, I inform you as follows: . . . merely to guard San Bernardino Strait while the enemy was coordinating his surface and carrier air force would be time wasted, so three carrier groups were . . . moved north for a surprise dawn attack on the carrier fleet; estimated the enemy force in the Sibuyan Sea too damaged to threaten Seventh Fleet, a deduction proved correct by events of 25 October off Surigao. . . . Commander Seventh Fleet sent urgent appeal for assistance just when my overwhelming force was within 45 miles of the crippled enemy; no alternative but to head south in response to call, although I was convinced his opponents were badly damaged from our attack of 24 October, a conviction later justified by events off Leyte.

The "events off Leyte" to which Halsey so cavalierly referred were the free entry of Kurita into the Leyte area. If Kurita had not lost his nerve, or become confused, or misestimated the ability of Oldendorf to arrive in Leyte Gulf in time (and with ammunition), the complete destruction of MacArthur's transports would have brought the battle to a disastrous conclusion.

The Japanese themselves had a rational explanation for the decision to break off the engagement. Interviewed after the war, Rear Admiral Koyanagi, Kurita's chief of staff, said:

One reason was that the Second Diversion Attack Force [Admiral Shima] reported the almost complete destruction of Admiral Nishimura's force. . . . The second reason was that Nishimura's force meant to go into the Bay in the morning and our force was to have entered at 0600 to coordinate but the approach of our force was greatly delayed. After the battle off Samar we finally decided that the cooperation of the two forces would not be effected at all, and if we ever decided to go into the Bay, the interval would be too much. The third reason, we intercepted a telephone message sent by your carrier to get reinforcements. We also intercepted an answer to the telephone call to the effect that it would be two hours before reinforcements of planes arrived; that is to say by the time we entered this Bay. We thought that planes would have come out and that warships would have come out and that the transports would have dispersed enough so that only a part would have been inside; they would escape from the danger zone. We figured by that time that the transports might have heard of the battle and started already in the morning. The fourth reason, we intercepted again a telephone message sent by carrier to the planes to the effect that all planes should go to Leyte shore strips; and also we thought reinforcement of the American carriers might come along and so your force would be very big, carriers and land-based planes, and it would not be advisable to go into this danger zone and be a target for attack by shore and reinforced carrier planes in narrow waters. The fifth reason, we surmised that your American Task Force might come down from the north; so after we failed to destroy this first American force, we thought that if we came back north now we might encounter another American Task Force, but we were very regretful that we failed to destroy your first American force. The sixth reason, if we continued the battle here at Leyte, it would consume more fuel; that was another reason for cruising north instead of staying around. We had no tankers anywhere around.

The rational explanation, however, cannot really cover Kurita's failure to make the most of his opportunity. For Leyte Gulf offered the "now or never" chance to defeat MacArthur at the very outset of his return to the Philippines. Once having lost this opportunity, the Japanese were never to get another one.

On land, while the battle for Leyte Gulf was being fought, Mac-Arthur's troops were without adequate air cover. The Japanese bombed and strafed from treetop level. They also landed 2,000 troop reinforcements from Cagayan under cover of the naval battle. One Japanese raid on the heavily congested Tacloban air strip destroyed 27 planes on the ground. The suicidal Japanese pilots sometimes followed American flight formations into the landing areas. The explosions of ammunition dumps and oil storage tanks were a nightly occurrence. Nor did Krueger's headquarters or Mac-Arthur's command post in Tacloban escape attention. Direct bomb hits were scored within a block of MacArthur's billet, Krueger's headquarters were struck on Thanksgiving Day, and tracer bullets ripped through MacArthur's office. When an aide pointed to the chipped wall, the General laughed and said: "The bullet that is designed for me has not been cast."

In response to a very recent question from Army Department

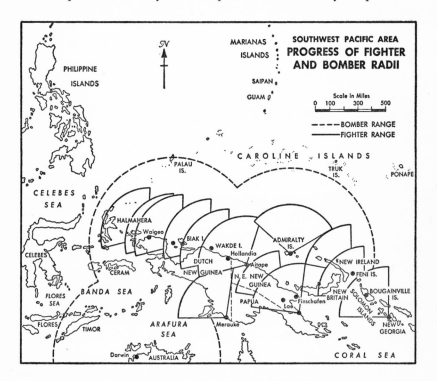

historians about the absence of a unified command in the Pacific, MacArthur made clear his feelings about the course of the battle for Leyte Gulf:

Of all the faulty decisions of the war, perhaps the most inexplicable one was the failure to unify the command in the Pacific. The principle involved is perhaps the most fundamental one in the doctrine and tradition of command. In this instance it did not involve an international problem. It was accepted and entirely successful in the other great theaters. The failure to do so in the Pacific cannot be defended in logic, in theory or even in common sense. Other motives must be ascribed. It resulted in divided effort, the waste of diffusion and duplication of force, undue extension of the war with added casualties and cost. The generally excellent cooperation between the two commands in the Pacific supported by the good will, good nature and professional qualifications of the numerous personnel involved was no substitute for the essential unity of direction of centralized authority. The handicaps and hazards unnecessarily resulting were numerous indeed but by way of illustration I will elucidate the one which produced the greatest jeopardy. It developed in the course of the Leyte landing.

It was suggested that if I moved direct on Leyte, naval air would cover me in landing. . . . The hop was double the usual distance and violated my basic concept never to risk having my ground forces uncovered from the air. Under the conditions, however, I decided on the movement. I believe this was probably the first time a ground commander ever placed his complete trust so absolutely in naval hands. . . . I was on the cruiser *Nashville* accompanying our convoys. It became evident to me that Halsey was too far to the north to properly cover the Gulf of Leyte and I so radioed Nimitz asking him to drop Halsey back. This would not only insure my base but would insure his fleet being in the action, as the magnetic attraction of my point of landing would draw the enemy's fleet there.

In the meantime, the enemy's forces acted with great skill and cunning . . . and moved on our base and rear naval echelons in the Bay off Tacloban. Probably two hundred or more vessels were there exposed. We instantly threw in our little flat tops, which gallantly and successfully repulsed the attacking Japanese forces. In doing so, however, the planes were practically destroyed and my potential air umbrella to protect my ground forces and operations disappeared. For the following month I was thereby in gravest danger, as the Japanese under General Yamashita regarded this as the crucial point of action. . . . Leyte came out all right, but the hazards would all have been avoided by unity of command.

Since Leyte "came out all right," MacArthur has been willing to let the event speak for itself. He even defended Halsey immediately after the battle for Leyte Gulf. When Halsey was being subjected to critical references by members of the MacArthur staff, Mac-

Arthur said: "Leave the Bull alone. He's still a fighting Admiral in my book."

The fury of the Japanese air attack, which persisted even after the defeat of the Japanese navy, made it abundantly clear that the fight for the Philippines was being waged at Leyte. Despite the Japanese commitment to make Leyte the win-or-lose fight for the Philippines, MacArthur managed to hold the initiative by constant pressure on all fronts. As Krueger's troops continued to drive inland, MacArthur decided on an amphibious landing, in rear of the Japanese positions, near Ormoc on the west coast of Leyte. On December 7, the third anniversary of Pearl Harbor, he got behind the Japanese at Deposito. The strategic implications of this were covered by MacArthur in words that were coming to have a familiar ring:

. . . by this maneuver we . . . have split the enemy forces in two. . . . Both segments are now caught between our columns. . . . The fighting in Ormoc itself before its fall was of the most desperate character, the entire defending garrison being destroyed.

After the war, when historians working under General Willoughby's editorial supervision in Tokyo were busy summing up phases of the four-year struggle, the Leyte victory seemed the place to pause for a long evaluation:

The battle for Leyte demonstrated to a greater degree than ever before in the Pacific war the coordinated striking power of the American land, air, and naval team. Despite heroic efforts and great courage, despite the use of unprecedented numbers of ships, planes and troops collected from all parts of their fast shrinking empire, the Japanese were unable to stand before the overwhelming drive of American combined arms.

The Japanese suffered complete defeat in the Leyte campaign. Every phase of their ambitious Sho plan for the defense of the Philippines met with complete and irretrievable failure. Driven to near panic by the threat of losing the Philippines, Japan's wartime leaders in Tokyo had risked their remaining offensive power in one last effort to save their empire. Whatever chance the Japanese had to regain the initiative in the Pacific was lost on Leyte.

In the largest and most widespread sea battle in history, Japan's naval power had been smashed. The losses sustained by the Japanese fleet are among the most staggering on record. After Leyte, Allied warships could sail with impunity anywhere in the Pacific. Japanese air power as an organized force also was destroyed in the Philippines. The employment of planes in suicide tactics not only reflected an extreme shortage of aircraft and trained personnel but also revealed the desperate plight of the minds that manipulated Japan's war strategy. The Kamikaze was the last fierce sputter of a burned out and dying air force.

On the ground General MacArthur's troops met the enemy for the first time en masse, with armies and corps pitted against each other in comparatively free maneuver. The Japanese, determined to retrieve their positions at any cost, dispatched troops from China and Manchuria and from all corners of the Philippines to the Leyte battlefront. Paralleling their performance in New Guinea and in the Solomons, the Japanese yielded nothing without a bitter fight and it took daring and skillful maneuver on the part of the American soldier to pry them out of their well prepared positions or break up their desperate counterattacks. All enemy efforts, however, proved in vain. Their movements were anticipated, their divisions decimated, and their troops forced to flee, starving and demoralized, into the hills and mountains of inner Leyte. General MacArthur's victory on Leyte was decisive and final. . . .

The battle for Leyte proved the advantages of General MacArthur's adherence to a master plan, which, though broad in scope, was flexible in execution. Extensive enough to cover operations from Port Moresby to Manila, his plan permitted rapid intermediate strokes along its operational axis such as the Admiralties operation, Hollandia, and even Leyte itself. The Allies had carefully selected definite objectives and concentrated their power in co-ordinated assaults. In comparison, Japanese planning was extemporized and spasmodic, and their leadership often vacillating.

The battle for Leyte brought other valuable lessons into sharp relief. Although past operations in the Pacific had demonstrated what could be accomplished with controlled air power, Leyte showed how lack of aerial supremacy, at a critical juncture, could change the whole complexion of an operation. The definite need for the establishment of forward air bases in the early stages of a campaign was emphasized more clearly in Leyte than in any previous operation. In the European theater, bombers could operate from the same fields over long periods of time in view of relatively short flight distance, but Southwest Pacific air units seldom stayed in one locality more than two months before they had to establish new fields 300 to 500 miles away. Consequently, Pacific operations demanded mobile and flexible tactical air combat teams that could transfer their base of operations at a moment's notice to keep pace with the rapid forward strides of General MacArthur's ground forces. . . .

With the defeat on Leyte the worst fears of the Japanese leaders had come to pass. Their empire was cut in two and the volume of sea traffic between Japan and the southern regions was ultimately reduced to a mere trickle. The Netherlands East Indies and Malaya—the Eldorado of the south—which had lured Japan's leaders into war in 1941, and which for four years had supplied much of the raw material for Japan's war machine, were now lost. With access to this region cut off, Japan lost every hope of successfully continuing the conflict.

General MacArthur had kept his faith. His return to the Philippines was a dramatic and singular fulfillment of historical destiny. A year before the assault against Leyte, his forces had been deep in the tangled jungles and swamps of New Guinea; almost 1,500 miles from the Philippines. Now he had led them into the very heart of the islands and in a position to become masters of the archipelago. On the third anniversary of the Japanese attack against the Philippines, General MacArthur's forces were organizing the final blows which would lead to the capture of Manila and the surrender of General Yamashita's troops on Luzon.

Just one last steppingstone was needed before the attack on Luzon could be mounted, and that was the island of Mindoro. As a central island below Manila, Mindoro would enable MacArthur to return to his strategy of never leaping ahead of his own air cover. Midway between Leyte and the Lingayen Gulf area of Luzon, an airfield on Mindoro could be used to cover the next landing at Lingayen. Accordingly, on December 12, even before Leyte had been made safe, Brig. Gen. W. O. Dunkel's task force, escorted by ships from the Seventh Fleet, sailed via Surigao Strait for Mindoro. The Japanese were quick to spot the convoy; a single-engined kamikaze plane

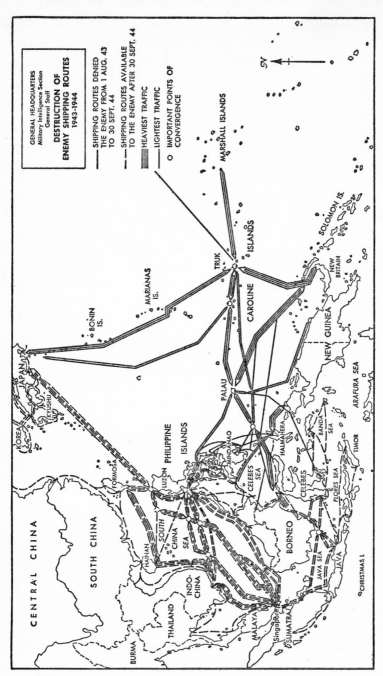

GENERAL HEADQUARTERS
Military Intelligence Section
General Staff
DESTRUCTION OF
ENEMY SHIPPING ROUTES
1943-1944

SHIPPING ROUTES DENIED
THE ENEMY FROM 1 AUG. 43
TO 30 SEPT. 44

SHIPPING ROUTES AVAILABLE
TO THE ENEMY AFTER 30 SEPT. 44

HEAVIEST TRAFFIC

LIGHTEST TRAFFIC

O IMPORTANT POINTS OF
CONVERGENCE

crashed headlong into the superstructure of the *Nashville*, flagship of the task force, killing 131 and wounding 158. Dunkel and his staff were hit by flying fragments; the *Nashville* itself was put out of action.

This setback did not stop the Mindoro expedition. Once again the Japanese were wrong about the Americans' destination; their patrols flew over the beaches of Panay and Negros—and only tumbled to the fact that Mindoro was our destination after the American ships had anchored off the chosen beachheads. The landing phase of the operation was accomplished without the loss of a single soldier. Kamikaze attacks did much damage to American shipping off Mindoro, and the destruction wrought by these suicidal assaults created a serious shortage of aviation gasoline for a period. But two American airfields were in operation on Mindoro as early as December 23.

With the loss of Mindoro, Japan halted shipments of reinforcements to the Philippines, and Manila Bay was abandoned as a stopover for convoys from the Netherlands Indies region. From now on Japanese shipping hugged the China coast. MacArthur's campaigns in the Southwest Pacific were approaching their climax. The battle for Luzon was at hand. Mindoro was the gate to Lingayen—and MacArthur held the keys.

11 Manila: MacArthur Returns

THE battle for Luzon was at hand—the climax of General Mac-Arthur's World War II campaigns, the long road from Corregidor and back again, a lapse of three years and a distance of thousands of miles. His opponent General Yamashita, the swaggering victor of Singapore, saw the handwriting on the wall; he transferred the Philippine puppet government to the mountain town of Baguio, the old summer capital of the islands, on December 22, 1944, and followed with his headquarters on January 4, 1945.

MacArthur's strategic plan of battle, as always, was aimed at the complete destruction of his foe. This was a ticklish and danger-ous problem, as Yamashita's ground forces were numerically greater than his own. His concept was as brilliant as it was to prove effective. MacArthur sums it up thus:

> With the Eighth Army off the southern coast of Luzon, with a firm hold on Mindoro, we would threaten landings at Legaspi, Batangas and other southern ports and draw the bulk of the Japanese into the south.
>
> This done, we would land the Sixth Army in an amphibious en-veloping movement on the exposed northern shore, thus cutting off the enemy's supplies from Japan. This would draw the enemy back to the north, leaving the Eighth Army to land against only weak op-position on the south coast in another amphibious movement.
>
> Both forces ashore with but minor losses would then close like a vise on the enemy deprived of supplies and destroy him. It worked like a charm.

In many respects, the scheme of maneuver for the invasion of northern Luzon paralleled the plan for the Leyte landings.

The naval forces were under Admiral Kinkaid, with subdivisions under Admirals Oldendorf, Berkey, Barbey, and Wilkinson. With General MacArthur in personal command, this represented the most powerful support grouping to date for the Sixth Army under veteran Walter Krueger.

As at Leyte, the army was to land with corps abreast, the I Corps on the left, Gen. Innis P. Swift commanding, the XIV Corps on the right, Maj. Gen. Oscar W. Griswold commanding.

The Fifth Air Force, with two bombardment and fighter wings, was under Maj. Gen. Ennis C. Whitehead, Kenney's able alter ego throughout the campaign of New Guinea. In addition, the army held out a strong reserve.

The initial changes of target dates, as between Mindanao and Leyte, affected supply, engineer, and shipping schedules. Pat Casey, MacArthur's engineer since the Bataan days, and Sam Sturgis, the Sixth Army engineer, had to perform prodigies of planning and organization within an unusually short span of time.

General MacArthur commented on the problems of this preparatory period:

Sixth Army engineers had begun planning for the Luzon operations in September. Not the least of the factors involved in all planning was the normal 90/150 days' gap—five months between "requisition" of supplies and their "delivery." For example, virtually no stocks existed in the Southwest Pacific area of such materials as Bailey bridging and floating equipage.

While there was an impressive bulk of engineer tonnage in the theater, it was not in well balanced depots and could not be shipped forward from rear bases in Australia and New Guinea. The engineers wanted more time.

MacArthur, whose branch of service is the Engineer Corps, settled these matters himself in a conference with the commanders of the Sixth Army, the Far East Air Force, the chiefs of operations, G-3, and the Engineer sections:

Air fields must be constructed within six days after landing; top priority was to be given for the unloading of treadway bridges equipment; landings directly seaward of airdrome areas were to be avoided; landing mats on at least five ships to begin unloading on the second day were to be provided; and many other stipulations which meant the narrow difference between success and failure.

It is interesting in this connection to know that fifteen years before, when MacArthur was commanding the Philippines Department, President Hoover, through Chief of Staff General Summerall, proposed to appoint General MacArthur, then the youngest major general in the Army, to the post of Chief of Engineers. General MacArthur's reply was typical. He said he had not practiced the engineering profession for so long that he doubted his ability properly to handle such a technical responsibility, and anyway there was a better man for it in his old instructor of engineering at West Point, Gen. Lytle Brown. Brown was appointed. The staff always liked this anecdote because it so truly reflected MacArthur's basic personal character—a character whose nobility and modesty have at times been so wantonly misrepresented.

It was expected that the Japanese would throw their remaining air power in the Philippines against the American landing and that they would intensify the suicide technique, the kamikaze attacks, so effectively introduced at Leyte. As predicted, the day after Admiral Oldendorf started his convoys en route to Lingayen, Japanese planes began to crash-dive into his ships. An escort carrier was damaged so badly it had to be sunk—a practice of our Navy, if immediate repairs were impossible. The following afternoon the *Louisville*, *Stafford*, *Manila Bay*, *Savo Island*, and the Australian *Arunta* and *Australia* suffered hits or damaging near-misses.

On January 5, the *Boise*, with General MacArthur aboard, became the target of two torpedoes from Japanese submarines; skillful maneuvering avoided the torpedoes, and the escorting destroyer rammed, depth-charged, and sank the enemy.

On January 6, the Navy reported that the fire-support groups "were attacked by the largest and most deadly group of suicide planes encountered during the operation." At least sixteen vessels were struck. Admiral Oldendorf's flagship *California* received serious damage, as did the battleship *New Mexico* and the cruisers *Columbia* and *Louisville*. The Japanese pilots appeared well trained and their deception measures were excellent; they made skillful use of land masses—flying at sea level, "window" (dropping metal tape to confuse our radar readings), and counterfeit identifications to escape detection. Bad weather had minimized the effectiveness of neutralizing air attacks by the Fifth Air Force and the Third Fleet.

Disregarding losses, the assault convoys pushed on, and in the early morning hours of January 9 all shipping arrived in Lingayen Gulf. The organizational planning of the Army and Navy was so perfect that four attack groups, one for each division, were simultaneously in position off their designated beaches along a front of twelve miles. The scheduled landing was 9:30 A.M. and by 9:40 A.M. all assault echelons had hit the beach. By late afternoon, the four division commanders had assumed control ashore.

In discussing the extraordinary speed of the operation, General MacArthur said:

There was no fixed timetable. I hoped to proceed as rapidly as possible, especially as time was an element connected with the release of our prisoners. I have always felt, however, that the endeavor to formulate in advance details of a campaign is hazardous, as it tends to warp the judgment of a commander when faced with unexpected conditions brought about by the uncertainties of enemy reaction or enemy initiative. I therefore never attempted fixed dates for anything but the start of operations. The rate of progress in this operation was fast and more than fulfilled all hopes and expectations.

The strongest resistance to the inland advance was encountered in the zone of action of the I Corps. The Japanese had developed a line of defenses along a series of ridges from Damortis, through Rosario and Urdaneta. By mid-January it was evident that the enemy was concentrated in strength in an area guarding the roads to Baguio and the Cagayan valley. Our troops faced heavily fortified and mutually supporting tunnel and cave systems, fully supplied with all types of weapons and ammunitions. In many places tanks, buried deep in the ground, were used as pill boxes in support of infantry positions.

On the right flank of the invasion front, in the zone of the XIV Corps, the open terrain and paved highways of the central plain

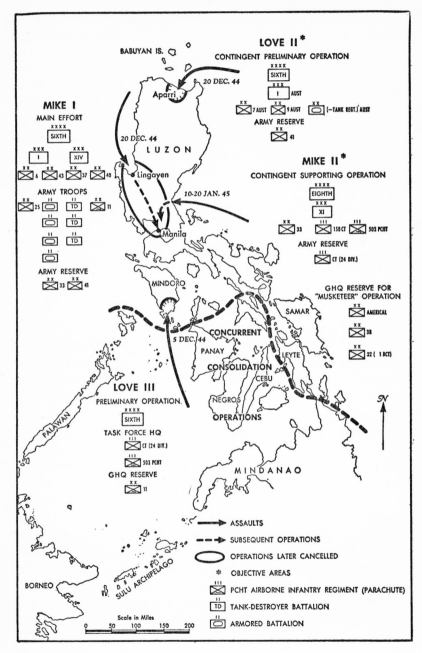

Luzon: plan of operations

made a more rapid advance possible. By January 15, the Agno River had been crossed. Advance patrols were applauded by excited Filipinos who lined the roads and shouted encouragement; but as the drive continued southward toward Ft. Stotsenburg, our troops began to encounter increasingly strong pockets of enemy resistance.

According to MacArthur's own outline of the situation, he was

. . . becoming concerned about his sea line of supply to Lingayen gulf. Washington had suddenly demanded that he return some one hundred ships, transports to be used across the North Pacific to Vladivostok, to carry munitions and supplies for the Soviet forces. He protested bitterly that the entire campaign for the Philippines might be seriously jeopardized. But it was without avail.

It was the staff's understanding that Harry Hopkins' influence in this decision overruled that of all others, though the General himself insisted that he could not believe President Roosevelt was aware of what was developing.

It was these supplies landed in Siberia, hundreds of millions of dollars worth, that later became the basis for fitting out the Red Chinese and the North Korean Armies.

The potential damage to the Western world was beyond estimate. The General understood this but his voice was powerless.

MacArthur's own summary of his strategy for the conquest of Luzon is as follows:

The only place the enemy could hope to counter our attack successfully, except on the actual battle line, was at Lingayen itself, to cut my line of supply. My beachhead and harbor base were exposed to attack from Formosa and the north. The Seventh Fleet had been reinforced from the Central Pacific by battleships with accessories, and as long as these powerful units defended the Lingayen roadstead, I felt my naval supply line, though somewhat attenuated, was secure.

Admiral Nimitz was preparing for the Okinawa attack, however, and he felt that these ships must be recalled as soon as possible.

I therefore decided to bring the XIth Corps of the Eighth Army, commanded by General "Chink" Hall, forward by sea and throw it in on the Zambales coast of West Luzon so that if Lingayen in its weakened naval state became jeopardized, I could shift my supply line to a more geographic secure position. In addition, this movement, a complete surprise to the enemy, would place Hall's forces so as to threaten the flank of the enemy's resistance in the Manila plain and would effectively bar any movement of the enemy to and from the Bataan peninsula.

I then intended when the resistance in the Manila plain crumbled to suddenly envelop from the other flank with the Ist Cavalry Division, which I was bringing up via Lingayen for that purpose.

Manila would thus be enveloped by this movement from the east, by simultaneous attack from the south by the Eighth Army, and by direct drive from the north by the main forces of the Sixth Army.

The plan worked perfectly. "All echelons of our forces performed admirably. Commanders were extraordinarily resourceful, the troops courageous and indomitable." MacArthur himself was everywhere. Operating on what was doubly hallowed ground for him, the scene of his father's great military triumph at the turn of the century and of his own epic resistance in the opening days of the war, he knew every inch of the terrain, every wrinkle of its topography. Constantly on the front line—at times well ahead of it—his sheer physical endurance and his reckless exposure of himself excited the native population and even his own forces to a pitch of effort that became the dismay of the enemy. Looking back on the Luzon campaign, the staff recalls an incident near Tarlac when General Kenney dropped in late one evening to report to MacArthur. Although a hustling mess sergeant had prepared a hearty meal, Kenney noticed that the General was eating practically nothing. "What's the matter with you?" he asked.

MacArthur replied, "George, I'm so tired that I can't eat."

Kenney had to leave early the next morning and started before daybreak. He called the orderly officer and told him to tell General MacArthur that he was sorry he could not wait to tell him good-by, that he was forced to get away early.

"Oh," said the officer, "General MacArthur left for the front two hours ago."

"Hell," said Kenney, "the guy must be nuts. If he works overtime, he'll lose his union card."

Many thousands of prisoners, military and civilian, women and children as well as men, Americans, British, and Filipino, were held by the enemy in concentration camps located at Cabanatuan at Santo Tomas University, at Bilibid Prison in Manila, and near Calamba on Laguna de Bay. Their condition was fast deteriorating from lack of food and the increasing savagery of their guards. General Mac-Arthur was determined to rescue these unfortunate people, although it seemed an almost hopeless task.

In a series of surprise movements made with stunning suddenness, he successively penetrated behind the enemy's lines at all four points, and without the loss of a single prisoner released them all. It was perhaps the most brilliant exhibition of minor tactics of this kind in the entire campaign.

Within Manila itself the enemy made a desperate stand before the city could be cleared. Corregidor was captured in a surprise parachute assault, which opened Manila Bay to our shipping, and on February 28 MacArthur re-established the Commonwealth government. To a provisional Assembly in Malacanan Palace, he said:

More than three years have elapsed since I withdrew our forces from this beautiful city that, open and undefended, its churches, monuments and cultural centers might be spared the violence of military ravage.

The enemy would not have it so. Much that I sought to preserve has been unnecessarily destroyed by his desperate action at bay, but by these deeds he has wantonly fixed the future pattern of his own doom. . . . The unleashed power of America, supported by our Allies, turned the tide of battle in the Pacific and resulted in an unbroken series of crushing defeats upon the enemy, culminating in the redemption of your soil and the liberation of your people. . . . My country has kept the faith. Its soldiers came here as an army of free men dedicated, with your people, to the cause of human liberty and committed to the task of destroying those evil forces that have sought to suppress it by the brutality of the sword. . . . Your capital city, cruelly punished though it be, has regained its rightful place—citadel of Democracy in the East.

The General spoke with deep emotion, and well he might. This beautiful palace of Malacanan with its noble halls must have seemed full of ghosts for him. Here his father had lived as Governor General to lay the foundations of a modern Filipino nation of liberty and prosperity. Here MacArthur had known and conferred through the years with Quezon, Osmena, Roxas, Romulo, Quirino, and a great host of Filipino leaders. Here he had broken bread with the Americans who had succeeded his father through the past forty-five years: William Howard Taft, Leonard Wood, Henry Stimson, Dwight Davis, Theodore Roosevelt, Jr., and all the others. Here is where, standing before a similar assemblage in brilliant array many years before, he had become the field marshal of the Philippine Army, first and only American to hold such foreign rank. Within the shadow of Malacanan's walls his mother, a valiant Virginia lady, contemporary of Robert E. Lee and Stonewall Jackson, had died. Here MacArthur had courted his wife, and here his only son had been born. From its windows he could still see the smoking ruins of his home, its priceless souvenirs of distinguished ancestry gone forever. No wonder that the resonant voice that has thrilled so many audiences broke at the end.

There were other reasons that might well have animated him, too. A staff summary of his views says:

The Secretary of the Interior, Harold Ickes, was bitterly opposed to setting up the Philippine Government Administration and proposed and actually planned to come himself to the Islands to administer its affairs. He claimed the functions of a High Commissioner and hoped to introduce many of the concepts then colloquially known in the United States as the New Deal. He had proposed this as soon as Mac-Arthur had landed in Leyte. The Secretary of War, Henry Stimson, had called on MacArthur for his views and recommendations. The General was entirely opposed. Said he had complete confidence in the Commonwealth Government to discharge its functions and loyally cooperate as it had always done. Recalled that at the outbreak of the war it had been suggested to him that he as Military Commander should assume general charge of all Philippine Administration. How he had opposed this concept, stating that these matters should be left to the Filipinos themselves, and how completely successful this cooperative arrangement had been. He further replied that the personality of Secretary Ickes was such as to insure friction, especially as he had never been to the Philippines and was utterly unacquainted with the Orient. Stimson acquiesced in this view and after a bitter quarrel in Washington, prevented Ickes from injecting himself into the local scene.

Ickes never forgave the General and was one of that vindictive group which never failed to misrepresent and prevaricate his position, his views and his accomplishments.

This smoldering, implacable enmity burst into open flame in 1949, when Tokyo intelligence reports disclosed the leftist writer Agnes Smedley as an accomplice of Richard Sorge, Soviet master-spy in the Far East. Ickes at once sponsored Smedley in his vituperative newspaper column. While his diatribe was directed against intelligence, MacArthur was the real target. Ickes' protégée died in 1950 and left her belongings to Chu-Teh, the Commander in Chief of the Red hordes at war with America. Her ashes were placed in a state shrine in Peking.

After the clearing of the Manila Bay area, the fighting still went on. The subsequent operations can be summarized as a coordinated three-pronged offensive: the I Corps, operating to north and east in the direction of Baguio and the Cagayan Valley; the XI Corps clearing the Sierra Madre, north and east of Manila; and the XIV Corps, charged with securing Batangas, Laguna, and Tayabas provinces, to the southeast.

The Japanese General Muto commented on MacArthur's tactics in this period:

Based on previous concepts of tactics, the terrain features of these areas provided impregnable fortifications. However, the Americans started attacking in the beginning of February and kept it up incessantly. The superior enemy bombardment and shelling gradually obliterated the jungle. Bulldozers accomplished the impossible. Tanks and artillery appeared in positions where we had thought they would never penetrate. Our front-line troops destroyed bulldozers, tanks and artillery in valiant hand-to-hand fighting. However, the enemy advanced inch by inch, capturing this mountain, taking that hill.

On May 13, the U.S. 25th Division broke through Balete Pass to Cagayan and the battle of Luzon entered its final phase. General Joseph W. Stilwell, on a visit to the Cagayan front, said of the difficulties of the Balete breakthrough:

This seems to be as tough as anything could be. . . . In Burma it was thick, almost impenetrable, jungle. Here there are cliffs that are almost impossible to scale as well as the worst sort of mountain terrain.

After the final clearing of the Cagayan Valley, MacArthur said, on June 28:

Our northern and southern columns have joined forces, securing the entire length of the Cagayan Valley, heart of northern Luzon. This juncture climaxes a campaign which overran the 200-mile valley in twenty-eight days. Battered enemy remnants have been driven into the rugged mountain ranges to the east and west cut off from all sources of supply.

Except for isolated operations this closes the major phases of the Northern Luzon Campaign, one of the most savage and bitterly fought in American history. No terrain has ever presented greater logistical difficulties and none has ever provided an adversary with more naturally impregnable strongholds. . . . Our troops comprised the I Corps and the north Luzon guerrillas, all of the Sixth Army, closely and most effectively supported by the Far Eastern Air Force and the Seventh Fleet. The entire island of Luzon, embracing 40,420 square miles and a population of 8,000,000 is now liberated.

Secretary of War Stimson cabled MacArthur appreciatively on July 3:

My congratulations go to you and all officers and men of your command for this most skilful and heroic accomplishment. . . . Your announcement that all Luzon has been liberated marks the achievement of a great military success. It has been brought about with a minimum of casualties. . . . Your great victory hastens the day when the last of the oppressors will have cleared Philippine soil.

And clear the entire Philippine Archipelago is just what Mac-Arthur proceeded to do with dazzling success. Using the elements of the Eighth Army under General Eichelberger, he instituted a series of amphibian thrusts with such lightning speed that the bewildered enemy, completely surprised, was successively over-

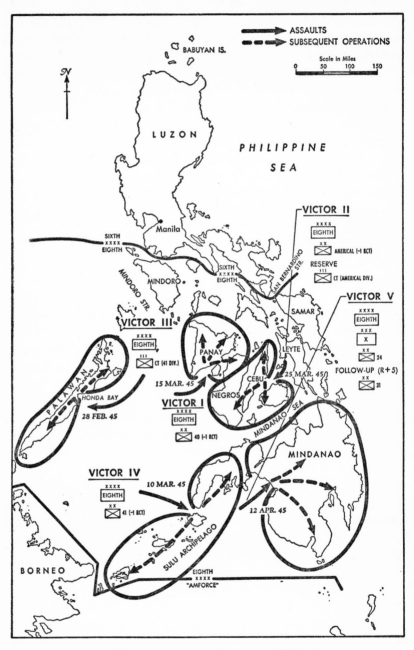

Montclair III: conquest of southern Philippines

whelmed. The islands of Panay, Cebu, and Mindanao, and the remainder of the Visayas and southern groups, were in rapid succession reconquered, liberated, and restored to civil rule.

The recapture of the southern islands, the story of which has been told in great detail in General Eichelberger's *Our Jungle Road to Tokyo*, was foreordained by the successes on Leyte and Luzon. The Japanese in the islands would have "died on the vine" in the long run anyway. Nevertheless, it was strategically necessary to push a line eastward through the southern archipelagoes. The importance of the operation was summed up in a statement by MacArthur after the capture of Tawi Tawi Island at the end of the Sulu Archipelago in April:

The seizure of Tawi Tawi secured the last link in the chain of blockading air fields which the recapture of the Philippines had made possible. Along the entire coast from the northern end of Luzon to the southern tip of the Sulu Archipelago, a distance of more than a thousand miles, our air fields flank the waters of the South China Sea between the coast of Asia and the Philippines, while our fields stretching for two thousand miles from New Guinea to the Philippines cover the waters necessary for communication from Japan to Java, Borneo, Celebes, the Moluccas and all the other islands in the Southwest Pacific. The width of the South China Sea averages only a few hundred miles so that its expanse as well as the coast line of the Asiatic mainland is easily covered by our bombers in addition to our submarines. This cuts off enemy sea traffic to the conquered possessions to the south and severs the so-called Empire lifeline to the East Indies. The effectiveness of this blockade results from its great depth, permitting multiplicity of successive fields to bear upon the target. The enemy can easily under favorable weather conditions slip through waters covered only from one set of bases, but when he runs into successive belts flanked by fields extending for thousands of miles he finds it impossible to pierce the blockade. He may well penetrate the thinness of a line blockade but it is difficult indeed to run the gauntlet of successive bases which cover the length of the way for thousands of miles. The campaign of the Southwest Pacific Area along the coast of New Guinea through the Halmaheras and throughout the length of the Philippines had this end in view as one of its primary strategic objectives. Already our blockade has sunk many hundreds of thousands of tons of enemy shipping and with the acquisition of the Tawi Tawi base is now in complete operation. For many weeks it has been difficult for Japan to ship oil, rubber or other essential military commodities from the Southwest Pacific to the homeland, or military supplies from Japan to garrisons in those waters, and as the air pressure of our blockade reaches its peak, such traffic will become practically impossible. The entire Dutch East Indies are now isolated not only for exploitation but from enemy reinforcement and supply. It is the culmination of one phase of the campaign which started from Milne Bay late in June 1943 and, progressing through Kiriwina, Salamaua, Lae, Finschhafen, Arawe, Gloucester, Saidor, Hollandia, Sarmi, Biak, Noemfoor, Sansapor, Leyte, Mindoro, Luzon, Palawan and Zamboanga, has now reached its far end at Tawi Tawi.

This done, with the same brilliant tactics but using the Australian Army under General Blamey, MacArthur landed in succession on the north, east, and south coasts of Borneo and reclaimed this great island with its limitless source of oil and other supplies. MacArthur went along personally on the cruiser *Boise* to watch the seizure of the Brunei Bay region of British Borneo. So confident was he that all would go off according to schedule that he told General Kenney: "You'd better come along with me. We'll have a good holiday and, besides, there will be chocolate ice cream sodas three times a day." But before he got his ice cream on one occasion, General Kenney, on his own confession, was scared half to death by MacArthur's personal reconnaissance of a Japanese outpost position. When a Japanese bullet caught an Australian Army photographer in the shoulder just a step away from MacArthur, it was enough for Kenney. He pleaded the importance of getting back to the *Boise* in time for dinner. "All right, George," said MacArthur. "I wouldn't have you miss that ice cream for anything."

If MacArthur had had his way, the Borneo campaign would have been extended to include the recapture of the Netherlands East Indies. Just recently General MacArthur made a comment of great historical significance:

I had planned to move immediately on to Java with the Australian troops and restore the Dutch Government under Van Mook, which would have rapidly brought law and order there as it had done in New Guinea.

For some reason never understood, this proposed movement was peremptorily called off and forbidden from Washington, in spite of my insistence of its complete success with little loss. This was one of the grave mistakes of the war and ultimately resulted in the chaotic conditions which followed in that part of Indonesia. It completely violated the basic principle of American foreign policy to support the orderly development of dependent areas toward self-government.

I foresaw this but my counsel was ineffective to change what I regarded as a political interference in a basically military problem. I was to find this deadly weapon in constant future use against me.

In connection with MacArthur's views on Indonesia, an earlier report to the General from the Dutch Admiral C. L. L. Helfrich, who commanded the naval forces in the battle of Macassar Strait in 1942, is extremely enlightening:

Batavia, 20th October, 1945

General Douglas MacArthur,
Commander-in-Chief Allied Forces Pacific,
G.H.Q.-AFPAC

I regret to have to intrude on your precious time but I feel I want to write to you personally, because conditions in the Netherlands East Indies are developing so unfavourably that, if no action is taken immediately, only a catastrophe can follow.

My return to this country after a long period of exile was none but a great disillusion. Political and military mistakes are made which seem unbelievable, but none the less are true, whilst there is no prospect yet of any improvement.

In the first place, I have to state that the N.E.I. [Netherlands East Indies] and its population had to wait for a long time before the British and Allies returned to the country. Only on the 15th of September *one* British cruiser and *one* Netherlands cruiser arrived and the first small British landing only took place on the 29th of that month.

Meanwhile Soekarno (the "President of the Indonesian Republic")

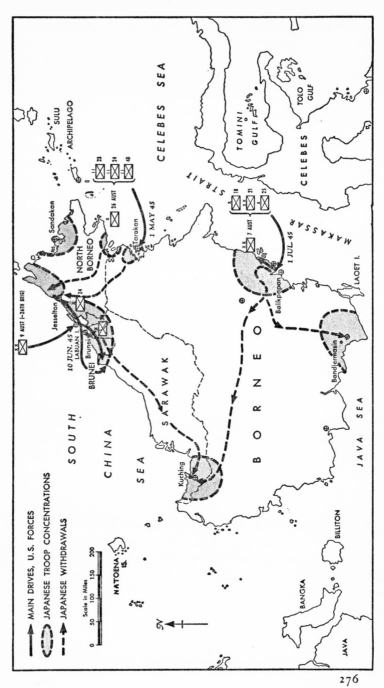

The Borneo operations: July 1945

with his satellites had moved about freely, taking advantage of the obvious proof of inability we showed.

On the 2nd of October I arrived at Batavia and noticed a hostile atmosphere which especially was marked by the Indonesian flags (red and white), as well as by the many insulting slogans on public buildings, streetcars and other means of transport.

In my opinion the British made their first political mistake when they did not declare immediately and clearly that they solely recognized the Netherlands Authority. On the contrary, at press conferences the general impression was made that they had nothing to do with "internal" politics, as a consequence of which one generally concluded that the Netherlands Authority and that of Soekarno were put on the same level. It is true that later on the Supreme Commander declared that the statements of the British General Christison had been interpreted absolutely wrongly, but the above mentioned impression had been made, and the reactions to it were very unfavorable.

I simply cannot understand that the British did not explain from the very beginning that first of all Netherlands Authority had to be restored. For had not Japan surrendered to the United Nations of which the Kingdom of the Netherlands forms an integral part? A Netherlands representative signed the Document of Surrender in Tokyo Bay on behalf of the Kingdom of the Netherlands. In the clause, which you personally signed, it is indicated clearly that this signing was also done in the interest of all United Nations at war with Japan.

The foundation of the Republic Indonesia by Soekarno, led and supported by the Japanese oppressors, was clearly unlawful and even a semblance of recognition thereof would mean a strengthening of the Japanese political game.

The untenable situation which at present exists is mainly created by this political weakness of the British. It is my firm conviction that nothing would have happened if it would have been stated from the very beginning that first the Netherlands Authority had to be restored and that only after that discussions would be held between this Netherlands Authority and the representatives of the Indonesian political parties concerning (a) the structure of the Government of the N.E.I., and (b) the place which this country would hold in the Kingdom of the Netherlands.

Moreover, it should have been stated that these discussions would be based on the radio speech delivered by Her Majesty Queen Wilhelmina on December 7, 1942, for in that speech Her Majesty made it clear that after the end of the war a conference would be held by representatives of all parts of the Kingdom (all members of the conference having equal rights) in order to discuss the new political structure of the Kingdom with a view to a higher grade of independence for all parts concerned. (It is very unfortunate that (a) through lack of proper propaganda, and (b) because Her Majesty made this speech in exile during the German occupation of Holland as well as the N.E.I., this speech could not then be made sufficiently clear to all of Her Majesty's subjects.)

However, when Soekarno noticed that one did not entirely reject the new Republic, he and his satellites automatically became encouraged to go on with their unlawful business, stimulated by British and Dutch military impotence and by an unbelievably weak British military generalship.

The reasons for the Dutch inability are well known to you. Through the late liberation of the Netherlands we were unable to strengthen our forces in time. Moreover, we did not get shipping at our disposal to transport the troops already available, and other reinforcements. One even denied us the ships under the Dutch flag, although during the whole war we put our entire shipping at the disposal of the Allied cause.

The British impotence could be explained by the fact that through the change of the boundaries of the war theatres they fairly suddenly were put before a much bigger commitment. I am convinced, however, that even with the available weak power one could have performed miracles if one would have taken action immediately.

Neither did I understand the British attitude towards the Japanese from the very beginning onward. The Japanese army soon backed out of their obligations to maintain law and order. The Japs interned themselves, withdrew into well-equipped camps, gathered big stores and even gave or sold their arms to the Indonesian rebels.

It is possible that there still are many moderate Indonesian leaders with whom one could talk, but I am strongly convinced that the whole movement tends to the side of the extremists, which is very powerful, and which under Japanese propaganda and leadership has created some sort of guerrilla army; moreover, this army at present is supplied with Japanese arms.

This guerrilla army, under fanatical leadership, mainly consists of youths of between 15 and 20 years of age, which I should like to compare with the "Hitler Jugend," and which adhere to complete independence free from any foreign influence or domination (Indonesia Merdeka!).

The things that happen, in the meantime, are unbelievable. At present the P.O.W. and Internee Camps for women and children are still overcrowded. Though of course the food situation has improved a little bit, the same misery exists as under Japanese domination, but what is more, the thousands and thousands of women and children in the camps in the middle and eastern part of Java are a prey for the armed Indonesian bands which in those parts are the absolute rulers. Fear for reprisals is the main reason which withholds us now, now that it is too late, to take powerful action, but even if I should like to maintain law and order myself, this is impossible to me because the British General wishes this to be done solely by British troops. Up till now the entry of Dutch troops was even forbidden for fear of reprisals in the above-mentioned camps.

One can even say that public life is entirely in the hands of the republicans; even in areas occupied by the British, such as Batavia, Buitenzorg and Bandoeng, all public works (telephone, telegraph, electrical supply, water supply, industries, railroads and means of transport) are in the hands of the rebels and the British declare themselves incapable to take over these works.

The weapons trade is in full swing. The "Hitler Jugend" disposes of the most modern small arms, machine guns, hand grenades and even tanks and armoured cars. Uninterrupted they build up supplies of arms, unpunished they terrorize the whole population, especially Europeans, Indo-Europeans, Ambonese and Menadonese.

Even Batavia is absolutely unsafe. Murdering and looting is the order of the day, even in full daylight. The entire British and Netherlands Authority is a farce and I am unable to undertake anything myself because I am under the orders of the Supreme Commander and because only he is fully responsible.

I need not tell you what value under these circumstances one has to attach to the Authority of the Netherlands Indies Government.

Even the Prisoners of War and Internee Relief Agency can only perform its duties with the permission of the Indonesians and during the last weeks it was even impossible for this organization to carry on with its work.

The rebels have the entire broadcasting system at their disposal which, undisturbed, extends its mischievous influence over the whole of the N.E.I. The British are doing nothing to prevent this.

In Tandjong-Priok harbour I had to unload ships with European personnel, because all native labour went on strike and because the British hesitated to use Japanese P.O.W.s for this work.

The whole situation is bewildering and greatly discouraging.

We will ultimately succeed, but only after a great loss of prestige, a hard struggle against extremists and an enmity between the white and coloured parts of the population which will only abate after a long period.

I am convinced that only strong political pressure by the well-meaning members of the United Nations on the British Labour Government could change the situation in a favourable way; this action should be combined with a clear statement addressed to the rebels that continuation of the present situation could only result in the use of powerful military means.

Finally, a quick removal of the Japanese troops will greatly contribute to the restoration of law and order.

The Netherlands East Indies in the hands of Soekarno and his followers or any other Indonesian party will only bring chaos to this country and will only create a permanent danger for peace in the Pacific. An independent Indonesia is impossible and will within a short time become a target for political and military powers which aim at upsetting the hard-won peace.

So much for the situation in the Netherlands East Indies.

Wishing you strength and courage in your extremely difficult task, which no doubt is also being made more difficult by outside subversive political influences, I am,

C. E. L. Helfrich
Admiral, R.N.N.

In all of the Philippine operations General MacArthur was habitually at the front. His continual exposure to enemy view was an incessant source of anxiety and worry to his staff. On one occasion, when his G-2 remonstrated with him at his personal reconnoitering in front of our lines, his reply was a laconic, "Thanks, Charlie, but I can't fight 'em if I can't see 'em!"

In his twenty campaigns with their innumerable battles, covering six wars as a participant or an observer, MacArthur has received more medals for courage than any officer or man who had ever served in the American Army: the Medal of Honor; the Distinguished Service Cross—three times; the Silver Star—seven times; the Distinguished Flying Cross; the Air Medal; the Bronze Star; the Purple Heart—twice; to say nothing of the Distinguished Service Medal—five times; the Navy's Distinguished Service Medal, and more than sixty foreign decorations, including the highest badges for bravery.

A visitor once admired a beautiful gold cigarette case on his desk. It was scrolled with the famous Rainbow insignia of World War I, a division MacArthur had commanded and whose bravery and service had been immortalized in the military annals of that time. And on it was this inscription:

From the Division
"To the Bravest of the Brave"

To those who knew him well, what was even more remarkable than his extraordinary physical courage was his moral courage. He decided problems not on the basis of whether they would be popular or not, nor because of the possible effects on his own future, nor in response to influential pressures, but solely and simply on what he judged to be right or wrong. Emotionally sensitive to the rights of the lowly and absolutely devoted to the welfare of the nation, he was the very embodiment of the West Point tradition of "Duty, Honor, Country." Meticulous in carrying out the directives he received, he was fearless in his outspoken frankness of view in the discussion period preceding a final decision. And it was to be this patriotic candor and devoted fervor which ultimately cost him his command. But nothing has, or ever can, take from him a serenity of conscience and composure of deportment that are without peer.

With his victorious liberation of the Philippines, General MacArthur reached a peak of acclaim. The Philippine Congress named him officially "Liberator and Defender" and directed that for all time his name should be placed on the muster rolls of its military units and the senior present should report, when his name was called, "Present in spirit." His image was placed on stamp and coin issues, and he received the Medal of Valor, Filipino equivalent of our Medal of Honor, the only person yet to receive this honor. The United States House of Representatives and the Senate gave him their thanks, as did the Australian government and others concerned. The Secretary of War called him the main architect of victory in the Far East, and our highest military authorities pronounced his campaigns "that rarest of all rare military phenomenons, flawless both in strategy and tactics—the product of pure genius."

Yet in replying to his selection as the "Father of the Year," MacArthur said:

By profession I am a soldier and take pride in that fact, but I am prouder—infinitely prouder—to be a father. A soldier destroys in order to build: the father only builds, never destroys. The one has the potentialities of death; the other embodies creation and life. And while the hordes of death are mighty, the battalions of life are mightier still. It is my hope that my son, when I am gone, will remember me not from the battle but in the home repeating with him our simple daily prayers: "Our Father Who art in Heaven."

Could anything more truly reflect the modesty and innate spirituality of character of this amazing man?

Within the Philippines a serious internal question was now coming to a head. It was called "collaboration." The Japanese during their occupation had set up a native government under Dr. José Laurel, which had nominally declared war on the United States. But neither the government nor the people had implemented this action. It was made under coercion and probably to obtain the least possible persecution and ravagement of their native land and its population.

The General forecast his successful methods in handling the occupation of Japan when he said:

When I overthrew the Japanese in the Philippines, I received orders from Washington which I believed were inspired by Secretary Ickes to arrest all so-called collaborators and bring them to trial.

I disagreed with this policy, holding that it would be a grave mistake for the United States itself to become involved in this punitive issue; that it was one for the Filipinos to settle themselves.

I expressed no views on the actual merits involved, but was anxious not to create any misunderstanding and friction between two allies. I was required to arrest those involved, but my views finally prevailed and the United States turned over to the Philippine Government the final disposition of the fate of those affected.

12 The Japanese Surrender

ADVANCE planning for the next operation was habitual with MacArthur. In the Philippines he began to outline his views on the invasion of Japan. The Tokyo records contain the salient points of the General's clear, strategic thinking:

He believed that the Pacific command required a complete reorganization. The arbitrary boundaries originally conceived for defensive purposes must be abolished altogether. The Ground, Air and Service forces were unevenly distributed, even inequitably distributed between the Southwest Pacific and the Pacific Ocean areas. Divided under two separate, independent commands, these forces could not be shifted with speed, nor could they be employed with maximum efficiency.

The invasion of Japan would demand the use of an Army group. He proposed a single commander for the coordination of such large bodies of troops. He reiterated the guiding principle "to retain under a single command all Army forces engaged in campaign against one enemy force. Any deviation from this merely weakens the potential, prolongs the war, and increases cost in blood."

Conversely, he believed in placing all naval forces under a naval commander. Unity of command for specific operations could be achieved by the creation of joint task forces. The task force commander was to be selected from the service having the paramount interest.

In general, such a definition of command would place the great land masses—Hawaii, New Guinea and the Philippines—under the Army, and outlying posts, such as Guam, Kwajalein and Manus Island, under the Navy.

On April 3, 1945, the Joint Chiefs of Staff approved a reorganization of the Pacific. MacArthur was designated as "C.-in-C. U.S.

284

Army Forces in the Pacific" and placed in control of all Army resources in the Pacific; all naval resources passed to the command of
Admiral Nimitz. Actually, the Twentieth (Strategic) Air Force
constituted a third command. It ran its private war from Washington, under Gen. H. A. Arnold. The separatist tendencies of our
armed services have more than nine lives. MacArthur's records contain references to several points of friction in this period:

The struggle for unified command (which was never challenged in
Europe!) continued to plague MacArthur in other directions. At a
Dominion conference in London, the British urged an Empire com-
mander for the Australian forces and drew a new pencil-line on the
patient maps of Southern Asia, to remove Australia, the Netherlands
East Indies and Borneo from MacArthur's command.

London underestimated the friendship between Curtin and Mac-
Arthur and the tradition of successful collaboration between their staffs.
Prime Minister Curtin refused the project.

Historically, this is probably the beginning of British rancor in influential quarters, ultimately to develop into corrosive opposition to
MacArthur in Japan and Korea.

The tendency of Washington to juggle boundaries between major
commands was one of the peculiarities of the war in the Pacific.
They simply ordered a draftsman to shift a pencil-line from one
parallel of latitude to another. This debonair method found its most
casual application in the now notorious 38th parallel in Korea. There
it eventually backfired—at the cost of more casualties than Mac-
Arthur sustained in going from Melbourne to Morotai.

Another problem inched into the open at the close of the Pacific
campaigns. Toward the end of 1944, Russian intervention in the
Pacific appeared as a factor in secret diplomatic understandings.
The General commented on this subject as follows:

From the viewpoint of my Headquarters, Russian participation was
not required. I had urged Russian intervention in 1941 to draw the
Japanese from their southward march and keep them pinned down in
Siberia. By 1945 such intervention had become superfluous.

Captured documents dealing with a general conference of Japanese ordnance experts in October 1944 clearly revealed a fatal degree of exhaustion of Japan's heavy and armaments industries. Concurrently, Washington was able to intercept the frantic appeals of the Japanese Ambassador to Moscow to the Soviet Foreign Minister to have Russia intercede "as a neutral" (*sic*) in developing a basis for an armistice and peace with the United States. There was an unmistakable note of shrill hysteria and despair in Sato's conversations with Molotov. Moscow drew realistic conclusions and smelled a cheap victory. The views of MacArthur's staff were substantially as follows:

Japan was ready for the *coup-de-grâce*—and it could have been administered with conventional weapons. There was not the slightest reason for permitting Russia to sneak into the war at the last moment—barely a week before the surrender!—and set up their preposterous claims that have since ripened into the communization of a large part of Asia.

With Japan's weakness completely revealed, the employment of the atomic bomb had even less justification. It is rare in military history that a nation has a monopoly on a hitherto secret weapon or of techniques of absolute supremacy. Had Truman kept the atomic bomb a secret, the American politico-military position today would be impregnable. Premature exposure led to intensified Russian espionage through a sinister factor of modern political decadence: the fifth column, the native traitor, the citizen saboteur.

MacArthur did not ask for the atomic attack. He did not even know of the existence of this bomb until a few days before its public use. Actually, the General's planning proceeded without consideration of the atomic bomb or of Russia's entry into the Pacific war.

The Soviets, however, made early use of that agreement in placing a strong military mission "in observation" with MacArthur's Headquarters in Manila. It was headed by Major General Derevyanko, an officer of considerable ability who later became the Soviet diplomatic representative in Tokyo and the perennially irascible member of the Allied Council. MacArthur's staff was thus able to study the "species" at first hand and learn that Soviet officials abroad can combine transient personal charm with bull-headed, exasperating obstinacy, depending on radio instructions from Moscow prescribing every nuance of diplomatic weather from day to day.

With MacArthur's authority in the new over-all command established, the plans for the invasion of Japan began to crystallize. The invasion scheme was given the cover name "Downfall" and consisted of two successive operations: "Olympic," the preliminary assault on the southern island of Kyushu, and "Coronet," the landing on Honshu, the heart of Japan. The exchange of strategic thought between Washington and Manila once more reflected MacArthur's known conviction that "there is no substitute for victory." The General analyzed three courses of action:

First, Japan could be encircled further by Allied expansion to westward and the collateral deployment of maximum airpower. A second course was to isolate Japan completely and endeavor to bomb her into submission without a landing. The third course open was to attack Kyushu directly, to install air forces to cover a subsequent assault of Honshu.

The first course involved diversion of strength from the main axis of advance and a negative involvement of American forces in China. The second course failed to utilize our resources for amphibious offensive movement. Air power as the sole means to conquer a people failed demonstrably in Europe. Germany was subject to more intensive bombardment than could be brought to bear on Japan; nevertheless, all available ground troops of the United States, Great Britain and Russia had to be committed in order to force a decision.

The third course would attain neutralization by placing our air power at the closest practicable distance from the final objective in Japan; it would permit application of full power of our combined resources, ground, naval and air, on that objective.

"I am of the opinion," said MacArthur, "that the combined resources in the Pacific are adequate to carry out the third course. The Japanese Fleet has been reduced to practical impotency. The Japanese Air Force has been reduced to uncoordinated, suicidal attacks. Its attrition is heavy and its power for sustained action is diminishing rapidly."

MacArthur recommended that the Kyushu assault could be expedited and he advanced the tentative landing date by one month. The Joint

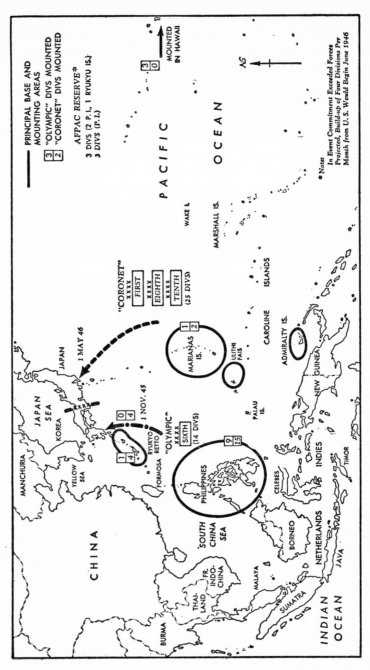

Downfall: plan for invasion of Japan

Chiefs of Staff concurred and issued the directive for "Olympic." General MacArthur was given the primary responsibility for the conduct of the entire operation. He assigned the assault on Kyushu to the veteran Sixth Army under General Krueger.

Against this background of incessant preparations for the invasion of Japan, international negotiations were under way which were ultimately to render "Olympic" unnecessary. The Potsdam conferences developed an Allied posture that gave Japan the single choice of surrender or destruction. With his habitual foresight, MacArthur had already envisaged the possibility of Japan's surrender, and his staff had been ordered to plan "for a possible peaceful occupation." The planners shifted promptly from "Olympic" to another code name, "Blacklist." The text of the plan was published on July 16 and presented four days later at Guam, for comparison with a concurrent plan for occupation termed "Campus" sponsored by the Navy. There was some pressure on Washington to adopt "Campus," which involved naval control of Tokyo, the seizure of "key positions ashore, including, if practicable, an operational air field in vicinity of each principal anchorage." MacArthur flatly rejected this concept as strategically unwise and tactically dangerous:

Naval forces are not designed to effect the preliminary occupation of a hostile country whose ground divisions are still intact. The occupation of large land areas involve operations which are fundamentally and basically a mission of the Army. The occupation should proceed along sound tactical lines, each branch of the service performing its appropriate mission.

I hold the firm belief that sound military judgment dictates that the occupation should be effected in force in order to impose our will and to avoid incidents which might develop serious proportions.

To accentuate the Potsdam "ultimatum," the interim air and naval offensives were stepped up. B-29s from the Marianas averaged 1,200 sorties a week. The Third Fleet roamed Japanese waters at will, shelling coastal cities with impunity. In the last fifteen days of the war, the Fifth and Seventh Air Force flew 6,372 sorties against Kyushu alone.

On August 7 President Truman electrified the world with a historic broadcast:

Sixteen hours ago, an American airplane dropped one bomb on Hiroshima. That single bomb had more power than 20,000 tons of explosive. It is an atomic bomb. It is a harnessing of the basic power of the universe. We are now prepared to obliterate more rapidly and completely every productive enterprise the Japanese have above ground in any city.

With the echo of this cataclysmic blast reverberating around the world, the Soviets declared war on the very next day, after having observed for four years an ostentatious neutrality which enabled Japanese divisions to move freely against New Guinea and the Philippines when they would otherwise have been immobilized along the Siberian border.

On August 9 a second atomic bomb destroyed the city of Nagasaki, wrapped in a cloud of dust and debris that rose 50,000 feet in the air and was visible for more than 175 miles. The selection of Nagasaki was an accident of weather. Kokura had been the real target. It escaped with the callous freakishness of fortune—but 100,000 citizens of Nagasaki died in the holocaust in less time than it takes to roll dice in a crap game.

With their military resources exhausted, their supply lines blocked, and their people and cities threatened with this new deadly weapon, the Japanese government instructed its Minister in Switzerland to inform the Allies that it was ready to accept the terms of the Potsdam ultimatum. The British, Soviet, and Chinese governments then concurred in the American proposal that General MacArthur be designated "Supreme Commander for the Allied Powers" (SCAP) to assume the over-all administration of the surrender.

It is comparatively rare to obtain an accurate insight into the motivations and viewpoint of leading or responsible personalities on the enemy side in war. Based on personal confidence rather than official pressure, American intelligence in Tokyo obtained confidential notes and observations by one of the highest functionaries in the Imperial entourage. Stripped of the slightly apologetic verbiage of the trained courtier, these notes constitute a remarkable historical document. Against the background of a tottering Empire there emerges a curiously intimate picture of the Japanese Emperor and his role at the time of the surrender:

I believe it was about February 1944 that His Majesty began to grapple with the problem of peace as the most urgent issue confronting the empire. I recall that one day after the war's end the Emperor, speaking to us his entourage, reminisced: "From the time when our line along the Stanley Mountain Range in New Guinea was broken through, I was anxious for peace. But we had a treaty with Germany against concluding a separate peace; and we could not violate an international commitment. This was a dilemma that tormented me."

In February 1945 we lost Manila. The Emperor summoned Baron Wakatsuki and several other ex-premiers and also Count Makino, former Lord Keeper of the Privy Seal, on different days, one at a time, and asked for their views. All these senior statesmen said peace was desirable but difficult to attain. None offered, it is said, any concrete suggestion.

It was toward the end of May 1945 when the *Yamato*, our newest and biggest battleship, despatched to save Okinawa, was sunk and all hope was gone in naval warfare. General Umezu, Chief of the General Staff, informed the Throne of the impossibility of land operations to recoup our reverses at the Yunnan and Burma fronts. His Majesty was then resolved to seek peace at all costs.

But in order to bring hostilities to an end it was necessary to persuade the officers and men, determined to fight to death, to lay down their arms. Here was a most delicate task. One false step would bring on domestic turmoil to the country threatened with an imminent enemy invasion. Defeat on Leyte, the fall of Saipan, and the loss of Okinawa had convinced the military leaders as well as all the Cabinet members of the pressing need of terminating the war. But they were at a loss as to how to go about it. In the face of the nation's volcanic temper at that time no one dared to voice his honest opinion, or even do anything that might arouse the suspicion of his entertaining such an opinion. At this juncture it was His Majesty who urged the government to sue for peace.

The Imperial Presence Conference of June 8, 1945, passed on the "Basic Program for Directing War" which declared the official decision of the government to continue the war. His Majesty was deeply shocked when this decision, in utter disregard of the developments at the front and the situation at home, was adopted by the supreme council presided over by Prime Minister Suzuki, who enjoyed Imperial confidence to the fullest degree. The Emperor wished to request the government as well as the military leaders to reconsider. But extraordinary caution was required for this. The Emperor was most reluctant to give out his personal opinion in the form of a command, for that would contravene the practice of our constitutional government and might produce grave repercussions. Herein lay the difficulty. The draft of the War Direction Basic Program contained an accurate description of both the war situation and the domestic conditions of the country, of which the impossibility of continuing the war should have been an obvious conclusion. But the document by an amazing twist of logic ended in advocating the continuation of war. At the June 8 conference the Emperor sensed the inconsistency at once, though he made no comment. He desired to leave the matter to be threshed out at another meeting. Thus, with the consent of the Prime Minister did he call the Imperial Presence Conference of June 22, at which he proposed peace.

"This is a critical moment," said His Majesty, "permitting no hesitation, no delay. Apart from the War Direction Basic Program of the June 8 conference, you will consider the question of ending the war as quickly as possible." To advocate peace, as His Majesty did, in those days of frenzied chauvinism was an act which required an extraordinary resolution, involving a grave risk even to the august person of an emperor.

What impressed those of us who were close to the Emperor was the steadfast and determined way His Majesty followed his own conviction. Thanks to the Imperial admonition, the government was now moving toward the termination of hostilities. But as to the time and method and also the terms of peace there was a wide divergence of views between the cabinet and the military. The Prime Minister and Navy Minister Yonai and Foreign Minister Togo were conspicuously active in working for peace. But the role of the Emperor should not be forgotten, who openly and covertly gave constant encouragement and support to these men.

The government wavered until the very last minute. It was at the Imperial Presence Conference of August 14 that the Emperor himself pronounced his decision in favor of immediate acceptance of the Potsdam Declaration. Thus did our nation emerge from the warfare of eight long years to hail the dawn of peace. At both conferences of August 9 and 14 His Majesty, summarizing in a lucid fashion the general situation relating to the war developments on land and sea, the extent of air raid damage, the defense of the home islands, the munitions production, and food supply, expounded why Japan should stop fighting and surrender. He was most deeply concerned not only over the sufferings of his subjects, which were being intensified each day, but also over the enormous waste in lives and property our futile resistance was causing our adversaries. These sentiments are partly revealed in the Imperial Rescript issued on the termination of war. I know well how heavily these matters weighed upon the mind of the Emperor throughout all the war years.

From the moment the Japanese threw in the towel and sued for peace, the air waves crackled with urgent radio messages between Manila and Tokyo. MacArthur directed the Japanese government to dispatch to Manila "a competent representative empowered to receive in the name of the Emperor, the Japanese government and the Japanese General Headquarters, certain requirements for carrying into effect the terms of surrender." Headed by Lt. Gen. Torashiro Kawabe, Vice-chief of the Imperial General Staff, a sixteen-man Japanese delegation left Japan on the morning of August 19. MacArthur's Tokyo papers contain glimpses of the ensuing conference:

Less than three hours after their arrival, the Japanese delegation was led by General Willoughby to MacArthur's Headquarters. The General made it a point not to be present. The conference was conducted by his Chief of Staff [Sutherland] instead. The meetings continued through the night. The translator unit, a work-horse of G-2, furnished linguists who scanned, translated and photostated the various maps, reports and charts which the Japanese had brought with them. These people worked through the night to put MacArthur's directives into accurate Japanese before morning. General Kawabe was handed the pertinent documents, and the party left at 1300 on August 20.

As the day of formal surrender drew near, all available air transport was massed on Okinawa to airlift the first contingents of the occupation forces. General MacArthur decided to go in himself:

It was a great but calculated military gamble. The Americans, outnumbered by thousands to one, were landing in hostile country when huge numbers of enemy soldiers still were fully armed and ready. There were twenty-two Japanese Divisions, more than 300,000 excellent combat troops, on the Kwanto Plain, into the midst of which MacArthur, unarmed and unattended except for a handful of his Staff, was to land.

The days before the actual arrival of the Americans had seen several outbreaks of violence among Japanese Army and Navy troops. Elements of the Imperial Guards Division in Tokyo tried to seize and isolate the Palace grounds and prevent the Imperial Rescript announcing the surrender from being broadcast. The attempted revolt was subdued and some of the rebellious participants committed suicide, but not before residences of the Prime Minister and the President of the Privy Council were attacked and burned.

Atsugi Airfield, the site of MacArthur's landing, was the scene of a five-day series of disorders during which naval kamikaze pilots dropped leaflets over Tokyo denouncing the Emperor's advisers. It was not until two days before the arrival of the American advance units that the rebellious groups were brought under control.

The first American landings at Atsugi came on August 28, when a small advance party of communications experts and engineers deplaned to make ready for swarms of four-engined aircraft that would shortly bring in the 11th Airborne Division. Next came thirty-eight troop transports with protective combat forces, gasoline, and oil. On August 30 the main phase of the airborne operation was begun: after dawn American planes landed every three minutes throughout the day, disgorging 4,200 troops by nightfall. General Eichelberger came in early on the 30th to take personal command of the situation and to make preparations for the arrival of MacArthur. At two o'clock in the afternoon a famous C-54—with "Bataan" printed in large letters on its nose—flew past the huge bronze Buddha of Kamakura, circled Atsugi, and made what Eichelberger has described as a "rubbery landing." MacArthur appeared at the door of the plane to be greeted by the spirited music of the 11th Airborne's military band. His shirt open at the throat, a corn-cob pipe in his hand, he grinned at Eichelberger and said: "Bob, this is the payoff."

When MacArthur's plane touched down at Atsugi, the world held its breath. But MacArthur knew his Orient thoroughly; forty years of foreign service had taught him the lessons of the Far East. And, perhaps even more significant, it taught the Far East of him. Thirty thousand Japanese troops, immaculate and immobile, lined both sides of the road, faced outward, from Atsugi all the miles to Yokohama. Not a sound broke the air but the chugging of his motor as this grave-faced man, symbol of Allied victory, made his way to his first headquarters on Japanese soil. Later, Winston Churchill told the American Ambassador, Winthrop Aldrich, that "of all the amazing deeds of bravery of the war, I regard MacArthur's personal landing at Atsugi as the greatest of the lot."

Japan's formal capitulation followed close upon MacArthur's landing. The ceremony took place on a misty Sunday morning, September 2, 1945, aboard the Third Fleet flagship, the U.S.S. *Missouri*. The decks of the battleship were crowded with repre-sentatives of the various nations that fought in the Pacific. Present also were the veteran members of MacArthur's staff who had served with the General since the beginning of the war, from Bataan to Brisbane and back again.

At 8:45 on that morning MacArthur and Sutherland drew up alongside the *Missouri* in a destroyer. They went aboard and dis-appeared into Bull Halsey's cabin to wait for the arrival of the Japa-nese delegates. Fifteen minutes later the Japanese emissaries came alongside the starboard gangway in a small launch. The first to climb up the ladder was the Japanese Minister of Foreign Affairs, Mamoru Shigemitsu. Dressed in a high silk topper, a frock coat, and striped trousers, a garb that was in marked contrast to the American khaki battle clothes, Shigemitsu had trouble on the ladder because of his wooden leg. Nobody greeted him. The second man of the Japanese delegation, Gen. Yoshijiro Umezu of the Imperial General Staff, and nine other representatives also came aboard the *Missouri* amid utter silence.

Inside Halsey's cabin, General MacArthur dallied for a long time while the Japanese were waiting, glum and bitter, on the deck.

Finally, MacArthur, Nimitz, and Halsey came out of the cabin. The sky still had a high overcast, but the sun was struggling to break through. All around the surrender ship, coveys of large and small vessels formed a tight cordon. Army and Navy planes maintained a protective watch overhead. With a calm but stern expression MacArthur looked at the Japanese, and spoke into the microphone:

We are gathered here, representatives of the major warring powers, to conclude a solemn agreement whereby peace may be restored. The issues, involving divergent ideals and ideologies, have been determined on the battlefields of the world and hence are not for our discussion or debate. Nor is it for us here to meet, representing as we do a majority of the people of the earth, in a spirit of distrust, malice, or hatred. But rather it is for us, both victors and vanquished, to rise to that higher dignity which alone befits the sacred purposes we are about to serve, committing all our peoples unreservedly to faithful compliance with the understandings they are here formally to assume.

It is my earnest hope . . . that from this solemn occasion a better world shall emerge . . . a world dedicated to the dignity of man. . . . The terms and conditions upon which surrender of the Japanese Imperial forces is here to be given and accepted are contained in the instrument of surrender before you.

At MacArthur's beckoning, Foreign Minister Shigemitsu signed twice, once in a book containing the surrender instrument in English, once in a book containing the same document in Japanese. The Japanese plenipotentiary had a little trouble with the pen, but finally managed to complete the job. Then General Umezu signed in behalf of the Japanese Army.

As the Japanese signatures were drying, MacArthur called the gaunt Gen. Jonathan M. Wainwright of Bataan, recently released from a Japanese prison camp, and Lt. Gen. Sir Arthur E. Percival, who had been forced to surrender the British stronghold of Singapore, to stand behind him as he signed his own name to the surrender documents. MacArthur used five silver-tipped pens to complete the signing. One pen went to Wainwright, another to Percival. Of the three remaining pens, one was for the *Missouri*, one for President Truman, and one for MacArthur himself.

It took only twenty minutes to complete the ceremony. Admiral

Nimitz signed on behalf of the United States, Gen. Hsu Yung-Chang for China, Admiral Sir Bruce Fraser for the United Kingdom, Lt. Gen. Kuzma N. Derevyanko for the Soviet Union, General Blamey for Australia, Col. L. Moore-Cosgrave for Canada, Gen. Jacques P. LeClerc for France, Admiral Helfrich for the Netherlands, and Air Vice-Marshal Leonard Isitt for New Zealand. The Japanese delegates then received their copy of the document, bowed stiffly, and set forth in their launch for the shore. Meanwhile, scores of planes roared in over the *Missouri* in one last warlike display of massed might. They had come from carriers off the coast, and from landing fields in Japan. General MacArthur said, as their roars died away: "Let us pray that peace be now restored to the world and that God will preserve it always. These proceedings are now closed."

To the world in general, as the Allied forces were disembarking from the huge flotilla that lined Tokyo Bay, General MacArthur broadcast his words of peace. But the shadows of Communist Russia already troubled his perceptive mind:

Today the guns are silent. A great tragedy has ended. . . . As I look back upon the long, tortuous trail from those grim days of Bataan and Corregidor . . . I thank a merciful God that He has given us the faith, the courage and the power from which to mold victory. . . .

A new era is upon us. Even the lesson of victory itself brings with it profound concern, both for our future security and the survival of civilization. The destructiveness of the war potential, through . . . scientific discovery, has . . . now reached a point which revises the traditional concept of war. Men since the beginning of time have sought peace. Various methods through the ages have been attempted to devise an international process to prevent or settle disputes between nations. . . . Military Alliances, Balances of Power, Leagues of Nations, all in turn failed, leaving the only path to be by way of the crucible of war. The utter destructiveness of war now blots out this alternative. We have had our last chance. If we do not devise some greater and more equitable system, Armageddon will be at our door.

It must be of the spirit if we are to save the flesh!

The General had previously defeated the Japanese in battle. Now, with these elevated concepts, he was to win them in peace.

INSTRUMENT OF SURRENDER

W e, acting by command of and in behalf of the Emperor of Japan, the Japanese Government and the Japanese Imperial General Headquarters, hereby accept the provisions set forth in the declaration issued by the heads of the Governments of the United States, China and Great Britain on 26 July 1945, at Potsdam, and subsequently adhered to by the Union of Soviet Socialist Republics, which four powers are hereafter referred to as the Allied Powers.

We hereby proclaim the unconditional surrender to the Allied Powers of the Japanese Imperial General Headquarters and of all Japanese armed forces and all armed forces under Japanese control wherever situated.

We hereby command all Japanese forces wherever situated and the Japanese people to cease hostilities forthwith, to preserve and save from damage all ships, aircraft, and military and civil property and to comply with all requirements which may be imposed by the Supreme Commander for the Allied Powers or by agencies of the Japanese Government at his direction.

We hereby command the Japanese Imperial General Headquarters to issue at once orders to the Commanders of all Japanese forces and all forces under Japanese control wherever situated to surrender unconditionally themselves and all forces under their control.

We hereby command all civil, military and naval officials to obey and enforce all proclamations, orders and directives deemed by the Supreme Commander for the Allied Powers to be proper to effectuate this surrender and issued by him or under his authority and we direct all such officials to remain at their posts and to continue to perform their non-combatant duties unless specifically relieved by him or under his authority.

We hereby undertake for the Emperor, the Japanese Government and their successors to carry out the provisions of the Potsdam Declaration in good faith, and to issue whatever orders and take whatever action may be required by the Supreme Commander for the Allied Powers or by any other designated representative of the Allied Powers for the purpose of giving effect to that Declaration.

We hereby command the Japanese Imperial Government and the Japanese Imperial General Headquarters at once to liberate all allied prisoners of war and civilian internees now under Japanese control and to provide for their protection, care, maintenance and immediate transportation to places as directed.

The authority of the Emperor and the Japanese Government to rule the state shall be subject to the Supreme Commander for the Allied Powers who will take such steps as he deems proper to effectuate these terms of surrender.

Signed at TOKYO BAY, JAPAN at 0904 I
on the SECOND day of SEPTEMBER ,1945.

重光葵
_____
By Command and in behalf of the Emperor of Japan
and the Japanese Government.

梅津美治郎
_____
By Command and in behalf of the Japanese
Imperial General Headquarters.

Accepted at TOKYO BAY, JAPAN at 0908 I
on the SECOND day of SEPTEMBER ,1945,
for the United States, Republic of China, United Kingdom and the
Union of Soviet Socialist Republics, and in the interests of the other
United Nations at war with Japan.

_____
Supreme Commander for the Allied Powers.

_____
United States Representative

_____
Republic of China Representative

_____
United Kingdom Representative

_____
Union of Soviet Socialist Republics
Representative

_____
Commonwealth of Australia Representative

_____
Dominion of Canada Representative

_____
Provisional Government of the French
Republic Representative

_____
Kingdom of the Netherlands Representative

_____
Dominion of New Zealand Representative

13 Japan: The Security Phase

MacARTHUR'S job as SCAP, or Supreme Commander of the Allied Powers, was to carry out the terms of a surrender conceived in a harsh image at Potsdam. His authority, as constituted by the Four-Power agreement of August 14, 1945, was virtually absolute:

From the moment of surrender, the authority of the Emperor and the Japanese Government to rule the state will be subject to you and you will take such steps as you deem proper to effectuate the surrender terms. You will exercise supreme command over all land, sea and air forces which may be allocated for enforcement in Japan of the surrender terms by the Allied forces concerned.

Later, on September 6, Washington reiterated its firmness:

Our relations with Japan [so MacArthur was told] do not rest on a contractual basis, but on unconditional surrender. Since your authority is supreme, you will not entertain any question on the part of the Japanese as to its scope.

Thus armed with a conqueror's power, MacArthur moved into an enigmatic land. No matter what was in his own mind in those first days of September 1945, his soldiers were apprehensive as they pushed out in the Yokohama area. "Carbines," to quote the MacArthur Tokyo papers, "were ready and faces were grim." But nothing happened. An official situation report of the period says:

No hostile military or civilian action during period as 112th RCT [Regimental Combat Team] landed Tateyma where 1,600 armed troops were reported: Jap Army, Navy and State Dept. officials met our forces and agreed to stipulation of the surrender. . . . CIC Detachment and Japanese Civil Police completed investigation of 2 Jap civilians found dead vicinity Grand Hotel, Yokohama, 1 Sep. Japanese Police satisfied deaths not result any American action.

On the fourth of September one reason for the Japanese docility became apparent: the Emperor wished it. To quote from the MacArthur papers:

While troops continued to unload in Tokyo Bay, an emergency session of the Diet was called to hear the Emperor's address and Prime Minister Prince Naruhiko Higashi-Kuni's explanation of the developments which led to the Imperial decision to surrender. The Emperor's opening address . . . was significant. It was the first time he gave direct orders to his subjects . . . the Emperor told them in person that, in his desire to improve Japan's difficult position, he had ordered capitulation. Thus, even in defeat, the unique traditional relationship of the Emperor-head of the Japanese Nation-family had been preserved. Peaceable fulfillment of Allied demands could mean continuation of this relationship. At the same time, it was hinted that this privilege might be lost if the Allied demands were not peaceably fulfilled. The Emperor ordered the people to abide by the terms of the surrender and to work toward regaining the trust and faith of the world. He stressed the need for coolness, self-discipline. . . . To the Japanese this was a clear directive to work in peace, an indication that a new chapter in the life of the nation was beginning.

Under Japanese armies, conquered populations, despite their poverty, had been expected to furnish not only full but even luxurious provisions for the invaders. The Japanese had no reason to expect anything better for themselves when the situation was reversed. But almost from the start MacArthur hinted that he intended to temper justice with mercy. His attitude on the *Missouri*, while stern, had not been devoid of charity. Following hard upon the signing of the surrender document came the Supreme Commander's General Order No. 1. This merely reiterated what had been decided two weeks previously in Manila, that Japanese troops were to surrender to SCAP representatives throughout the Pacific Theater and in China. Significantly, however, General Order Number 1 exempted the Japanese police force from surrender—an indication that MacArthur, while "absolute" in his authority, intended to make full use of the Japanese themselves in "ruling the state."

Directive No. 2, which came on September 3, was a comprehensive document designed to guide the occupation forces in their relations to the Japanese. But this, too, gave indication that the Japanese "Imperial Government" was to be used, not displaced. In other words, the fabric of traditional civil rule was not to be rudely ripped apart.

While occupation forces were being deployed, general headquarters moved into Tokyo. At a simple ceremony in front of the American Embassy, MacArthur gave an order to General Eichelberger:

Have our country's flag unfurled and in the Tokyo sun let it wave in its full glory, as a symbol of hope for the oppressed and as a harbinger of victory for the right.

Once ensconced in Tokyo, the General proceeded somewhat ostentatiously to follow a "correct" line vis-à-vis the Emperor. Their first meetings were shrouded in secrecy, although the local and foreign press were bursting with curiosity. The General has never chosen to discuss those meetings. A staff officer, recalling the first days in Tokyo, says:

Since MacArthur is one of the few great figures in public life remaining who still have the intangible thing that marks the "grand seigneur," the approach of a monarch was made easy, subtly painless. There was no "loss of face." . . . MacArthur took no initiative whatever; there was no suggestion of pressure, of militaristic necessity. There was no publicity. . . . No one was present at the interview. The Emperor brought his own interpreter, a court official. No one knows to this day what transpired. MacArthur can be ruthless but he can also exercise the most exquisite tact and courtly manners. They came into play to ease an hour that might have been bitter.

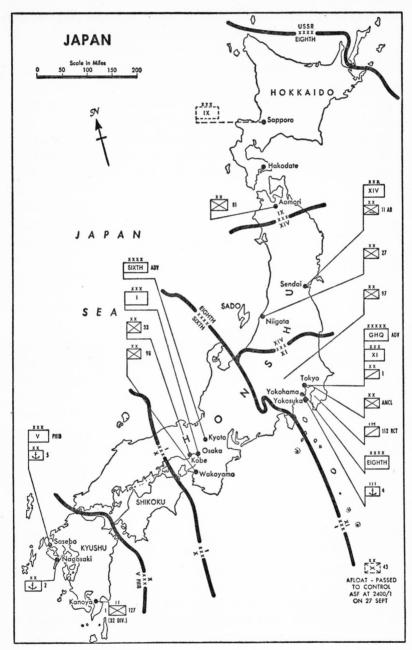

Japan: location of major occupation units, 1945

What the Japanese public sensed in all this was a basically friendly disposition. Friendly intentions were borne out by the behavior of the occupation forces themselves. The veteran American troops proved themselves equal to the task of reassuring a nervous populace. Personal kindliness and official consideration from the Americans were wholly unexpected by the Japanese.

Shortly after the surrender, twenty truckloads of flour, rolled oats, canned goods, and rice arrived at the Yokosuka municipal office to be used as relief for the local people. The next day eleven more trucks appeared with medical supplies, blankets, tea, and other goods. Mayor Umezu was completely overwhelmed. Meanwhile, American soldiers on patrol or merely sightseeing in jeeps circulated through the occupied areas. Amused by Japanese children, they handed out chocolate bars, hardtack, chewing gum, and candy drops. Three soldiers gave first aid to a girl knocked down by a streetcar. They hailed a passing Army vehicle and took the injured girl to a hospital. The friendly boyishness of the "conquerors" eased the general tension.

With the friendly note established by the Americans, the Japanese "authorities" changed their attitude from one of correct politeness to one of an open trust in the future. A Domei broadcast reassured the populace that the Allies had no intention of confiscating private property. The police advised the people to stop worrying. And the press, which had been dubious at first, now began to voice unanimous praise.

Without ever making an issue of it, MacArthur had, in effect, repudiated the harsh spirit of Potsdam. Morgenthau planning, which had its punitive impact on Germany, never took hold in MacArthur's headquarters in the Dai-Ichi Building in Tokyo.

Looking back on the Occupation, MacArthur thinks of it as the humanist capstone of his achievement. He said:

If the historian of the future should deem my service of some slight reference, it would be my hope that he mention me not as a Commander engaged in campaigns and battles, even though victorious to American arms, but rather as one whose sacred duty it became, once the guns were silenced, to carry to the land of our vanquished foe the solace and hope of faith of Christian morals.

Could I have but a line a century hence crediting a contribution to the advance of peace, I would gladly yield every honor which has been accorded to war.

Never in history has a nation and its people been more completely crushed than were the Japanese at the end of the struggle. They had suffered more than a military debacle, more than the destruction of their armed forces, more than the elimination of their industrial bases, more even than the occupation of their land by foreign bayonets. Their entire faith in the Japanese way of life, cherished as invincible for many centuries, perished in the agony of their total defeat. Into the ensuing spiritual vacuum flowed the American concept of honor and justice and compassion drawn from our Christian teachings.

If it was still "unconditional surrender" in Japan, it was unconditional surrender with a subtle difference. To begin with, there *was* a tacit condition implied in the Japanese response to Potsdam: they had accepted the surrender with an "understanding that the said declaration does not comprise any demand which prejudices the prerogatives of His Majesty as a sovereign ruler." MacArthur's aloof but humane treatment in Manila of the Japanese peace emissaries on August 19 and 20 had been in marked contrast to General Homma's treatment of Wainwright in 1942; the implication was that the Japanese had a basis for hope. While the Allied Powers reserved the right to define the "prerogatives" of the Emperor, they let it be known in due course that Hirohito might remain on his throne in British fashion, as a symbol of continuity. The Soviets clamored for a trial of the Emperor as a "war criminal," and even hoped to hang him, but in this instance, for the first time in the "peace" wrangles of 1945, they failed to carry their point. The Soviet Union was nominally one of the victor powers in the Far East, but with MacArthur in command as SCAP the Communists never got more than token representation in Japan itself.

The docility of the Japanese was assured once the continuity of Hirohito's reign was established. But though the Emperor continued to reign, it was MacArthur who ruled. He ruled through SCAP—which shortly came to connote MacArthur's headquarters staff in the Dai-Ichi Building as well as the General himself. While Hirohito was nominally head of the Japanese state, MacArthur himself carried on Japanese diplomatic functions with the outside world. Moreover, MacArthur's word, whether to Hirohito or to any Japanese cabinet member, had an authority that was never questioned. In Washington eleven to thirteen nations sat on something called the Far Eastern Commission, which issued occasional instructions, but MacArthur ran things in Tokyo as the sole executive of the Allied Powers' will.

His method of ruling in Tokyo was in obvious contrast to his habits of generalship as practiced throughout the Pacific war. On Corregidor MacArthur had stood contemptuously in the open when the bombs were falling; in Australia he had visited the camps, his cap atilt; in New Guinea he had accompanied his paratroops to the scene of their first important drop; at Leyte he had gone ashore through the surf with the Filipino leaders. Throughout the war the *presence* of the "old man" was visible. But in Tokyo, MacArthur withdrew his presence. Although he never explained it definitely as such, it was as though he had decided that the Japanese liked the *mystique* of the unseen ruler. They had always looked upon Hirohito as the Son of Heaven, and, while MacArthur never pretended to be anything like that, he knew his authority would be the greater if it came from a Jovian distance.

Thus began a seven-days-a-week routine that was to last to the outbreak of the Korean War. For the first time the "conqueror" had quarters suitable to his station. In Melbourne and Brisbane he had used hotels and commercial office buildings; in New Guinea it had been a colonial governor's cottage and a plywood hut; in Manila, headquarters was in the old City Hall, half of which had been bombed to rubble. But in Tokyo MacArthur took up residence in the American Embassy, with his office in the walnut-paneled insurance building of the Dai-Ichi.

Every morning MacArthur would leave the Embassy around nine or ten, following the identical route by car with no military escort. Once at his desk in the Dai-Ichi he would work until one-thirty or two, then go home to lunch, which his wife would endeavor to keep warm until he got there. The military aides—Colonel Bunker and Colonel Huff—would undertake to solve the domestic problem by phoning the Embassy periodically on the General's whereabouts. Sometimes he would entertain visiting notables at lunch. Afterward came the siesta, as sacred to MacArthur as to Winston Churchill. The return to the Dai-Ichi would come around four, and ordinarily MacArthur would work on until eight in the evening. Sunday was a working day like any other, though with perhaps an hour's difference on the short side. The office itself, though austere, had its personal touches: a stand of Allied flags, a small table for the General's pipes, a portrait of Lincoln, an old-fashioned glass-fronted bookcase for reports, a comfortable leather couch for visitors.

For five years MacArthur saw very little of Japan beyond the Embassy, the office, and the route connecting the two places. He did manage to get some relaxation, however, his favorite form being to sit through a Western movie with his son Arthur.

Meanwhile, he gleaned information from his staff and gave orders through the SCAP organization. The rule of SCAP was made relatively easy and painless by several factors that did not pertain in Europe. In Germany the entire government structure had dissolved when the Nazi functionaries committed suicide or fled for their lives before Patton's tanks. In addition, Germany had been physically cut to pieces by the invasions from both the west and the east. The presence on German soil of occupying armies from four nations— Britain, the United States, France and Russia—meant the inevitable partition of the shattered Reich into zones. And the absence of any government apparatus, or even the very forms of communal life, meant that the invading armies had to create governments in the various zones *de novo*.

In Japan, by way of contrast, there had been no armed invasion, no partitioning of the nation into sectors. And the government itself was intact. To quote from MacArthur's Tokyo records:

Since the Japanese civil government was capable of operating, Occupation authorities were relieved from directly administering a "conquered" country; instead, they were charged with seeing that the Japanese government complied with SCAP's directives. Military Government was also to advise Japanese officials on matters in which they had no previous experience under a totalitarian regime. In effect, there was no "military government" in Japan in the literal sense of the word. It was simply a SCAP superstructure over already existing government

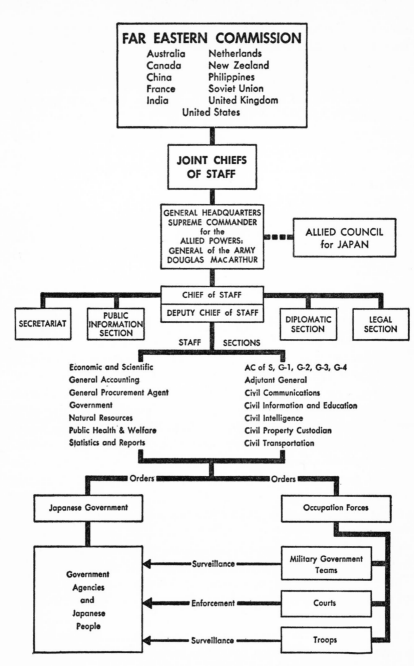

The Occupation: channels of command

308

machinery, designed to observe and assist the Japanese along the new democratic channels of administration.

On the day of surrender, the Imperial Japanese Forces totaled 6,983,000 troops, an aggregate of 154 army divisions, 136 brigades and some 20-odd major naval units. Stationed within the home islands were 2,576,085, comprising 57 divisions, 34 brigades and 45 regiments; the remainder of the Japanese forces were spread in a great arc from Manchuria to the Solomons and across the islands of the Central and Southwest Pacific.

In view of expert knowledge of the structure of the Imperial Japanese Forces, MacArthur's G-2 played a prominent role in the surrender negotiations in Manila in August 1945, when basic conditions were laid down to demobilize and disarm the Imperial forces. Completely familiar with the make-up of the Japanese Army after four years of intensive combat observation, G-2 and G-3 took over the initial planning, policy development, and staff surveillance of the demobilization of the Japanese units in the homeland.

The actual task of the demobilization and disarmament was charged to the then existing Japanese Army and Navy Ministries in order that the inherent technical and administrative skill, indispensable for a vast demobilization process, could be fully exploited. Coordination and supervision of this complex operation ultimately involved general headquarters, the Eighth Army, and the Navy.

The enormous initial military risks of landing with "token forces" on the Japanese mainland, at that time a colossal armed camp, and the obvious gamble of landing with only two and a half American divisions—confronted by 57 Japanese divisions, 34 brigades, and 45-odd regiments—will probably only be appreciated by military professionals. All strategical landing areas on the east coast of Japan were completely organized by the Japanese, and each one of these areas had the potentiality of another but greatly enlarged Okinawa. There were five or six such areas along the east coast of Japan— on Honshu, Kyushu, and Shikoku. The Japanese General Staff had enough local divisions and brigades to make an attack expensive everywhere. At Okinawa two and a half Japanese divisions exacted a total of 40,000 to 60,000 American casualties on land. This came on top of the shattering kamikaze attacks on the Fleet. The conclusions are inescapable. In the face of these suggestive military possibilities, our peaceful entry into Japan without a shot being fired or a single American casualty is nothing short of miraculous.

The terrific tension was resolved, as by magic, by the shatteringly simple formula of utilizing the existing Japanese government, the person of the Emperor, and the psychic force of tradition. No other formula was practicable. General MacArthur was able to make calculated use of its expected effectiveness because of expert intelligence on existing political, military, and social factors, and through his own brilliant appraisal of the Japanese mind.

By the tactful utilization and suitable modification of existing Japanese government organs, all Japanese armed forces in the homeland were physically disarmed by early December 1945. The War and Navy Ministries, initially responsible for demobilization, were demilitarized, placed under a civilian head, and renamed the "First Demobilization Bureau" (Army), whose principal job was the reception and demobilization of overseas troops as they arrived at repatriation ports; and the "Second Demobilization Bureau" (Navy), which was charged with the manning and operation of repatriation vessels, mine sweeping, and the maintenance of former naval vessels held at the disposal of the Allied Powers. By the middle of 1946, a total of about 2,170,000 Army and Navy personnel had been demobilized in the homeland and some 3,880,000 on repatriation from overseas.

Beginning with a handful of U.S. soldiers in late August 1945, the American Eighth Army had moved three corps and seven combat divisions into Japan for occupation duty within less than a month, to an aggregate of 232,379 men. The Sixth Army had mustered an approximately equal number. However, this was the high-water mark; the ebb tide of U.S. demobilization soon set in. Unaware of what was going on, critics at home began to be heard. General MacArthur remarked:

I have noticed some impatience based upon the assumption of a so-called soft policy in Japan. This can only arise from an erroneous concept of what is occurring. The first phases of the occupation must of necessity be based upon military considerations, the deployment of forward troops, the disarmament and demobilization of the enemy. This is coupled with the paramount consideration of withdrawing our former prisoners of war and war internees from the internment camps. . . .

During this interval of time, safety and complete security must be assured. When the first phase is completed other phases as provided in the surrender terms will infallibly follow. It is well understandable in the face of atrocities committed by the enemy that there should be impatience. This natural impulse, however, should be tempered by the fact that security and military expediency will require an exercise of some restraint. The surrender terms are not soft and they will not be applied in kid-glove fashion.

The inconsistency of armchair strategists, who clamored for punitive measures while weakening American military strength through a madly accelerated demobilization, was to be one of the marks of the period. One result was that by the end of 1945 the Eighth Army shrank to less than 200,000 men and was still shrinking. The Sixth Army was soon to vanish entirely.

It was in MacArthur's character as a humanitarian that all prior considerations gave way initially to the immediate relief of Allied prisoners of war and civil internees. Within a few hours of his arrival at Atsugi Airfield, the first American prisoners became free men. Three weeks later, virtually all those held prisoners on the Japanese mainland were on their way back home. The speed of liberation put the Eighth Army weeks ahead of the most enthusiastic estimates made for this enterprise.

The "recovered personnel detachment," an adjutant general's project, organized and trained teams to accompany our field forces; the recovery teams were set up on the basis of one for each 500 prisoners. Highest priority on transportation went to the prisoners, with air movements used at a maximum. Sick and wounded had special priority, but there was no discrimination because of rank, service, or nationality. It was estimated that thirty days might be required for complete evacuation of prisoners from Japan, which made it desirable for immediate relief measures to ease the last days of incarceration. Air drops seemed the most feasible method of bringing supplies to prison camps. Flight crews came in from all over the world for this Samaritan operation; they were called in from the

Presque Isle to Paris run; from the Wilmington to India run, and from North Africa via India and the Philippines. Some 63,000 needed cargo parachutes were rounded up; crews were briefed to drop bundles above 1,000 feet; the capacity of a B-29 was forty individual drop units, or a 10,000 pound load. Drops were made in three-, seven- and ten-day units. The three-day supplies included juices, soups, clothing, and medical supplies; the ten-day drops consisted almost entirely of food.

The Navy pitched in. The Third Fleet in Tokyo Bay had immediately available three hospital ships, thirty doctors, ninety corpsmen, and food for 3,000 patients. This was only a drop in the bucket: over 30,000 Allied prisoners had to be eventually fed and succored in inland camps. However, the Fleet could and did reach prisoner camps in the immediate vicinity of the waterfront. At Yokosuka naval base, 1,000 emaciated Allied prisoners were taken aboard the S.S. *Ancon.* Among them were survivors of Wake and Bataan who had withstood months of solitary confinement. At least 80 per cent of them were suffering from malnutrition; many were medical and surgical cases. The conditions in Omori and Shinagawa camps had been abominable; the third camp, Ofuna, had been the Gestapo center of Japan. A record of maltreatment and barbarities was established, leading to the eventual arrest and trial of the war criminals. Here was the forerunner of Oriental brutality that was still to reach satanic depths in the Korean and Chinese war.

An American surgeon, inmate of one of these camps, gave a graphic account of the reactions of our prisoners to the relief operations:

Flying low, six planes wove back and forth in single file. At a height of five thousand feet they roared over the camp. Three hundred ragged prisoners ran up and down the little compound waving their arms hysterically and yelling themselves hoarse. The fliers missed the signs in the heavy ground mist. They disappeared as we moaned and cursed. An hour later they appeared again, lower this time. Down through the cleft in the mountain, the flight leader dove straight for the enemy camp. We howled, cheered and pounded each other.

A black object hurtled down from the flight leader's plane: an orange parachute fluttered open. A suspended 55-gallon drum pendu-

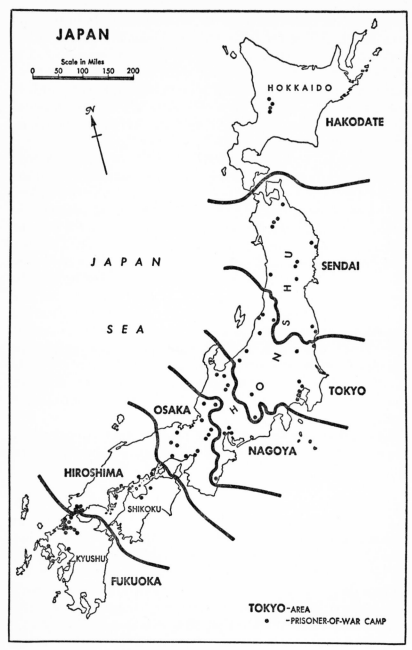

Japan: location of Allied prisoner-of-war camps, 1945

lumed back and forth three times and dropped with a thud in a clearing between the Nip administration and the galley—a bull's eye! One after another the planes roared down and dropped their loads. Something red fluttered down. The men high-tailed it. There was a note stuck in a sandbag which had a long red cloth streamer. It read: "Hello folks: The crew of the U.S.S. *Randolph* send their best. Hope you enjoy the chow. Keep your chin up. We'll be back."

Our first contact with American forces in three and a half years!

While the rescue of our prisoners went on, the occupation forces fanned out to their stations in Japan, from Kyushu in the south to Hokkaido in the north. This was comparable to a distribution of garrisons from Los Angeles to Seattle. Their silent purpose was control, security, and the supervision of demobilization and disarmament of Japan's armed millions.

The homeland demobilization proceeded with remarkable smoothness; American units in the field, on the regimental level within each Japanese prefecture, kept an eye on the military installations, barracks, warehousing, etc., while the disciplined Japanese military engineered their own disarmament. The experience of an American officer in an encounter with a Japanese armored column is typical of the casual atmosphere of the period:

A jeep bearing a lieutenant of the 43rd U.S. division was spinning along the road to Kumagayo when an approaching cloud of dust resolved itself into a Japanese tank column. As the lead tank stopped to permit passing on the narrow road, the soft shoulder crumbled and the jeep slid gently into the muck of a rice paddy. Climbing out, the officer scratched his head and pointed to a cable attached to the side of the tank. Meanwhile a Japanese officer had come running up and asked in broken English if the tank driver had been at fault. Assured of the contrary, he barked orders to his men and the tank driver jockeyed his tank into position, hooked the cable on the jeep and pulled it back on the road. The Japanese captain bowed politely, accepted a cigarette with thanks, ordered his tank column to continue, and waving amiably to the American, disappeared in a cloud of dust . . . en route to the nearest demobilization center!

MacArthur had every reason to chalk up an unqualified success when he reported on demobilization as follows:

I know of no demobilization in history, either in war or peace, by our own or by any other country, that has been accomplished so rapidly and so frictionlessly. Everything military, naval or air is forbidden in Japan. This ends its military might and its military influence in international affairs. It no longer reckons as a world power either large or small.

Approximately seven million armed men, including those in outlying theaters, have laid down their weapons. In the accomplishment of the extraordinarily difficult and dangerous surrender of Japan, not a shot was necessary, not even a drop of Allied blood was shed.

Again I wish to pay tribute to the magnificent conduct of our troops. They could easily—and understandably—have emulated the ruthlessness which their enemy have freely practised when conditions were reversed but their perfect balance between their implacable firmness of duty on the one hand and resolute restraint from cruelty on the other, has taught a lesson to the Japanese civil population that is startling in its impact. Nothing has so tended to impress Japanese thought—not even the catastrophic fact of military defeat itself. They have for the first time seen the free man's way of life in action and it has stunned them into new thoughts and ideas.

Less than four years later, the General was compelled to lay the foundation for rearmament and reorganization of a Japanese Army in order to protect his lines of communication when he had to throw his occupation troops into South Korea to block the communist invasion.

The destruction of surrendered war material, weapons, and ammunition boomeranged in a similar fashion. Japan had a highly developed prewar armament industry. Under the terms of the Potsdam Agreement its factories were dismantled and the complex machinery scrapped. Weapons were destroyed or dumped into the sea. American industry and the American taxpayer now make up the deficiencies. The Russians, on the other hand, repaired and preserved the matériel which the Japanese forces surrendered to them after their five-day war, and later turned the weapons over to the Chinese Communists, which tipped the balance in their favor at a critical juncture.

Amid the vindictiveness engendered by the Potsdam Declaration, MacArthur insisted on a modicum of hard common sense in the return to the Japanese civil economy of such military stores as could be reasonably converted to civilian use—food, uniforms, rubber boots, overcoats, and medicines. More than 21,000,000 pairs of socks, about 7,000,000 woolen blankets, and over 5,000,000 pairs of military shoes were returned to the Japanese government for distribution to Japanese citizens. Engineering and automotive equipment, vital in rebuilding devastated areas, was specifically excluded from the list of matériel to be destroyed. Initial requirements of the occupation forces for such articles as nails, ropes, cement, wire, and plywood were met, but, in general, were later returned for civilian use.

At the end of the war more than six million Japanese were scattered throughout the Pacific islands and on the Asiatic mainland. Their repatriation, desirable for purely humanitarian reasons as well as easing the economic burden on the liberated countries, became one of the major problems confronting General MacArthur. G-3 supervised the mass repatriation of these men, but the work was done by Japanese demobilization bureaus. By 1946 the bulk of overseas repatriates had been handled with relatively little shipping, reaching a weekly peak of nearly 200,000 persons. Thereafter followed the dilatory repatriation by the Soviets, a mere trickle floundering along over several years. MacArthur had to furnish the shipping. He offered to evacuate 300,000 a month, but the Russians reduced this figure to about 50,000: they had other plans.

These plans centered on the Soviet need for slave labor in the first instance, and for "brain-washed" and thoroughly indoctrinated Japanese Communist agents in the second. Stalling on the repatriation of Japanese military and civilians in Manchuria, the Soviets were soon involved in an international scandal of maltreatment and brutalities that matched anything on the dockets of the Allied War Tribunals proceeding against the Japanese or Germans. The Soviets refused information on their prisoners, and the subject matter became one of constant wrangling with Gen. Kuzma Derevyanko, the Soviet member of the Allied Council in Tokyo.

The Allied Council, like the Far Eastern Commission which sat in Washington, was presumably a "control" body for setting policy for the Occupation. Like the Far Eastern Commission, however, it functioned mainly as a "talk shop." It consisted of four members: the Supreme Commander, who was Chairman and U.S. representative; a representative each from China and the U.S.S.R.; and a member in joint representation of Great Britain, Australia, New Zealand, and India.

The Allied Council met every two weeks "to consult and advise" the Supreme Commander. But MacArthur soon made it plain that he was not anxious to seek the counsel of a body that contained an obstructionist Soviet element. He understood perfectly that General Derevyanko was there for discord, not for amity. After briefly inaugurating the first meeting of the Council, MacArthur designated the U.S. Ambassador to Japan, William J. Sebald, as his "deputy" and was never seen at a Council meeting thereafter.

Sebald handled matters adequately without MacArthur's prompting. When the Russians demanded an accounting of the "purges" in financial and industrial circles, Sebald countered this obstructionism by summoning General Whitney to read an alphabetical record of the organizations then purged. By nightfall the list was half finished, and the audience was in a state of exhaustion. On another occasion the Russians wept over the depressed state of Japanese labor. Whereupon Ambassador Sebald opened a searching inquiry into the missing Japanese prisoners in Siberia.

The obstructionism practiced by Derevyanko in the Allied Council soon reduced that body to a state of complete impotence. But it served to put MacArthur thoroughly on his guard about Soviet tactics in regard to prisoners. Intelligence had compiled numerous reports on the subject of Soviet slave labor and indoctrination camps; these reports disclosed many sinister things, chief among them being the systematic practice of "brain-washing" techniques. The most immediately horrifying thing about the report, however, was the discrepancy which it disclosed between Japanese and Russian figures bearing on the number of war prisoners in Siberia. According to the Japanese estimates, close to half a million Japanese were still unaccounted for as late as April 1949. More than 300,000 Japanese had been swallowed up in Siberia; approximately 100,000 had disappeared in Sakhalin and the Kuriles, and some 50,000 were "lost" in Chinese Communist controlled areas.

From 1946 to 1949 MacArthur had pressed periodically for the repatriation of the missing half-million. Idle ships were kept waiting, steam up, to report to Soviet ports. But nothing happened as Derevyanko and his mates kept stalling. Then, in May 1949, to quote the MacArthur report:

. . . came a shattering Soviet announcement. A *Tass* press release in Moscow on 20 May 1949, indicated that only 95,000 former Japanese troops remained to be repatriated. This figure was at complete variance with official Japanese Government Demobilization Bureau compilations. . . . These records listed a total of 469,041 persons still to be repatriated from Soviet controlled areas as of 26 May 1949.

For years repeated efforts by MacArthur to obtain precise statistical information from Soviet authorities on general prisoners of war totals or on deaths of Japanese internees had been abortive. Soviet repatriation authorities had refused to allow repatriates to carry ashes of their dead back to their homeland, an old Japanese tradition, and had suppressed the transmittal of Japanese rosters of deceased internees to offset this official silence. . . .

The difference between the Soviet and Japanese figure is roughly 374,000 persons. Though this figure appears staggering, it must be remembered that the prisoners were held for over four years under unbelievably hard working and living conditions conducive to an extremely high death rate.

To ascertain the fate of these people, MacArthur's intelligence section started questioning returned prisoners of war. Repatriates promptly reported that intolerable conditions found in Soviet prison camps resulted in thousands of fatalities. The enslaved Japanese had undergone incredible sufferings. In a cross-section survey of 209,-300 prisoners in over a hundred Soviet camps, sworn statements by survivors indicated that 51,332 had died from malnutrition and communicable diseases. The mortality rate thus obtained was 24.5 per cent. In certain areas the mortality rate ran as high as 60 per cent.

Typical of the reports was that of a repatriate employed as a gravedigger at one of the district hospitals:

So many died from starvation and disease that a crew of 50 men could not keep up with the job of burying the dead. According to a medical officer, the deaths between 1945 and 1947 ran as high as 30 per cent in that area.

Discounting the initially high death rates reported in certain localities as applying uniformly to all camps, such macabre percentages easily explain the discrepancies in Japanese and Russian figures. These men died under slave-labor conditions far worse than those in the days of the Czars. The element of Soviet barbarity was clearly established by the MacArthur findings, which were duly forwarded to Washington.

Summarized later in a notarized eyewitness report under the title of "Life and Death in Siberian P.W. Camps," the whole story was placed before the United Nations. The United Nations chose to ignore it, but General MacArthur was able to use it effectively in his private "cold war" with the Russian Embassy in Tokyo. Whenever General Derevyanko tried to pose as the "protector of Japanese labor, and individual rights," Ambassador Sebald threw the mass murder of Japanese captives in the Russian's teeth. His arguments collapsed forthwith.

To complicate MacArthur's difficulties further, the Russians were "brain-washing" and converting to communism certain carefully selected individuals among their Japanese prisoners with the object of returning them to Japan to operate as leaders of the Soviet fifth column. MacArthur's report spoke of a communist indoctrination program that functioned as a

. . . vast centrifugal machine designed to reconstruct the lives and political future of every prisoner within its scope. It was skillfully adapted to the Japanese form and habit of thought. Carefully paced to the prisoner's current circumstances and to each stage of his development, it was implemented in the prison camps by a group of Japanese Communists, working under Soviet direction. Fellow prisoners, early converts to Communism through conviction or expediency, they combined the unsavory roles of propagandists and informers.

The positive indoctrination of selected "brain-washed" Japanese prisoners began with an offensive on the Emperor and military caste systems. Then a "Japan newspaper" was introduced into the scheme. This newspaper, edited by a Japanese staff, kept the prisoners in a ferment of anxiety by printing calculated lies and half-truths about the fate of their families under the American Occupation. When the prisoners had become convinced of the "horrors" of life in Japan under the American "exploiters," they were ripe for taking a pledge:

"To overthrow the Emperor system."
"To establish a communist government in Japan."
"To join and support the Japan Communist Party."

The newly fledged Japanese Communist agents and group leaders were then given special training for future work in Japan. Selected and tried converts took special courses in the four important training centers: The Moscow Indoctrination School, and the Democratic School, the Youths' School, and the Political School, the latter three at Khormorin. Only the most advanced students of communism were enrolled at the intelligence school at Moscow, a training center for special intelligence agents.

Kikan Toso, or "struggle upon returning home," was the name given the program which the "brain-washed" repatriates were supposed to carry out. They were taken in tow by investigation squads charged with determining each man's degree of progress in communist indoctrination. If an individual was found to be below required standards, he was sent to a labor battalion for an indefinite period. Survivors of the program underwent an intensive propaganda course based on the assumption that one and all loved and revered the Soviets and were reluctant to leave Siberia. Strenuous efforts were made to smarten up the appearance of the indoctrinated repatriates as they took ship for Japan, though little enough could be done with what remained of their clothing.

The Russians chose 1949 as the test year of their plan to inject 95,000 communist-indoctrinated repatriates into the blood stream of Japan. There is no question that this was a plan of almost scientific quality engineered by the Soviet Embassy in Tokyo—though it boomeranged in the end. Aboard ships the repatriates showed their Soviet training in complete non-cooperation: they refused to sign personnel cards, indulged in dancing and capering, displayed insolence in food and clothing issues, and practiced every kind of chicanery to try the patience of ships' crews and reception-center authorities. They boarded special trains only to leave them at unauthorized stops to join rowdy demonstrations of local communist organizations; there was hardly a railway station in even the most remote areas where the returnees failed to shout communist songs, to the shocked bewilderment of their waiting families. These tactics demonstrated to the Japanese people as nothing else could have done the corrosive character of communism. They also furnished a test of the efficiency of the Japanese police, under G-2 management in its "Public Safety Division." In a single executive session of police chiefs, local ordinances were invoked that kept repatriates under military control until delivered to their home towns. Within twenty-four hours heavy penalties put a stop to unauthorized absences or

Nippon Times

第二十四年二月十七日　　TOKYO, FRIDAY, AUGUST 5, 1949　　第三種郵便物認可 ●

Nippon Times

Published by
The Nippon Times, Ltd.
KIYOSHI TOGASAKI, President

TOKYO OFFICE
1. Ichome Uchisaiwai-cho, Chiyoda-
ku Central P.O. Box 144, 352, 359
Telephones: Ginza (57) 303, 403, 5851,
5858, 5852, 1003.
Telegraphic Address: "Times To-
kyo-yubin"

OSAKA: Dojima Bldg. Tel.: Bori-
kawa (35) 177.

SUBSCRIPTION RATE:
¥2.945 per copy ¥0.055 charges
incidental to sales tax Thursday
issue with supplement ¥4.906
¥0.099 charges incidental to sales
tax One month ¥89.00. ¥1.65
charges incidental to sales tax
Obtainable directly from all newspaper agents in Japan. By mail
¥104.5 per month. ¥1.79 charges incidental to sales tax. For foreign
countries postage ¥150.00 per
month extra.

TOKYO, FRIDAY, AUG. 5, 1949

echoed and re-echoed many times since the begining of this year's repatriation program.

These questions are asked because the repatriates have shown time and again that they apparently lack the basic sentiments and feelings which differentiate human from beasts. For almost a week with their native land in sight and with loved ones waiting, a shipload of repatriates have sullenly refused to land. Others have snarled and snaped at the warm words of welcome and

Men or Beasts?

Are these men or beasts the Soviets are sending back to Japan from their prison camps? It is no wonder that an anguished mother welcoming her long - absent son should cry out, "What have they done to my son?" That cry has been

the kind hands extended in heartfelt sympathy. Still others have stonily brushed aside their families, who have been impatiently waiting these many years to have them back under their family roof, to stay with the pack. Moving as animal herds, they move and act at the direction of the pack leaders whatever the action or course may be.

Where is their individuality? Where is their feeling for family and home? Where is their sentiment for their native land? Where is their respect for law and order?

Perhaps the repatriates themselves should not be judged too severely for they are the products of Communist training. They are the ones so well indoctrinated that the Soviets allowed their return. They are Communists.

It is small wonder that the families of the repatriates should ask, "What have they done . . . ?" The Japanese know now, if they did not know before, what communism does to men. What sensible, freedom-loving people would take in an ideology which robs men of their individuality and their sensibility as human beings?

public demonstrations. Eventually, the repatriates could see for themselves that they had been fed outrageous lies about the Occupation and the Americans. With returning sanity they wrote hundreds of personal apologies to MacArthur.

The influx of communist agitators created a security problem that could not be met by the mere presence of troops; it called for the operation of open and covert intelligence agencies. MacArthur's G-2 promptly oriented his wartime apparatus toward "civil" rather than "military" intelligence. A newly created "Civil Intelligence Section" operated in fairly well defined channels, and the old G-2 "work horses" pulled in fresh harness.

The 441st Counter Intelligence Corps supplied almost all the information on subversive activities in Japan, with special emphasis on communist agitators, saboteurs, and foreign espionage agents. Its work was roughly analogous to that of the American FBI. In the tense period following the initial occupation, its personnel handled the job of "securing" headquarters and other important installations. A network of detachments spread through Japan, eventually maintaining an observation unit in every prefecture.

In December 1945 the former headquarters of the Japanese Military Police (Kempei-Tai) was taken over in Tokyo. The Kempei-Tai was the enemy counterintelligence agency which G-2 had to combat from Papua to the Philippines. It was an impressive and ironic occasion when the American unit took over as its own the former main headquarters of the Kempei-Tai and named it after Capt. John H. Norton, an officer killed on Okinawa.

During the first months of the Occupation, the Civil Intelligence Section was responsible for effecting the release of those individuals who had been imprisoned, or held under "protection and surveillance," for violation of the multitudinous laws, decrees, and regulations which for so many years had restricted the freedom of speech, thought, religion, and assembly of the Japanese people. Actually, they went overboard in at least one case: the release of Japanese Communists and the members of the Sorge espionage ring—a fabulous Russian spy organization with important American ramifications which were finally exposed.

The Sorge case has profound historical significance: it contained proof that the communization of China was engineered by American brains. Along with Gerhart Eisler, most of the wheelhorses of the American Communist Party operated in Shanghai: Earl Browder, Eugene Dennis, W. Haskell, Katherine Harrison, George Hardy, J. H. Dolson, Sam Darcy, and Harry Berger. The press was eager for publication of the facts, but the case was virtually suppressed at that time through the intervention of Kenneth Royall, the Secretary of War; Gen. Omar Bradley, the Chief of Staff; and the Secretary of the Interior, Harold Ickes. Their motivation is still unexplained. No one, of course, suggests that this miscellany of high dignitaries were Communists, but Tokyo headquarters felt that they must be naïve and gullible to lend the enormous prestige of their offices to shield communist traitors and saboteurs from exposure in the press.

Concurrently, leftists and fellow-travelers were hired in the States and unloaded on the civil sections of general headquarters, although the majority of civil occupation personnel were entirely satisfactory. MacArthur had no choice of selection or refusal. Derogatory reports eventually reached Tokyo from various security agencies in Washington. Then began a time-consuming local process to get rid of these people, often made abortive by "Loyalty Boards" that failed to function. Some of these individuals were later haled before Congressional committees that were interested in the Institute of Pacific Relations; the leftist infiltration of general headquarters was in full swing. The situation is obvious in a partial tabulation of critical information below; names are withheld under current security regulations; only eight typical "case histories" of individuals in key positions are shown; there were many, many others:

Summary of Derogatory Information	A	B	C	D	E	F	G	H
FBI reports, derogatory	x	x		x				
G-2 reports, derogatory	x	x	x	x	x	x	x	x
Local investigations, derogatory	x	x	x			x	x	
State Department reports, derogatory							x	
Association with Institute of Pacific Relations	x	x	x		x			x
Membership in Communist Party	x						x	
Membership in Communist-front organizations	x		x		x			
Local Red press contacts		x	x			x	x	
Local Russian contacts	x						x	

Summary of Derogatory Information	A	B	C	D	E	F	G	H
American League for Peace and Democracy		×	×					
Open Letter for Co-operation with U.S.S.R.			×					
American Peace Mobilization				×				
American Friends of Chinese People		×						
Washington Book Shop				×			×	
Workers' Alliance				×				

Despite the fact that troops could hardly assist directly in the ferreting out of communist agents, the decrease in the occupation forces represented a steadily mounting internal security risk. As of 1949 the total American military strength in Japan was set at 117,-580, of which only 68 per cent were combat troops available for emergencies. This shrunken force, plus the lightly equipped Japanese police with 122,673 men, constituted the only control force for almost 80,000,000 people. The Communist Party of Japan, following the usual pattern, infiltrated labor, communications, and the intelligentsia. They concentrated on basic industries as they have done in all countries they seek to subvert: transportation, communications, electric power, and coal mining. With the strike as the habitual weapon of coercion, though it was broken in the first collision with MacArthur, the Communists had the power in 1948 to disrupt major industries and services on a percentage basis, as follows:

Rail Transportation	50% stoppage through interruption of key points
Communications	80% stoppage of telephone, telegraph, wireless and postal services
Electric Power	50% stoppage
Coal Mining	30% stoppage

The Communists concentrated on five areas in Japan in which there were particularly heavy concentrations of repatriates, *i.e.*, trained, disciplined, organized bodies. With roughly one Japanese policeman to 300 population and one American soldier to 1,000 population, MacArthur had little enough "muscle." Such insignificant numbers could hardly have prevailed against a restless population with a 10 per cent nucleus of militarized communist-minded repatriates, a hard core to furnish organized leadership.

Fortunately, the Japanese Communists never quite dared to make any overt move to capture either industrial or political power in the 1945–1950 period. In obeisance to Moscow, they stuck to their propagandistic functions in so far as above-ground action was concerned. Spying and fifth-column activities were, however, another story.

The free world has recently learned something of the communist fifth columns operating in every country. The disclosures of espionage and subversion are incontrovertible, though fellow-travelers and leftists still wage a bitter fight against the truth. The intelligence services, of course, have always been aware of this creeping menace, but their reports over the years were ignored in an era of myopic official appeasement or were pigeonholed by traitors in key administrative positions. The experience of Tokyo was no exception. Long before McCarthy or Velde became nationally known, the silhouette of Soviet espionage and communist penetration in the Far East had been sharply etched in intelligence channels—only to be ignored or suppressed in Washington. An extract from a report of the period reads:

. . . the Soviet diplomatic Mission in Japan is no exception to the world-wide pattern [of Soviet espionage]. It began with a small Military Mission, attached to MacArthur's Headquarters in 1945; it numbered 16 persons. Following the occupation of Japan, it expanded to 467, exclusive of dependents. MacArthur applied pressure in 1948 and the number was reduced to 172.

The plan to unload thousands of agitators on the economy of Japan, in the repatriation of 1949, was a joint Soviet-Japanese Communist party scheme. An increasing number of "sleeper" agents were discovered amongst the repatriates. The approach used by the Soviets seldom varied. Under pressure, the individual joined the Soviet secret service. He was given a code name and informed in great detail what method would be used to transmit information.

It was no surprise to G-2 that the "sleeper" missions were focussed on military intelligence with special emphasis on Hokkaido and Northern Honshu. Hokkaido is separated by a narrow channel only from

Soviet-held Sakalin—one of the lush prizes given the Soviets for their five-day picnic in Manchuria at the end of the war.

Specific interest was shown in:

a. Location, strength and command personnel of U.S. Forces in the area.

b. Ship and cargo movements; identification and movement of warships.

c. Railroad terminals, equipment and repair facilities.

d. Disposition and organization of the Japanese Police and Coast Guard.

e. Details on installations of the American Air Force.

On the mechanics of tracking down these individuals or taking countermeasures, security regulations as well as common sense prevent too detailed disclosures.

In the field of international surveillance, *i.e.* counterespionage dealing primarily with the Russians and their communist affiliates, investigative agencies sometimes drifted into ambitious duplication if not direct competition. A memo by Captain E. J. L., an "ace" operator, is typical:

Beginning with the outbreak of the Korean war, we got fake reports from all sorts of swindlers that the Russians were "burning their documents"; the information if true would normally be vital: a precaution by diplomatic personnel prior to joining the Korean war. *Tokyo got this bit of news from Washington!* That meant that some independent agency had sent this "canard" without clearing it with G-2. It was up to us to disprove it. It was not too difficult. The Soviet Embassy employed Japanese labor, including a carpenter shop. Personnel transferred from Japan would normally crate their belongings about ten days in advance of departure. We were able to spot any major dislocation in that way.

The proof that the Soviet Embassy was financing espionage was more complex and it took time. The Japanese Government furnished a certain amount of Yen per capita, to every Allied Mission, chargeable against the War Reparations Account. The Finance Section handled the payments. We arranged to list the serial numbers of the banknotes. When they appeared in the hands of "double agents," the Russian link was established.

One of the most important counterintelligence tasks during the first months of the Occupation was the apprehension of the "Class A" war-criminal suspects. The first from a list of several hundred of these suspects were placed behind bars during September 1945. A spectacular apprehension was that of former Gen. Hideki Tojo, Prime Minister during most of the war. When officers arrived at Tojo's home on September 11, 1945, he barricaded the door, seated himself in an overstuffed chair, and unsuccessfully attempted suicide.

While MacArthur was bent on eliminating all militaristic influence from the Japanese government, he kept himself aloof from the juridical proceedings of the International War Crimes Tribunal which condemned the Japanese war criminals. An attempt was made to link the Occupation—and MacArthur—with the Tokyo counterpart of the Nuremberg body, but MacArthur never countenanced it. Actually, the trial and conviction of the Japanese war leaders was an Allied governmental action on the highest level. It was the work of the artisans of Yalta, Teheran, and Potsdam, not of any group connected with the Occupation. The members of the Allied Council attended the grisly, shattering hanging of the principal Japanese figures, but they attended as representatives of their respective governments, not as judges or executioners. MacArthur kept his own counsel about the whole business. The staff had the impression that he was not in agreement with the excessive punitive measures of the Morgenthau philosophy. As a historian, he was aware of the deep resentment of the defeated South—decades after the War of Secession. He anticipated the day when strong allies would again be needed in the East and West to contain the growing communist threat, when Japan and Germany would be asked to rearm in their traditional role of a bulwark against Soviet imperialistic encroachments.

14 Japan: The Political Phase

MacARTHUR'S implied mandate in Japan had a threefold aspect. One aspect, that of military security, was dealt with in the preceding chapter; the other aspects were reform and recovery. As we have seen, the years 1945 to 1946 were largely taken up with problems of disarmament and repatriation of Japanese overseas troops. Then came the big police reforms and the purges of top-level individuals with militarist records from government, business, and banking. Overlapping the purge period in 1947–1948 came the civil reforms, the remaking of parliament under a far more representative balance of power, and so on. Finally, there came the more positive aspects of economic reconstruction, a job that was gathering headway when the Korean War broke out.

In a special study in 1949 entitled "Japan: An Economy of Survival," General MacArthur commented on the functional evolution of the first three years:

It is a mistake to assay the results of the Occupation solely in terms of economic recovery. A fair evaluation can only be made with reference to the objectives of the Occupation. For many years Japan's greatest asset—and liability—has been her population, which now numbers over 81,000,000 or more than half that of the United States, crammed into an area about equal to California. Since only one-sixth of the land area of Japan is arable and the rest mountainous, the population in the arable plains is about 2,840 persons per square mile. Thus, with the utmost intensive cultivation, Japan is still unable to meet the minimum requirements for her survival. . . .

In these circumstances, I proceeded as rapidly as possible to accomplish the given mission. I decided at an early date to permit the Japanese authorities to carry responsibility and to exercise initiative in administering Japan's internal affairs. Physical disarmament and demilitarization were begun at once and soon completed. In the political field, the first important moves were toward the abolition of restrictions on the basic freedoms. . . .

Given the docility of the Japanese under the Emperor, most phases of keeping order were not too difficult, though no chances were taken. One of the first acts of MacArthur was to abolish the dread "Thought Police" which had long maintained an iron grip on Japanese society. Along with the "Thought Police" went other special bodies and powers of the police; for example, their tendency to exercise absolute control over the economic and social life of a community.

As between reform and recovery, there was, of course, the age-old problem of which logically should come first. Decision on this problem was taken out of MacArthur's hands by orders from Washington to concentrate on reform once certain basic measures had been taken to keep the Japanese from starvation. While MacArthur was personally charged with "democratizing" Japan, the methods of democratizing could not be those of *force majeure*. The post-surrender operational directive read:

This [the Japanese] government should conform as closely as may be to principles of democratic self-government but it is not the responsibility of the Allied Powers to impose upon Japan any form of government not supported by the freely expressed will of the people.

Whether this was to be interpreted to mean that the Japanese had powers of initiation, or merely of ratification by consent, was somewhat vague. MacArthur's own desire was to have the Japanese do the democratizing for themselves, under their own free will. If they would only pick up the ball and run with it, nothing would please MacArthur more; if, on the other hand, they showed apathy, SCAP stood ready to "suggest."

Some things were naturally preordained by the very nature of MacArthur's mandate to "insure that Japan will not again become a menace to the United States or to the peace and security of the world." The Japanese had nothing to say about the instructions from Washington that called for the dismissal of all Regular Army officers, the abolition of the Japanese General Staff, and the liquidation of all veterans' pension rights. They had nothing to say about the dissolution of the Kempei-Tai—the notorious Japanese secret police. They had nothing to say about certain "Bill of Rights" provisions that are basic to any good democracy or republic; nor did they have any rights about defining purge requirements.

On October 4, 1945, barely a month after MacArthur's landing at Atsugi, SCAP told the Japanese government to remove "restrictions on political, civil and religious liberties." Political prisoners, including Communists, were ordered released. The Ministries of Home and Justice were ordered abolished, and a Civil Liberties Bureau was set up. By way of piquant reminder to those who call MacArthur a "reactionary," Roger Baldwin, veteran head of the American Civil Liberties Union, visited Japan before the Korean War and found MacArthur's philosophy of civil liberty very much to his own taste.

The purges, which were decreed as part of the Potsdam Agreement, were designed to eradicate every trace of militarist influence from the Japanese government. The first purge struck drastically at a thousand or more members of the national government, including a few members of the cabinet. Concurrent purges removed "militarist" officials in the villages, the cities, and the forty-six Japanese prefectures. Businessmen who had been involved in the military and financial penetration of Manchuria, Formosa, and Indo-China were separated from their jobs. Militant patriotic societies were abolished. Finally, journalists and other "public service" people who had militaristic records were told they must move to other lines of business. Aside from the convicted military criminals, those purged were not deprived of property or general civil rights; what was prohibited to them was the right to hold political office or jobs designed to influence public policy in certain specified fields.

Naturally, since some very able Japanese were affected by the purges, SCAP was accused of "removing the best brains of Japan." But the whole business was handled with enormous tact and restraint. In successive removals or disqualifications, the record of each individual was carefully examined by American and Japanese investigators and reviewed by Japanese screening boards. Actually, only 8,000 persons were removed or barred from political office, about 600 from key positions in business and finance, and about 200 from the field of public information. The Japanese themselves recognized MacArthur's restraint and tolerance in this matter. The Justice Minister, Yoshio Suzuki, spoke for a considerable segment in and out of government when he said:

It is regrettable that there are people in this country who do not consider the purge question sternly enough. In Germany 100,000 people have been thrown into jail and 1,000,000 fined, sentenced to menial labor, their property confiscated. In our country, however, those who precipitated the nation into war are only barred from office, which, we must explicitly bear in mind, is due to General MacArthur's generous occupation policy.

MacArthur welcomed the banishment of the Tojo clique and the Pearl Harbor men from the public life of Japan. And, though he is a traditionalist, he did not boggle at the idea of limiting the Japanese peerage to members of the Emperor's family. But he suspected the hand of the Russians in the provisions calling for the liquidation of veterans' pensions—after all, some of those pensions were being paid to soldiers and sailors who had served the Allied cause in 1917 and 1918. Moreover, while he wanted the General Staff abolished, he did not wish to force starvation upon regular officers. It was a dangerous restriction since the Communist Party offered all sorts of inducements to the dispossessed. With an eye to the Communist Army of the future, they realized that an officer corps is hard to improvise.

Once the requirements of submission to the Potsdam Declaration had been carried out, the Japanese had all the latitude in the world to create their idea of a nation conforming as "closely as may be" to democracy. As soon as it was practicable, MacArthur shifted his emphasis from direction to leadership. He saw from the start that the shadow of Allied bayonets was not conducive to democratic evolution. The staff was cautioned that all measures taken by the Japanese themselves were to be reviewed only in the light of broad principles. SCAP itself was organized to encourage and assist the Japanese in putting the stamp of their own thought on all acts of civil government. A government section under Gen. Courtney Whitney stood ready to help with the writing of a new constitution —which at MacArthur's suggestion, incidentally, was to be adopted as an *amendment* to the old constitution, thus emphasizing the idea of a great nation's continuity. An Economics and Scientific Section was set up under General Marquat, MacArthur's amiable anti-aircraft officer in New Guinea and the Philippines. Col. H. G. Schenck, on loan from the University of California, headed a Natural Resources Section; Gen. Crawford F. Sams was in charge of the Public Health and Welfare Section; a Civil Information and Education Section was established under Col. D. Nugent, a former educator in Japan.

By June 1950, the date of the outbreak of the Korean War, SCAP had achieved an enviable record in encouraging the Japanese to reform themselves in accordance with democratic concepts. Habeas corpus, which had been brought to the Philippines by Arthur MacArthur in 1900, became part of Japanese law under son Douglas forty-five years later. The new Japanese constitution, promulgated in 1946, had become effective in May of 1947. Shinto was disestablished as a state religion. Agrarian reform had been just about completed: practically all of the acreage chosen for redistribution to small holders had been taken over at forced-sale prices from the big landlords, which meant that 90 per cent of the land had become owner-operated as compared to 54 per cent in 1945. A labor movement had been established on Western lines, with a membership of close to 7,000,000. Women's suffrage had become a reality; education had been decentralized, and the textbooks rewritten by the Japanese themselves to exclude militarist interpretations.

If the record was good, however, it had taken considerable missionary work by SCAP-ists as well as willing cooperation by the Japanese.

The writing of the constitution represented the first hazard of new fortunes which the Japanese had to face. It was also the biggest hurdle which Gen. Courtney Whitney's Government Section had to take. But Whitney and his men were up to it. Whitney had had a spectacular rise in the MacArthur headquarters organization, be-

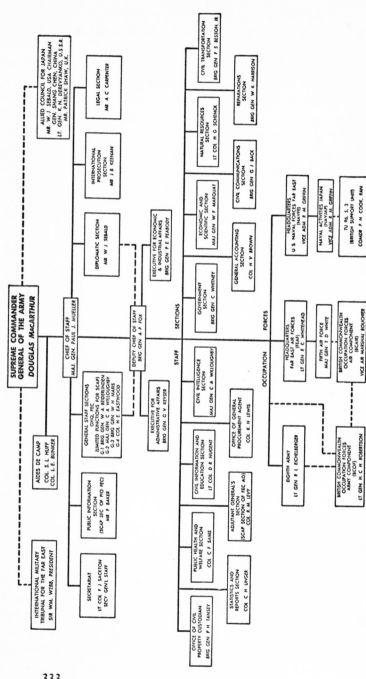

The staff of SCAP

ginning with 1943 when he appeared in Brisbane, in the grade of lieutenant colonel, to develop and expand the Philippines guerrilla system that was initiated as a G-2 activity in 1942; a successful and prominent corporation lawyer in prewar Manila, General Whitney had exceptional background for this particular assignment, as he was familiar with every facet of economic and political conditions in the Philippines. After the liberation of the Philippines he headed the civil-affairs organization that did much to rehabilitate the islands. When MacArthur moved on to Japan, it was in character that Whitney should undertake high-level governmental reforms as head of the Government Section. He assembled a group of clever and able assistants: Charles L. Kades, Frank Rizzo, Justin Williams, Alfred Hussey, Cecil Tilton, and others.

Whitney's report on the work of the Government Section stressed the "catalytic" nature of the work done by MacArthur in stirring the Japanese to create their own democracy. He says:

MacArthur set the pattern for peace while engaged in the violence of war. The initial Philippines Campaign was conducted without superseding the civil by the military power. From Corregidor President Quezon conducted affairs of his government in complete freedom and authority. MacArthur continued to adhere scrupulously to this concept after he reached Australia and never failed to refer all civil problems of the Philippines to President Quezon for decision, even though the latter was in exile in Washington.

Later on, just three days following MacArthur's landing in Leyte, the General formally restored all of the civil powers within conquered territory, to President Osmena. Thereafter, as other Philippine areas became liberated, they automatically reverted to civil control.

With such a background of rigid adherence to a distinction between the civil and military power, the pattern for the Occupation was basically designed long before hostilities ended: It was a foregone conclusion that MacArthur would elect to utilize the existing machinery of civil government.

The Japanese officials, however, did not catch their cues with the alacrity shown in the Philippines by Osmena after MacArthur had landed at Leyte. They moved slowly and tentatively. Nevertheless, there was movement. After Prince Konoye, the last man of peace to hold office before Pearl Harbor, had sought MacArthur's advice about revising the old Meiji constitution, a meeting between George Atcheson, Jr., MacArthur's political adviser, and Konoye was arranged. Atcheson specified several changes that were close to MacArthur's heart, such as extension of the authority of the Japanese House of Representatives over the budget, abolition of the Emperor's power of veto and curtailment of his authority to legislate by rescript, provision for a bill of rights defining the relations between citizen and government, establishment of independent judges, democratization of the House of Peers, and so on. A Japanese committee under Dr. Joji Matsumoto was appointed to draft a revised constitution, and the various political parties and other unofficial groups were invited to express their views.

What happened was a heartening commentary on the Japanese people themselves. The official Matsumoto Committee backed and filled whenever it came to changing the basic nature of the Meiji constitution, but the unofficial groups came out with far more progressive proposals. In the light of public reaction against the Matsumoto draft, which left the old Emperor system very much where it was, SCAP insisted on a new approach. MacArthur's own notes stipulated three major constitutional changes. The rights and duties of the Emperor, said MacArthur:

. . . will be exercised in accordance with the Constitution and [be] responsible to the basic will of the people as provided therein. . . . War as a sovereign right of the nation is abolished . . . and no rights of belligerency will ever be conferred upon any Japanese force. . . . The feudal system of Japan will cease.

General Whitney passed the MacArthur notes on to Colonel Kades and the other officers of the Government Section in charge of constitutional reform, and the Shidehara Cabinet was told that the Matsumoto draft must be done over again.

When Dr. Matsumoto expostulated that "some of the roses of the West, when cultivated in Japan, lose their fragrance," a crisis developed in the Japanese Cabinet over meeting MacArthur's three points. The Cabinet attitude was expressed in a fearful "What will the Emperor say?" But when Prime Minister Shidehara and Foreign Minister Yoshida finally called on Emperor Hirohito for his views, they were dumfounded to learn that the Emperor himself backed all the MacArthur proposals, even those which would deprive the Imperial institution of all political authority. Hirohito had caught an inkling of what a Whitney Government Section report called

. . . the urge of the common man toward freedom from oppression [which] . . . had not been stifled . . . but became almost a triumphant shout. . . . The Japanese people looked on the surrender almost as a liberation . . . that faced real . . . democratization.

After that, the rest was foreordained: General Whitney's Government Section had relatively easy sailing. Whitney assembled texts of the important constitutions of the outside world. The combined Japanese and SCAP experts then made a comparative analysis of constitutions and drafted an entirely new constitutional document that was offered as an amendment to the old document. The judicial system was made independent of the executive; the Emperor's authority was limited to persuasion and personal influence. And the Japanese forbade themselves to make war: the constitution proclaimed that "war, as a sovereign right of the nation . . . is forever renounced as a means of settling disputes with other nations. The maintenance of land, sea, and air forces, as well as other war potential, will never be authorized. . . ."

This document was approved by Hirohito, accepted by the parliament, and finally promulgated as basic law. When the public prosecutor of Tokyo dismissed *lèse majesté* charges against five people who had publicly criticized the Emperor, it was a sign that the Japanese had grasped the nature of a "government of laws, not of men," under which the Emperor himself was simply another man bound by law. MacArthur took the opportunity to comment on the dismissal of the *lèse majesté* charges:

The decision of the Japanese procurators to drop accusations against men charged with *lèse majesté* is a noteworthy application of the fundamental concept, embodied in the new Constitution just adopted by the National Diet, that all men are equal before the law, that no individual in Japan—not even the Emperor—shall be clothed in legal protection denied the common man. It marks the beginning of a true understanding of the lofty spirit of the new National Charter, which affirms the dignity of all men, and secures to all the right freely to discuss all issues, political, social, and economic, of concern to the people of a democratic nation. For the free interchange of ideas, the free expression of opinion, the free criticism of officials and institutions is essential to the life and growth of popular government. Democracy is vital and dynamic, but cannot survive unless all citizens are free thus to speak their minds. Such action, moreover, emphasizes the fact that from this land, broken and ravaged by war, there is emerging a free people and a free nation. As the Emperor becomes under this new Constitution the symbol of the State, with neither inherent political power nor authority, the Japanese men and women are raised to a new status of political dignity and, in fact, will become the rulers of Japan. In his new role, the Emperor will symbolize the repository of state authority—the citizen. The dignity of the State will become the dignity of the individual citizen, and the protection accorded him as the symbol of the State ought to be no more and no less than the protection accorded the citizen. To hold the contrary would constitute a direct negation of one of the basic principles of democratic government. It would but serve to perpetuate the pattern of feudalism, and autocracy, and do violence to those basic freedoms acknowledged by Japan and to which the Emperor himself has given most hearty accord. It should be needless to point out that it is for an enlightened public opinion to exert its great moral influence to the end that this right freely to criticize be exercised with decorum and restraint—that all public officials be protected against unwarranted defamation or vilification in licentious disregard of the respect to which they as free individuals in a free society and as the public representatives of a free people are fully entitled.

MacArthur's pride in the new constitution was expressed formally in his speech on the second anniversary of its adoption. He said:

Today marks the second anniversary of the birth of new Japan— a Japan conceived in the impoverished aftermath of war's violence, seeking political stability and social progress through concepts which hold to the primacy of individual liberty, equal opportunity, and personal dignity. These have been fruitful years as you progressively have come to understand and live by the new and enlightened constitutional precepts. Your basic laws have been recast and your public institutions redesigned. Your selected architects and builders have worked arduously to fabricate a citadel of freedom from those imperishable human norms drawn from the experience of the ages. And your house now rests upon a political and social foundation which, if well fortified by the human spirit, should remain impervious to the ideological stresses and strains which threaten all about you. Your farmers now own the soil they and their forebears long have tilled—and your women now exercise influence upon the political and social course of Japan's destiny, all beneficiaries of human rights and fundamental liberties rendered inalienable by your constitutional mandates. These changes in the moral values of Japanese life have brought about a regeneration of the Japanese edifice. This edifice, if it firmly stands as an impregnable barrier against the forces bent upon its destruction, will strengthen the faith of all peoples in the spirituality of human freedom. And in proportion as you value this freedom, you must understand, cherish, and preserve it.

MacArthur is also proud of the laws enacted by the Japanese parliament to establish local government on an autonomous base; of these laws, he said:

Democracy cannot be imposed upon a nation. It is a thing of the spirit which to be lasting and durable must impregnate the very roots of society. It is not to be instilled from above. It must have its origin in the understanding and faith of the common people. It must well up from the people's will to be free, from their desire and determination to govern their own local affairs without domination by their own strongmen, by minority pressure groups, or by entrenched bureaucracy. It is essential, therefore, that the people in every prefecture, city, and village be given complete opportunity to express their will, and by assuming full responsibility to learn procedures of democratic government. Such direct participation in local government will profoundly influence the shaping of national policies—will provide a checkrein against arbitrary governmental controls and a safeguard to individual freedom. . . . It is axiomatic that such experience in government will develop the dynamic and enlightened leadership and intiative essential to the vigorous and progressive building of a democratic nation.

The form of the new Japanese government, however, might not have made so much difference if the leadership had not been reconstructed almost from the beginning to match it. There wasn't time to wait for local autonomy to train new leaders. By screening out the chauvinistic wartime faces as a means "of creating new democratic leadership responsive to the will of the people," SCAP changed the balance of power in the nation almost at the start. New faces began to appear progressively in public and electoral positions. A tabulation of the results of the general election in January 1949 is significant of the "trend toward renovation." There was a total of 1,365 candidates, divided as follows:

Party	New Faces	Holdover from 4th Diet (1947)	Holdover from 3d Diet (1945)
Democratic Liberal	207	152	28
Social Democratic	65	107	12
Democratic	109	85	17
Peoples' Cooperative	33	26	4
Social Renovation	14	15	0
Labor-Farmer	32	12	1
Communist	107	4	4
Minor parties	63	20	3
Independents	232	7	6

And did the "roses of the West," to repeat Dr. Matsumoto's phrase, tend to lose their fragrance in Japan as the Occupation relinquished its authority? Summing up political developments prior to the end of the Occupation, General Whitney's able assistant, Frank Rizzo, said:

In both the Japanese and the American press there have been expressions of skepticism concerning the genuineness of the Japanese postwar reformation, and alarm at an apparent tendency to revert to the old order. To some extent the alarm and skepticism arise from an overstatement of the Occupation's initial aim. U.S. basic Occupation policy, later indorsed by the Far Eastern Commission, wisely refrained from directing that any specific form or system of government be established in Japan but required only that the government be peacefully inclined and responsible, conforming as closely as may be to democratic principles, but that it accord with the freely expressed will of the Japanese people. Further, the policy required the removal of obstacles to the revival and strengthening of democratic tendencies. This broad but definitely limited objective led to the corollary that political and social reforms induced by the Occupation should not be forced but should be brought about by persuasion and through Japanese acceptance of the underlying principles, and further, that they should insofar as possible be Japanese in character, if not by origin or inspiration, then at least by adaptation. To the extent that these principles were followed, Occupation-inspired reforms might be expected to take root in Japan. Otherwise they would not outlast the authority of the Occupation. The soundness of these precepts is being thoroughly demonstrated. The Japanese Government and Diet are in the process of revising many Occupation-inspired laws and reforms, some of them substantially. This is a perfectly normal readjustment. It does not mean reversion to the old order. . . .

In all the current talk of possible change there is no evidence to show that any branch of the government or any responsible segment of popular opinion advocates restoring the sovereignty to the Emperor, or reducing the Diet to its former status of impotence, or depriving the women of the right to vote. The fact that these basic reforms were inspired by foreigners does not damn them in Japanese eyes because they are responsive to Japanese needs and desires and because the Japanese consider them their own. The National Diet, which is defined by the Constitution as the highest organ of State power, is the keystone in the arch of popular sovereignty. The Government Section view on this institution might be considered biased. I quote therefore from . . . Sir George Sansom in the September 1951 issue of *Pacific Affairs:*

"With regard to the position of the Diet under the new Constitution, its absolute control of every aspect of national policy is in such striking contrast to the helplessness of parliament under the old regime that it is difficult to imagine its members surrendering any of their newly-gained authority. It has more power than the Congress of the United States, and . . . only slightly less power than the House of

Commons. Of course, the power of an elected assembly is not a measure of its wisdom; but it is a safeguard against most forms of arbitrary rule. This feature of the new Constitution is likely to prove the most important of all of the reforms sponsored by the Occupation."

The reorganization of the Japanese police system, while it was a phase of "security," was definitely related to the shift in governmental forms. Every effort was made to key it in with respect for the new liberties of the citizen. From the United States, police experts—former Police Commissioner Lewis J. Valentine of New York and Oscar Olander, Commissioner of State Police in Michigan—were introduced to advise on the reform of the Japanese public-safety organizations. Most of the men operating the Public Safety Division, a G-2 subdivision, were civilians or military personnel with wide experience in the public-safety field; full credit should be given to Col. H. E. Pulliam, who headed this division.

The fundamental special police reports of the New York and Michigan experts were completed by the end of June 1946. Much of the work of the Public Safety Division during the year which followed was aimed at getting these reports accepted as official policy and putting their recommendations into practical effect. Police brutality and corruption were curtailed, and the Japanese police inspectors were trained to continue the new program on their own initiative.

The success of American police methods is evident in a comparison of crime rates, per thousand, as between Japan and Germany under Occupation conditions. In such a statistical appraisal it must be borne in mind constantly that the American Sector in Germany comprised only about 16,000,000 people and a surface area about one-fifth that of Japan; the administrative problems were correspondingly lighter, viz.:

Ratios	Japan	Germany
Crime rate per thousand	190	390
Ratio of police to population	1 : 843	1 : 437

In other words, the crime rate in the American zone of Germany was double that of Japan; conversely, the police density per population in Japan was half that of Germany. These figures speak well for the discipline of the Japanese under their new law; they also speak well for the methods followed in controlling crime.

Considering the present international situation and the future of Japan, perhaps the most important feature of the new police system was the so-called "National Rural Police," initially set at 30,000 men in 1947, since grown to 120,000, with the probability of further expansion. It can be termed a sort of "rural constabulary" in transition to a "lightly armed mobile security force": it is in fact the

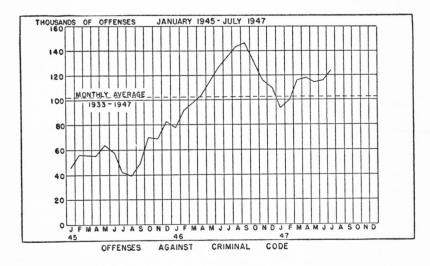

OFFENSES   AGAINST   CRIMINAL   CODE

nucleus of Japan's defense establishment, the army of the future. The initial policy was decentralization of the police on the American pattern, to state, county, or municipal autonomy. Like many American reforms, this was theoretically perfect, but in Japan many communities lacked the funds to maintain separate police establishments. G-2, in its police subdivision, took a strong stand against the all-out decentralization which General Whitney's government section championed. With the abolition of army and navy, the central government, *i.e.*, the prime minister, lacked any means of internal defense if local police forces failed. The "national rural police" scheme would give him that means.

Quite in keeping with the changes in the nation's political orientation were the reforms in education. Reporting on these reforms toward the end of the Occupation, Col. D. Nugent, head of SCAP's Education and Information Section, said:

Most Japanese educators, as well as many parents, had long resented the centralized, regimented controls over education exercised by the pre-Occupation Ministry of Education. As a major step toward local control, a Board of Education Law was passed in 1948, providing for a large measure of educational control by locally elected Boards of Education. These boards are functioning in all the prefectures, the five major cities, and such other cities, towns, and villages as exercise the option of establishing them. Further to get away from centralized control, the textbook monopoly long exercised by the Ministry of Education was discontinued, and the preparation, publication, and sale of textbooks left to private initiative, with choice of textbooks to be used exercised by the local community.

Under this system, Japan's textbooks, re-written in their entirety by Japanese educators, have shown remarkable improvement and, in the opinion of educators in other countries, compare favorably in both content and format with those published anywhere in the world. The Ministry of Education, no longer an agency of centralized control and administration, has been reorganized as an effective professional service agency, providing assistance to educators and educational organizations.

While the Government Section of SCAP was busy with developing a legal framework for a government of limited powers, and while the Education Section was helping to free the Japanese mind, other SCAP sections were working to make it possible for the Japanese to remain alive. The most remarkable performance was turned in by Gen. Crawford Sams's Public Health and Welfare Section. Prior to 1945 there was only a primitive Public Health and Welfare organization in Japan. Sams organized Health and Medical Service Districts based upon the population flow, or trade center, idea—districts that are now jointly financed by city, town, village, or county groups. With sewage systems dislocated by the bombings, with "environmental sanitation . . . virtually non-existent," General Sams was faced with the almost certain probability of smallpox, dysentery, typhoid, and typhus epidemics. What he proceeded to do in the way of mass immunizations almost staggers the imagination: millions and millions of Japanese were vaccinated and inoculated during the Occupation. When a smallpox epidemic developed in March 1946, there was no vaccine available. Starting with a little vaccine from America, Sams reported that his organization

. . . succeeded in bringing the epidemic under control in the spring and early summer of 1946, but not until more than 17,800 cases had occurred among the civilian population. The entire population of Japan, now 83,000,000, has been immunized three times within the past six years. In the year 1950 there were only five cases of smallpox.

Typhus, diphtheria, cholera, tuberculosis, enteric diseases, and venereal diseases represented challenges almost as great as that of smallpox. For typhus, diphtheria, and cholera, General Sams's organization carried out heroic mass immunizations similar to those for smallpox. And to get tuberculosis, the number-one killer in Japan, under control, Sams's organization worked a revolution in the whole subject of the Japanese diet. This involved changing a food pattern that was based on the religious tenets of Buddhism, which prohibits the consumption of flesh or milk from animals. Says Sams:

Japanese children did not drink milk once they had been weaned. . . . Their entire agricultural economy had been for many years oriented toward the raising of grain crops (rice) for which that mountainous country is poorly adapted. . . . But eventually over 7,100,000 school children were receiving milk as a base of their school lunch. The increased growth, both in height and weight of these children, as contrasted to those who had not been placed on this program, was visual evidence to the Japanese themselves as to the need for adequate nutrition for their children. . . . To carry out this selling program was no easy matter, since it involved a change in thinking, not only of the Japanese, but also a continuing battle with others who insisted that we should concern ourselves only with the importation of grain for the Japanese. . . . The Japanese will reap the benefits of this reorientation in their nutritional pattern and in the reorientation of the agricultural economy of their country for many years to come.

The sum total of Sams's work is best expressed in the life-expectancy statistics. Between the years 1895 and 1946, the life expectancy of Japanese men remained stationary at 42.8 years. The life expectancy for women during the same period was increased only from 44.3 to 51.1 years. But between the years 1946 and 1951 the life expectancy at birth for males took an astounding jump from 42.8 to 60.8 years, and that for women increased from 51.1 to 64.8. This constituted a gift of life of 18 additional years for men and 13.7 for women—a phenomenon, as Sams says, that has been "unequaled in any country in the world in medical history in a comparable period of time."

The conclusion of Sams's report to MacArthur has a significance that transcends the merely medical. For, as Sams says:

I know of nothing more important in demonstrating to the people of Japan and other nations of the world—particularly those in the Far East—what we mean by the worth of the individual, which we consider to be the essence of democracy, than the literal gift of life which the Occupation has brought to some 3,000,000 Japanese who would have died between 1945 and 1951 had these modern programs not been established and had the prewar death rate continued at its normal level.

The gift of life to 3,000,000 Japanese might seem a mixed blessing in a land whose 83,000,000 population is bottled up in an area of 147,690 square miles. And it is precisely on the subject of economic rehabilitation that the record of SCAP has been most severely criticized. MacArthur, however, has always held it a mistake to judge the results of the Occupation in terms of economic recovery. Recovery was impossible in the five-year span between 1946 and 1950 for the simple reason that the war had dragged Japan down too far. As MacArthur has always seen it, Japan in 1945 was faced with a stark problem of survival. Defeat had forced the nation backward fifty years to the surface area of 1896, when the population was approximately half of what it was in 1946. Japan's loss of territory—Sakhalin, Okinawa, the Caroline and Marshall Islands, Korea, Manchuria—was exacted as punishment for aggression; SCAP was powerless to change that even if it had wanted to. The problem was to feed the 83,000,000 Japanese, and to keep the basic services and utilities going, until the Japanese themselves could figure out a way of peacefully gaining a livelihood by trade. In Mac-Arthur's own words:

> The Occupation was charged with a basic economic directive: "You will not assume any responsibility for the economic rehabilitation or the strengthening of the Japanese economy." This basic directive was not altered until December, 1948. For over three years, controlling policy prescribed this limitation, and the Japanese economy received no financial support from the United States other than that necessary to prevent "widespread disease and unrest."

Even so, the prevention of unrest was interpreted in terms that did allow a good measure of rehabilitation. As a staff report from Tokyo put it:

> There is much ado about the recovery of West Germany under the benevolent aegis of American assistance. The American sector happens to represent only 16,000,000 inhabitants, or roughly one-fifth the population of Japan. But this small European fragment received three times the amounts that were granted Japan year by year.

With much less outside money than was made available to the Occupation in Germany, MacArthur did some astounding things toward insuring economic survival to Japan.

This point was completely confirmed on a high level in the comments of Joseph M. Dodge, formerly budget director to the Eisenhowever Administration and financial adviser to the American Military Government in Germany:

> The actual and projected appropriations for Germany are approximately twice that for Japan. On a population basis, they are three times the amount per capita. The proposed allocations for 1951 for Germany are twice the amount of aid requested for Japan. We should note the substantial progress that has been made in Japan, on relatively modest appropriations. In no other nation has so much been accomplished with so little.

There was the rehabilitation of the coal-mining industry, for example. In 1945, to quote from the MacArthur records:

The mines were in need of drilling equipment . . . and were operated by slave labor which was immediately eliminated. Stockpiles of coal had dropped to less than two million tons by the end of 1945. Following the SCAP instructions to repatriate the Korean coal miners, the shortage became so serious that the mining industry was placed under special study. . . . Through development of unions, higher wage rates, use of special food rations for the miners, and release of incentive goods such as American cigarettes and clothing, coal production was gradually increased. . . . The production for 1946 was . . . 22,000,000 tons. For 1948 . . . actual production was 34,791,300 tons.

The fishing industry was also brought back under MacArthur's guidance:

Initially, the greatest need was for boats. Another serious shortage was in twines and nets, but with the partial rehabilitation of the spinning industry and the importation of hemp from the Philippines, this shortage was overcome . . . the amount of fish available increased steadily.

MacArthur's economic mandate was to change the structure of Japanese economic life so that the people as a whole would benefit from revival when it came. As the General himself said:

A land reform program of vast proportions was initiated. Tenant farmers who had lived in a condition of serfdom were enabled to buy from the landlords the land they lived on and worked on. . . . In the economic field the great combines of the *zaibatsu*, which had monopolized the commercial, financial, and industrial facilities of the nation, were dissolved. . . . The organization of industrial workers into labor unions of their own choice was encouraged and their right to bargain collectively was guaranteed.

Toward the end of the Occupation, Dr. Sherwood Fine, General Marquat's right-hand man in his Economic and Scientific Section, summed up the economic progress of Japan under MacArthur. He said:

Japan's industrial recovery to date can be said to have achieved most impressive proportions when viewed in the light of the abnormally depressed immediate postwar circumstances. The industrial levels of the prewar base period (1932–1936) were substantially exceeded and total exports, thanks to the demand stimulated by the Korean war, finally attained a volume sufficient to balance the foreign exchange accounts. However, the precipitation of a new inflationary trend, particularly pronounced with respect to export prices with attendant loss of sales, raises serious doubt concerning the lasting character of the boom. Actually, with the decline of world prices during the first half of 1951, manufacturers and export merchants heavily stocked with peak-priced raw material inventories and completed merchandise were confronted with prospective large scale losses and possible bankruptcy. The business community, acutely aware of the war-generated nature of their prosperity, has been seized with well justified anxiety upon indications of a possible political settlement of the Korean conflict.

American aid appropriations to Japan which totaled $2 billion were terminated at the close of fiscal year 1951. In the light of Japan's current foreign exchange balances and export levels, no case can be made either for dollar loans or for any other type of economic aid to Japan. While there is every indication that Japan is eager to exploit to the maximum the United States' stated interest in her future due to our political and military concerns in South East Asia as a whole, it is not believed possible to argue that Japan requires economic aid at this time. It is impossible to forecast the likelihood of returning to a situation where American aid may again become an imperative requirement. Such an eventuality should by no means be precluded.

In the area of institutional reform remarkable success was realized in implementing: (*a*) a democratic land reform program which transformed large numbers of tenant farmers into land owners; (*b*) a program transferring to fishermen control of their fishing areas; (*c*) the growth of a democratic labor movement strongly opposed to communist ideology. With respect to implementation of the directives concerning the democratization of corporate enterprise, complete elimination of the Zaibatsu holding company structure was achieved. However, the activities of the numerous industrial control associations never completely disappeared and there is good reason to expect their full re-emergence before very long. Unfortunately, very little support was found in influential circles for the program to achieve a democratic competitive enterprise structure to replace the preponderantly noncompetitive prewar and wartime business structure. In this sphere in-

stitutional forces were effective in resisting substantial attainment of
the goals sought by the democratization of Japanese corporate enterprise program.

There are many uncertainties confronting Japan economically. The
importance of the foreign trade makes her exceedingly sensitive to
significant fluctuations in the volume of world trade. The marginal nature
of a number of her important export industries makes her particularly
vulnerable to increased competition. The obligation of having to provide for substantial defense requirements will have an important bearing
on her future standard of living. Much depends upon Japan's ability
to improve the efficiency of her industrial plant. If Japan concentrates
on maintaining a competitive position in international trade through
improvements in the efficiency of her democratic production and by
maintaining effective economic stabilization, her prospects are at least
reasonably bright. There is an enormous potential for increases in trade
with the South East Asiatic orbit which may very well be able to absorb
the slack resulting from the cessation of Korean military operations. In
the final analysis Japan, a relatively poor, second-rate industrial power,
is acutely dependent upon the prevailing level of world trade. If there
is enjoyed a reasonably prosperous world economy, Japan will undoubtedly be able to persevere. In the absence of such favorable conditions, her future is fraught with serious uncertainties and challenges.

A principal bar to Japan's attempt to build up its competitive
position in the world under the Occupation was the attitude of the
British, who sought by one means or another to bring Japan under
the control of the sterling bloc. MacArthur always refused to allow
the British to have their will in this matter at a time when the United
States was subsidizing Japanese recovery with dollars. Because of his
pertinacity in combating British attempts to place permanent fetters
on Japan's industrial capacity, MacArthur encountered increasing
animosity in No. 10 Downing Street. His closest advisers always
suspected that the fight over London's suggested strait jacket on
Japan's import-export economy played a very important part in
setting the stage for his dismissal. These secrets are locked in the
archives, but members of MacArthur's Tokyo staff are certain that
British pressure helped to bring Mr. Truman to the sticking point
in the great drama of the recall.

15 The North Korean Communist Invasion

BARELY five years after the spectacular defeat of one of the world's great military powers, Imperial Japan, MacArthur, the victor in that conflict, was to be faced by Soviet satellites, the North Korean and Chinese Communists, in a powerful combination of inexhaustible Asiatic cannon fodder and Soviet technical "know-how." It was the right kind of war for the illiterate Chinese coolie under the opiate of the Red gospel, reinforced with modern Russian tommy guns.

One of MacArthur's old armies with a brilliant record in the Southwest Pacific, the Eighth Army, fought again with accustomed skill but against numerical odds at times as high as ten to one. It was severely handicapped, at various stages of the fighting, by a wave of distorted and unwarranted "defeatist" publicity without parallel in the annals of this proud nation.

When Secretary of State Dean Acheson testified before Congress in 1951, he was queried by Sen. Styles Bridges on warnings by Mac-Arthur's headquarters of the impending North Korean invasion. Acheson made some carefully pruned selections from a single intelligence report, dated March 8, 1950—about four months in advance of the Communist attack. Actually a similar report had already been made as early as December 8, 1949.

Bridges said to Acheson:

This record shows—even the record that you read here shows—that they reported there was to be an attack in June, even though they did qualify it afterwards. That would be a fair analysis, would it not?

Acheson replied coldly:

350

Not only qualified it. They said it is believed that it will not occur.
That is a little more than qualification.

By arguing a point of phraseology in a single report, Acheson left
the senator ignorant of the fact that a secret agency in Korea, sent
there from MacArthur's headquarters in Tokyo, filed 1,195 con-
secutive reports in the period from June 1949 to June 1950. In the
critical six months immediately before the outbreak of the war, 417
special reports were filed. Tokyo headquarters held receipts indicating their arrival in Washington. This total represents an average of
one hundred reports per month, or three reports every single day for
an entire year. All of them were of increasing urgency and covered
every facet of the North Korean Communist threat, from tanks
which Rhee's forces did not have, to airplanes which the South
Koreans likewise had not been furnished.

The extent of Acheson's elisions becomes apparent even from the
most random check of the Tokyo intelligence files on the subject of
a probable North Korean invasion:

Sept. 1, 1949: Chinese Communist troops, disguised as war refugees,
enter Pyongyang almost daily, since June 1949. A division [of such
troops] entered North Korea from Manchuria, by way of Antung.

December 8, 1949: North Korean government and their Chinese
allies are under complete domination of Russia. Soviets will not permit
the indefinite existence of a non-Communist state in the Korean Peninsula. . . . Patterned on the master plan, the North Korean government is merely a puppet of Soviet Russia. Acting as overseer is a Soviet
mission of 300 persons in Pyongyang. . . . The army is composed of
4 to 8 Divisions and Ind. Brigades and possesses normal infantry weapons, howitzers of 76-mm and 122-mm calibers, 30 to 40 tanks, model
T-34, and 36 to 70 aircraft. All equipment is of Soviet origin. Recent
influx of Chinese Communist troops makes up an [unidentified] divi-
sional unit. . . . Capitalizing upon [the] weakness of the democratic
system, the Communist-dominated S.K. Labor Party is the instigator
of practically all civil disturbances [in South Korea]. . . . North
Korean sponsored guerrilla forces are creating fear and unrest in the
South Korean populace. . . . To the Communist, an armed invasion
of South Korea is probably considered as the final resort to gain con-

trol of the Peninsula. . . . With the conclusion of the Chinese Communist campaign in China, more troops and supplies may be channeled into North Korea. [The] danger to the Southern Republic will mount at that time. . . . Climatic conditions most favorable for military operations have passed [December]. [The] next favorable period for [any such] action will occur in April and May 1950.

Jan. 5, 1950: North Korea has set March and April 1950 as the time to invade South Korea. Such threats should be viewed in relation to military activities. By this criterion, the movement of the 3rd N.K. Division into the western 38th Parallel, the arrival of Chinese Communist personnel, the southward displacement of the N.K. 2nd Division and expansion of Border Constabulary seem significant in terms of military action in the spring.

March 10, 1950: N.K. [People's Army] will be prepared to invade South Korea by fall or possibly by spring of this year [1950] as indicated by armed forces expansion and major troop movements. . . . Soviet intentions in Korea believed closely related to the Communist program in Southeast Asia. If checked in their operations in these countries, Soviets may divert their efforts to Korea. . . . Latest reports received that the North Korean P.A. will invade South Korea in June.

April 15, 1950: In mid-March, the Communist government ordered evacuation of all civilians residing in an area within three miles of the 38th Parallel. Vacated housing in latter area then occupied by troops and guerrillas. Purpose reported as "preparation for war and to interfere with South Korean intelligence operations."

May 25, 1950: National Inspection teams have completed field inspections of all units of the armed forces in North Korea (a preparatory war measure). Positive identification of seven Army divisions. . . . Note the existence of several regular Army divisions, located roughly in a cross-country belt between the 38th and 39th Parallels. . . . Previous evidence of the entry from Manchuria of trained Communists of Korean ethnic origin would furnish the necessary manpower [for additional divisions]. In addition, there is continuous compulsory recruitment; estimates indicate as many as 100,000 to 150,000 of N.K. youths.

These reports that went to Washington by way of Tokyo could be termed "gratuitous": MacArthur was not officially concerned

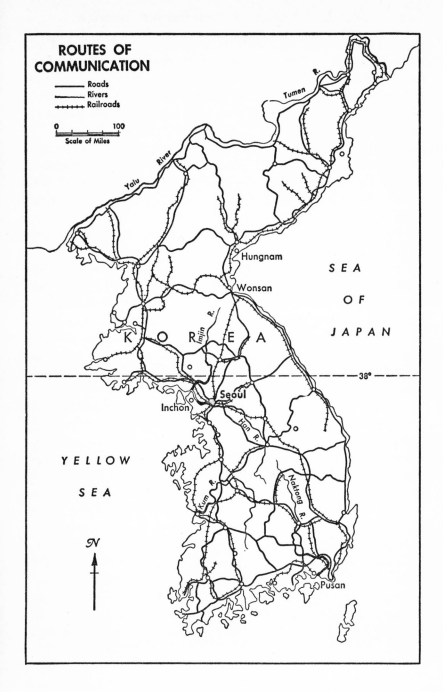

ROUTES OF
COMMUNICATION

——— Roads
━━━ Rivers
+++++ Railroads

0   100
Scale of Miles

Tumen R.

Yalu River

Hungnam

Wonsan

K O R E A

Imjin R.

SEA

OF

JAPAN

38°

Seoul

Inchon

Han R.

YELLOW

SEA

Kum R.

Naktong R.

N

Pusan

with Korea, which had become a jealously guarded State Department enclave. The territorial boundaries of the Far East Command pointedly eliminated Korea from MacArthur's responsibilities, including intelligence collection. His G-2, of course, could not remain indifferent to the general military situation in an adjacent area, and quietly maintained a small surveillance unit in Korea, the K.L.O., or "Korean Liaison Office."

Even the Central Intelligence Agency, though normally sheltered by powerful influences in Washington, could not escape criticism for the North Korean invasion. This Agency had quite recently come into Japan, though its interests were primarily on the Asiatic mainland. The G-2 organization in Tokyo immediately ranged itself with the Agency in fraternal solidarity: their inflexible "joint position was that Washington had been fully informed." Admiral Roscoe H. Hillenkoetter, the CIA director in that period, wired General Willoughby:

Greatly appreciate your fine personal message. I want, particularly at this time, to express special appreciation of the help and cooperation you have extended to our people in the F.E.C. area. Your understanding of the mutuality of interest of our organizations in the over-all intelligence goal, which has to be achieved by many different methods, has served to advance the aims of U.S. intelligence centrally.

As the war grew closer, John Foster Dulles, then on a mission to the Orient, stood on the 38th parallel in company with the South Korean Minister of War. A substantial portion of Syngman Rhee's army was already physically in position along the parallel. Helping Rhee was General Roberts, with about 500 American military instructors who had worked with the Korean Army for two years. The Embassy in Seoul maintained military attaché groups—Army, Navy, and Air, as well as their own diplomatic and political specialists whose sole business was to gauge the trend of events.

In spite of all the warnings from G-2 Tokyo, the visit of Dulles, and the fact that the American Embassy in Seoul was well equipped as a listening post, the invasion of South Korea came as a jolt to Washington. When the Reds struck, General Roberts happened to be on "transfer status" on the high seas. The South Korean Army did the best it could without high-level advice. The chips were down, with Russian training and Russian weapons suddenly and brutally matched against a headless army of trainees who inevitably lost the first round.

General MacArthur's views on this dramatic collision, as outlined to a staff officer, are substantially as follows:

The South Korean forces consisted of ten divisions. They had been well trained and the personnel was brave and patriotic, but had been equipped not so much as troops of the line but more as a constabulary. This inexplicable decision was made in Washington without consultation with General MacArthur's Headquarters, which was in entire disagreement, a fact which could hardly have been unknown. This basic error was immediately exploited by Communist North Korea. Behind a front of light units on the 38th Parallel, equipped much as the South Koreans, there was built a powerful striking force, ready and waiting. The blow came suddenly and swept all before it.

Censure should not be directed at an alleged failure to pinpoint the exact day and hour of the Communist assault, but at the military failure to prepare South Koreans to meet the attack effectively when it came. The potential of attack was inherent in the fact that the North Korean forces had tanks, artillery, and fighter aircraft with which South Korea was not equipped. It was a vital and a fatal error.

At the time the North Koreans struck, General MacArthur's only responsibility in Korea was "to evacuate Americans there." This he was to do when requested by the American Ambassador John Muccio. The movement was well planned and more than two thousand persons were flown out immediately without a single casualty. General Headquarters had no faintest inkling that it was to be further involved. It was not consulted in any way when suddenly General MacArthur received orders from President Truman to intervene. The President characterized the situation as "a police action." This reflected a fatal misunderstanding of the strength and character of the enemy's forces. Washington completely underestimated both. It seemed to believe that a show of force by our Air and Navy would be sufficient to solve the problem and restore Korea to unity and peace.

The United Nations, at first not involved, supported in lukewarm fashion the intervention and directed the United States to act as its agent. General MacArthur was appointed Commander of the United Nations Forces and was *directed to restore peace, order, and unity to the entire Korean Peninsula*. Statements so frequently made later that our purpose was merely to drive the enemy out of South Korea are completely at variance with the truth. The documentation, the orders, the directives, the action of the campaign—all show this beyond challenge or debate. It was only later that political policies corrupted the original purpose and chose to attempt to mislead public opinion accordingly. [Italics added.]

Hugh Baillie, President of the United Press and one of the most objective of reporters in Korea, has made an interesting comment on the early stages of the war:

We had a narrow escape being thrown out of Korea altogether. We, as usual, were caught unprepared. This was not due to any lack of knowledge of what the North Koreans were planning. Intelligence knew what the Communists were scheming and knew South Korea was going to be invaded in June, but the policy decided on was to abandon Korea and make a stand against Communism elsewhere.

MacArthur told me he was very surprised when he was called on telecon at 4 o'clock in the morning and directed to undertake the defense of Korea on behalf of the United Nations. That was a complete switch. Now he was confronted with the necessity of going to war and halting the Reds already over the border and smashing southward with fifteen divisions.

Immediately on receiving his orders from Washington, General MacArthur flew to the Korean front. It was a hazardous trip. In his unarmored, unescorted plane he landed at Sinwon, some 20 miles south of Seoul, even as the airfield was being bombed by enemy planes. Motoring forward under the constant air bombardment, he encountered all the dreadful backwash of a defeated and dispersed army. The South Korean Forces were in full flight. He reached the banks of the Han River just in time to be caught up in the last rearguard action to defend its bridges. Seoul was already in enemy hands, and he found himself once again the inheritor of a massive disaster, leader of yet another forlorn hope. For full twenty minutes the General stood on a little mound just off the road, clogged with retreating, panting columns of disorganized troops interspersed with ambulances filled with groaning, broken men, the sky resonant with shrieking missiles of death and everywhere the stench and misery and utter desolation of a stricken battlefield. His trained eyes missed nothing—but in this brief interval his desperate plan was made. And desperate indeed it was! Completely outnumbered though he would be, he would bring his occupation force from Japan and rely upon strategic maneuver to overcome the great odds against him.

How could he accomplish this when, in fact, nothing stood in the way of the enemy's rushing his tank columns straight down the road from Seoul to Pusan at the end of the Peninsula? He reflected on Japan, which was his primary responsibility to secure and protect. How could he denude this great bastion of troops without inviting Soviet entry from the north? Could he salvage the time necessary to bring his forces to the Pusan area? Could he improvise native forces in Japan sufficient to deter any abortive seizure of that country by an enemy? Could he find the transportation to carry the troops to Korea, the munitions and supplies to sustain them in combat, the minimum equipment to create and organize a Japanese protective force? Could he rally, reorganize, and reinspire the defeated South Korean Army? Could he, if all this were accomplished and the enemy's tenuous supply lines extended to dangerous limits, cut these lines and then envelop and destroy his main forces with only a handful of troops available? In these reflections, which he recalled vividly at a later date, is to be found the genesis of the Inchon operation.

Probably never in history was a commander faced with so complex and desperate a situation—and no commander in history rose to greater heights of genius in meeting and surmounting such unprecedented obstacles. First and foremost, he must delay and impede the enemy's headlong rush. He had four woefully understrength occupation divisions scattered from Kyushu to Hokkaido, about the same distances as from Seattle to Los Angeles, and one battalion of Australians. Washington authorized the American troops to move on June 30. The first elements of the 24th Division, Maj. Gen. William F. Dean commanding, reached Korea on July 1 by air. Outnumbered one hundred to one, they roadblocked the enemy immediately just north of Osan. Dean's forces were destroyed in fiercest combat—but the first great gamble of MacArthur's had been won.

As MacArthur predicted, the entry of American troops and the ferocity of their defense slowed the North Korean Army to a walk. Instead of driving his tanks forward on the roads in exploitation, the enemy paused to bring up his artillery across the river and deploy his divisions in extended line of battle. Nearly ten days to get his guns forward! Precious days! Every ship, every plane, every train, every vehicle was commandeered by MacArthur. His moves were like lightning. No mobilization toward a battlefield ever equaled it in speed. It is doubtful that American divisions at any point in the United States, with the best rail and road net in the world, could have moved faster than MacArthur threw his garrison troops into battle.

Early reports from the front were all bad. Russian medium tanks, Model T-34, were chewing up the Korean infantry. The 24th U.S. Division had seventeen obsolescent light tanks, the M-24; five of the seventeen were worn out. The only tanks that could stop the Russian model were medium-type, the "Pershing," weight 43 tons, armed with 90-mm guns, and the "Sherman," 37 tons, armed with 76-mm guns. There were only 92 of these types in Japan; all of them had been in storage and were unserviceable. Fortunately, the Eighth Army Ordnance operated a magnificent salvage and repair depot that successfully rebuilt the old wrecks of the Pacific war, incidentally saving the taxpayer hundreds of millions of dollars.

The failure to provide proportionally enough troops and proper armament for this risky UN adventure must be laid to Washington. The bulk of our military strength continued to be sent to Europe under the patently apparent delusion that the U.S.S.R. was about to attack there. No professional military mind could fail to discern that the Soviet's position in Europe was plainly defensive, that they labored under the illusory concept that we were building to strike them there. As the staff in Tokyo saw it, the same old curse of World War II was back again: concentration on Europe to the exclusion of other global interests with equal or predominant demands and necessities, as in this case with war in the Orient blazing and no fighting in Europe.

MacArthur's Tokyo records of the period contain a miscellany of staff officers' notes and observations on the unequal struggle:

Criticism of the South Korean forces is pointless, considering the

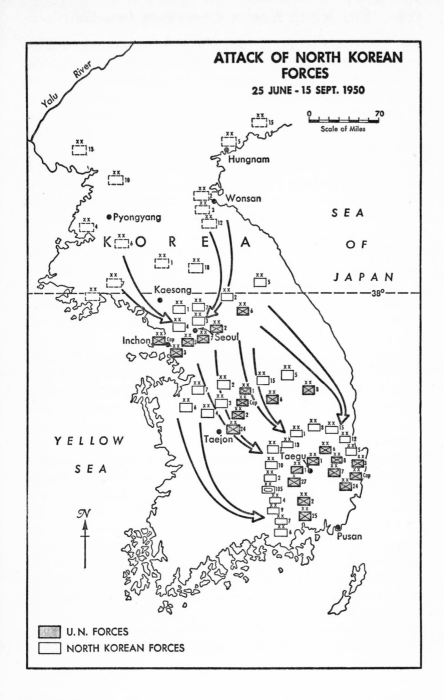

ATTACK OF NORTH KOREAN
FORCES
25 JUNE - 15 SEPT. 1950

relative strength of friend and foe. The Reds had tanks and planes to start with. The planes disappeared but the tanks remained. They even sliced through the advance battalions of the 24th U.S. Division, right smack into their artillery. Reports were received that the 75-mm of the American M-24 bounced off the 3-in. steel Russian turrets. The small "bazooka," the 2.36-in., expected to be an effective anti-tank weapon, was disappointing. The troops called for 3.5-in. types in a hurry. This is uncomfortably reminiscent of the defective American torpedoes in the first year of the Pacific War.

The occupation infantry in Japan was kept habitually one-third below strength. The American regiments had only two instead of three battalions. Housewifely, the Pentagon tried to make "both ends meet," to keep some divisions largely on paper or in skeleton shape, and fill them up as required. This characteristic American bluff was predicated on our last wars when we always found some ally to hold the line somewhere, give us a few months to get ready, and then move in. Lesson number one of the Korean War is probably a unique "first" for the American Army: it is old stuff for the Europeans, glaring at each other for generations across armed frontiers. When they cross, they are combat ready.

The Korean War meant entry into action "as is." No time out for liberty-loan drives and for recruiting rallies. It was move in—and shoot. So we moved—with two instead of three battalions, with light tanks instead of heavies. That put the bee on that hardy perennial—the infantry, Mauldin's Willie and Joe—the great expendable G.I.

The story of the infantry soldier taking it on the chin is not a new one. The cards are stacked against him. He carries his home with him—and often his grave. Somehow he has to drag along the whole paraphernalia of fighting as well as domesticated living; the grocery store (the ration dump); the hospital (the Medical Corps); the garage (the motor-pool); the telephone exchange (the signal service). He must sleep and eat and fight and die on foot, in all weather, rain or shine, with or without shelter. It is a wonder that the morale of these uniformed gypsies holds out at all.

The ratio of killed is proportional to time of exposure. This factor operates primarily against the infantry. In combat, the doughboy is vulnerable day and night. Death has his finger on him for twenty-four hours, in battle, going toward it, and retreating from it. Periodical War Department reports on relative casualties tell their own mute and irrefutable story: The dates are unimportant; the relative percentages remain about the same—November 1950 or April 1953:

Service	Nov. 1950	Per cent	Mar. 1953	Per cent
Army	39,500	82.0	104,476	77.3
Marines	7,588	15.8	26,897	20.1
Navy	566	1.4	1,984	1.5
Air Force	381	0.8	1,448	1.1
Aggregate	48,035		134,085	
Monthly average	9,607		4,085	

When the period of piecemeal entry into action was over, when the painful rear-guard type of retreat under pressure of overwhelming numbers was ended, when the fight for time and space was won, MacArthur made a characteristic public statement:

With the deployment of major elements of the Eighth Army now accomplished, the first phase of the Campaign has ended and with it the chance for victory by the North Korean forces. The enemy's great opportunity depended upon the speed with which he could overrun South Korea, once he had temporarily shattered South Korean resistance with overwhelming numbers and superior weapons. . . . I do not believe that history records a comparable operation which excelled the speed and precision with which the Eighth Army, the Air Force, and the Seventh Fleet have been deployed to a distant land for immediate commitment to major operations. . . . This finds added emphasis in the fact that the Far East Command had no slightest responsibility for the defense of the free Republic of Korea. . . . The issue of battle is now fully joined and will proceed along lines of action in which we will not be without a choice. Our hold upon the southern part of Korea represents a secure base. Our casualties despite overwhelming odds have been relatively light. The enemy's supply line is insecure. He has had his great chance but failed to exploit it. We are now in Korea in force and, with God's help, we are there to stay.

Accent on infantry brings out sharply the period of crisis in the perimeter defense of the Eighth Army during August. The enemy made a most serious major effort against Lt. Gen. Walton H. Walker's thin lines around Pusan, in repeated savage and bloody attacks which lead to the partial penetrations of the defensive arc in the Pohang-Dong area, in the Waegwan corridor, and along the Nak-tong River. For a time, it was touch and go. The Cassandras of the world gloomily speculated on a vast "Asiatic Dunkerque."

The enemy then operated with thirteen divisions at the front, massing in complete freedom at any selected point of the perimeter for overwhelming local assaults. The American division at that time, with six battalions only, building up with hasty replacements, was at a terrible disadvantage in men and tanks. It is with this yardstick of deficiencies that Walker's stubborn defense and the fighting capacity of the American draftees must be measured.

In August, Walker's divisions maintained frontages that were simply fantastic. Each South Korean division occupied from 12 to 20 miles; the American divisions were compelled to cover even greater frontages: the 1st Cavalry, 28 miles; the 24th Division, 16 miles; the Marines and the 25th Division, approximately 25 miles as the crow flies. The over-all distances are probably one-third greater if the natural convolutions of the ground are included. Mac-Arthur's staff commented on this technical point, regretting that it was generally ignored or not fully appreciated:

These are terrific distances to defend, or hold, or even keep under patrol surveillance; penetrations, deep behind friendly lines, were fre-quent and menacing, though, in fact, they were not penetrations at the point of the bayonet but leisurely infiltrations, at night, through some valley that was not guarded.

There are specific historical statistics that will bring into sharp relief the defense picture of the Pusan perimeter. The yardstick employed is density per yard of front, *i.e.*, the actual battlefield frontage in relation to total infantry employed thereon; . . . this line of thought is com-mon to all analytical military literature.

Date	Location	Div.	Front Yds.	Infantry
Aug. 1918	St. Die	5th	32,500	12,000
July 1918	Baccarat	77th	18,500	12,800
Aug. 1918	Lucey	89th	17,500	12,000
Aug. 1918	Alsace	29th	15,500	12,800
Aug. 1918	Sazerais	1st	11,500	13,000

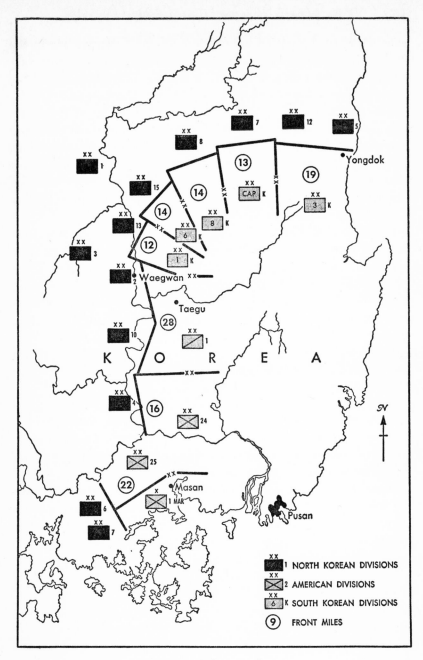

The Pusan defense perimeter

The frontages held by the American-Korean divisions (about half the infantry strength of 1918) along the Pusan-Taegu perimeter are most revealing:

Date	Location	Div.	Front Yds.	Infantry
Aug. 1950	Yongdok	3rd ROK	70,300	5/6,000
Aug. 1950	Kusangdong	Cap ROK	38,100	4/5,000
Aug. 1950	Uisong	8th ROK	41,800	5/6,000
Aug. 1950	Kurwi	6th ROK	41,800	6/7,000
Aug. 1950	Hajang	1st ROK	34,400	5/6,000
Aug. 1950	Waegwan	1st US	103,600	6/7,000
Aug. 1950	Naktong	24th US	59,200	6/7,000
Aug. 1950	Masan	25th US	81,400	6/7,000

The density per yard factor represents an average of one or two riflemen every ten yards and nothing behind them; of course, there is no such rubber-band distribution; there were miles of gaps through which the enemy infiltrated. . . . It is a miracle that the perimeter held at all, though caving in locally, here and there, to be patched up by General Walker shuttling his weary reserves from one crisis to the next.

It was apparent that no military decision could be reached in that perimeter, and "hanging-on" was not good enough. The prestige of the Western world wavered in the balance. Oriental millions were watching the outcome. The test was not in Berlin, Vienna, London, or Washington: it came along the Naktong River in South Korea. The Kremlin watched the performance of their stooges, their "lend-lease armament"; they watched their guns and tanks and planes, anticipating an easy victory. One could almost hear the ticking of the second hand of destiny: something had to be done.

No one at the seats of government wanted to do anything. The fervor of the United Nations "to stop aggression" had perceptibly cooled. The Joint Chiefs of Staff began to talk vaguely about "the wrong war, at the wrong time, and in the wrong place." That was the intellectual equivalent of a municipal fire chief noting calmly that a conflagration in the slums was in the "wrong part of the city"; unchecked, the fire might spread to the business districts or the exclusive residential sections.

With reference to Walker's situation, the daily intelligence summaries threw light on the enemy supply system and the principal routes of rail and truck deliveries. These summaries revealed the pattern and densities of his supply movement, principally along the west coast. It was obvious that enormous tonnages were still driving down from the north, from Chinese Manchuria and Russian Siberia, en route, through Seoul, to the south in spite of our strafing and bombing. The elusive enemy moved habitually at night. His ingenuity and tenacity in repair of bridges and tracks was astounding. Under the nose of the Air Corps, the Reds delivered at least two fresh divisions and two tank brigades, from North Korea to the Naktong River, for Walker's infantry to take on. Supply, food, and ammunition went forward without a letup, by train and motor, by oxcart and *cargadores*.

With Walker, his back to the sea, clinging grimly to his Pusan beachhead; with a Japanese force, the reorganized police reserves of 100,000 men, mustered and well on the road toward securing the safety of Japan from sudden seizure by the U.S.S.R.; with Japan proving its utter loyalty by its well-ordered conduct; with his air and naval forces unopposed, MacArthur was now finally ready for the last, great stroke to bring his plan into fruition. His Han River dream as a possibility had begun to assume the certainties of reality—the maneuver of Inchon in the classical Napoleonic pattern. Throughout his career, Napoleon maintained an absolute confidence in the efficacy of the maneuver against the rear of the enemy. In 1813 Prince Eugene was holding the Adige with 40,000 men; the Austrians were facing him frontally. The Prince wrote Napoleon for advice. The master replied:

"Do not give up the Adige without a fight. This is the maneuver which I would undertake: Move via Brondolo—on the Piave (a turning movement). . . . You can expect incalculable results. The enemy's communications run via Trevise: cut them. . . . Perhaps I should not insist on this bold maneuver, but it is my style, my manner of doing things."

Substitute the Pusan perimeter for Adige; Inchon for Trevise— and the Napoleonic maneuver in northern Italy in 1813 was successfully repeated in Korea in 1950.

It was also MacArthur's style, his manner of doing things. Every operation along the New Guinea–Philippines axis was a turning movement deep into the flank and rear of the enemy. As we have seen, Hollandia was such a maneuver. It was repeated at Inchon even to the point of applying the same ruse: enemy attention was concentrated on the port of Kunsan, through American commando landings, leaflet drops, preliminary air attacks, etc. When Admiral Struble's convoy passed Kunsan en route to Inchon, it was too late to make sizable troop displacements; the bulk of the Reds was committed down south, along the perimeter.

The general plan and the decision to take Inchon were entirely MacArthur's. He had made similar decisions throughout his military career, but none more momentous, none more fraught with danger, none that promised to be more vitally conclusive if successful. His plan was opposed by powerful military influences in Washington. The essence of the operation depended upon a great amphibious movement. General MacArthur recalled that the chairman of the Joint Chiefs of Staff, Gen. Omar Bradley, had but recently given it as his considered opinion that such amphibious operations were obsolete—that there would never be another great movement of this sort. The Chief of Staff of the Army, General Collins, and the Chief of Naval Operations, Admiral Sherman, had flown on a special trip to Tokyo for the express purpose of persuading MacArthur against this operation.

Apparently the top brass had forgotten the lessons of military history. Were they content to let Walker's men stay in the bloody Pusan perimeter like cattle in an abattoir? Did this reflect the influence of Secretary Acheson who had publicly checked off the defense of Korea and Formosa? How deep must "the dust settle" in the Far East? When queried on this formative period of staff calculations, MacArthur's Chief of Staff, General Almond, who was soon to command the X Corps, commented:

About mid-July, during the course of a visit by Lieutenant General Shepherd, Marine Corps, then Admiral Radford's Pacific Fleet Marine Chief, General MacArthur discussed the prospect of Marine reinforcements, even to the extent of an entire Marine Division; General Shepard was enthusiastic and offered the suggestion that provided the Army authorities would make the request, "as much as a full division could be assembled on the Pacific Coast of the U.S. in a period of three weeks;

and provided the shipping was made available, this force could be in Japan or in Korea in an additional three weeks' period."

This gave some substance to General MacArthur's ideas; he immediately made his plan known to Washington and requested the Marine reinforcements, stating that he would reconstitute the depleted 7th Inf. Div. in the meantime; that with such a force at his command, the bold stroke at the enemy's vital communications center promised the greatest assistance that could possibly be rendered to General Walker's beleaguered force.

This request met with a cool reception on the part of the Chief of Staff of the Army. He offered numerous reasons why this use of Marines was inopportune and unfeasible—none of which seemed to be in the least valid to General MacArthur and his principal staff advisers. General Collins's failure to grasp the significance of the plan and the means of practical effectuation thereof marked his stature and his incapacity to meet the real problems facing the Commander-in-Chief in the field.

One of the principal items of the conference in Tokyo centered around the "impossibility" of finding sufficient ship tonnage to bring the 1st Marine Division to Korea. Fortunately, Admiral Sherman had brought along his newly appointed commander of the Military Sea Transport Service. Just as fortunately the Tokyo Staff had prepared, in anticipation of a "roadblock" from Washington, a complete list of all ships at sea and in harbor in the Pacific, on the U.S. coast, in Japanese waters, and even in Philippine waters. When General Collins raised his question of "impossibility," General MacArthur turned to Admiral Sherman, referring to the list of ships in the Pacific, and asked if "sufficient tonnage could not be made available by a shift in loadings."

Admiral Sherman, immediately grasping the significance of the possibility, turned to his chief aide and directed that he radio the Chief of Naval Operations in Washington to determine the availability of the required shipping; that, if it was possible, orders be sent forth at once by the Navy Department for earmarking this shipping. Within the next hour an affirmative reply was received and the shipping to send the Marines to reinforce the Far East was made available.

This incident is cited merely to show how studied were the efforts of the Washington military authorities to deny the means that were practicable for supporting the Far Eastern Command to the fullest. An exception to this attitude was that of Admiral Sherman; he constantly sought to aid General MacArthur to the fullest; the example just cited is only one of a number of instances. Admiral Sherman's opposition to Inchon as a landing place was mainly the result of technical difficulties, magnified by Sherman's advisers, both in Tokyo and in Washington. He overrode them when he had the necessary assurances from General MacArthur that "nothing rash" was intended and that if "weather, tide, or other reasons arose" the operation could either be terminated or diverted to less vulnerable strategic spots. Sherman understood the larger aspects of General MacArthur's concepts.

In a recent summary, MacArthur said:

There were no optimistic views to an early end of the Korean war when our beleaguered, outnumbered forces clung desperately to the Pusan perimeter, with their backs to the sea. The only prediction from Washington at that time warned of impending disaster. Disaster was avoided by the Inchon operation which was only grudgingly approved on my desperate insistence over the most serious professional doubts from higher authority.

With President Truman already planning his dismissal, MacArthur courageously set his eyes on greater goals: to salvage the reputation of Allied arms, to bring into sharper focus the colossal threat of imperialist Mongoloid–Pan-Slavism under the guise of communism, and to smash its current challenge in one great blow.

In early July he ordered Admiral James T. Doyle, his amphibious expert, to make an examination of the technical details of a landing at Inchon. Doyle said: "Our research listed every known geographical and naval handicap—Inchon had 'em all." G-2 turned out Terrain Study No. 13 and Handbook No. 65, "Seoul and Vicinity," comparable in every facet to the famous pocket-sized "Baedekers" that were a conspicuous feature of MacArthur's amphibious assaults in New Guinea.

The Marine Division staffs, old hands at assault landings from

New Ireland to Okinawa, were quite unhappy about Inchon. This
is what they said:

We regarded this maneuver as very hazardous since it required a
landing in the heart of a city. When we first looked at Inchon, we
thought it preposterous—the city was poison!

The ability of our troops to gain sufficient ground for a beachhead
was obviously restricted, while all the advantages of shoreline defense
lay with the enemy. There was hardly enough time to organize for the
night. The Marine landing was scheduled at 5:30 in the afternoon.
Sunset was at a quarter to seven. . . . The biggest navigational handicap was the incredible tidal conditions—easily the worst in the Far
East. The average rise and fall of the sea was 29 feet. The sea approach
to Inchon is a land-locked "pocket." The Yellow Sea surges into narrow channels; the tides are "piled up." On September 15, the tide rose
to its full height of 30 feet in six hours; in the next six hours the tide
fell to only six feet.

Any landing had to be made at high tide. The American landing
craft required from 23 to 29 feet to clear mud flats. The planners calculated that there were only three possible dates in the fall of 1950 "when
the tides would be right": September 15, October 11, and November 3.
Conversely, the Reds were equally aware of the practical implications
of these dates.

Two additional problems were mentioned: one tactical—in the appearance of Russian magnetic mines; the other political—the possible
intervention of China. Chinese entry into action on or about the date
of the Inchon landing might become fatal. Speed in timing and execution might neutralize the menace. Even then, however, it was perfectly
understood that half a dozen American Divisions could hardly undertake to offset the half-million Chinese, even then known to be on the
move through Manchuria and toward the Yalu.

These unquestionable risks and objections were presented to
MacArthur in a series of high-level conferences. The General was
patient, polite, and firm.

The final conference took place at 5:30 P.M. on August 23. It
was as important a gathering of military celebrities of the period as
any assembly in any war: General MacArthur; Gen. J. Lawton

Collins, the Army Chief of Staff; Maj. Gen. Edward M. Almond, MacArthur's Chief of Staff, who was already designated as Commander of the X Corps to land at Inchon; Lt. Gen. George E. Stratemeyer, the Air Commander; Admiral Forrest P. Sherman, the Navy Chief of Staff; Lt. Gen. Lemuel C. Shepherd, Jr., Marine Corps; Admiral Arthur D. Struble; Admiral C. Turner Joy; Admiral James T. Doyle, the brilliant Amphibious Group Commander; and a miscellany of senior military, naval, and air staffs. Eyewitness statements cover this meeting:

The conference room was not large enough to accommodate all the personnel. "Briefers" waited in the adjacent Chief of Staff's office until called for to put on their act. Doyle opened the briefing. He felt that excessive technical details, ordinarily frowned on by the General, were important in this instance. The staff then followed with about an hour's presentation, supported by maps and charts.

MacArthur sat relaxed and attentive during the long briefing, intermittently pulling on his famous pipe. Now and then he would stab into the flow of arguments to ask a brief question. When the naval staff terminated, MacArthur took command of the conference. He is a magnificent speaker; a quiet low voice that rose imperceptibly to a great dramatic nuance, at crucial points of his argument; precise, impeccable English without waste of a single word. The room was completely silent. Wisps of cigarette smoke drifted across the huge battle maps along the walls.

The General emphasized that the vulnerability of the enemy was his supply position. Every step southward extended his transport lines and rendered them more frail and subject to dislocation. The several major lines of enemy supply from the north converged on Seoul and then by diverging and radiating lines distributed munitions and supplies to his advancing front. It was MacArthur's plan to seize Seoul and thus completely throttle his entire supply system coming and going. This in turn would completely paralyze the fighting power of the [invader's] troops. Without munitions and food they would become helpless and disorganized and easily overpowered by our outnumbered but supplied forces. And this is exactly what happened.

The General reminisced on Wolfe's capture of Quebec, an operation which took the defenders by surprise. He felt that the North Koreans would not seriously consider Inchon as an American target.

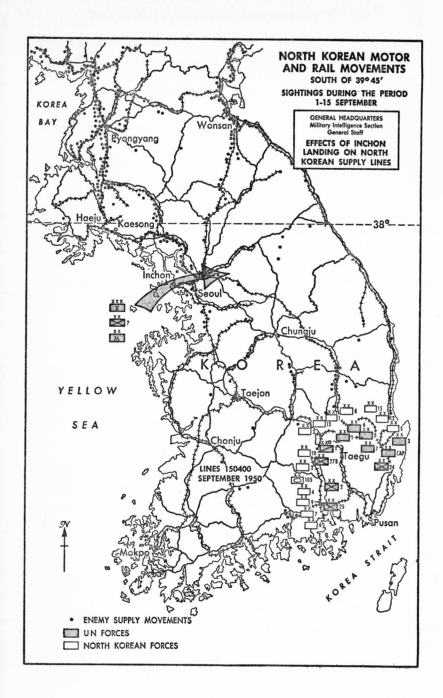

**NORTH KOREAN MOTOR
AND RAIL MOVEMENTS**
SOUTH OF 39° 45'
SIGHTINGS DURING THE PERIOD
1-15 SEPTEMBER

GENERAL HEADQUARTERS
Military Intelligence Section
General Staff
**EFFECTS OF INCHON
LANDING ON NORTH
KOREAN SUPPLY LINES**

KOREA
BAY

Pyongyang

Wonsan

Haeju   Kaesong

— — 38° — —

Inchon

Seoul

Chungju

K   O   R   E   A

YELLOW

Taejon

SEA

Chonju

LINES 150400
SEPTEMBER 1950

Taegu

Pusan

N

Mokpo

KOREA STRAIT

• ENEMY SUPPLY MOVEMENTS

☒ UN FORCES

☐ NORTH KOREAN FORCES

Finally, with complete confidence in the Navy, their rich experience in staging amphibious landings in the Pacific, he considered the amphibious landing as the most powerful tool of warfare in an insular area.

Sherman was lukewarm; Collins remained skeptical. The latter wished to compromise in favor of a more southerly landing at Kunsan. Such a short envelopment, however, would not have severed or destroyed the enemy's supply lines or distributing center and would therefore have served little purpose. MacArthur was adamant and finally won a most reluctant assent. The die was cast: Operation "Chromite" went into high gear immediately. Planning for the Solomons had required several months; the preliminaries for the landing in Africa consumed the better part of a year; Inchon took less than a month.

Intelligence had already entered the picture. The Eighth Army had no specialists at the time. General headquarters furnished linguists for interrogations of prisoners and for translations of documents. It furnished trained counterintelligence teams. It sponsored cryptanalysis. As in Brisbane in 1942, headquarters had to initiate and control "clandestine operations"; it established a "Joint Special Operations" staff (J.S.O.), with all intelligence agencies from Tokyo to Taegu pooling their meager resources, including the Central Intelligence Agency and certain South Korean groups. Maj. Gen. Holmes K. Dager, a veteran of the European Theater retired for wounds in action, represented G-2. High rank was necessary to deal with intransigent high-powered civil and military agencies. The whole thing had to be a repetition of the wartime Allied Intelligence Bureau. The flavor of their operations is contained in extracts from Dager's reports:

Parallel with the tactical planning for the Inchon landing, G-2 directed several clandestine operations to cover the Inchon-Seoul area, primarily to determine the influx of Red reinforcements and expansion of beach defenses. The Joint Special Operations planners set up a special project, "Trudy Jackson." Command and staff personnel involved several services and C.I.A.: Colonel H. Kae and Commander F. Youn, South Korean Army and Navy; Major Norberg, G-2; Lieutenant Clark, U.S.N.; Mr. F. Kluckhohn of Yokosuka, and two Signal

Corps Lieutenants. Kae and Youn naturally played a decisive role, since we were dealing with Korean natives. Kae collected twenty-two local agents to infiltrate the Inchon area; most of them came out again, with about ninety "target" descriptions.

The "Jackson" unit, with portable and hand-generated two-way radios, were flown to a port in southern Japan where they boarded the British destroyer *Charity*. The group was transshipped to the South Korean frigate P.C. 703 and delivered to one of the many small islands in the mouth of the Inchon harbor, arriving there on September 1. The information to be sought was primarily as a check against hundreds of air photos then being developed by the Air Corps.

It was also a check against other sources—a routine and time-honored intelligence precaution. Concurrently, J.S.O. had ordered about 250 parachute drops prior to the Inchon landing. Only half returned in time; others trickled in after that date. What reached us was excellent. Emphasis was on last-minute Red reinforcements.

In addition, J.S.O. had furnished the G-2 Geographical Branch with over thirty separate topographical studies of beaches, approaches, and entry data into Korean port areas, with numerous sketches and maps, developed by individuals who had lived and worked in those areas prior to the surrender.

With the Inchon landing still in progress, G-2 directed another expedition to be set up to cover the mouth of the Yalu River. The march north, across the 38th Parallel, had already been decided on. We got busy to set up "Operation Racketeer" posthaste. It was this group that reported the October crossing of Chinese "volunteers" into Korea.

One of the greatest hazards to the success of the operation was our lack of manpower. We did not have the troops. MacArthur with unprecedented boldness had partially built up our divisions by enlisting thousands of native Koreans and incorporating them in our skeletonized companies, battalions, and regiments. But even then he was woefully outnumbered. He just did not have enough men anywhere to make an envelopment without taking the Marines from the Pusan perimeter, which just at that moment was exposed to the enemy's most violent thrusts. It called for men of iron nerves to take such a step, but MacArthur and Walker were that sort of men.

As MacArthur was boarding Admiral Doyle's flagship, the *Mt. McKinley*, two great storms broke out threatening disaster—one on the seas, the other bred from opposition to his plan in Washington. He received a peremptory message "expressing doubt of success and implying the whole movement should be abandoned." MacArthur understood perfectly that this was "an anticipatory alibi in case the expedition should run into trouble." His reply was a masterpiece of reasoned logic. It overcame "the Bradley-Acheson thesis of inertia and passive defense" and won him a reluctant and depressing assent. Said MacArthur: "The incident was pessimism at its worst."

At dawn of September 15, the X U.S. Corps, Maj. Gen. E. M. Almond commanding, landed in the Inchon port area. Under heavy naval fire, a battalion of the 5th Marine Regiment seized Wolmi-do, a small, gun-studded enemy island that dominated the harbor. The remainder of the 1st Marine Division landed in the port area and swept into the city.

General Almond describes the action as follows:

The Marine Division's original objective had been the city of Seoul and it was to be secured on its right flank against Red forces being withdrawn from the Pusan front by the 7th U.S. Inf. Div. operating southeast and south of Seoul as far as Suwon and its important air field. Due to the stubborn resistance being put up by the fanatical North Korean defenders and the urgency of capturing the city for the psychological reason of restoring President Rhee to his capital as soon as possible, we decided to narrow the Marine Division's objective to the northern two-thirds of the city and to maneuver the enemy out of his entrenched position where the Marines were having so much strong opposition, by using the 7th Inf. Div., then well east of the southern outskirts of Seoul, to strike across the Han River, on the morning of the 25th, against South Mountain, an important terrain feature in the rear of the enemy line.

This maneuver was immediately successful and the enemy defenses in Seoul collapsed, except for some sporadic attacks of his covering forces. The Marine Division and elements of the 7th Inf. Division swept the enemy eastward and out of the city on the 26, 27 and 28 of September. . . . The Xth Corps secured the area south of Seoul, including the important air field at Suwon, and the 1st Marine Division was driving the retreating Red forces northward towards Ouijonbu, which they had rushed through to the capture of Seoul just three months before.

The entire Red Army was in a state of collapse; although sporadic and diehard fighting was being employed against the Eighth Army, then moving rapidly to join forces with the Xth Corps in the vicinity of Osan—the same Osan where the small force of General Dean's 24th Inf. Div. had met and been overrun by the victorious Reds almost three months to the day, on 4 July.

MacArthur, with his naval commander, Admiral Struble, went in on the afternoon of the assault to oversee the operation. The General immediately directed the prompt seizure of Seoul to be followed by an advance toward the south. This would place the bulk of the enemy's army between the two giant prongs of MacArthur's forces—the X Corps from the north, the Eighth Army from the south. He had forged the pincers, both the anvil and the hammer, and was ready for that strategist's dream—the stroke of complete annihilation.

MacArthur's insistence on speed and his selection of the earliest date for favorable tidal conditions represented split-second timing. Had the assault landing been delayed another month, the enemy's preparations for beach defense would have taken a heavy toll. Our landing, a "deep envelopment of the enemy's flank and rear," was coordinated and timed superbly with a "frontal breakthrough" of the Pusan perimeter. The Eighth Army launched its main attack on September 16. Some of the most severe fighting of the entire war resulted. But with his supplies gone, caught between the "pincers" and without retreat routes available, the enemy gave way at an accelerated rate. Precipitate withdrawal carried him rapidly northward over 70 miles. Soon complete disintegration set in. He was cut off from supply, command, and communications. Red regiments ceased to exist as organized units. Arms and equipment were abandoned; tanks, artillery, mortars, and small arms littered the highways and trails. Prisoners surrendered or were captured by the thousands. Within a month, the total of Red captives rose to 130,000. More than 30 per cent carried "psychological warfare leaflets" promising them fair treatment if they surrendered.

As he had done earlier with Osmena in Manila, MacArthur moved the government of Syngman Rhee into the shattered capital city of Seoul on September 29. None who were present will ever forget

that emotion-packed moment when MacArthur led that great assemblage in the Lord's Prayer. With his spirituality and innate
modesty, he believed and stated that such an astounding success,
under such abnormal difficulties, could only be the result of Divine
intervention. But the hard-bitten professionals who had followed
him so long, through so many trials and tribulations, through so
many "forlorn hopes," had other views.

Official congratulations were pouring in from the White House,
from the Pentagon, from the London War Office. Harry Truman
wired:

> I speak for the entire American people when I send you my warmest
> congratulations on the victory achieved under your leadership. Few
> operations in military history can match either the delaying actions
> where you traded space for time, or the brilliant maneuver which has
> now resulted in the liberation of Seoul.

The Joint Chiefs of Staff shifted suavely from their earlier misgivings about the Inchon landing:

> The J.C.S. are proud of the great successes you have achieved. They
> would have been impossible without brilliant and audacious leadership.
> From the sudden initiation of hostilities, you have exploited to the ut-
> most all capabilities and opportunities. Your transition from defensive
> to offensive operations was magnificently planned, timed and executed.

Frank Pace, Jr., Secretary of the Army, who was to be the General's guest in Tokyo on the day of MacArthur's dismissal, wired:

> The successes of your forces are deeply gratifying. I doubt that the
> response of your forces in the crucible of Korea to your inspired,
> courageous leadership has ever been surpassed. May God grant to you
> and the magnificent forces you command the full fruits of victory
> which their unfailing courage and determination so richly merit.

The British Chiefs of Staff, *i.e.*, the British Government, followed
the verbal pattern thus set:

> We have admired not only the skill with which you have conducted

an extremely difficult rear-guard action against great odds over many anxious weeks, but equally the bravery and tenacity with which the forces under your command have responded to your inspiring and indefatigable leadership. We believe that the brilliant conception and masterly execution of the Inchon counter-stroke which you planned and launched while holding the enemy at bay in the south will rank amongst the finest strategic achievements in military history.

But even as these messages of extraordinary praise came pouring in, General MacArthur had begun to have misgivings as to the concepts of their authors for the future of Korea. He outlined his fears to General Walker, whom he held in the highest esteem and regard:

The whole purpose of combat and war is to create a situation in which victory on the battlefield can be promptly translated into a politically advantageous peace. Success in war involves political exploitation as well as military victory. The sacrifices leading to a military victory would be pointless if not translated promptly into the political advantages of peace.

The golden moment to liquidate a war which had already been won militarily now presented itself—to immediately transmute the Inchon victory with its destruction of the North Korean Army into a political peace. This did not mean merely the imposition of our arbitrary will on the defeated North Korean Army. Our diplomacy must be capable of convincing Red China and the Soviet Union that we had no ambition, no mission further than to clear Korea and give it a chance for its own independent existence.

But instead it seemed to him [MacArthur] that the inertia of our diplomacy was failing utterly to utilize the victory as a basis for swift and dynamic political action to restore peace and unity in Korea. He feared a tremendous political failure to grasp the glittering possibilities of ending the war and moving decisively toward a more enduring peace in the Pacific. He feared our political and diplomatic lassitude would be regarded as timidity and appeasement and might well incite further military efforts against us. This he felt would not end the war but would extend it.

Walker agreed completely. Their fears were to become all too devastatingly true.

16 The Chinese Communist War

WHEN, after Inchon, no diplomatic action looking toward peace seemed to be forthcoming, there was a lull in the Korean War. Diverse views shortly began to appear among the members of the United Nations. The United States took the position that if the North Korean Army was not completely destroyed and peace and order restored in the northern half of the peninsula, South Korea would live indefinitely beneath the threat of renewed communist aggression. Many others, led by the British, were opposed to sending United Nations forces into Northern Korea.

On October 6 the question was decided by the General Assembly of the United Nations which voted explicit approval to make the crossing of the 38th Parallel. *General MacArthur then received definitive orders to move north.*

This decision presented MacArthur with problems of the greatest moment. It immediately raised the shadow of Red Chinese intervention. Actually, the possibility of such an intervention had existed ever since the amazing order from Washington, issued to the Seventh Fleet in June, to "neutralize" Formosa, which in effect protected the Red China mainland from attack by Chiang Kai-shek's force of half a million men. This released the two great Red Chinese Armies assigned to the coastal defense of central China and made them available for transfer elsewhere. They were reported to be moving north toward Manchuria. It was undoubtedly this "concept of sanctuary immunity" which tipped the scales in Red China's future decisions.

Red China would represent for MacArthur new conditions and a totally new war. The United Nations chose to ignore this uncomfortable problem. No means were ever furnished or even considered

378

to meet it, although the sinister implications were perfectly understood by all governments concerned. Unquestionably the failure, through inertia, of our diplomacy to utilize the victory of Inchon and destruction of the North Korean Armies as the basis for swift and dynamic political action to restore peace and unity to Korea was one of the great contributing causes to the subsequent new war into which we were soon to be plunged by Red China.

Behind the Red Chinese, of course, stood the Kremlin, ever alive to its chances of pushing to the warm waters of the Pacific. The prospect of a clash between America and Russia in Asia had been foreseen by those two prescient members of the Adams family, Henry and Brooks, at the very beginning of the century. But even before the prediction of the Adamses, an American naval officer, Commodore M. C. Perry, made a startlingly accurate forecast of the war to come. Speaking in a mild and innocuous setting before the American Geographical and Statistical Society of Massachusetts on March 6, 1856, Commodore Perry said:

It seems to me that the people of America will, in some form or other, extend their dominion and their power, until they shall have . . . placed the Saxon race upon the eastern shores of Asia. And I think, too, that eastward and southward will her great rival in future aggrandizement Russia stretch forth her power to the coasts of China and Siam: and thus the Saxon and the Cossack will meet. . . . Will it be in friendship? I fear not. The antagonistic exponents of freedom and absolutism must thus meet at last, and then will be fought the mighty battle on which the world will look with breathless interest; for on its issue will depend the freedom or the slavery of the world. . . . I think I see in the distance the giants that are growing up for that fierce and final encounter: in the progress of events that battle must sooner or later be fought.

The Commodore had just returned from his epochal trip to Japan. He could not foresee that an American commander would at some time be in occupation of Japan or that the American troops would face Russian puppets across an imaginary line, the 38th Parallel, thin as horsehair and as silly as fumbling diplomacy could possibly devise.

By a curious twist of alliteration, they were "Chinese" and not

"Cossacks" that "met the Saxon"—but the Commodore was right about Russia. Unfortunately, the Commodore's astonishing prophecy was not remembered in Washington.

The failure to remember Perry or the Adamses, however, need not have been fatal. For there was evidence much closer in time to prove that Red China—and, behind her, Soviet Russia—were preparing for a move. MacArthur's intelligence summaries of August 27, 1950 contained a miscellany of highly suggestive and completely ominous reports from Chinese Nationalist channels:

High level meeting held in Peking. Chinese Communists ordered to assist North Korea.

Lin-Piao to command Chinese forces in Korea. Communist troops continue to move north from Canton.

New China Co-Operative Society established. Includes China, Soviet Russia and North Korea.

Soviets order Communists to threaten Hong Kong. British warships fired on while entering Hong Kong. Communist merchant vessels depart Hong Kong.

The prospective geographical range of the Chinese Communist conspiracy as established in these reports was impressive—from Hong Kong to North Korea. There were to be many other reported instances of "saber rattling." In the light of the August 27 warning, MacArthur's comment at a later date is historically pertinent:

It is now plainly evident that the intervention by Communist China was responsive to basic decisions reached even before the North Korean attack last June, Communist China unquestionably having pledged herself to use her full military resources in support of the North Korean effort, should the necessity arise. Thus it is perfectly clear now that whether our troops crossed the 38th Parallel or had remained south thereof, the Chinese forces would have been utilized to rectify the situation resulting from the North Korean defeat. It would be naive indeed to believe that such an imaginary line would have influenced the Chinese in the slightest degree.

In a convenient post-mortem, a great deal of political propaganda has been made of the Truman-MacArthur conference on Wake

INTELLIGENCE HIGHLIGHTS

DECLASSIFIED
By No. 2909
C of S, G-2
GHQ, FEC Command

(1) JAPAN

CHIBA meets ASANUMA, proposes three party discussions on foreign affairs. ASANUMA says his party will not abandon "peace drive." Applications for police reserve total 321,000 (Page 2)

New Leftist Korean organization succeeds banned Choren. Korean Liberation Relief Society follows same Communist line. Leftist women's organization also prominent in Korean affairs. (Page 3)

Management dismisses 2,137 leftist Densan members. CIC source claims non-Red union members can control possible disturbances. Power cable fire reported in Fukui Prefecture. (Page 4)

Analysis of today's Tokyo dailies.

Weekly Prefectural Press Analysis.

(2) COMMUNIST CHINA

High level meeting held in Peking. Chinese Communists ordered to assist North Korea. Soviet officer to command combined Communist forces. Taiwan and Indo-China to be invaded. LIN Piao to command Chinese forces in Korea. LIU Po-cheng to command invasion forces for Indo-China. Chinese Communists reluctant to undertake further adventures. (Page 5)

USSR orders Communists to threaten Hong Kong. CNAC aircrews ordered to Tientsin. Hong Kong border remains quiet. Communist troops continue to move north from Canton. (Page 5)

British warship fired on while entering Hong Kong. Foreign ship strikes mine while leaving Shanghai. Communist merchant vessels depart Hong Kong. (Page 6)

Chinese Communists make preparations to aid Indo-Chinese rebels. Chinese Communist guerrilla units join Viet Minh forces. Second Field Army troops rumored will take part in Viet Minh offensive. (Page 7)

New China Co-operative Society established; includes China, USSR, North Korea. (Page 7)

Reconstruction of highway between Szechwan and Sikang Provinces underway. (Page 7)

Daily Summary 2909: Aug. 27/1950

Island in this period. Presumably this was planned to seem like an exact replica of the famous Roosevelt-MacArthur meeting in Hawaii. Actually the two were not in the same category.

With an eye to the coming elections, it was expedient for the President to smooth over the differences, if any, with his principal field commander—especially as a shooting war was then in full swing. It was equally expedient to exploit politically the smashing victory of Inchon and directly link the Administration with this impressive success.

There could have been no other motives. There were no obscure areas to explore. There was nothing to discuss that was not already known. Minute information on Korea went to Washington daily.

MacArthur himself placed this meeting of "slightly more than an hour's duration" in its proper perspective when he left it without waiting for luncheon and without bothering with the draft of a "public statement" that was then being laboriously composed by Ambassador Philip C. Jessup. Staff notes covering the meeting read as follows:

The item of Chinese intervention was brought up almost casually. Truman and his advisers had known from intelligence reports for some time that a build-up of Chinese forces in Manchuria was a *fait accompli*. On October 5 G.H.Q. reported 18 Red Divisions along the Yalu, while an over-all total of 38 Divisions was carried in Manchuria. They also knew that the Eighth Army mustered only 4 American and 4 S.K. Divisions at the time. To determine if the Red hordes were on the move or not, by day or night, was made impossible by Truman's own suicidal orders that kept our planes twenty miles south of the river border.

It was the general consensus of all present that Red China had no intention of intervening. This viewpoint had previously been advanced by the Central Intelligence Agency and Secretary of State Acheson. General Bradley went so far as to extract an agreement from General MacArthur to return two American Divisions before Christmas for disposal on the European front. Plans were outlined to MacArthur covering the administration of Korea as a united country and its rehabilitation from the ravages and destruction of the war. General MacArthur's views were asked as to the chance of Red China's intervention. He replied that the answer could only be "speculative"; that neither the State Department through its diplomatic listening posts abroad, nor the Central Intelligence Agency to whom a field commander must look for guidance as to a foreign nation's intention to move from peace to war, reported any evidence of intent by the Peiping government to intervene with major forces; *that his own local intelligence (which he regarded as unsurpassed anywhere) reported heavy concentrations near the Yalu border in Manchuria whose movements were indeterminate;* that his own military estimate was that with our largely unopposed air forces, with their atomic potential capable of destroying at will bases of attack and lines of supply north as well as south of the Yalu, no Chinese military commander would have dared hazard the commitment of large forces upon the Korean Peninsula. The risk of their utter destruction through lack of supply would be too great. [Italics added.]

Another staff commentary on the significance of Wake meeting reads:

How little did MacArthur realize that by one process or another it would be conveyed to the Red Chinese that even though they entered the fray in large forces, it would be under the sanctuary of being immune from any destructive action by our military forces within their own areas; that not even to save the lives of our men or insure the safety of our Army would we permit the Air Force to drop the atom bomb on military targets and enemy installations and troops, even though such a limitation upon available military force to repel an enemy attack would have no precedent either in our own history or the history of the world. That the Red Chinese commander apparently knew such a decision would be forthcoming while General MacArthur did not, represents one of the blackest pages ever recorded.

The episode at Wake Island was later completely misrepresented to the public and an effort made through an alleged eavesdropping report of a concealed State Department stenographer to pervert the position taken by General MacArthur.

The orders issued to General MacArthur after Inchon directed the destruction of the North Korean armed forces. To attain this objective he was to conduct military operations, including amphibious and airborne landings or ground operations, north of the 38th Parallel in

Korea. "Under no circumstances, however, will your forces cross the Manchurian or U.S.S.R. borders of Korea and, as a matter of policy, no non-Korean ground forces will be used in the North East provinces bordering the Soviet Union or in the areas along the Manchurian border. Furthermore, support of your operations, north or south of the 38th Parallel, *will not include air or naval action against Manchuria or against U.S.S.R. territory*. When organized armed resistance by the North Korean Forces has been brought substantially to an end, you should direct the R.O.K. forces to take the lead in disarming remaining North Korean units and enforcing the terms of surrender. Circumstances obtaining at the time will determine the character of occupation of North Korea. Your plans for such an occupation will be forwarded for approval to the J.C.S. . . . You will submit your plan for further operations north of the 38th Parallel to the J.C.S. for approval." [Italics added.]

In the light of this order, the charges made in the press of the world "that MacArthur crossed the parallel and went into North Korea on his own initiative and in reckless defiance of superior authority" were fantastically false. It is equally reprehensible that no voice from that superior authority was ever raised to correct this false propaganda. On the contrary, the "smear" was fed by the vulgar phrase used later to refer to the General as "too big for his breeches."

Previous orders had already forbidden both "hot pursuit" by our planes when attacked and the bombing of a number of electric-power installations in North Korea which furnished current to Manchuria and Siberia.

Especially incomprehensible to those in the field was the refusal of General Stratemeyer's request to bomb the important supply center of Rajin in the northeast. It was the place to which the Soviet forwarded tanks, artillery, and other heavy equipment from Vladivostok for the North Koreans.

Taken at face value, Washington's refusal to permit the bombing of a Russian supply point located well within North Korea is quite consistent with its complaisant refusal to face the fact of Allied trade in war materials with Red China through channels that ran from Ceylon and Indonesia to Macao and Hong Kong. Indeed, collateral information from Hong Kong about this trade was noted by MacArthur's staff and commanders with the paralyzing knowledge that they were forbidden either to blockade the sources or to strike at these supplies as they reached the Yalu border at a leisurely pace.

Hong Kong has become important as a supplier of strategic material to the Chinese Communists. Total trade in Hong Kong for 1950 amounted to over seven billion Hong Kong dollars ($500,000,000) an increase of almost 50% over 1949 and more than 600% over 1939. Chinese Communist imports from non-Communist countries amount to over four hundred million American dollars (U.S. 415,000,000) as compared to $53,000,000 in 1948. During last quarter of 1950, the Chinese Communists obtained vehicles and transport equipment, rubber, chemicals and drugs, iron and steel, non-ferrous metals and products, electrical and other machinery. . . .

The [listed items] imported during February 1951 totalled 146,214,-691 Hong Kong dollars. . . . The total export for the first two months of 1951 exceeded the total for the last two months of 1950 by 78,200,000 Hong Kong dollars.

It is against the uneasy background of United Nations inconsistencies, evasions, and contradictions, as well as against the indications of Red intervention, that MacArthur's advance toward the Yalu must be appraised. In addition to the warning from Chinese Nationalist sources on August 27 that intervention was coming, there were the continuing evidences of Chinese Red troop movements. As early as June 5, 1950, a G-2 report was filed that "North Korea received reinforcements from the Chinese Communist Forces through Manchuria." This was the first of a continuous succession of reports and comments on the Chinese potential. These reports were disseminated in large numbers of copies to our staffs and to Washington. Note random extracts from Tokyo "Daily Intelligence Summaries" special reports, "telecons," and radio exchanges with the Pentagon. Allied liaison officers in Tokyo received copies for daily dispatch to their governments:

June 6: A memorandum to the Chief of Staff: Without weakening their control of the China mainland the Communists are capable of redeploying a considerable force of regular troops for the assistance of the North Koreans. Estimates on Manchuria list 115,000 Regulars and 374,000 local Militia and Security forces.

July 8: Chinese Communist troops have already arrived at An-tung Yalu area on the Sin-Korean border.

August 15: W. Averell Harriman was given a report for presentation to the United Nations that "build-up of Chinese Communist troops in Manchuria was continuing and that China had agreed to furnish military assistance to North Korea."

August 31: Troop movements from Central China to Manchuria over a considerable period suggest preliminary to entering the Korean theater. Total Chinese strength in Manchuria estimated to be 246,000 Regular and 374,000 Militia Security forces.

September 8: If the North Korean forces are unsuccessful in driving U.N. forces from Korea within a reasonable period of time, or if success of the N.K. Army appears doubtful, the forces of General Lin Piao's Fourth Army [Chinese] will probably be committed.

October 5: The interest of all intelligence agencies is focussed on the Yalu river and the movements of Lin-Piao. A build-up of Chinese forces along the Korean-Manchurian border has been reported in many channels. The potential of massing at An-tung and other crossings appears conclusive. This mass involves a possible 9/18 Divisions organized in 3/6 Corps within a total strength of 9 Corps and 38 Divisions now carried in Manchuria.

October 14: Re the fine line of demarcation between enemy "intentions" and enemy "capability," recent declarations by Chinese Communist leaders, threatening to enter N.K. if the Americans were to cross the 38th Parallel, are probably in the category of diplomatic blackmail. The decision is beyond the purview of combat intelligence: it is a decision for war on the highest level, i.e. by the Kremlin and Peiping.

However, the numerical troop potential in Manchuria is a *fait accompli*. A total of 24 Divisions are disposed along the Yalu river, at crossing points. The grouping in the vicinity of An-tung is astride a suitable road for deployment southward.

October 28: Regular Chinese Forces in Manchuria now number 316,000 organized into 34 Divisions, in 12 Corps, as per Map A-3 att. In addition, there are 347,000 "irregulars" or Security forces.

All Regulars could be deployed in the Korean War. The bulk of these forces are now in position along the Yalu river at numerous crossing sites. They assemble in complete safety since U.N. air forces are forbidden to cross the border. Twenty-nine Divisions, or two-thirds of the total forces known to be in Manchuria, are immediately available.

The quality of the Chinese Communist fighting is probably similar to that of the well trained North Korean soldier in mid-campaign.

After the capture of the first Chinese soldiers, identifications began to emerge strongly indicating that the so-called "volunteers" were advance elements of the same regular divisions already spotted along the Yalu.

Intelligence is like a mosaic in which many colored chips are fitted until suddenly the pattern is revealed. The Wake Island conversations had not "played down" the Chinese threat; the subject simply was not static. The figures of Chinese strength were subject to change, fluctuating from day to day, as cumulative intelligence began to pile up. Truman and MacArthur would be confronted by Chinese forces not in strength as of Wake Island on October 15, but as of Sinanyu on November 24. In the meantime, the Chinese hordes had only fifty miles to march and had thirty-nine days in which to make it.

We have here an accepted distinction in intelligence parlance between enemy "capabilities," *i.e.*, physical ability to march into Korea in overwhelming numbers, and enemy "intentions," *i.e.*, was Peiping really prepared to march and thus risk open war with half the Western world? Obviously the "intentions" of the enemy would be determined by Peiping and Moscow as a diplomatic tour de force and not by the commanders along the Yalu. Military-political research dealing with the intentions of a foreign nation normally was handled by the State Department or the Central Intelligence Agency. There is a curious example of controversial Washington reporting on this elusive topic; it was obviously "planted":

Many people in Washington including several European Diplomats know of an overall intelligence report on Korea prepared by the Central Intelligence Agency. This report took a very grim, foreboding view of the numbers and intention of the Communist Chinese in Korea. Completed on November 21. It was available to MacArthur's staff before the offensive was launched. . . .

This report was mailed on November 21 and took more than a week to reach Tokyo. It was neither "overall" in scope nor "grim and foreboding"; rather it conceded "that there was no information at hand of a Chinese intervention of serious proportions" and concluded "that there was no evidence available that the Chinese were committed to an all-out military action."

In fact, MacArthur had to take steps to force the enemy to tip his hand: MacArthur's attack of November 24 was a reconnaissance in force but with freedom of action to advance or to withdraw.

MacArthur's strategic plan for the movement into North Korea was approved in Washington. It provided for a direct movement forward by the Eighth Army toward the enemy capital of Pyongyang and an amphibious movement of the X Corps to the east-coast port of Wonsan to bring flank pressure if necessary for the capture of Pyongyang. The so-called "waistline" between the east and west coasts of Korea is cut by a spinal mountain range which renders lateral communication extremely difficult between the two coastal areas and the movement of supplies across the peninsula completely impracticable. It was essential to secure both areas thus separated by the mountainous divide, as otherwise the entire eastern sector of the peninsula would have been left unguarded against an enemy flanking movement to the southeast—a similar course was followed previously by the North Koreans in their initial attack!—and the entire northeastern section of the peninsula would also have been left open for enemy maneuver against the Eighth Army's right.

The terrain was such that there was little prospect that an enemy might drive an effective wedge between the two forces and initiate flanking operations against either or both, and no such attempt was made. The maneuver planned by MacArthur was the classical one made famous by von Moltke: action by separated forces off the enemy's axis of movement. Both the Eighth Army and the X Corps were under direct control and central coordination of general headquarters until they were to meet in the north, when the united command would pass to General Walker. Until these two forces could

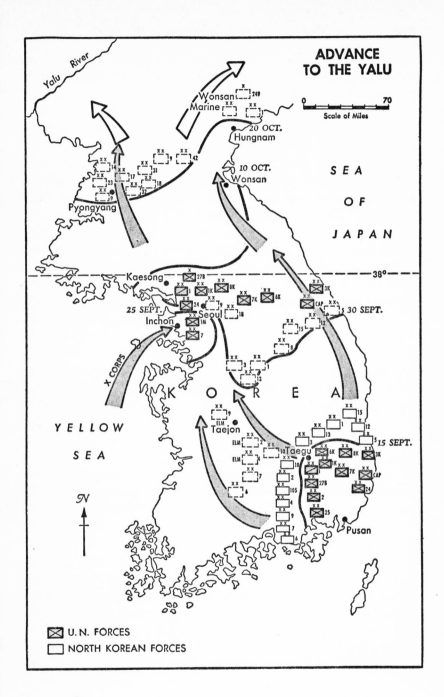

ADVANCE TO THE YALU

SEA OF JAPAN

YELLOW SEA

KOREA

Yalu River

Pyongyang

Wonsan Marine

20 OCT. Hungnam

10 OCT. Wonsan

38°

Kaesong

25 SEPT. Inchon Seoul

30 SEPT.

X CORPS

Taejon

15 SEPT. Taegu

15 SEPT.

Pusan

Scale of Miles
0 — 70

⊠ U.N. FORCES
☐ NORTH KOREAN FORCES

N

unite, it would have been impossible for Walker in the west area to attempt command responsibility and coordination of the east coastal area. The logistical maintenance of an entirely separate and different supply line from Japan to the east coast would have been beyond him.

The movement started on September 30, with two divisions of the R.O.K. forces, destined later to join the X Corps, pushing 100 miles along the east-coast road net. In ten days these divisions had taken Wonsan with but light resistance.

In the west, the Eighth Army drove sharply forward toward the southern environs of Pyongyang. The parachute drop of the 187th Airborne regiment 25 miles north of the city on October 20 was almost a duplicate of the famous maneuver in New Guinea when the gap was closed near Lae. Both General MacArthur and General Walker accompanied the paratroopers and met on the Pyongyang air strip. Both were disturbed by the supply situation which faced the Eighth Army.

Supply is the nervous system of any military operation. The rail lines north from Pusan, our naval base for overseas deliveries, had been thoroughly worked over by our air during the months of our perimeter defense. The port of Inchon, the sea harbor of Seoul, was restricted by the same adverse tidal conditions which had aroused such violent opposition to our initial amphibious attack there. As for the port of Chinnampo, the sea harbor of Pyongyang, it had only limited capacity. The net result of all these adverse logistical factors was materially to slow down the advance northward. The lack of supply facilities in the western sector was one of the prime reasons for the transfer of the X Corps to the east coast, where it could establish a new and independent sea-borne supply line direct from Japan to Wonsan.

General MacArthur, along with his field commanders, was worried by the growing indication of the startling build-up of Red Chinese troops in Manchuria, just north of the Yalu. In fact, the General was so concerned that he flew in an unarmed plane along the entire length of the Yalu River to observe for himself, applying his wise theory that "you can't fight 'em if you can't see 'em." The MacArthur flight itinerary ran over Sinuiju where as many as seventy Migs had occasionally been sighted. The very audacity of the flight was perhaps what saved him. The air has never seen a more daring flight. MacArthur found no concentrations, however, this side of the river. Nothing but subfreezing temperatures, glazed roads, and a landscape somber and barren almost beyond belief.

After the capture of the North Korean capital, General Mac-Arthur summoned the defeated Korean commander to surrender, with the sharp injunction to "liberate all UN prisoners of war and civilian internees and to make adequate provisions for their protection, care and maintenance." He had already warned the Communists previously. He had every reason to be worried.

When our troops overran the Red positions in Korea in our counteroffensive, they picked up mounting evidence of the brutal murder of our men behind the communist lines. They found the bodies of our teen-age boys flung into roadside ditches like so much rubbish, hands tied behind their backs and their heads blown in by pistol shots behind the ears—the classical Soviet-Mongoloid form of execution. General headquarters promptly filed medical reports and photographs. The gruesome record did not jibe with political remarks about a "police action."

MacArthur's concern was based on experience. Two years earlier he had conclusively established the Soviet pattern of calculated brutalities against Japanese prisoners of war—maltreatment, medical inefficiency, death marches, slave labor, brain washing, and kangaroo courts, the same story now haltingly revealed by a few hundred American soldiers. MacArthur's report about the earlier atrocities was designed to warn our men what to expect in war with communist assassins. The staff hoped eventually to force the United Nations to acknowledge the diabolical nature of one of their charter members—Soviet Russia. Tokyo headquarters wryly noted at the time that Congress had recently moved to a legalistic indictment of the Russian massacres of Polish officers in the Katyn Forest in 1943. Congress could have saved time and rhetoric had it made use of the immediate Tokyo report, on "life and death" in Soviet prisoners-of-war camps.

MacArthur's summons to the Korean commander was ignored and our mopping-up advance continued. Almond's X Corps swept rapidly forward; leading elements of his command were the first to reach the Yalu River on November 21, 1950. Reconnaissance elements of the Eighth Army did the same, but General Walker began to experience difficulties. His report to MacArthur was as follows:

On October 26th, the Army was advancing on a broad front in widely separated columns in pursuit of the defeated North Korean forces. The advance north of Pyongyang was based on a calculated logistical risk involving supply almost entirely by airlift. Supplies available were sufficient only for bare maintenance of combat operations . . . against light opposition, with no possibility of accumulating reserves to meet heavier opposition. . . .

An ambush and surprise attack began a sequence of events leading to the complete collapse and disintegration of the II South Korean Corps of three divisions. The Corps retreated in confusion to a position 13 miles from the only crossing area into the 1st U.S. Corps combat zone before some semblance of order could be restored.

The collapse on the East flank, together with heavy attacks on the 1st Korean division and the 8th U.S. Cavalry Regiment on the East flank of the 1st U.S. Corps, seriously threatened the only road supplying the 1st Corps and dictated temporary withdrawal of exposed columns of the 24th U.S. Infantry divisions on the West, a regrouping of forces, an active defense, a build-up of supplies pending resumption of offensive and advance to the border. By intense efforts progress is being made in reorganization and stabilization of the II South Korean Corps.

Chinese soldiers continued to be captured at this time. As did the earlier Chinese captured, they claimed to be "volunteers," but their identifications, too, indicated strongly they might be advance elements of the regular Chinese divisions already spotted along the Yalu River. On November 2 MacArthur reported urgently:

Recent captures of soldiers of Chinese nationality and information obtained from their interrogations, together with increased resistance being encountered by advancing U.N. forces, removes the problem of Chinese intervention from the realm of the academic and turns it into a serious proximate threat. . . .

The following day MacArthur furnished Washington a revised communist battle order, listing in complete numerical detail strength and locations in Manchuria of 56 Regular Army divisions, in 16 corps—a total of 498,000 men. In addition, there were District Security Forces of 370,000, or an aggregate of 868,000 in all. Meanwhile, other forces were still converging northward from central China.

Chinese Communist Regular Ground Forces (Cont)			
Unit and Location	Unit Strength	Area Strength	Unit Commander
YALU RIVER AREA:		109,000	
38th Army (4FA)(f)	23,000		LIANG Pi-yeh
Hq & Army Troops	5,000		?
112th Division	6,000		CHIANG Yung-hui
113th Division	6,000		TANG Ching-shan
114th Division	6,000		PENG Chin-wen
39th Army (4FA)(f)	30,000		LIU Chen
Hq & Army Troops	6,000		?
115th Division	8,000		CHEN Chin-yu
116th Division	8,000		CHUNG Wei
117th Division	8,000		CHANG Tien-yun
40th Army (4FA)(f)	30,000		HAN Kuang-chu
Hq & Army Troops	6,000		?
118th Division	8,000		TENG Yueh
119th Division	8,000		NING Hsien-wen
120th Division	8,000		HSU Kuo-fu
41st Army (-)(4FA)(g)	26,000		WEN Yu-cheng
Hq & Army Troops	2,000		?
121st Division	8,000		TSAI Cheng-kuo
122d Division	8,000		CHOU Kuang
123d Division	8,000		CHIANG Hsieh-yuan
ANTUNG AREA:		78,000	
46th Army (4FA)	28,000		CHAN Tsai-fang
Hq & Army Troops	3,000		?
136th Division	9,000		TSENG Yung-ya
137th Division	8,000		HSIAO Chuan-fu.
138th Division	8,000		JEN Chang-hui
55th Army (4FA)	25,000		
Hq & Army Troops	4,000		?
163d Division	7,000		?
164th Division (e)	7,000		?
165th Division	7,000		?
57th Army (4FA)(h)	25,000		
Hq & Army Troops	4,000		?
169th Division	7,000		?
170th Division	7,000		?
171st Division	7,000		?
CHENGTE AREA:		26,000	
70th Army	26,000		?
Hq & Army Troops	5,000		?
208th Division	7,000		?
209th Division	7,000		?
210th Division	7,000		?
Total Chinese Communist Regular Ground Forces in Manchuria:		415,000 (+)	
Armies:		16	
Divisions:		56	

Chinese Communist Regular Ground Forces (Cont)			No.2977 3 Nov
Unit and Location	Unit Strength	Area Strength	Unit Commander
Total Chinese Communist Regular Ground Forces in Manchuria:		415,000 +	
Total Military District Troops in Manchuria:		370,000	
Total Military Forces in Manchuria:		785,000 +	
Total Other Forces Reported in Manchuria:		48,000	
Aggregate:		833,000	

(a) Location tentative.

(b) Location in Manchuria confirmed. Exact location within Manchuria uncertain.

(c) Identified in Korea.

(d) Reports persist that elements of the 45th Army are in Kwangsi Province. These units may be the 48th or 88th Independent Divisions which are formerly carried as attached to the 45th Army and later dropped through lack of evidence of their existance.

(e) PWs confirm that these divisions were redesignated the 5th and 6th North Korean Divisions. They have probably since been reconstituted.

(f) Special units formed from each of these Armies consisting of 3,000 men each have been identified in North Korea.

(g) Elements in Kwangtung, possibly 121st Division. Now en route north.

(h) Also reported in the Yenchi Area.

(i) Two divisions are reported to be in the Hankou area. Elements in Manchuria.

(j) En route north. Elements in Manchuria.

This cumulative intelligence was made available not only to Washington, which furnished the "substance of force," but to the United Nations, which supplied "the label." Either Washington or the UN could have stopped our troops at any point in North Korea if they had taken the mounting Chinese threat seriously. Instead, each preferred the opiate of wishful thinking, the myopic resignation of the ostrich. Modern general staffs do not normally philosophize about "wrong wars in the wrong places." They advise their governments not to stumble into that kind of war, or if pushed in, they argue for adequate military means to end them: "In war, there is no substitute for victory."

MacArthur's concern was increasing daily. There was no Joint Chiefs of Staff clarification or change of his orders of September 27, which read ". . . you will continue to make special efforts to determine whether there is a Chinese Communist or Soviet threat to the attainment of your objective." There was no slightest indication of direct Soviet intervention. The sole question was Peiping's action.

Did the fiction of "volunteers" mask the projected entry of the Red Regular Army of China into the foray? Was Communist China prepared to take the stunning gamble of throwing its ground forces into war against a country possessing the atom bomb and complete air control of the campaign area? Could she afford to risk the destruction of her flimsy industrial base and the severance of her tenuous supply lines from the Soviets, which would deny her the resources to support modern war or to sustain large military forces in the field and in turn so weaken the Peiping Communist government's hold in Asia as to threaten the eventuality of a Red debacle?

Staff notes of the period cover the General's thought and actions substantially as follows:

At this juncture MacArthur carefully reappraised the disposition of his forces. They were completely adequate to encompass the destruction of the remnants of the North Korean forces and the restoration of order throughout North Korea was unquestionable. So far as North Korea was concerned, it had been a "mopping up" operation. His problem was how to pass from an "operation on the offensive" to the best possible "posture of security" in case of an unannounced and sudden attack by the Red Chinese hordes in the manner of a Pearl Harbor.

They already outnumbered his forces nearly five to one and every day that passed increased this discrepancy. By the end of the year, it would be ten to one—and still growing.

MacArthur had already been informed by Washington that he could expect no major addition to his own forces. His plea for Chinese Nationalist reinforcement was submitted [to] and denied by the Joint Chiefs of Staff because of the possibility ". . . that it would disrupt the united position of the nations associated with the United States in the United Nations and leave the United States isolated. It may be wholly unacceptable to the Commonwealth countries to have their forces employed with Nationalist China. . . . Our position of leadership in the Far East is being most seriously compromised in the United Nations. The utmost care will be necessary to avoid the disruption of the essential Allied line-up in that organization. . . ."

The question the General posed for himself was this: Should he withdraw the Xth Corps to Wonsan and have it incorporated with the Eighth Army with the hope of holding a line across the Peninsula? Such a defensive attitude he felt would be fatal. He did not have the force to permit "a defense in depth." At the narrowest neck each of his divisions would have to assume responsibility for fronts of over twenty miles. With no reserve dispositions in depth, the attempt to hold such a line against the tactics of infiltration so frequently and efficiently employed by the Chinese could easily have subjected the entire line to piecemeal destruction. When a line was established after the truce negotiations began, the U.N. forces had more than doubled in strength.

Moreover, MacArthur could not afford to wait on the defensive—a "Maginot line of action." Time would be with the enemy. If the Reds were allowed to continue their build-up and our forces compelled to remain unaugmented, the discrepancy would eventually become so great as to destroy any chances we might have. He must act—and act without delay. He felt that the practical effect of the deployment of the Xth Corps in the northeast would be to place it squarely upon the flank of the Chinese supply lines and build-up operations and thus force them to split up their forces to counter this Xth Corps threat. This would materially weaken the force that could be hurled at the 8th Army. An entire Chinese field army would have to be detached from their main stroke, which could not fail to be against Walker.

MacArthur consulted his staff and his field commanders, and general consensus was that a *"limited advance that kept the Army free to maneuver" was the best solution to an extraordinary situation.* General Walker was especially vehement. He wrote the General: ". . . there has never been and there is not now an intention for this Army to take up or remain on a passive perimeter or any other type of defense. Every effort is being made . . . to facilitate the resumption of attack as soon as conditions permit. All units continue to execute local attacks to restore or improve our lines. Plans have been prepared for resumption of the offensive employing all forces available to the Army. These plans will be put into effect at the earliest possible moment."

MacArthur approved the plans of field commanders and reported to Washington accordingly. If Red China was not going to intervene, it would spell the end of the war. If such were not the enemy's intention, the movement would serve as an "army reconnaissance in force" with the object of "unmasking" the Chinese Government, demolishing the fiction of "volunteers" and identifying "the Red Regular Army."

MacArthur directed Walker to prepare and have ready for instant use a plan for immediate retreat if the Chinese should intervene. [Italics added.]

General MacArthur flew to the Eighth Army as it began its cautious forward movement. In talking with one of his old friends, he quipped about the desire of Washington as expressed at the Wake Island conference, to "send two divisions back and to get the boys home for Christmas." The remark was misconstrued by the press of the world as a bona fide "official estimate." Actually it was not intended to have any relation to realities. It was an unfortunate misinterpretation—although psychologically and politically it may have been of value as a final public reassurance to China that the "U.N. command was not interested beyond the borders of North Korea." Peiping chose to ignore MacArthur's bid. On November 26, 1950 the Red Commander Lin-Piao launched his full forces across the Yalu and into battle. Red China thus entered upon open war against United States forces and those allied with us.

In the space of hours, the presence of two Chinese Army groups with overwhelming forces was established, the Fourth under Lin-Piao operating against Walker; the Third under Chen-Yi colliding with Almond. To add insult to injury, Lin-Piao's Chief of Staff was permitted to harangue the UN Security Council and "complain of American aggression against China."

MacArthur summoned his field commanders to Tokyo for a brief conference. An eyewitness to this historical meeting reported:

The conference was held in the salon of the American Embassy. Walker and Almond, showing the strain of the front-line, in worn field uniforms, clashed discreetly with the opulent decor. Present were Generals Whitney, Doyle Hickey (the Chief of Staff), Wright (G-3), and Willoughby (G-2).

The overwhelming enemy strength in Manchuria was accepted by all concerned. A fifty mile hop would bring them into the American outposts.

The commanders were bitter (against Truman) to be compelled to fight another unfair ratio of five or ten to one against the Red Armies which had supply bases protected by an inviolate frontier.

The conferees considered various intermediate positions, such as the line: Pyongyang-Wonsan. The only touch of humor in an otherwise grim atmosphere was the recollection that this was "the thin waist of Korea," a current popular hoax. When scaled via Yangdok, along the only decent crossroad in North Korea, the waist was no thinner than the Seoul-Chonchun line. The Eighth Army would have to be supplied via Chinnampo, a poor harbor at best. The Chinese had enough divisions to surround the Eighth Army, if it remained stationary, as well as to pour other divisions southward in the direction of Seoul. This was in fact the grandiose Chinese plan.

Both Walker and Almond had fought with distinction in Europe. They were too experienced to overlook the odds in this situation. General Hickey, MacArthur's able Chief of Staff in this period, a man of ripe judgment and distinguished service in Europe, called for speed in withdrawal and to expedite Almond's movements to cover the east flank of the Eighth Army. MacArthur promptly made the decision to withdraw and fight delaying actions long enough to enable Almond to pull out from the east coast and join Walker in a defensive line further south.

With full confidence in the Navy's superior skill in handling amphibious operations, MacArthur decided on the withdrawal of the Xth Corps by sea.

With the junction of the Eighth Army and the Xth Corps accomplished, the General expected to resume the offensive. He shrewdly counted on forcing the Chinese supply lines from their Yalu "sanctuary" into the open, where he could hit them with incessant air attacks.

The withdrawal, as such, did not worry anybody. A modern army does not disintegrate overnight. This was the same battlewise army that had taken 135,000 prisoners of war only a few weeks before.

The Red Fourth Army attacked near the junction of the Eighth Army and the South Korean II Corps. The South Korean divisions were thrown back, exposing the flank of the American Eighth Army troops. MacArthur promptly ordered the Eighth Army and the X Corps to withdraw. His advance of November 24 had upset the enemy's timetable, causing the Red Chinese to move prematurely, and threw off balance their preparations aimed at surreptitiously massing the power capable of destroying our forces with one mighty

---

The map on the facing page must be read in the light of the following data:

1. In early October, prior to the crossing of the 38th parallel by UN forces, Communist China's Premier Chou En-lai made a statement over the Peking radio warning that the Chinese people "would not stand supinely by while their neighbor was being invaded." This statement followed a vitriolic propaganda campaign against the United States, wherein Peking stated that China "will always stand on the side of the Korean people" and "cannot but warmly sympathize with and support their liberation of Korea." It was about this same time that a Chinese delegation headed by Kuo Mo-jou, Chairman of the Committee for Culture and Education, visited Pyongyang and assured the North Korean people of Chinese Communist support in their war of "liberation."

2. Concurrent with the propaganda broadcast, *i.e.*, intensive psychological and political preparation for war, Chinese Communist forces in Manchuria were being steadily increased. On July 8 there were an estimated 116,000 regulars in Manchuria. By August 8 these troops had been increased to an estimated 217,000 and by August 30 to 246,000. By September 21 this number had almost doubled, through transfers from south and central China, with a total of 450,000 reported to be in Manchuria. Another substantial increase in this troop strength was noted during the period from September 21 to November 16, at which time there were an estimated 850,000 Chinese Communist troops in Manchuria and Korea, of which about 350,000 were Internal Security troops.

blow. Had we not acted when we did, the Eighth Army would have
been a "sitting duck" doomed to eventual annihilation.

A headquarters report on the situation reads:

When the Chinese crossed the Yalu, MacArthur instantly ordered
the bridges—six of them!—destroyed by our air force. Within hours
his orders were countermanded from Washington. Those bridges still
stand. Their planks have echoed to the tramping feet of hundreds of
thousands of men, and millions of tons of supplies and ammunition
have crossed them, either to support the enemy or blast our own ranks.

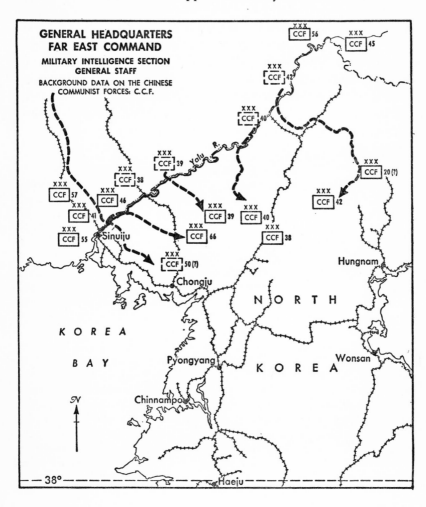

They are still there inviolate, intact. In his bitterness, General Mac-Arthur exclaimed: "I realized for the first time that I had actually been denied the use of my full military power to safeguard the lives of my soldiers and the safety of my army. To me it clearly foreshadowed a future tragic situation in Korea and left me with a sense of inexpressible shock."

Chiang's ambassador in Tokyo, Gen. Ho Shai-Lai, called on General MacArthur early in November on behalf of his government to state that "the Chinese Regular Army had entered Korea, in great strength." The ambassador, who had been graduated from Ft. Leavenworth, class of 1933, was thoroughly indoctrinated in American combat methods. Now a delegate to the United Nations in New York, his views, as of 1950, are of more than casual significance today.

He agreed with General MacArthur that the communist supply lines, especially the Yalu bridges and bases adjacent to the river, could and should be destroyed by American air, provided that the current sanctuary was discontinued—a privilege completely unintelligible to the American-trained diplomat. He felt that some assurance must have reached the Reds, on that point, in devious channels. He discounted the current alibi that the Russians would intervene.

Ho Shai-Lai recalled that reports had already been received since March 1950 that communist troops were moving into Manchuria and that many divisions were massing on the Korean border. Since the North Koreans appeared to be winning, at the time, their employment was not considered.

When General MacArthur succeeded in the spectacular landing at Inchon, in September 1950, the fate of the North Koreans was sealed—but the Chinese Reds chose to wait until the end of October, *i.e.*, at least six weeks, before they started crossing the Yalu. Why did they fail to come to the assistance of the North Koreans immediately? For the simple reason that after Inchon, they had to face the probability that the Yalu bridges and their adjacent bases would be bombed, which would have jeopardized successful intervention.

So for six weeks all they did was to hint that if UN troops crossed the 38th Parallel, they might enter the war. Communist supporters and dupes promptly yielded to this blackmail. The Korean War would have terminated if the U.S. had issued a warning to the effect that any entry of the Chinese Communists into Korea would be considered an act of hostility. They would have stayed on the other side of the Yalu. Instead—through a weak policy and for fear of Russian intervention—information must have been relayed to the other side, guaranteeing that those bridges would enjoy sanctuary and their bases left intact. And so, Ho Shai-Lai concluded, the Communists were not only assured that there was no real intention to win—but they were also guaranteed against the risk of losing. No better assurance could have been furnished. They marched on that assurance. . . .

General MacArthur reiterated that he "planned the air-interdiction of the Yalu bridges and expected to slow down the Reds through this measure." As it turned out, the General was expressly forbidden all-out air bombardment, on Washington orders, and half a dozen American divisions were consequently exposed to the full onslaught of overwhelming numbers. Was this a calculated sacrifice to some obscure diplomatic motivation?

The withdrawals of the Eighth Army were made with consummate skill. MacArthur himself regarded the whole operation as one of his best . . . if not the best! He felt that the hard decisions he had made and the skill displayed by his field commanders in their implementation had saved not only the Eighth Army but Korea itself and, with it, our future hopes for the Far East. MacArthur was fully aware that the entire situation would be misunderstood and misrepresented but merely said dryly: "I've always been able to take care of the enemy in my front—but have never been able to protect myself from shafts from the rear."

After the entry of China into the war, the American Army was compelled to take odds never before encountered in the entire military history of the nation. There is nothing even remotely comparable in recent wars. However, the impact of the disaster school of war reporting on public opinion in the fall of 1950 was such that it must now be driven home forcefully that the frightening stories of the time represent a distortion of history. We fought harder in Korea than in Europe, and, given the circumstances, just as successfully. A brief parallel shows this vividly, for the Allied campaign in Italy had some similarities to that in Korea. Topography and road net were similar. The Italian front was approximately 100 miles as compared with 140 miles in Korea. In Italy, however, the Allies employed two armies, the American Fifth and the British Eighth with thirty-one first-class divisions to fight against a variable twenty to twenty-seven Italo-German divisions somewhat battered and usually half the Allied troop strength. Italy was a strategic sideshow. Nothing vital was at stake. The war could not conceivably be won there. One need not strain one's imagination to guess what thirty-one Anglo-American divisions, instead of only nine, would have done to the Chinese in Korea, at any stage of the war.

Nevertheless the Allied high command, the Joint Chiefs of Staff, the American and British "brass" in Italy threw in a great superiority of means. It is a point of historical importance that the same "brass," still powerful in Washington during 1950 and 1951, apparently changed the basis of their military calculations between the Anzio and the Yalu. It is impossible to understand on a professional basis how the General Staff in Washington could placidly accept the staggering odds piled on the Eighth Army in Korea. Instead of a pat on the back for our teen-age draftees of a few months' training who were fighting rather forlornly in an alien land, an inexplicable wave of defeatist reports engulfed the Eighth Army with wide repercussions at home and abroad. Here is a cross section of some characteristic comments of the period:

The flight of our troops before Chinese peasant soldiers was the most shameful disgrace suffered by American arms since the first Battle of Bull Run in 1861. . . .

It was America's worst licking since the battle of the Bulge and maybe even Pearl Harbor. Barring a military miracle, the Army might have to be evacuated in a new Dunkerque, from being lost in a new Bataan. . . .

An explosion of white-hot wrath was spontaneous throughout the rank and file of the Eighth Army. Petitions were circulated by enlisted men of the 2d Division, demanding a retraction and denouncing these reports as "vicious lies and slander upon thousands of American war dead."

A cold statistical comparison of dead, wounded, and missing with battle-action losses of World War II is a complete refutation of the deadly nonsense which was fed to an anxious and bewildered public. A reference to the Tenth Army in the Ryukus during World War II is enlightening, since some of the divisions involved in the three months' fight for Okinawa also appeared in the Yalu operations, *viz.*, the 1st Marine and the 7th Infantry Division.

COMPARISON OF LOSSES
TENTH ARMY (RYUKUS) AND EIGHTH ARMY (YALU)

Ryukus Operations	1945	Yalu Operations	1950
XXIVth Corps	34,736	Eighth Army	7,337
7th Division	10,893	2d Division	4,131
27th Division	. 5,224	1st Cav. Div.	443
77th Division	7,126	24th Division	146
96th Division	10,247	25th Division	1,606
Corps Troops	1,246	Other U.N.	1,011
III Amph. Corps.	26,724	Xth Corps	5,638
1st Mar. Div.	13,002	1st Mar. Div.	2,891
2d Mar. Div.	95	3d Division	650
6th Mar. Div.	12,815	7th Division	2,097
Corps Troops	812		
Tact. Air Force	520		
Tenth Army Troops	1,015		
Army Garrisons	2,636		
Total	65,631		12,975

On the average, individual divisions on Okinawa sustained from *two to five times the losses incurred in the withdrawal from the Yalu* five years later. The Eighth Army in 1950 took on extraordinary numerical odds, facing from twenty-four to thirty-nine Chinese divisions; the Tenth Army in the Ryukus was involved with only one Japanese corps of three divisions. Bastogne in Belgium was not unlike Anju in Korea, and Anzio in Italy was not unlike Inchon.

In the Bulge operations in 1944, the 108th Division, directly in the line of advance of the German penetration, lost 8,490 men of its total strength of 14,032 in a period of fourteen days.

In the Anzio campaign in the spring of 1943, American losses for the four-month period amounted to an aggregate of 43,000. Casualties of the 3d Division alone were 3,131 during an eight-day period. That same division was in the Hamhung-Wonson withdrawal in Korea eight years later: it lost 650 men.

The evacuation of the X Corps from the port of Hungnam, with the 1st Marine, 3d and 7th Divisions fighting heroic rear-guard actions that stopped three Chinese corps in their tracks, was exposed to unwarranted comments. This remarkably smooth and efficient amphibious operation was loudly proclaimed "a second Dunkerque." The absurdity of this classification is self-evident:

| | Ships | | Personnel | Equipment |
	Total	Sunk	Evacuated	Salvaged
Dunkerque	841	163	338,000	—
Hungnam	163	—	205,000	350,000 tons
				17,500 vehicles

About Dunkerque, Churchill said:

More than 300,000 British and French troops scrambled for boats and ships of the rescue fleet. An estimated 2,000 men were lost at sea, as well as over 200 ships and most of the Army equipment, including 120,000 vehicles, 2,700 artillery pieces and 90,000 rifles. Our armies at home were almost unarmed except for rifles. There were hardly five hundred field guns of any sort and hardly 200 tanks in the whole country. Months must pass before our factories could make good even the munitions lost in Dunkerque. . . .

Compare this tragic description of real disaster with the terse radio from General Almond, commander of the American X Corps, on December 24:

The Xth Corps, reinforced, has completed evacuation by air and sea from Hungnam at 14:36 Hrs. 350,000 tons of supplies and equipment have been withdrawn. Nothing has been left to the enemy. 105,-000 troops, including S. Korean units and approximately 100,000 refugees, have been evacuated to safety in South Korea. Structures of possible military value to the enemy have been destroyed. The enemy paid heavily for his attempt to interfere with our operations. The losses of our forces were comparatively light.

When General MacArthur, during his visit with General Almond at Yonpo Airport (near Hamhung) on December 8, asked, "How long can the X Corps maintain its position in this area with Hungnam Port as the base of supply?" General Almond replied:

For as long as you desire; the X Corps is now established in a tactically strong position with a secure base and line of supply by sea; we can stay here as a threat to the enemy's flank and should do so, unless there are no other troops available to support the Eighth Army from the U.S.

But higher authority had decreed that sufficient forces should not be sent from the United States and General MacArthur had to bow to the inevitable. He was forced to use the X Corps to strengthen the badly used Eighth Army in the south instead of maintaining it as a dagger in the enemy's flank at Hungnam and Hamhung.

MacArthur stabilized his lines early in January at a position midway in South Korea. General Walker had been killed in an accident and the Eighth Army was now under command of Gen. Matthew B. Ridgway. MacArthur flew to Korea on January 20, nullified any suggestion that the enemy might drive our forces into the sea, and issued orders for the counteroffensive.

His field strategy had involved breaking contact with the enemy and a rapid withdrawal to lengthen and expose the latter's supply lines. What resulted was a pyramiding of logistic difficulties for the Reds and an almost astronomical increase in the destructiveness of our air power. Soon the balance was restored between the opposing forces. MacArthur's objective was again to be the enemy's supply lines.

For psychological as well as other reasons MacArthur proposed by constant thrusts to regain the Seoul line for a base of operation from which to clear North Korea of enemy forces. This could be accomplished through the air destruction of enemy concentration and installations, the closing of major lines of enemy supply and communication through the sowing of defensive fields of suitable radioactive materials available as by-products of atomic manufacture, and simultaneous amphibious landings at the upper ends of both coasts of North Korea. For these amphibious landings, he would employ the new divisions just ordered to the Far East and picked veteran troops from Formosa which had been offered. It was to be Inchon again—only on a larger scale!

In frequent visits to the front, General MacArthur made his own lucid appraisal of the chronology of the fighting and accurately forecast the slow deterioration and eventual defeat of the Chinese hordes:

February 13: I am entirely satisfied with the situation at the front. The enemy has suffered a tactical reverse. His losses are amongst the bloodiest in modern times.

February 20: The enemy is finding it an entirely different problem fighting 350 miles from his base than when he had sanctuary in his immediate rear. He is paying now for the illusion so falsely but effectively propagandized that he had defeated our Eighth Army decisively. I note that Marshal Stalin has just predicted the annihilation of our forces in Korea—but his Comrades will have to do lots better than they have yet done, to prove him a prophet.

March 24: It is increasingly evident that the heavy destruction of the enemy's lines of supply, caused by our round-the-clock air and naval bombardment, left his troops in forward areas deficient in requirements. The enemy's human-wave tactics have failed. He is showing less stamina than our own troops under the rigours of climate, terrain and battle. Of even greater significance has been the revelation that this new enemy, Red China, of such exaggerated and vaunted military power, lacks the industrial capacity essential to modern war.

Expansion of our operations to the enemy coastal areas and interior bases would doom Red China to imminent military collapse. These basic facts established, there should be no insuperable difficulty in arriving at decisions on the Korean problem if the issues are resolved on their own merits. . . .

To the very moment of General MacArthur's dismissal, Washington was informed of the fluctuating situation in Korea and the enormous potential of victory inherent in the last two months. As early as March, a blueprint was drawn: expansion of our operations to the enemy coastal and interior bases; the threat of aerial reprisal—a concept which was new to Truman but has since become a commonplace item, under Eisenhower, as a deterrent for war. MacArthur personified this threat. Somehow MacArthur had to be eliminated. The enemy made one last convulsive, bloody effort to discredit him in the field and so to convince the Western world that the fiction of military power that they and their stooges had established was real.

The enemy staged an abortive offensive in April. The Eighth Army anticipated it by fifteen days and was ready; our troops "rolled with the punch" and then counterattacked with brilliant success. The Reds tried again in May—and for the last time. They suffered crippling losses. Of twenty-one Chinese divisions which started the attack, sixteen lost half or more of their effectives and were *hors de combat;* the XII, XV, XXVII, and LX Corps had disappeared; only one corps, the XX, was able to continue in action. It must be realized that the Chinese Third and Fourth Armies were the best they had; the seventy to eighty divisions, stuck in Korea and literally consumed in this holocaust, were the best divisions they had; in all of China, from Tibet to Siberia, there remained about 120 second-rate divisions of variable quality, from fair to poor—and the Korean drain was endless, relentless, and killing.

The Chinese recognized the implications: just short of collapse, they called for a truce for the sole purpose of physical recovery, and they obtained it through the crafty, superbly timed intervention of the Soviets in the gullible and lukewarm United Nations. President Truman added the final touch by relieving his ablest field commander on the eve of another victory. The effect of these incongruous measures coalesced to eliminate the one man in the Far East whom communism had reason to fear. Truman had played right into the Communists' evil hands.

We also missed a military opportunity that may never return: the failure of the Reds in their violent offensives, and their slow deterioration since February, were not explicable on grounds of superior Allied tactics alone, since our collective strength in infantry was always far below that of the enemy. There was an important

No	Unit	Position	Name	Arms	Serial Number	Model	Belongings 1 2 3 4 5 6 7	Remarks
1	1 Sqd 1 Plat	Gunnery officer	LEE Hung Chol	Inf rifle	440168	1917		
2	"	Gunner	LEE Sok Pin					
3	"	2nd gunner	KIM Yong Kwan	Inf rifle	589254	1917		
4	"	3rd gunner	LEE Chun Kil	"	533421	"		
5	"	4th gunner	KIM Suk Che	"	350842	"		
6	"	5th gunner	CHOI Wal Hyon	"	414221	"		
7	"	6th gunner	HONG Hyong Jin	"	711501	"		
8	"	7th gunner	SONG Sa Tok	"	553531	"		
9	"	8th gunner	LEE Bong Son	"		"		
10	"	Driver	CHANG Hak Pin	"	441348			
11	"	"	PANG Hyong Kil		262353	"C.2		
12	"	"	PANG Bak Chong					
13	"	Gun carriage man	CHUNG In Hong	Inf rifle		1917		

ITEM 26 Loose sheet, mimeographed, containing an order, in Chinese, is-
202487 sued by Medical Section of unknown unit, CCF, dated 8 March.

Captured: Place unknown - 30 Mar 51

Recd ATIS: 5 Apr 51

Full translation:

Diseases

The following is a report on the "disease situation" existing among the native people and troops in the area where our Regiment is stationed.

1. An NKA hospital is located in the vicinity of our Medical Section. The number of patients in this hospital has increased to over four hundred. Most cases are typhoid and recurrent fever. Several patients have died lately. The hospital announced that these diseases have been reaching epidemic proportions, and that two-thirds of the staff of this hospital have been infected.

2. In the area surrounding the Supply Section, Medical Section, Guard Company and 1st and 2nd Bns, many native families were infected with these diseases and three children died from them.

3. There are some cases of pneumonia, bad colds, and recurrent fever in our Regiment. In 1st Bn, there are five or six cases of recurrent fever. A first sergeant of 3rd Bn, a supply sergeant of Regimental Headquarters, and a culture officer of the SMG Co had pneumonia. Besides these, quite a few have "soreness of waist and legs" and scabies.

4. The main factors causing these diseases are:

a. Some slept in native houses during encamping, and were infected with typhus by lice in blankets. Others contacted recurrent fever by staying in the rooms where patients had stayed previously (like NKA cases).

b. Some who became heated from heavy work during marching, removed their clothes immediately or went out at night without sufficient clothing and caught cold and influenza which may develop into pneumonia (such as KE Hsiu Sheng (*1) and HSU Wen Kuang (*2) developed pneumonia from a cold).

c. Some who often stay in air raid shelters or are on duty in defensive position, sometimes develop sore waist and legs and scabies.

5. Methods of prevention:

a. Clean a house thoroughly before staying there. Basins and bowls borrowed from the natives should be dipped in boiling water several times.

b. To make effective the "Kill the lice movement," since we lack DDT powder, we have to wash our clothes and sun the straw bed cushions as often as possible.

c. Don't remove clothes and hat when perspiring from heavy work; put hat and enough clothes on when going out at night.

d. When in air raid shelter or on duty in defensive position, lay more dry straw at the spot where you happen to stay for a while. During the night, sleep on a "stoved bed" if possible.

e. Exercise constantly and effect preventions strictly by watching each other.

Close cooperation between military and political cadre and medical organizations is needed to fight diseases and secure the health of our troops.

Med Sec, Regt Hq

(*1) etc:-

(1) 郭秀生   (2) 徐文光

collateral factor: the scourge of epidemic disease—one of the four horsemen of the Apocalypse.

After our withdrawal from North Korea, General MacArthur feared the potential of epidemics of smallpox, typhus, and typhoid fevers. The foci of infection were already smoldering. We doubted that the Communists were able to control epidemics. Their vaccines, made under Russian supervision, were found to be practically worthless.

In order to explain their medical failures to their own troops and to a restless, frightened population, the Chinese launched the flimsy lie that "the Americans had engaged in germ warfare, in dropping disease germs." But captured Chinese documents, containing their own front-line medical warnings, proved the local character of these epidemics. The following document, dated March 8, 1951, was received by ATIS on April 5; a mimeographed sheet, issued by the medical section of a Chinese unit, it was translated and reads significantly:

DISEASES

The following is a report on the "disease situation" existing among the native people and troops in the area where our Regiment is stationed.

1. An NKA hospital is located in the vicinity of our Medical Section. The number of patients in this hospital has increased to over four hundred. Most cases are typhoid and recurrent fever. Several patients have died lately. The hospital announced that these diseases have been reaching epidemic proportions, and that two-thirds of the staff of this hospital have been infected.

2. In the area surrounding the Supply Section, Medical Section, Guard Company and 1st and 2nd Bns, many native families were infected with these diseases and three children died from them.

3. There are some cases of pneumonia, bad colds, and recurrent fever in our Regiment. In 1st Bn, there are five or six cases of recurrent fever. A first sergeant of 3rd Bn, a supply sergeant of Regimental Headquarters, and a culture officer of the SMG Co had pneumonia. Besides these, quite a few have "soreness of waist and legs" and scabies.

4. The main factors causing these diseases are:

    a. Some slept in native houses during encamping, and were infected with typhus by lice in blankets. Others contacted recurrent fever by staying in the rooms where patients had stayed previously (like NKA cases).

b. Some who became heated from heavy work during marching, removed their clothes immediately or went out at night without sufficient clothing and caught cold and influenza which may develop into pneumonia (such as KE Hsiu Sheng and HSU Wen Kuang developed pneumonia from a cold).

c. Some who often stay in air raid shelters or are on duty in defensive position, sometimes develop sore waist and legs and scabies.

5. Methods of prevention:

a. Clean a house thoroughly before staying there. Basins and bowls borrowed from the natives should be dipped in boiling water several times.

b. To make effective the "Kill the lice movement," since we lack DDT powder, we have to wash our clothes and sun the straw bed cushions as often as possible.

c. Don't remove clothes and hat when perspiring from heavy work; put hat and enough clothes on when going out at night.

d. When in air raid shelter or on duty in defensive position, lay more dry straw at the spot where you happen to stay for a while. During the night, sleep on a "stoved bed" if possible.

e. Exercise constantly and effect preventions strictly by watching each other.

Close cooperation between military and political cadre and medical organizations is needed to fight diseases and secure the health of our troops.

Med Sec, Regt Hq

As far as the Eighth Army was concerned, it was urgent to infiltrate a highly qualified expert behind the enemy lines to obtain smears and slides. Brig. Gen. Crawford F. Sams, chief of the Public Health and Welfare Section in the occupation of Japan, volunteered for the job. Getting a general into Chinese territory was not a question of selling a Fourth of July excursion ticket. A secret trip was promptly set up by the G-2 clandestine operations section. General Sams was quietly delivered on the east coast of North Korea for a "medical raid" into an enemy-held village. It was a hazardous journey. Here follow extracts from his personal report:

Because of the great hazard to our troops and the civilian people, it was necessary for us to know quickly and accurately whether these reports made by laymen agents indicated that plague had actually been brought into Korea, because if it had, we must move at once and begin a tremendous program to protect our troops and the civil population. After about twelve days of efforts to get into the Wonson-Hamhung area where these cases were reported among the Chinese troops, we finally succeeded after some nine Korean groups had been captured and killed with the exception of two men. As you know, the Wonson Harbor area was organized against amphibious operations as our Navy was trying to pin down troops there by implying the threat of such an amphibious operation. Therefore, it was not a simple matter of landing on an undefended shore. Not only did they have the water mined in the area, but they had the beaches mined and the beaches defended with the usual small arms and artillery, so it was impossible to get close to the shore in any boat that they could see, without drawing fire.

On our next to the last attempt in which we took a destroyer and went down the coast opposite the village of Chilbo-ri, we were warned off by one of the surviving agents that the Communists had laid a trap for us. As you know, they have a nice habit of torturing people under those circumstances before killing them, and one of the agents had given them the information that we were trying to get in. On the following night we did succeed in getting through the beach defenses at Chilbo-ri and met with the G-2 agents in a little cave on the edge of the village, which was being used as a hospital by the Chinese Communists. I wanted to go, not only to that village, but two others which were west of the coast road, but was unable to get across the road because unfortunately our Air Force, not having been informed of our activities, was bombing a Chinese convoy on this road. You know what happens when a convoy is bombed; the personnel detruck with great rapidity and scatter, and we had Chinese running all over the place in addition to those who were already there, so we had to confine our activities to interrogation of the G-2 agents and first-hand information of what was happening in Chilbo-ri.

The boys eliminated one small Chinese patrol with the usual wire and knife technique, since we could not fire our pistols or use hand grenades without bringing more Chinese into the picture. In addition to confirming the fact that these people did not have plague, but had hemorrhagic smallpox, it also confirmed previous reports that these diseases were sweeping not only the civil population, but the military forces not only in the Wonson area, but the Pyongyang area. I wanted to stay on for a couple of days, hoping to get further inland to visit these other villages which were being used as hospitals, but the Koreans with me did not go along with the idea. Great credit is due to the courage of Commander Yun and Lieutenant Clark, G-2, representatives . . . who went with me, because they did not have to go but volunteered. The results, I believe, were important to the military operations and justified the expedition because as you well know, negative information in intelligence is frequently as important as positive information.

In this case, the knowledge that we were not faced with plague was most important. On the other hand, it did confirm our previous bits of information that the enemy were hard hit by smallpox, typhus and typhoid, but principally smallpox and typhus, which they could not control.

As you know, following our "medical raid," the Communists killed about twenty-five people in the village who they thought might be contacts of ours, and then immediately charged us with introducing biological warfare. The facts are these: Of course there was great unrest among the people because there is unrest in any population when they are dying like flies and no one does anything about it, and the Communists were doing nothing and are incapable of doing anything. In their effort to alibi to their own people for their own non-effectiveness, they of course accused us of having started the epidemics. They ignored the facts that the foci of these diseases were already smoldering when we were in North Korea five months before, and that these foci flared up due to the incompetence of the Communists, after we had withdrawn south of the parallel. I don't believe that the people who were ill or dying of these diseases throughout those months were in any way influenced by the Peiping radio or Pravda in announcing we had started the diseases the following March.

On another little island in Wonson Harbor, as an example, I went ashore and found about 124 survivors of typhus and smallpox, and there were still about twenty cases of typhus on the island. In other words, these were not small outbreaks. That was simply an illustration of how these diseases were affecting the entire population on the mainland. Our own people have missed the boat in not throwing this fact back at the Communists by constant repetition through Voice of America and other means familiar to you in psychological warfare. If I had anything to say about it, I would be constantly hammering the fact that diseases were sweeping North Korea not only among civilian, but also military forces, because the Communist military and civil people were incompetent and unable to control them. I would hammer then to the other people in Asia that if the Communists invade their country, they can expect widespread epidemics, because they don't know how to control them. On the other hand, the United Nations Forces were able to control these diseases on their side of the lines. . . .

So far as Tokyo headquarters knew, this evidence was not used in UN rebuttals; the defense instead was a lukewarm offer of an "impartial investigation."

MacArthur recognized the symptoms of weakness of the Reds, drew common-sense conclusions, and pressed for a military decision through attack on the Chinese sanctuary. He recommended to Washington that he be permitted air-bombardment in due course of military installations north of the Yalu then actively employed against us, naval blockade of the coast of China to cut off enemy supplies, and renewed his request for the utilization of Nationalist Chinese troops available on Formosa. These recommendations were actually approved by the Joint Chiefs of Staff, but somewhere between the offices of the Secretary of Defense, Gen. George C. Marshall, the Secretary of State Dean G. Acheson, and President Truman, they were pigeonholed; and we took the course leading to the stalemate of positional warfare, by all odds the most costly and least productive method of waging war.

To his staff, General MacArthur said:

The overriding deficiency incident to the conduct of the war in Korea by the United Nations lies in its lack of will for victory. Underlying the whole problem has always been the indeterminate question as to whether or not the Soviet contemplates the conquest of the world by military means rather than by those of more peaceful persuasion.

If it intends to use force, the time and place will be at its own initiative and could not fail to be influenced by the fact that in the atomic area, the lead of the United States is being steadily diminished with the passage of time. So likewise is the great industrial potential of the United States as compared with the Communist world.

In short, it has always been my own belief that any action we might take to resolve the Korean problem could not in itself be a controlling factor in the precipitation of a world conflict. It is quite probable that the Soviet masses are just as eager for peace as are our own people. They probably suffer the delusion that there are aggressive intentions against them on the part of the capitalist world and that they would welcome an imaginative approach which would allay this false impression. . . .

On January 14, 1952 President Truman sent a personal message to General MacArthur finishing with these words: "The entire nation is grateful for your splendid leadership in the difficult struggle in Korea and for the superb performance of your forces under most difficult circumstances." Less than three months later, on the eve of another victory, he suddenly, without warning, relieved MacArthur of his command in a most savage and brutal way. The peremptory order did not permit him even to bid good-by to his troops. Superbly trained, they carried on under other generals, one of whom, James A. Van Fleet, was fully as certain as MacArthur himself that victory over the Chinese Communists could have been had if the politicians had simply given the soldiers the word.

17 The Dismissal

AS far as MacArthur's own knowledge of its circumstances is concerned, his dismissal is still shrouded in considerable mystery. His first information of it came over the public radio. But in summarizing, ex post facto, the possible reasons for it, MacArthur has listed three things which members of the Truman Administration seized upon to prepare a case for ridding themselves of their foremost general.

The decision [said MacArthur] was arbitrary. I warned of the dangers of Formosa falling under Communist control. This was said to be contrary to existing policy. The Secretary of State has since declared that it was long-standing policy of the United States.

The second reason given was my readiness to meet the enemy commander to discuss terms. This identical proposal was received enthusiastically when made by the Soviets.

The third reason was my reply to a Congressman. There is a law that no member of the Armed Forces shall be restricted from communicating with members of Congress.

In retrospect, it must seem that all of the Administration's "reasons" masked something deeper. General Bradley, presumably speaking for the Joint Chiefs of Staff, said on one occasion that MacArthur "was not in sympathy with the decision to try to limit the conflict in Korea. The J.C.S. had decided to try to avoid a third war." Yet MacArthur desired only to destroy the enemy where he had chosen to attack, in Korea. His proposals to bomb the Yalu bridges, to avail himself of the right of "hot pursuit" of enemy aircraft, and to utilize his own air and naval forces to carry the war to the enemy's supply and communications, were hardly a prescription

418

for a third *world* war. They were merely the prescription for ending the war he had been ordered to fight. In no case was he in favor of sending American troops to fight on Chinese soil. "Anybody who advocates that," so MacArthur said, "should have his head examined."

The first inkling of trouble with the Administration came when MacArthur made a reply to an inquiry by the Veterans of Foreign Wars about the strategic value of Formosa. The letter, written on August 27, 1950, is hardly startling, for its contents are today an accepted part of our Far Eastern strategy. But it constitutes an interesting footnote to history, by a military commander of the first rank who has spent many years in the Far East:

Any appraisal of Formosa's strategic potential, requires an appreciation of the changes wrought in the course of the past war. Prior thereto the Western strategic position of the United States lay on the littoral line of the Americas with an exposed island salient extending out through Hawaii, Midway, and Guam to the Philippines. That salient was not an outpost of strength but an avenue of weakness along which the enemy could and did attack us. The Pacific was a potential area of advance for any predatory force intent upon striking at the bordering land areas.

All of this was changed by our Pacific victory. Our strategic frontier then shifted to embrace the entire Pacific Ocean, which has become a vast moat to protect us as long as we hold it. Indeed it acts as a protective shield for all of the Americas and for all lands of the Pacific Ocean area. We control it to the shores of Asia by a chain of islands extending in an arc from the Aleutians to the Marianas held by us and our former allies. *From this island chain we can prevent any hostile movement into the Pacific.* Our line of defense is a natural one and can be maintained with a minimum of military effort and expense. It envisions no attack against anyone, nor does it provide the bastions essential for offensive operations, but properly maintained would be an invincible defense against aggression. If we hold this line we may have peace. If we lose it, war is inevitable.

The geographic location of Formosa is such that in the hands of a power unfriendly to the United States, it constitutes an enemy salient in the very center of this defense perimeter. There is on Formosa a concentration of operational air and naval bases which is potentially greater than any similar concentration on the Asiatic mainland. Our air supremacy at once would become doubtful. Formosa in the hands of a hostile power could be compared to an unsinkable aircraft carrier and submarine tender. Submarine blockade by the enemy would become a virtual certainty.

As a routine courtesy to journalists, copies of this letter were sent to the press some days before it was scheduled to be read at the Veterans of Foreign Wars annual convention in Chicago. To MacArthur, the letter seemed sheerest common sense about geographical factors as they relate to strategy. But the President, for reasons that are still inexplicable, took violent exception to the letter and ordered it withdrawn. MacArthur complied with the order. It was too late, however, to keep its contents from reaching the public; *Life* magazine and David Lawrence's *U.S. News and World Report*, for example, had already printed it and committed it to the mails. *Life*, in fact, had made it its editorial for the week.

Within twenty-four hours of the "withdrawal" that failed to withdraw the letter's contents, Truman summoned Louis Johnson, his Secretary of War, to discuss ways and means for the relief of MacArthur "as Korean commander." Johnson revealed this in testimony before the Joint Senate Investigating Committee on June 14, 1951. After discussion, however, the conclusion was reached not to do anything "at that time." MacArthur did not have the lightest suspicion of what was going on.

Considering that Formosa was a touchy subject with both State Department and White House, MacArthur's previous staff visit to Formosa and brief consultation with Chiang Kai-shek in 1950 must be considered a contributory cause to the smoldering hostility in Washington.

There was no real cause for resentment, however. MacArthur had no plenary power to arrive at political understandings. He was not an ambassador charged with negotiating for the State Department. On the other hand, it was well within his prerogatives as a regional commander in the Far East to visit adjacent strategic areas for purposes of obtaining firsthand impressions of their military and geographic potentials. When he could not go himself, he habitually sent senior staff officers or commanders. General Stratemeyer of the Air Force, accompanied by General Willoughby, made just such an exploratory staff journey to Hong Kong, Hai-phong, Bangkok, and Singapore.

MacArthur thus flew to Formosa. Washington was advised and made no objections. The General met Chiang and his principal civil and military staff. He attended a briefing of the map-room variety which outlined the Nationalist Chinese concept of the situation. He attended a ceremonial dinner—and then returned to Tokyo: *Tant de bruit pour une omelette?*

The Inchon victory followed MacArthur's temporary "reprieve" by Truman and Louis Johnson—and naturally nothing much could be done to push immediately for the removal of a commander who had just won a decisive battle. But on March 20 of the following year, when the fighting in Korea had reached the "accordion" stage, Washington plucked up its nerve. The occasion for moving decisively against MacArthur presented itself on the 20th when MacArthur wrote a mild enough answer to a letter from Joe Martin, leader of the House Republicans. It read:

Dear Congressman Martin:

I am most grateful for your note of the 8th forwarding me a copy of your address of February 12th. The letter I have read with much interest, and find that with the passage of years you have certainly lost none of your old-time punch.

My views and recommendations with respect to the situation created by Red China's entry into war against us in Korea have been submitted to Washington in most complete detail. Generally these views are well known and clearly understood, as they follow the conventional pattern of meeting force with maximum counter-force as we have never failed to do in the past. Your view with respect to the utilization of the Chinese forces on Formosa is in conflict with neither logic nor this tradition.

It seems strangely difficult for some to realize that here in Asia is where Communist conspirators have elected to make their play for global conquest, and that we have joined the issue thus raised on the battlefield; that here we fight Europe's war with arms while the diplomats there still fight it with words; that if we lose the war to Communism in Asia the fall of Europe is inevitable, win it and Europe most probably would avoid war and yet preserve freedom. As you point out, we must win. There is no substitute for victory.

With renewed thanks and expressions of most cordial regard, I am

Faithfully yours,

Douglas MacArthur

MacArthur had been saying the same sort of thing for months, in both letters and statements. But this time it was "different" for one simple reason: Truman had decided to act. The Administration was making ready for its great "peace" play; Acheson was even then busy circulating peace proposals to the UN nations which had troops in Korea. It was at this point that MacArthur called upon the Chinese Communist commander in Korea to surrender—"or else." MacArthur offered the Chinese commander an opportunity to meet with him for a discussion in the field. He stressed the reserve strength which the United Nations could bring to bear upon the enemy if he insisted upon continuing the war.

MacArthur construed his own "peace" offer as (*a*) a smart stroke of psychological warfare and (*b*) an effort to back up the peace campaign that was being waged in the United Nations. To Truman, however, it was an impertinence. Two days after the Martin letter had been published, Truman conferred with Acheson, Bradley, Marshall, and Averell Harriman. The generals were uneasy at first about touching a soldier who was a popular idol, but Acheson and Truman carried the day. After sounding out the Joint Chiefs of Staff, who formulated some "military considerations" which made the firing of MacArthur desirable, Bradley was in a position to tell Truman that the high brass "concurred" with his decision to relieve MacArthur. Truman's own reasons for taking the step were subsequently summed up as (*a*) the letter about Formosa, (*b*) the Martin letter and (*c*) the offer to deal with the Chinese in the field.

As a fitting irony, Truman then turned over to the "European-minded" Marshall the job of drafting a dismissal message for the Presidential signature.

I deeply regret [the message said] that it becomes my duty as President . . . to replace you as Supreme Commander. . . . You will turn over your commands, effective at once, to Lieut. Gen. Matthew B. Ridgway. . . . My reasons for your replacement will be made public concurrently with the delivery to you of the foregoing order, and are contained in the next following message.

Harry S. Truman

It was originally planned to let Secretary of War Frank Pace, Jr., who was then in the Far East, deliver the dismissal note to MacArthur at the Tokyo Embassy. But the April 12 radio got there ahead of Pace. MacArthur and his wife were entertaining visitors at luncheon when Sid Huff, the General's aide, picked the dismissal notice from a news broadcast. With tears in his eyes he called Mrs. MacArthur from the table. She returned to break the news.

Not a flicker of emotion stirred MacArthur's face. When the General subsequently read the official confirmation, he turned to his wife and said serenely, "Jean, we're going home at last." To the press, Gen. Courtney Whitney said: "I have just left the General. He received the word magnificently. He never turned a hair. His soldierly qualities were never more pronounced. I think this has been his finest hour."

The Communists reveled in the news when they heard it. In a "Proclamation of the Japanese Communist Party concerning General MacArthur's Dismissal," they said:

MacArthur's dismissal most plainly reveals that due to the strongly growing discrepancy and divergence of opinion amongst the imperialistic nations, a cornerstone of their war-provocative policy seeking world control has crumbled before the peace-loving masses composed of over a billion people.

One of Premier Stalin's great predictions, that "all meddlers will no doubt meet with certain failure," has come true.

It is also clear that as a result of this dismissal the separatist peace group [pro U.S.] is now in a state of confusion, and the Yoshida cabinet and their clique have lost their staunch supporter of the past several years.

We now have an opportune moment. By taking advantage of the confusion, an all-out peace and antiwar preparation movement can be strengthened.

In co-ordination with a poll of 40,000,000 [Japanese] voters on the general peace issue, efforts will be made to expose thoroughly the maladministration of the Yoshida cabinet, sweeping from local autonomy the Liberal party influence advocating a separate peace [with the U.S.] at the same time bringing about the downfall of the Yoshida cabinet.

The plain people of Japan, however, spoke with a different voice. The dismissal dominated news and editorial columns in Tokyo and other Japanese cities more completely than any world event since the surrender. The initial reaction was shock and disappointment, regret and fear. The final phase was one of resolutions of national gratitude and sincere editorial tributes to MacArthur's efforts in behalf of Japan. Said *Mainichi Shimbun* (circulation 3,970,000):

MacArthur's dismissal is the greatest shock since the end of the war. He dealt with the Japanese people not as a conqueror but a great reformer. He was a noble political missionary. What he gave us was not material aid and democratic reform alone—but a new way of life, the freedom and dignity of the individual. . . . We shall continue to love and trust him as one of the Americans who best understood Japan's position.

Said *Asahi Shimbun* (circulation, 4,074,000):

The removal is a great disappointment to the Japanese, especially when the peace settlement is so near. Japan's recovery must be attributed solely to his guidance. We feel as if we had lost a kind and loving father.

On the day of MacArthur's departure the 20-mile roadway to Haneda Airfield was lined by thousands of Japanese, of every social class, bearing American and Japanese flags. People wept as the General's car rolled past them. And *Mainichi Shimbun* provided the final commentary:

We wanted your further help in nurturing our green democracy to fruition. We wanted your leadership at least until a signed peace treaty had given us a send-off into the world community.

The citizens of Kanagawa Prefecture, embracing the great port city of Yokohama, put into words what was latent in many Japanese hearts. On the base of a bronze bust which Japan's leading sculptor had been commissioned to create, the words foretold the judgment of history: "General Douglas MacArthur—Liberator of Japan."

The reaction of America to the General's homecoming was no less affecting than that of Japan to his departure. When he landed in San Francisco, he had spent twenty-five years on foreign service, longer than any officer or man of the U.S. Army. On Friday afternoon, in Japan, he had first heard the news of the dismissal. He was gone on Monday to receive at home the greatest welcome ever accorded an American. His staff thrilled to the echo of his closing words as he said farewell in the halls of Congress:

I have just left your fighting sons in Korea. They have met all tests there and I can report to you without reservations, they are splendid in every way.

It was my constant effort to preserve them and end this savage conflict honorably and with the least loss of time and a minimum sacrifice of life. Its growing bloodshed has caused me the deepest anguish and anxiety. Those gallant men will remain often in my thoughts and in my prayers always.

I am closing my fifty-two years of military service. When I joined the Army, even before the turn of the century, it was the fulfillment of all my boyish hopes and dreams.

The world has turned over many times since I took the oath on the plain at West Point, and the hopes and dreams have long since vanished, but I still remember the refrain of one of the most popular barracks ballads of that day, which proclaimed, most proudly, that "Old soldiers never die. They just fade away."

And like the old soldier of that ballad, I now close my military career and just fade away—an old soldier who tried to do his duty as God gave him the light to see that duty.

Goodbye.

Index